FOOL'S ERRAND

Time to End the War in Afghanistan

Scott Horton

Eva,

For peace.

Advance Praise for Fool's Errand

"In *Fool's Errand*, Scott Horton masterfully explains the tragedy of America's longest war and makes the case for immediate withdrawal. I highly recommend this excellent book on America's futile and self-defeating occupation of Afghanistan." — Daniel Ellsberg, *Pentagon Papers* whistleblower and author of *The Doomsday Machine: Confessions of a Nuclear War Planner*

"The real story of the disastrous U.S. war in Afghanistan must be written so that future generations may understand the folly of Washington's warmongers. Scott Horton's Afghan war history is an important contribution to this vital effort." — Ron Paul, M.D., former U.S. congressman and author of *Swords into Plowshares: A Life in Wartime and a Future of Peace and Prosperity*

"Scott Horton's *Fool's Errand* is a deeply insightful and well-informed book on America's longest war, explaining why it remains as unwinnable as it ever was. It appears at an important moment as the Trump administration is once again reinforcing failure." — Patrick Cockburn, Middle East correspondent for the *Independent*, author of *The Age of Jihad: Islamic State and the Great War for the Middle East*

"An incisive, informative analysis of the Afghan fiasco and how we got there, scrubbed clean of propaganda and disinformation. Horton captures the situation very well indeed. I much enjoyed reading it." — Eric S. Margolis, author of *War at the Top of the World: The Struggle for Afghanistan, Kashmir and Tibet* and *American Raj: Liberation or Domination? Resolving the Conflict Between the West and the Muslim World*

"*Fool's Errand: Time to End the War in Afghanistan* by Scott Horton is a spectacularly researched and sourced book, and it provides a refreshingly rational analysis of America's Afghan quagmire. I would recommend this book to anyone who wants to know the truth of this nation's longest war." — Lt. Col. Daniel L. Davis, U.S. Army (ret.), senior fellow at Defense Priorities

"Scott Horton has a far better record on Afghanistan than the Pentagon or the White House. He has been pointing out the follies of U.S. intervention there since it started half a generation ago. *Fool's Errand* vividly exposes the pratfalls, atrocities, lies and incorrigibility of our never-ending Afghan crusade." — James Bovard, columnist at *USA Today* and author of *Attention Deficit Democracy*

"Scott Horton's *Fool's Errand: Time to End the War in Afghanistan* is a definitive, authoritative and exceptionally well-resourced accounting of America's disastrous war in Afghanistan since 2001. Scott's book deserves not just to be read, but to be kept on your shelf, because as with David Halberstam's *The Best and Brightest* or Neil Sheehan's *A Bright Shining Lie*, I expect Horton's book to not just explain and interpret a current American war, but to explain and interpret the all too predictable future American wars, and the unavoidable waste and suffering that will accompany them." — Capt. Matthew Hoh, USMC (ret.), former senior State Department official, Zabul Province, Afghanistan, senior fellow at the Center for International Policy

"*Fool's Errand* is a hidden history of America's forgotten war, laid bare in damning detail. Scott Horton masterfully retells the story of America's failed intervention, exposes how Obama's troop surge did not bring Afghanistan any closer to peace, and warns that the conflict could go on in perpetuity — unless America ends the war. As Trump threatens to send more troops to Afghanistan, Horton shows why the answer to a brutal civil war is not more war, which makes Fool's Errand a scintillating and sorely needed chronicle of the longest war in American history." — Anand Gopal, journalist and author of *No Good Men Among the Living: America, the Taliban, and the War through Afghan Eyes*

"Scott Horton's *Fool's Errand: Time to End the War in Afghanistan* is a brilliant achievement and a great read. I recommended it to the faculty at the Army Command and General Staff College to be part of the course work. It's that important." — Col. Douglas Macgregor, U.S. Army (ret.), author of *Warrior's Rage: The Great Tank Battle of 73 Easting*

"In *Fool's Errand*, Scott Horton informs us of just how non-masterful has been the U.S. approach to Afghanistan — policy-wise, strategically, and even tactically. Two presidents and several Congresses have failed, the Pentagon has failed, and the military has failed. Moreover, there is nothing we can do about it except withdraw, cut our losses, and put as brave a face on it as possible. Horton tells us that President Trump, having indicated as much himself in his campaign, should do just that, get out. Having watched this debacle from very close-by for four years and for twelve more in academia, I totally agree with Mr. Horton, but he has done a much better job than I could of telling every single American citizen precisely why." — Col. Lawrence Wilkerson, U.S. Army (ret.), visiting professor of government and public policy at the College of William and Mary and former chief of staff to Secretary of State Colin Powell

"A lot of people think of the war in Iraq as the bad war, but Afghanistan as the good and justifiable war. That convenient view does not survive Scott Horton's careful and incisive demolition." — Thomas E. Woods Jr., author of *Nullification: How to Resist Federal Tyranny in the 21st Century* and *Rollback: Repealing Big Government Before the Coming Fiscal Collapse*

"Scott Horton is the first to pull together all the strands of the story of America's longest war in one book. He tells it straight, with an unblinking eye for all the lies that have accompanied each twist and turn of the war. Read it if you dare to know the full truth about this sordid exercise in American imperial power." — Gareth Porter, historian and journalist, author of *Perils of Dominance: Imbalance of Power and the Road to War in Vietnam* and *Manufactured Crisis: The Truth Behind the Iran Nuclear Scare*

"Scott Horton's new book *Fool's Errand: Time to End the War in Afghanistan* has a title that tells you where it is going, but to think that is all it is about would be to sell short a comprehensive work that takes the reader on a long journey starting in the 1980s. Indeed, if there were a university course on what went wrong with Afghanistan, starting with Ronald Reagan's Holy Warriors and continuing with George W. Bush's ouster of the Taliban leading to 15 years of feckless nation building, this book could well serve as the textbook. Horton provides insights into key decision-making along the way as he meticulously documents the dreadful series of misadventures that have brought us to the latest surge, which will fail just like all the others. The book is highly recommended both for readers who already know a lot about Afghanistan as well as for those who want to learn the basics about America's longest war." — Philip Giraldi, former CIA and DIA officer, executive director of the Council for the National Interest

"Unlike some liberals who go wobbly when confronted with U.S. military intervention done in the name of 'human rights,' the principled libertarian Scott Horton consistently opposes American aggression abroad. Read his *Fool's Errand* to find out why the U.S. never should have invaded Afghanistan and should get out now." — Reese Erlich, foreign correspondent and author of *Inside Syria: The Backstory of Their Civil War and What the World Can Expect.*

"America's longest war — in Afghanistan — has until now been among America's least documented. Horton brings together far more than 16 years of conflict, drawing in sources from well before most Americans even heard of Osama bin Laden to show how the Afghan quagmire's roots are deep. The title tells it all, however: this war cannot be won, and 'victory' will be in the form of escape. Meticulously researched and footnoted, *Fool's Errand* is required reading." — Peter Van Buren, retired foreign service officer and author of *We Meant Well: How I Helped Lose the War for the Hearts and Minds of the Iraqi People* and *Hooper's War: A Novel of WWII Japan*

"Why is the United States still fighting in Afghanistan? In this timely new book, Scott Horton explains why America's longest war is strategically misguided and why getting out would make the United States safer and advance America's broader national interests. Even readers who do not share Horton's libertarian world-view are likely to find themselves nodding in agreement: the war in Afghanistan has indeed become a 'fool's errand.'" — Stephen M. Walt, professor of international affairs, Harvard University, co-author of *The Israel Lobby and U.S. Foreign Policy*

"Scott Horton has written a superb, encyclopedic history and policy analysis of the U.S. Global War on Terror. This should be essential reading for all Americans involved with foreign and national security policy, especially 'mere' citizens in what is supposed to be a democracy. Mr. Horton's book provides the information we must have to understand Clausewitz's words that 'war is never an isolated act' and that we as decision-makers must 'know the nature' of a conflict, especially to end it when that is called for. This includes knowing how successive administrations have distorted the law in presenting lawlessness as legitimate, and subverting the country from within, which Mr. Horton explains. It is plain to see after sixteen years of aggressive war that our alleged experts are anything but in understanding real strategic thought, which, in Clausewitz's view, called for a nation to seek peace as the strategic objective, not perpetual war as U.S. policy is today. Mr. Horton's book fills that strategic void for citizen and 'expert.'" — Maj. Todd Pierce, U.S. Army Judge Advocate General (ret.)

"Scott Horton has been a scrupulous critic of American militarism since 2001. His full-length case study of the 'good war' in Afghanistan is a chronicle of warnings unheeded, lessons not learned, and the relentless pursuit of a policy whose futility was always apparent. Every detail of this story is backed by an impressive depth of documentation, and the final verdict spares neither the ambition of generals nor the cowardice of presidents." — David Bromwich, professor of literature, Yale University, editor of Edmund Burke's selected writings *On Empire, Liberty, and Reform*

"Scott Horton has written an impassioned plea against the insanity of the endless, hopeless war on terror. He shows that the war in Afghanistan was and is unnecessary, and links its bipartisan prosecution and the use of torture to the American rulers' dream of world hegemony. It skewers the hype about the dangers of radical Islam and terrorism. This book is needed now more than ever!" — Jeffrey S. Kaye, author of *Cover-up at Guantánamo: The NCIS Investigation into the "Suicides" of Mohammed Al Hanashi and Abdul Rahman Al Amri*

"Outstanding! Highly readable and fascinating summary of the longest war in U.S. history, and why it never worked. Well researched and organized, *Fool's Errand* should be mandatory reading for every military officer serving today and be placed in President Trump's hands immediately. Trump's pre-election instincts on this ugly, corrupting and unnecessary war were certainly correct. Scott Horton's well-documented timeline of waste, illogical strategies and neoconservative fantasy in Afghanistan all show why Trump's gut feelings, and those of most Americans for the past decade, have been dead-on. Using careful, fair-minded and patriotic prose, the author exposes the Afghanistan experience as a high-tech, networked Vietnam. *Fool's Errand* is the true story of the direct, undeniable result of a newer generation of 'smart' bureaucrats, in and out of uniform, their shockingly bad advice and their astonishing willingness to repeatedly lie to sitting presidents. Whether you want to wake up, stay woke or just be remembered as the president who made America great again, this book is a must read!" — Lt. Col. Karen Kwiatkowski, U.S. Air Force (ret.), founding member of Veteran Intelligence Professionals for Sanity

"Scott Horton's *Fool's Errand* is an elegantly written, scrupulously researched and timely history of the American war in Afghanistan. Horton casts a critical eye over some of the Beltway's most cherished myths and successfully challenges what too often goes unchallenged in Washington. Horton calls into question the morality and efficacy of counterinsurgency doctrine and nation-building and warns of the possible consequences of staying in Afghanistan forever. Horton's arguments will be cheered by principled anti-interventionists on both the Right and the Left — and if there is any justice in the world (an increasingly dubious proposition) his arguments will resonate with the current crop of policymakers charged with overseeing what is now, tragically, America's longest war. Here's to hoping *Fool's Errand* gains a wide, influential readership." — James Carden, contributing writer at *The Nation* and the executive editor for the American Committee for East-West Accord

"Scott Horton has tapped an incredible number of sources and insights from his thousands of expert interviews. He presents an original, compelling, and ultimately damning indictment of the U.S. invasion and occupation of Afghanistan." — Grant F. Smith, director of the Institute for Research: Middle Eastern Policy and author of *Big Israel: How Israel's Lobby Moves America*

"Scott Horton's *Fool's Errand* makes a well-researched and compelling case that American policies in Afghanistan were ill conceived from the outset and doomed to fail. Chronicling one unsuccessful American initiative after another in a seemingly endless war, Horton argues that our continued military efforts now yield little more than revenge-minded blowback. There is no light at the end of the tunnel, and no one can imagine realistically that one will appear. It will no doubt be a bitter pill to acknowledge that the Beltway fantasy of a united, democratic, pluralist and feminist Afghanistan will never be achieved, but it is one we will have to swallow eventually. Since the cost of pursuing unrealistic goals is exorbitant in blood and treasure, the sooner our failure is faced up to, the better." — Scott McConnell, founding editor of *The American Conservative* magazine

"Scott Horton's book on the U.S. war in Afghanistan — its origins, its failures, its ongoing travesties — is an indispensable guide to the latest conflict taking place in the 'graveyard of empires.' Horton provides useful detail on the self-defeating campaign against al Qaeda and the tragicomic pursuit of Osama bin Laden, the malign impact the war has had on U.S. civil liberties and conduct of international relations, and the destruction of a proud but poor country. He navigates expertly between the micro level of tribal politics and the macro level of geopolitics, providing compact analysis of counter-insurgency doctrine, drone warfare, and the backdraft of the war's consequences for the United States. An important contribution to analyses of the forever war." — John Feffer, director of Foreign Policy in Focus, Institute for Policy Studies and author of *North Korea/South Korea: U.S. Policy at a Time of Crisis* and *Crusade 2.0: The West's Resurgent War on Islam*

"*Fool's Errand*, Scott Horton's well-researched, fine-grained chronicle of the U.S. debacle in Afghanistan, reveals how foreign policy elites seized the post-9/11 opportunity to pursue their neocon agenda. What is now the perpetual-motion U.S. war machine has been maintained since 2001 by the entrenched bureaucracy of three successive administrations under easily manipulable presidents. This deep-state engine has proven to be devoid of any mechanism of self-correction, fueled as it is by a lethal alloy of opportunism, vanity, and short-term political expediency. Anyone wondering how Afghanistan became the United States' longest war will find the disturbing answer in this important and timely book." — Laurie Calhoun, research fellow at the Independent Institute and author of *We Kill Because We Can: From Soldiering to Assassination in the Drone Age*

"Scott Horton's *Fool's Errand: Time to End the War in Afghanistan* is a remarkable book. Backed up by massive and meticulous research and informed by compelling analysis, Horton marshals a devastating case against America's longest war. If this book ever becomes required reading in international relations courses and military academies, a great deal of harm in the future might be avoided." — David T. Beito, professor of history, University of Alabama, co-author of *Black Maverick: T. R. M. Howard's Fight for Civil Rights and Economic Power*

"Bovardian!" — Anthony Gregory, author of *The Power of Habeas Corpus in America*

FOOL'S ERRAND

Time to End the War in Afghanistan

Scott Horton

The
LIBERTARIAN
INSTITUTE

Published in the United States of America by
The Libertarian Institute
205 W. Randolph St., Suite 1305
Chicago, IL 60606

LibertarianInstitute.org
ISBN-13:978-1548650216
ISBN-10:1548650218

In Memory of

William Norman Grigg

For my girls

Contents

Detailed maps available at FoolsErrand.us/maps

Introduction

A brutal civil war continues to destroy Afghanistan in the aftermath of the U.S. invasion and regime change of 2001. Years after President Barack Obama's promised 2014 deadline for the final withdrawal of American and NATO forces, the U.S. military dares not declare victory and come home. Without the aid of American dollars, air power, special operations forces and infantry, the "National Unity Government" the U.S. has installed in the Afghan capital of Kabul would quickly collapse. And so the longest foreign war in American history rages on toward the 2020s.

Yet Operation Enduring Freedom, now Operation Freedom's Sentinel, was doomed from the start. After President George W. Bush's initial failure to capture or kill those guilty of attacking the United States on September 11th, he ignored his own warnings against intervention and nation-building. Instead Bush installed a U.S.-friendly government in Kabul, one he claimed would secure the Afghan people's freedom by destroying the forces of terrorism and Islamist fundamentalism. By the time he left office, after more than seven years of war in Afghanistan, Bush's advisers were warning him that the Taliban regime he overthrew in 2001 was making a strong comeback and that the U.S.-backed government in the capital city was on the verge of unraveling.

President Obama came to power criticizing Bush's supposed inattention and negligence, calling Afghanistan "the war that has to be won," which he vowed to do. Obama then escalated and lost anyway. The vaunted, rewritten counterinsurgency doctrine (COIN), promoted by U.S. Army General David Petraeus and the think-tank cheerleaders at the Center for a New American Security, turned out to be a complete flop. These "COINdinistas" said they could "change entire societies" into becoming compliant with U.S. goals. All they had to do in Afghanistan was "surge" in tens of thousands more American troops to win over the nice people in the daytime while sending special operations forces on house raids to hunt down the bad guys at night. These tactics, combined with a renewed push by the State Department and its contractors to rebuild Afghanistan and its local governments from the ground up, would save the country, or so they promised.

All this so-called counterinsurgency "surge" accomplished was the loss of thousands more American and allied lives, along with the lives of tens of thousands of Afghans. The escalation did not decrease the power of the Afghan Taliban, their allies in the Haqqani Network or other insurgent groups. The Taliban is as powerful now as it has been at any time since the war began, controlling nearly half of the country at night, and not much less during the day. When it was revealed that the Taliban's former leader, Mullah Omar, had died back in 2013, the group split. Since then, room has been created for the growth of factions now declaring themselves loyal to the "Caliph Ibrahim," Omar Baku al-Baghdadi, the self-proclaimed leader of the Islamic State (ISIS).

The year 2016 saw the most civilian deaths in Afghanistan since the United Nations started counting. Violence in the country was so bad that Obama halted the military's drawdown at 8,500 troops, a number 4,000 higher than originally planned. In January 2017, during the final week of his presidency, he ordered 300 more marines back to the Afghan south in a desperate effort to shore up security in the capital of Helmand Province.

In August of 2017, President Donald Trump ordered thousands more troops to "break the stalemate" there. In reality, the new troops were desperately needed to try to halt the momentum of the Taliban-led insurgency before the U.S.-backed government there lost entire regions of the country permanently. If American forces could achieve a stalemate now, it would be an improvement.

Some prominent think tank experts are calling for another full-scale troop escalation to 100,000 men to again attempt to implement the "hearts and minds," nation-building, counterinsurgency doctrine.

America's Afghan war may have officially ended on December 31, 2014, but for the people of Afghanistan, and the U.S. and allied forces stationed there, it continues regardless.

America's generals in charge of managing the occupation come and go, but their advice remains the same: we can't leave now — we can't leave ever. As long as total defeat can be staved off with drones and special operations forces, the U.S. will stay and the war will continue. On the other hand, that may be assuming too much. With troop levels being determined largely by office politics in Washington, D.C., rather than tactical concerns in Kabul, a forced withdrawal of American troops after a Fall of Saigon-type disaster remains at least a possibility in the near to medium term.

What began as a punitive raid in response to the September 11th attacks quickly escalated. Initially launched in the name of targeting al Qaeda, a small group of Saudi and Egyptian terrorists hiding out in far-away Afghanistan, and the Taliban government that had given them safe-haven, this action soon turned into a broader military occupation, nation-building project and endless war. The government the U.S. installed in the capital city of Kabul has been dominated by a coalition of the political leaders and warlords of the ethnic minorities from the Afghan north — Tajiks, Hazaras, Uzbeks, Turkmen and others — in alliance with the worst sorts of warlords and criminals from the predominantly Pashtun south and east of the country. This coalition does not represent their people or provide them security. Consequently, a mostly Pashtun insurgency, led by remnants of the old Taliban government, has been waged against the United States, its allied military forces and the new Afghan government since the early years of the occupation. And the insurgency has only gotten stronger in response to escalated efforts against it. No longer just a militia, or even a shadow government acting unofficially, the Taliban is now, once again, the only actual government in operation in much of the predominantly Pashtun regions. Even America's highest-ranking war commanders, such as Gen. Petraeus, have conceded that the insurgents' systems of criminal and civil dispute resolution are fairer than those imposed by the American-backed government. As a result, the insurgents enjoy far more popular support in those areas.

After more than a decade and a half, the results are in. The U.S. government has been unable to achieve its goals in Afghanistan. Even worse, what state it has been able to establish there is completely unsustainable and is certain to fall apart when the occupation is finally called off, and America does come home. The politicians, generals and intelligence officers behind this unending catastrophe, who always promise they can fix these problems with just a little bit more time, money and military force, have lost all credibility.

The truth is America's Afghan war is an irredeemable disaster. It was meant to be a trap in the first place. America is not only failing to defeat its enemies, but is destroying itself, just as Osama bin Laden and al Qaeda always intended.

Fool's Errand is an attempt to present the American people with the reality of this forgotten war, because only the ignorance of pride and the refusal to admit they have been deceived can prevent Americans from realizing they have supported a policy that is destructive to the United States as well as Afghanistan. The first chapter of this book addresses the history of the al Qaeda movement and the nature of the terrorists' war against the United States. Chapter 2 examines the initial stages of the invasion of Afghanistan, the escape of Osama bin Laden and other al Qaeda leaders, as well as the abandonment of the rule of law and some of the other complicating factors that have fueled continued conflict there. Chapter 3 is a discussion of some of the external forces at work in Afghanistan, poor decision-making that has helped to drive the insurgency against the U.S.-installed government and some of the consequences for U.S. troops and innocent Afghan civilians. Chapter 4 is a short history of President Obama's "surge" escalation and its inevitable failure. Finally, chapter 5 recounts the costs and consequences of our government's failed policies and argues that President Trump should reverse his escalation and end the war now.

Introduction

If the U.S. is to ever get out of this mess, the American people will have to force the issue and insist upon withdrawal. Otherwise, both the U.S. government and the Taliban could conceivably keep the fight going for many more years.

Let us stop and take a fresh look at how things came to be the way they are now before they get too much worse.

Chapter One: Getting into This Mess

"If we don't stop extending our troops all around the world in nation-building missions, then we are going to have a serious problem coming down the road."
— Texas Governor George W. Bush, October 3, 2000

"They hate our freedoms." — President George W. Bush, September 20, 2001

Problems

On September 11, 2001, there were no more than a few hundred al Qaeda members in the world.[1] Three months later, when the Central Intelligence Agency's paramilitaries, the U.S. Army Delta Force and the U.S. Air Force finished bombing them, and Osama bin Laden had escaped to Pakistan, there were not enough left alive to fill a seventeenth-century pirate ship.[2]

Now, 15 years after that brief, one-sided victory, there are tens of thousands of bin Ladenite jihadists thriving in lands from Nigeria to the Philippines. Recently, and for a period of almost three years, some even claimed their own supposedly divinely ordained caliphate, or Islamic State, in western Iraq and eastern Syria.[3] Local chapters of their group keep popping up all over the region.[4] Year after year, the State Department reports a vast increase in the number of global terrorism incidents compared to the pre-September 11th era.[5] In recent years, al Qaeda, the Islamic State in Iraq and Syria (ISIS) and their "lone wolf" copy-cats have carried out multiple, deadly attacks in more than a dozen major cities in the West, including Brussels, Paris, Berlin, London, San Bernardino, Orlando and New York City. In 2014, then-Marine Corps General, now White House Chief of Staff, John F. Kelly echoed former Vice President Dick Cheney's statements from more than a decade before[6] when he said the United States must remain at war with terrorism for "generations" into the future.[7]

---

[1] Cynthia Storer, interviewed by the author, *Scott Horton Show*, radio archive, March 13, 2017, https://scotthorton.org/interviews/31317-cynthia-storer; Robert L. Grenier, *88 Days to Kandahar: A CIA Diary* (New York City: Simon & Schuster, 2016), 43-44.

[2] Robert Dreyfuss, "The Phony War," September 12, 2006, *Rolling Stone*, http://truth-out.org/archive/component/k2/item/65441:robert-dreyfuss--the-phony-war; Gary Berntsen and Ralph Pezzullo, *Jawbreaker: The Attack on Bin Laden and Al-Qaeda; A Personal Account by the CIA's Key Field Commander* (Portland: Broadway, 2006), 308.

[3] Mark Tran and Matthew Weaver, "ISIS Announces Islamic Caliphate in Area Straddling Iraq and Syria," *Guardian*, June 30, 2014, https://www.theguardian.com/world/2014/jun/30/isis-announces-islamic-caliphate-iraq-syria.

[4] Daniel Boffey, "Boko Haram Declares Allegiance to Islamic State," *Guardian*, March 8, 2015, https://www.theguardian.com/world/2015/mar/07/boko-haram-suicide-bombers-50-dead-maiduguri; Sudarsan Raghaven, "Islamic State Loses Its Stronghold in Libya, but More Chaos Could Soon Follow," *Washington Post*, December 7, 2016, http://wapo.st/2vG6A6z.

[5] "US State Department Country Reports on Terrorism," United States Department of State, accessed May 23, 2017, https://www.state.gov/j/ct/rls/crt/.

[6] James Sterngold, "Cheney's Grim Vision: Decades of War," *San Francisco Chronicle*, January 15, 2004, http://www.sfgate.com/politics/article/Cheney-s-grim-vision-decades-of-war-Vice-2812372.php.

[7] Rowan Scarborough, "General: Millennial Marines Shun Self-absorbed Culture," *Washington Times*,

Something must be wrong.

The problem is that our government is ignoring and misrepresenting the real causes of the terrorists' war against the United States. They then exploit the population's ignorance and fear to advance their own unrelated and counterproductive political agendas.

More than a decade and a half after the September 11th attacks, America is deeply invested in a terrible lie: al Qaeda and Islamic State terrorists want to kill Americans because their belief in "radical" Islam makes them hate and wish to destroy all innocent and virtuous people and things.[8] Faced with such an implacable and irrational enemy, we are told there is only one option: "Fight them over there so we don't have to fight them over here."[9] When foreign-planned or foreign-inspired attacks then take place in the U.S. anyway, the answer remains: "Fight them over there some more."[10]

After all, even if the "collateral damage" from U.S. counter-terrorism efforts causes some "blowback," inspiring more terrorist attacks against our country, *they still started it*, right? What are we supposed to do, refuse to defend ourselves?

But this is all wrong. As the late libertarian activist, Harry Browne, used to say, for the purposes of the War on Terrorism, our political leaders would have us believe "history began on September 11th."[11] The truth is U.S. intervention in the Middle East long precedes al Qaeda's war against America and is the primary cause of our terrorism problem. Then, in a seemingly endless cycle, virtually everything the government has done in the name of defending us from terrorists has continued to make matters worse.

The September 11th attacks were no first assault by the "Muslim World," or even "Radical Islam," intent on invading the middle part of North America to overthrow the U.S. government, destroy our society and freedom or convert us to their religion. Instead, it was a last-gasp, desperate measure taken by a tiny group of formerly U.S.-backed Arab insurgent fighters, most of them from Saudi Arabia and Egypt, who had

May 7, 2014, http://www.washingtontimes.com/news/2014/may/7/general-millennial-marines-shun-self-absorbed-cult/.

[8] George W. Bush, "Address Before a Joint Session of the Congress on the United States Response to the Terrorist Attacks of September 11," 37 Weekly Comp. Pres. Doc. 1347 (September 20, 2001), http://www.presidency.ucsb.edu/ws/?pid=64731.

[9] George W. Bush, "President's Radio Address," 39 Weekly Comp. Pres. Doc. 1329 (October 4, 2003).

[10] Peter Baker and Eric Schmitt, "Paris Terror Attacks May Prompt More Aggressive US Strategy on ISIS," *New York Times*, November 14, 2015, https://www.nytimes.com/2015/11/15/world/europe/paris-terror-attacks-response-islamic-state.html.

[11] Harry Browne, "As Usual, the Wrong Question Is Being Asked," April 9, 2004, http://www.harrybrowne.org/articles/TerrorismReason.htm.

been exiled to the wilderness of Afghanistan's Hindu Kush mountains. Their strategy was to goad the United States government into helping accomplish their goals for them: destabilization, radicalization and revolution in *their* countries.

Leftist activist Saul Alinsky wrote that in all asymmetric, radical political acts, "the real action is in the reaction of the opposition."[12] Bin Laden understood this well. And though his stated plans once seemed grandiose to the point of absurdity, it turns out that in the last 15 years, America's War on Terrorism has already accomplished more of al Qaeda's agenda than they could have ever dreamed of managing on their own.

For years before the September 11th attacks, bin Laden told the world exactly what his grievances were, what he was going to do about them and how he expected his plan to work. His problem was U.S. military intervention in the Middle East. His plan was to wage war against the United States with the goal of forcing our military out of the region, thus making it possible to achieve al Qaeda's long-term goals of carrying out revolutions in their own countries without American interference.

John Miller, an ABC News reporter who later became an FBI counter-terrorism agent, interviewed bin Laden at his mountain camp near the border between Afghanistan and Pakistan in 1998.[13] Miller later described his incredulous reaction after hearing bin Laden declare his intentions for war against America and revolution throughout the region. "I thought, 'Yeah, you and what army?'"[14]

The answer, it turned out, was the U.S. Army, brought into the ranks of al Qaeda's forces by 19 very persuasive recruiters on September 11, 2001.

Blowback Terrorism

According to liberal Democrats like Obama-era State Department spokesperson Marie Harf, fighters rally to groups like al Qaeda and the Islamic State because they "need jobs."[15] Conservative Republicans, such as Texas Senator Ted Cruz, insist that no, it's Islam! Radical Islamic

---

[12] Saul David Alinsky, *Rules for Radicals: A Practical Primer for Realistic Radicals* (New York: Random House, 1971), 75.

[13] Osama bin Laden, interviewed by John Miller of ABC News, posted on Frontline website, May 1998, http://www.pbs.org/wgbh/pages/frontline/shows/binladen/who/interview.html.

[14] Peter L. Bergen, *The Osama Bin Laden I Know: An Oral History of al Qaeda's Leader* (New York: Free, 2006), 216.

[15] Jessica Mendoza, "State Department Rep Says Jobs Could Be Key to Eradicating Islamic State," *Christian Science Monitor*, February 17, 2015, http://www.csmonitor.com/USA/Foreign-Policy/2015/0217/State-Department-rep-says-jobs-could-be-key-to-eradicating-Islamic-State.

extremism! They hate us! They want to kill us![16] These explanations for our problems would be simply laughable if they did not help contribute to the formation of such deadly policies.

As "extreme" as al Qaeda and the Islamic State's version of Islam may be, what has clearly motivated their war against the U.S. from the beginning are American foreign policies they viewed as detrimental to their interests in the real, political world. Osama bin Laden repeatedly explained his motivations in his "fatwas" (religious edicts), speeches and media interviews leading up to the September 11th attacks.[17] From his 1998 "Declaration of War Against Jews and Crusaders":

> First, for over seven years the United States has been occupying the lands of Islam in the holiest of places, the Arabian Peninsula, plundering its riches, dictating to its rulers, humiliating its people, terrorizing its neighbors, and turning its bases in the Peninsula into a spearhead through which to fight the neighboring Muslim peoples. If some people have in the past argued about the fact of the occupation, all the people of the Peninsula have now acknowledged it. The best proof of this is the Americans' continuing aggression against the Iraqi people using the Peninsula as a staging post, even though all its rulers are against their territories being used to that end, but they are helpless.

> Second, despite the great devastation inflicted on the Iraqi people by the crusader-Zionist alliance, and despite the huge number of those killed, which has exceeded one million... despite all this, the Americans are once again trying to repeat the horrific massacres, as though they are not content with the protracted blockade imposed after the ferocious war or the fragmentation and devastation. So here they come to annihilate what is left of this people and to humiliate their Muslim neighbors.

> Third, if the Americans' aims behind these wars are religious and economic, the aim is also to serve the Jews' petty state and divert attention from its occupation of Jerusalem and murder of Muslims there. The best proof of this is their eagerness to destroy Iraq, the strongest neighboring Arab state, and their endeavor to fragment all the states of the region such as Iraq, Saudi Arabia, Egypt, and Sudan into paper statelets and through their disunion and weakness to guarantee Israel's survival and the continuation of the brutal crusade occupation of the Peninsula.[18]

---

[16] Julia Harte, "Cruz Chairs Contentious US Senate Hearing on 'Radical Islam,'" Reuters, June 28, 2016, http://www.reuters.com/article/us-usa-congress-islam-idUSKCN0ZE2U4.

[17] Osama bin Laden, *Messages to the World: The Statements of Osama Bin Laden*, ed. Bruce Lawrence, trans. James Howarth, annotated ed. (New York: Verso, 2005).

[18] Osama bin Laden, "Jihad Against Jews and Crusaders, World Islamic Front Statement," February

There you have it. Foremost among al Qaeda's grievances against America were the U.S. Army and Air Force combat forces stationed permanently at Saudi Arabian bases since the preparations for the first Iraq war in 1990, as well as their presence in other countries on the Arabian Peninsula. National borders between these countries are a distinction without a difference to bin Laden and his followers, for whom the entire peninsula is not just their homeland, but holy land — birth place of the Prophet Mohammad and the religion of Islam. According to a Saudi poll conducted after the September 11, 2001, attacks, 95 percent of educated Saudi males between the ages of 25 and 41 agreed with bin Laden's goal of driving Americans off the peninsula.[19] The U.S. was using these military bases, bin Laden complained, to enforce the long-term sanctions policy against Iraq and the bombing of its "no-fly zones" throughout the 1990s.

Bin Laden also routinely cited America's unconditional support for Israel, which both occupied Jerusalem — considered to be the third holiest site in Islam — as well as the property of millions of Palestinians in the rest of the West Bank and the Gaza Strip. Additionally, he objected to Israel's 1982 invasion and subsequent 18-year occupation of southern Lebanon, as well as what he characterized as Israeli-centric plans to destabilize antagonistic states in the region, such as Iraq.

Another part of al Qaeda's public case justifying its war against America was U.S. support for corrupt dictatorships in the Middle East, which included Jordan, Saudi Arabia, Kuwait, the United Arab Emirates, Bahrain, Oman, Qatar, Yemen and Egypt. This support, bin Laden complained, came with the condition that these regimes kept oil prices artificially low and spent their profits on large purchases of American arms instead of using it for the benefit of the people.[20] At one point, bin Laden referred to the old joke that the people of Arabia cannot drink the oil. Therefore, he said, it would always be for sale to the rest of the world, even if the head terrorist himself ruled all of Arabia — but then only at market prices.[21]

Is it a surprise then that all of the September 11th hijackers were from countries with governments friendly to our own — Saudi Arabia, Egypt, Lebanon and the United Arab Emirates — and that none of them were from America's designated enemy states of Iran, Iraq or Syria?[22]

23, 1998, https://fas.org/irp/world/para/docs/980223-fatwa.htm.

[19] Robert Pape, *Dying to Win: The Strategic Logic of Suicide Terrorism* (New York: Random House, 2005), 82.

[20] Michael Scheuer, *Imperial Hubris: Why the West is Losing the War on Terror* (Washington, DC: Potomac, 2007), 241.

[21] Abdul Bari Atwan, *The Secret History of al Qaeda*, updated ed. (Oakland: University of California Press, 2008), 33; Abdul Bari Atwan, "My Weekend with Osama bin Laden," *Guardian*, November 11, 2001, https://www.theguardian.com/world/2001/nov/12/afghanistan.terrorism2.

[22] "September 11th Hijackers Fast Facts," CNN, last modified September 5, 2016,

Osama bin Laden was a mass-murderer, deserving the utmost contempt. Why should we listen to what he says? Why would *anyone* listen to him? The reality is that no matter what bin Laden really believed, this list of grievances was his successful recruitment pitch[23] — the tale he told to motivate young men such as the September 11th attackers to carry out his war against America. As former CIA bin Laden unit chief Michael Scheuer has emphasized, when Iran's Ayatollah Khomeini spent the 1980s denouncing America's corrupt popular culture, the region more or less yawned. Were conservative religious leaders concerned about Hollywood polluting young minds? Yes, of course. Was this enough to motivate men to want to kill and die in a war against the United States? Of course not. Bin Laden chose instead to harp on real, tangible, largely destructive U.S. government policies in Arab countries. This enabled him to recruit a small army of terrorists willing to do his bidding, even at the cost of their own lives.[24]

For one example, in April 1996, after Israel launched their Operation Grapes of Wrath campaign in Southern Lebanon, future lead September 11th hijacker, Mohammad Atta, signed his last will and testament, a symbol of his willingness to die in the fight against those he blamed for the war.[25] As journalist Terry McDermott explains in his book on Atta's so-called "Hamburg cell" of September 11th plotters, they had all agreed it was the Americans who were responsible for what Israel was doing since the U.S. government gives Israel so many billions of dollars in military equipment and other financial aid.[26]

It was just a few months later, in August of 1996, that Osama bin Laden released his first "fatwa" against the United States, entitled "Declaration of War Against the Americans Occupying the Land of the Two Holy Places." In it, there was no mention of a hatred for liberty, democracy, action movies, tacos, motherhood, the county fair or any other wonderful thing. What it did mention was the presence of U.S. military bases on the Arabian Peninsula, the bombing and blockade of Iraq from those bases and Israel's occupations — especially Operation Grapes of Wrath, including what is now called the First Qana Massacre, during which 106 Lebanese civilians were killed when Israeli forces shelled a United Nations

---

http://edition.cnn.com/2013/07/27/us/september-11th-hijackers-fast-facts/; "Official: 15 of 19 Sept. 11 Hijackers Were Saudi," *USA Today*, February 6, 2002,
http://usatoday30.usatoday.com/news/world/2002/02/06/saudi.htm.

[23] "Compilation of Usama Bin Laden Statements 1994-January 2004," FBIS, January 2004, https://fas.org/irp/world/para/ubl-fbis.pdf; Osama bin Laden, *Messages to the World*.

[24] Scheuer, *Imperial Hubris*, 112, 211.

[25] Lawrence Wright, *The Looming Tower: Al-Qaeda and the Road to 9/11* (New York: Vintage, 2007), 307.

[26] Terry McDermott, *Perfect Soldiers: The 9/11 Hijackers: Who They Were, Why They Did It* (New York: Harper Collins, 2009), 67-68, 86-87.

compound where they had sought shelter.[27]

> It should not be hidden from you that the people of Islam had suffered from aggression, iniquity and injustice imposed on them by the Zionist-Crusaders alliance and their collaborators; to the extent that the Muslims' blood became the cheapest and their wealth as loot in the hands of the enemies. Their blood was spilled in Palestine and Iraq. The horrifying pictures of the massacre of Qana, in Lebanon are still fresh in our memory. ...

> The youths hold you responsible for all of the killings and evictions of the Muslims and the violation of the sanctities, carried out by your Zionist brothers in Lebanon; you openly supplied them with arms and finance.

As journalist James Bamford later noted, "[Bin Laden] frequently mentioned Qana during those times. It was a very inflaming incident in terms of his own development of his hatred for the United States, and as well for other people throughout the Middle East."[28]

When Atta and his best friend and co-conspirator, Ramzi bin al-Shibh, found out how closely Osama bin Laden agreed with their own view, they decided his war was to be their path. The next year, Atta and bin al-Shibh traveled to the training camps in Afghanistan to meet with bin Laden and volunteer their services.[29] Their potential must have been obvious to al Qaeda; upper middle-class graduate students studying engineering in Germany would have easy access to the United States...[30]

These pilot hijackers cited U.S. military, financial, and diplomatic support, not simply for Israel's existence, but for its violence against the people of southern Lebanon — invaded and occupied by Israel between 1982 and 2000 — and against the occupied Palestinian population of the West Bank and Gaza Strip — areas conquered and ruled under Israeli military control since the 1967 Six Day War.

This obviously does not mean the leaders of al Qaeda have ever indicated they would be happy to settle for a return to 1967 borders and a two-state solution for an independent Palestine. Bin Laden himself consistently railed against Israel's very existence.[31] However, virtually every

---

[27] Osama bin Laden, "Declaration of War Against the Americans Occupying the Land of the Two Holy Places," PBS, August 1996, https://web.archive.org/web/20120201053344/http://www.pbs.org/newshour/terrorism/international/fatwa_1996.html.

[28] James Bamford, interviewed by author, *Scott Horton Show*, radio archive, August 14, 2004, http://scotthorton.org/interviews/2004/08/14/august-14-2004-hour-1-james-bamford/; Osama bin Laden, *Messages to the World*, 51, 114.

[29] McDermott, *Perfect Soldiers*, 88-89.

[30] Ibid., 177-179.

[31] Bin Laden, *Messages to the World*, 107, 114, 128, 162-163.

government in the region has said they would make a permanent peace with Israel on those terms,[32] including Hamas, the fundamentalist militant movement that rules the Gaza Strip.[33] This leaves little doubt that if the Palestinians were granted independence or equal rights as citizens within Israel, a huge part of the controversy would be eliminated, just as outrage and attacks from Hezbollah have subsided since the withdrawal of the Israeli military from Lebanon in the year 2000.[34]

Israel has a huge military advantage in terms of modern high-tech arms, transport, training and virtually any other measure, over all their neighbors, most of which are Israel-friendly dictatorships such as Jordan, Egypt and Saudi Arabia.[35] So any argument that an end to foreign aid to Israel would amount to "abandoning" Israel's Jewish population to a second Holocaust at the hands of the Arab hordes cannot be taken seriously. As far as that position goes, military-oriented Israeli leaders, such as Prime Minister Benjamin Netanyahu, have said dependence on the United States ultimately weakens the Israeli state. American aid is arguably counterproductive, even from the point of view of Israeli and pro-Israel hawks, much less from American victims of terrorism.[36]

---

[32] "The Arab Peace Initiative: Full Text," *Guardian*, March 28, 2002, https://www.theguardian.com/world/2002/mar/28/israel7.

[33] Kevin Liffey, ed., "Hamas Renews Offer to End Fight if Israel Withdraws," Reuters, May 30, 2010, http://www.reuters.com/article/us-palestinians-israel-hamas-idUSTRE64T2AM20100530.

[34] Robert A. Pape, interviewed by Eleanor Hall, "Analyst Says Israel Missed Chance for Diplomacy," *World Today*, ABC (Australia), August 9, 2006, http://www.abc.net.au/worldtoday/content/2006/s1710684.htm; "Suicide Attack Database," accessed May 16, 2017, Chicago Project on Security and Terrorism (CPOST), http://cpostdata.uchicago.edu/search_new.php; "Hezbollah," Mapping Militant Organizations, Stanford University, https://web.stanford.edu/group/mappingmilitants/cgi-bin/groups/view/81?.

[35] "Joint Press Conference with Secretary of Defense Ash Carter and Israeli Minister of Defense Moshe Ya'alon," United States Department of Defense, July 20, 2015, https://www.defense.gov/News/Transcripts/Transcript-View/Article/612945/joint-press-conference-with-secretary-carter-and-minister-of-defense-yaalon-in; "Ensuring Israel's Qualitative Military Edge," Andrew J. Shapiro, remarks to Washington Institute for Near East Policy, November 4, 2011, https://web.archive.org/web/20170121040853/https://www.state.gov/t/pm/rls/rm/176684.htm.

[36] "Israeli Prime Minister Benjamin Netanyahu's Speech to the US Congress," Israel Ministry of Foreign Affairs, July 10, 1996, http://mfa.gov.il/MFA/MFA-Archive/1996/Pages/default.aspx; Amos Harel, "Israel's Evolving Military: The IDF Adapts to New Threats," *Foreign Affairs*, July/August 2016, https://www.foreignaffairs.com/articles/israel/2016-06-08/israel-s-evolving-military; William Wunderle and Andre Briere, "US Foreign Policy and Israel's Qualitative Military Edge: The Need for a Common Vision," Washington Institute for Near East Policy, January 2008, http://www.washingtoninstitute.org/uploads/Documents/pubs/PolicyFocus80Final.pdf; Eli Lake, "Some of Israel's Top Defenders Say It's Time to End US Aid," Daily Beast, July 18, 2014, http://www.thedailybeast.com/articles/2014/07/18/some-of-israel-s-top-defenders-say-it-s-time-to-end-u-s-aid.html; Richard Perle et al., "A Clean Break: A New Strategy for Securing the Realm," Information Clearing House, July 8, 1996, http://www.informationclearinghouse.info/article1438.htm; Barbara Opall-Rome, "Ex-Israeli General: US Aid Harms and Corrupts," Defense News, July 25, 2016, http://www.defensenews.com/story/defense/policy-budget/budget/2016/07/25/israel-general-us-military-aid-idf/87526182/; Yori Yanover, "Naftali Bennett: Stop US Aid, Slash Israel's Military Budget," *Jewish Press*, January 8, 2013,

The true costs and consequences of U.S. intervention in the region, then, extend far beyond the unnecessary billions of dollars spent on "Made in the U.S.A." brand F-16s and M-16s for Israel's military occupation over the Palestinians, to innocent American lives lost as well.[37]

U.S. support for Israel's violence in the occupied territories and Lebanon were cited again and again as motivation for al Qaeda attacks against American civilians. As bin Laden said in his 1997 interview with Peter Arnett of CNN,

> We declared jihad against the U.S. government because the U.S. government is unjust, criminal and tyrannical. It has committed acts that are extremely unjust, hideous and criminal whether directly or through its support of the Israeli occupation of the Prophet's Night Travel Land [Palestine]. And we believe the U.S. is directly responsible for those who were killed in Palestine, Lebanon and Iraq. The mention of the U.S. reminds us before everything else of those innocent children who were dismembered, their heads and arms cut off in the recent explosion that took place in Qana.[38]

FBI agent James Fitzgerald, when questioned by the September 11th Commission about the enemies' motives, testified:

> I believe they feel a sense of outrage against the United States. They identify with the Palestinian problem; they identify with people who oppose oppressive regimes, and I believe they tend to focus their anger on the United States.[39]

In fact, after the September 11th attacks, Secretary of State Colin Powell believed President Bush's approval ratings were high enough, and the problem of anti-American terrorism was important enough, to move the issue of the creation of a Palestinian state in the occupied West Bank and Gaza Strip to the front burner. He was soon disappointed to discover that the hawks' counter narrative that the Israelis were simply innocent victims of Islamic terrorism — like us — was far more appealing to the president. They convinced Bush that "the road to Jerusalem runs through Baghdad" — that regime change in Iraq would be the panacea that would

---

http://www.jewishpress.com/news/naftali-bennett-time-to-stop-us-aid-slash-israels-military-budget/2013/01/08/.

[37] Shirl McArthur, "A Conservative Estimate of Total US Direct Aid to Israel: Almost $138 Billion," *Washington Report on Middle East Affairs*, October 2015, http://www.wrmea.org/2015-october/a-conservative-estimate-of-total-u.s.-direct-aid-to-israel-almost-$138-billion.html.

[38] "Transcript of Osama Bin Ladin Interview by Peter Arnett," Information Clearing House, March 1997, http://www.informationclearinghouse.info/article7204.htm.

[39] James Bamford, "Intelligence Test," review of *Without Precedent: The Inside Story of the 9/11 Commission,* by Thomas H. Kean and Lee H. Hamilton, *New York Times,* August 20, 2006, http://www.nytimes.com/2006/08/20/books/review/20Bamford.html.

end all support for terrorism in the region and allow the U.S. and Israel to negotiate from a much stronger position in the future.[40]

Eric Alterman, columnist for the liberal *Nation* magazine, recognized the problem as well:

> I think that bin Laden, and 9/11, was to some degree inspired by U.S. support for Israel. I think the great deal of terrorist attacks, and the sort-of pool of potential terrorists who want to attack the United States are inspired by United States support for Israel. I'm not saying we shouldn't support Israel for that reason. I'm saying "Dammit, if that's the price we have to pay, then I'm willing to pay it." … I'm just saying let's be honest about it.[41]

One may acknowledge this reality and yet persist in the belief that the U.S. should support Israel's occupation, keep troops stationed at bases in Arabia, continue to bomb Iraq and provoke terrorist enemies in various other ways. It is notable, though, when hawks occasionally admit the truth: our enemies' motives for attacking the United States are rooted in our government's foreign policies rather than the pale tone of the American majority's skin, predominantly Christian religious beliefs, personal freedoms, republican political system or unseemly height of our skyscrapers. The issue has always been the military occupations and support for dictatorships.[42]

Islam

There are those who seek to put the West on a course for a total clash of civilizations with all Muslims[43] by blaming faith in Islam itself for

---

[40] Karen DeYoung, *Soldier: The Life of Colin Powell* (New York: Vintage, 2007), 388.

[41] Jane Eisner et al., "Why We Need a Liberal Israel Lobby," YouTube Video, 1:16:54, from a panel discussion at the 92nd Street YMCA, New York, on March 16, 2009, uploaded March 18, 2009, posted by 92nd Street Y, https://www.youtube.com/watch?v=bcq8rsgetm8#t=2359.

[42] Wright, *The Looming Tower*, 245-247; Berntsen, *Jawbreaker*, 67; Robert A. Pape, "It's the Occupation, Stupid," *Foreign Policy*, October 18, 2010, http://foreignpolicy.com/2010/10/18/its-the-occupation-stupid/; United States Department of Defense, "Report of the Defense Science Board Task Force on Strategic Communication," Federation of American Scientists, September 2004, p. 40, https://fas.org/irp/agency/dod/dsb/commun.pdf; Stephen Zunes and Richard Falk, *Tinderbox: U.S. Foreign Policy and the Roots of Terrorism* (Monroe, ME: Common Courage, 2002); Johnny Spooner, "Islamic Terrorists, in Their Own Words," Drifters and Parking Spaces, November 16, 2015, https://driftersandparkingspaces.wordpress.com/2015/11/16/49/.

[43] Wajahat Ali et al., "Fear, Inc.: The Roots of the Islamophobia Network in America," Center for American Progress, August 26, 2011, https://americanprogress.org/issues/religion/reports/2011/08/26/10165/fear-inc/; Max Blumenthal, "The Great Fear," TomDispatch, December 19, 2010, http://www.tomdispatch.com/post/175334/tomgram:_max_blumenthal,_the_great_fear_/; Nathan Lean, *The Islamophobia Industry: How the Right Manufactures Fear of Muslims* (London: Pluto, 2012); David Noriega, "Brigitte Gabriel Wants You to Fight Islam," BuzzFeed News, September 27, 2016, https://www.buzzfeed.com/davidnoriega/meet-the-charming-terrifying-face-of-the-anti-

turning sane men into irrational terrorist psychopaths bent on total war against anyone who happens to be good. We have heard variations of this message day in and day out for years now.

What does "radical Islamic extremism" have to do with anti-American terrorism? It plays some role, but not in the way the hawks claim. There are more than 1.6 billion Muslims, making up more than one-fifth of the planet's population. Of these, there are at least hundreds of millions of deeply committed believers in Islam in the world, including several million Americans. Sunni and Shi'ite Muslims — and a number of other, smaller schools — can be either fundamentalist or moderate, conservative or radical, and represent different nationalities and races from across the world. It is safe to say that since fewer than 100,000 bin Ladenites have emerged out of a global Muslim population of over one and a half billion, even in all the chaos of the U.S.-created Middle Eastern battlefields of the last 15 years and at the height of the so-called Islamic State in Iraq and Syria,[44] there must be another explanation, since the vast majority of even Salafi and Wahhabi fundamentalists would rather solve problems peacefully and have no interest in supporting or engaging in terrorism whatsoever.[45]

There is also the plain fact that many actual al Qaeda and ISIS terrorists are not religious fundamentalists or "radicals" at all.[46] Over the last 25 years, many of these bin Ladenite terrorists have had a distinct lack of religiosity. This includes some of the perpetrators of the first World Trade

islam-lobby; Jack Shaheen, *Reel Bad Arabs: How Hollywood Vilifies a People,* 3rd ed., (Northampton, MA: Olive Branch, 2014).

[44] Ali Soufan, "Al Qaeda is Stronger Now Than When Bin Laden Was Killed," Daily Beast, May 7, 2017, http://www.thedailybeast.com/articles/2017/05/07/al-qaeda-is-stronger-now-than-when-bin-laden-was-killed; "Al-Qaeda," GlobalSecurity.org, http://www.globalsecurity.org/military/world/para/al-qaida.htm; "Al Qaeda," Mapping Militant Organizations, Stanford University, https://web.stanford.edu/group/mappingmilitants/cgi-bin/groups/view/21; Jim Sciutto et al., "ISIS Can 'Muster' Between 20,000 and 31,500 Fighters, CIA Says," CNN, September 12, 2014, http://cnn.com/2014/09/11/world/meast/isis-syria-iraq/.

[45] John L. Esposito and Dalia Mogahed, *Who Speaks for Islam? What a Billion Muslims Really Think* (Washington, DC: Gallup, 2008); Najam Haider, interviewed by the author, *Scott Horton Show,* radio archive, January 7, 2016, https://scotthorton.org/interviews/1716-najam-haider/.

[46] Scott Wilson et al., "Boston Bombing Suspect Cites US Wars as Motivation, Officials Say," *Washington Post,* April 23, 2013, https://www.washingtonpost.com/national/boston-bombing-suspect-cites-us-wars-as-motivation-officials-say/2013/04/23/324b9cea-ac29-11e2-b6fd-ba6f5f26d70e_story.html; Patrick Tucker, "Why Join ISIS? How Fighters Respond When You Ask Them," *Atlantic,* December 9, 2015, http://theatlantic.com/international/archive/2015/12/why-people-join-isis/419685/; Alan Travis, "MI5 Report Challenges Views on Terrorism in Britain," *Guardian,* August 20, 2008, https://www.theguardian.com/uk/2008/aug/20/uksecurity.terrorism1; Arun Kundnani, "A Decade Lost: Rethinking Radicalization and Extremism," Claystone, January 2015, http://mabonline.net/wp-content/uploads/2015/01/Claystone-rethinking-radicalisation.pdf; Fareed Zakaria, "Today's New Terrorists Were Radical Before They Were Religious," *Washington Post,* March 31, 2016, https://www.washingtonpost.com/opinions/todays-new-terrorists-were-radical-before-they-were-religious/2016/03/31/9cb8e916-f762-11e5-9804-537defcc3cf6_story.html; Pape, *Dying to Win,* 209-210.

Center bombing in 1993,[47] at least a few of the September 11th hijackers,[48] and many Islamic State fighters in Iraq and Syria,[49] as well as the Paris,[50] Brussels[51] and Nice[52] attackers of 2015 and 2016.[53] Even among those terrorists who can be considered fundamentalists or believers in "radical" branches of Islam, we again find explicit, repeated claims of secular motivations, namely, revenge against Western governments for specific, violent foreign policies.[54]

A 2008 study of those who became involved with terrorism by the British domestic intelligence service, MI-5, found that

---

[47] John Parachini, "Religion Isn't Sole Motive of Terror," RAND Corporation, September 16, 2001, http://www.rand.org/blog/2001/09/religion-isnt-sole-motive-of-terror.html.

[48] "Manager: Men Spewed Anti-American Sentiments," *USA Today*, September 14, 2001, http://usatoday30.usatoday.com/news/nation/2001/09/14/miami-club.htm; Dave Wedge, "Terrorists Partied with Hooker at Hub-Area Hotel," *Boston Herald*, October 10, 2001; Tony Harnden, "Seedy Secrets of Hijackers Who Broke Muslim Laws," *Daily Telegraph*, October 6, 2001, http://telegraph.co.uk/news/1358665/Seedy-secrets-of-hijackers-who-broke-Muslim-laws.html.

[49] Lizzie Dearden, "ISIS: Islam is 'Not Strongest Factor' Behind Foreign Fighters Joining Extremist Groups in Syria and Iraq," *Independent*, November 16, 2016, http://www.independent.co.uk/news/world/europe/isis-foreign-fighters-british-european-western-dying-radicalised-islam-not-strongest-factor-cultural-a7421711.html; Aya Batrawy et al., "Leaked ISIS Documents Reveal Recruits Have Poor Grasp of Islamic Faith," *Independent*, August 16, 2016, http://www.independent.co.uk/news/world/middle-east/isis-documents-leak-recruits-islam-sharia-religion-faith-syria-iraq-a7193086.html; Arie Perliger and Daniel Milton, "From Cradle to Grave: The Lifecycle of Foreign Fighters in Iraq and Syria," Combating Terrorism Center at West Point, November 2016, https://www.ctc.usma.edu/v2/wp-content/uploads/2016/11/Cradle-to-Grave.pdf; Musa al-Gharbi, "Don't Think of the 'Islamic State' in Religious Terms," Middle East Policy Council, October 31, 2014, http://www.mepc.org/articles-commentary/commentary/dont-think-islamic-state-religious-terms; Lydia Wilson, "What I Discovered from Interviewing Imprisoned ISIS Fighters," *Nation*, October 21, 2015, https://www.thenation.com/article/what-i-discovered-from-interviewing-isis-prisoners/.

[50] Camille Turner, "Paris Attacks Suicide Bomber 'Drank, Smoked and Ran Drug Den,'" *Daily Telegraph*, November 16, 2015, http://www.telegraph.co.uk/news/worldnews/europe/france/11999576/Paris-attacks-suicide-bomber-drank-and-ran-drugs-den.html.

[51] Lizzie Dearden, "ISIS Claims Responsibility for Brussels Attacks 'In Revenge for Belgium's Role Fighting Militants in Syria and Iraq,'" *Independent*, March 22, 2016, http://www.independent.co.uk/news/world/europe/isis-claims-responsibility-for-brussels-attacks-explosions-bombings-at-airport-and-maalbeek-maelbeek-a6946136.html.

[52] "Terrorist Behind Nice Attack a Creepy Loner; Not Overtly Religious, Say Neighbors," Fox News, July 15, 2016, http://www.foxnews.com/world/2016/07/15/terrorist-behind-nice-attack-creepy-loner-not-overtly-religious-say-neighbors.html.

[53] Anne Aly, "The New Breed of Terrorists: Criminals First, Islamists Second," Conversation, March 31, 2016, http://theconversation.com/the-new-breed-of-terrorists-criminals-first-islamists-second-56996; Davide Lerner, "It's Not Islam That Drives Young Europeans to Jihad, France's Top Terrorism Expert Explains," *Ha'aretz*, June 4, 2017, http://www.haaretz.com/world-news/europe/1.791954?v=FBAED08735812BD2447429DD931B773A.

[54] US Department of Defense, "Report of the Defense Science Board Task Force on Strategic Communication," September 2004, https://fas.org/irp/agency/dod/dsb/commun.pdf, p. 40; William Blum, "Myth and Denial in the War Against Terrorism: Just Why Do Terrorists Terrorize?" in *Freeing the World to Death*, (Monroe, ME: Common Courage, 2004), https://williamblum.org/chapters/freeing-the-world-to-death/myth-and-denial-in-the-war-against-terrorism.

far from being religious zealots, a large number of those involved in terrorism do not practice their faith regularly. Many lack religious literacy and could actually be regarded as religious novices. Very few have been brought up in strongly religious households, and there is a higher than average proportion of converts. Some are involved in drug-taking, drinking alcohol and visiting prostitutes. MI5 says there is evidence that a well-established religious identity actually protects against violent radicalization. ...

The security service also plays down the importance of radical extremist clerics, saying their influence in radicalizing British terrorists has moved into the background in recent years. ... The MI5 authors stress that the most pressing current threat is from Islamist extremist groups who justify the use of violence "in defense of Islam," but that there are also violent extremists involved in non-Islamist movements.[55]

A 2010 report by the UK think tank Demos found that young Muslims, including religious radicals, rejected terrorism, and that, on the contrary, those who did embrace violence in the name of the religion tended to have a "simpler, shallower conception of Islam." They continued:

Radicals refused to defend violent jihad in the West as religiously obligatory, acceptable or permitted. The same was true of the young Muslim sample. Young Muslims rejected al Qaeda's message and often use simple, catchy sayings from the Qur'an or Hadith to express that rejection. However, there was widespread support among radicals and young Muslims for Iraqi and Afghan people "defending themselves" from "invaders," framed in the language of self-defense, just war and state sovereignty.[56]

Religion's most important role in the situation is simply that it creates a *shared identity*, or basis for solidarity, between the victims of violence and those who fight in their names. None of the September 11th hijackers were Iraqi, but al Qaeda's Saudi and Egyptian ringleaders had made it clear for years that they were fighting the U.S. in part to defend or avenge the Iraqis — their fellow Arabs and Muslims — who were being slaughtered and starved under the American no-fly zones and blockade of the 1990s. Iraqi civilian victims were still seen by them as part of the "ummah," or greater Muslim community, regardless of where former European empires had drawn the modern national borders.[57]

---

[55] Travis, "MI5 Report Challenges Views on Terrorism in Britain."

[56] Jamie Bartlett et al., "The Edge of Violence: A Radical Approach to Extremism," Demos, 2010, http://www2.gsu.edu/~crirxf/Edge%20of%20violence.pdf.

[57] Osama bin Laden, "Full Text: Bin Laden's 'Letter to America,'" *Guardian*, November 24, 2002, https://www.theguardian.com/world/2002/nov/24/theobserver.

This is no different than the many American Christians, Jews, and, yes, Muslims, from Florida, Texas, Colorado and California who felt the need to join the American armed forces that were retaliating for the September 11th attacks against far-away New York and Washington, D.C., believing they were defending Western Civilization, or at least their country, from the terrorist enemy.

Yes, it is true that al Qaeda infuses their message with theology, citing scriptures and religious leaders to justify their positions and actions. It makes sense that those most committed to literalistic interpretations of scripture and belief in the afterlife might be some of the first to sign up to fight, but there is no reason to suppose this is unique to Christians, Jews or Muslims. If the U.S. had bombed, blockaded and occupied the Indian subcontinent for the last generation, "radical Hindu extremists" would very likely be leading the resistance against it. We would then be hearing endless warnings about the dangers and influence of this radical Hinduism among our insurgent enemies, which makes people go insane and want to murder strangers halfway around the world just for the crime of being free and living in the Western Hemisphere.

Osama bin Laden did often invoke religious justifications for his ultimately political purposes. Typical is this example, from his fatwa of 1998, "Declaration of War Against Jews and Crusaders":

> All these crimes and sins committed by the Americans are a clear declaration of war on Allah, his messenger, and Muslims. And ulema [religious leaders] have throughout Islamic history unanimously agreed that the jihad is an individual duty if the enemy destroys the Muslim countries. This was revealed by ... the shaykh of al-Islam in his books, where he said: "As for the fighting to repulse, it is aimed at defending sanctity and religion, and it is a duty as agreed [by the ulema]. Nothing is more sacred than belief except repulsing an enemy who is attacking religion and life."

> On that basis, and in compliance with Allah's order, we issue the following fatwa to all Muslims:

> The ruling to kill the Americans and their allies — civilians and military — is an individual duty for every Muslim who can do it in any country in which it is possible to do it, in order to liberate the al-Aqsa Mosque [in Jerusalem] and the holy mosque [in Mecca, Saudi Arabia] from their grip, and in order for their armies to move out of all the lands of Islam, defeated and unable to threaten any Muslim.[58]

This is clearly politics invoking religion. It is a call for a defensive war, not an attempt to recruit people who do not even control their own

---

[58] Bin Laden, "Jihad Against Jews and Crusaders."

countries to try to violently force a system of totalitarian Islamist rule on ours.

When U.S. military officers have said publicly they believe they are fighting a religious war for Christianity against the forces of Satanic darkness,[59] it has not caused us to forget that terrorists attacked us. Nor have we understood them — and all others who join the army or support the war — to be simply motivated by extreme Christian-Crusader religious views that mandate the eradication or suppression of all Muslims and the occupation of all their lands. That would be stupid. Even when President Bush himself invoked religious justifications for the second Iraq war,[60] few considered these statements to reveal his true motivations for the invasion. They were seen instead as obvious attempts to rationalize an earthly, political policy.

Try to imagine for a moment Americans tolerating foreign military bases and combat troops stationed inside the United States, even at the invitation of our president or governors. The population would go to war against them and stay at war until they forced the occupiers out, no matter the cost, just as America's founders fought for independence from England in the Revolutionary War "for quartering large bodies of armed troops among us."[61] Many ministers, priests, rabbis and imams would bless the cause, too.

As ex-CIA analyst Scheuer has observed, identifying the method al Qaeda uses in its war against us as "terrorism" is correct; terrorism being properly defined as "the unlawful use of violence and intimidation, especially against civilians, in the pursuit of political aims."[62] But this can obscure an important point. Rather than simply a terrorist group, the movement is more correctly described as an insurgency — yes, led by Islamists — against our nation's domination of their region of the world, which uses terrorism as one of its tactics.[63] This seems obvious enough in terms of the Sunni Arab insurgency in the second Iraq war and the Taliban insurgency in Afghanistan. Yet these two current, major invasions and occupations can obscure the fact that America was the dominant power in the Middle East long before 2001.

---

[59] "Rumsfeld Praises Army General Who Ridicules Islam as 'Satan,'" Reuters, October 17, 2003, http://www.nytimes.com/2003/10/17/world/rumsfeld-praises-army-general-who-ridicules-islam-as-satan.html; Robert H. Reid, "Attacks Rock Central Iraq," *South Coast Today*, November 7, 2004, http://www.southcoasttoday.com/article/20041107/News/311079978.

[60] Ewen MacAskill, "George Bush: 'God Told Me to End the Tyranny in Iraq,'" *Guardian*, October 7, 2005, https://www.theguardian.com/world/2005/oct/07/iraq.usa.

[61] Thomas Jefferson et al., "Declaration of Independence of the Thirteen united States of America," National Archives, July 4, 1776, https://www.archives.gov/founding-docs/declaration.

[62] "Definition of Terrorism in English," Oxford Dictionaries, https://en.oxforddictionaries.com/definition/terrorism.

[63] Scheuer, *Imperial Hubris*, p. x.

Abu Musab al Zarqawi, the first leader of al Qaeda in Iraq, and his successors in the Islamic State of 2014–2017 that grew out of it have had a far more apocalyptic religious view, preaching about the end of the world and an ideology which holds virtually genocidal views toward Shi'ites and other supposed heretics.[64] And they act on them, ruthlessly massacring and enslaving minority civilians in areas where they have dominated. In practice, however, even ISIS — whose leadership is comprised mostly of former Iraqi Ba'athist military officers and local insurgent leaders from the second Iraq war — fights first and foremost for territory here on earth.

Rather than driving the movement, ISIS's apocalyptic frame of reference is mostly just the thin war propaganda of a corrupt, nihilistic and ultimately doomed force; to justify their war crimes and help rally fighters to their side, the terrorists invoke holy texts. A war of conquest must be framed as a war of religious defense as well.[65] Why fight modern Iraqi Shi'ite forces when they can all be characterized as evil, heretical "Safavids" of a long-lost Persian empire from the sixteenth century? Why struggle under aerial bombardment from America and its banal European Union allies, when they can be characterized as the Roman Empire of ancient history, whose defeat will presage the end of the world?[66] Why settle for an identity as a run-of-the-mill criminal, raping women and girls as spoils of war, when your debauchery can be spun as doing the Lord's work against the infidels?[67]

Of course, when it comes to religious doctrines, there is always a mix of charlatans and true believers among the leaders of the groups espousing them. Certainly, many al Qaeda and ISIS members have deep devotion to their religion and to various political doctrines about their people's place in the world. But it is the destabilizing chaos of war that makes the radical sidewalk preacher who calls for violence seem like he must be something other than a raving nut. As British filmmaker Adam Curtis argued in his documentary, *The Power of Nightmares*, the American interventionists and the al Qaeda terrorists act as mirror images, or a transmission belt of power, for each other. Each group of radicals needs the violent chaos their

---

[64] Abu Bakr Naji, "The Management of Savagery: The Most Critical Stage Through Which the Umma Will Pass," trans. William McCants, John M. Olin Institute for Strategic Studies at Harvard University, May 23, 2006, https://azelin.files.wordpress.com/2010/08/abu-bakr-naji-the-management-of-savagery-the-most-critical-stage-through-which-the-umma-will-pass.pdf; Lawrence Wright, "ISIS'S Savage Strategy in Iraq," *New Yorker*, June 16, 2014, http://www.newyorker.com/news/daily-comment/isiss-savage-strategy-in-iraq.

[65] Doug Bandow, "The Islamic State Attempts to Eradicate Christians While Creating Killer Caliphate," *Forbes*, March 22, 2016, https://www.forbes.com/sites/dougbandow/2016/03/22/the-islamic-state-attempts-to-eradicate-christians-while-creating-killer-caliphate/.

[66] "Dabiq: Why is Syrian Town So Important for IS?," BBC Monitoring, October 4, 2016, http://www.bbc.com/news/world-middle-east-30083303.

[67] Rukmini Callimachi, "ISIS Enshrines a Theology of Rape," *New York Times*, August 13, 2015, https://www.nytimes.com/2015/08/14/world/middleeast/isis-enshrines-a-theology-of-rape.html.

enemies create to rally populations and portray themselves as the leaders of the new defensive war which must be fought.[68]

This is where the hawks on both sides benefit from highlighting the worst aspects of the other. ISIS complains about what they call the "Grey Zone,"[69] otherwise known as modern Western Civilization, where people's respect for individual rights — especially freedom of religion — allows millions of Muslims to live harmoniously among those of different faiths. This peaceful coexistence is anathema to the terrorist leaders. They explicitly order their followers to commit attacks against Western targets for the very purpose of forcing our governments to overreact, yet again — to clampdown upon and alienate Muslims in our societies where they have assimilated well, by and large, especially in the United States.[70]

This is similar to the tactics used by European, communist terrorists of previous generations, who used attacks on civilian targets to "sharpen the contradictions" between the left and the right, alienating the moderate middle and helping to drive both sides to extremes.[71] It is unfortunate so many American hawks have found reason to abet such fringe criminals and murderers as al Qaeda and ISIS, legitimizing their claims to represent the true faith in their careless attempt to blame Islam for our terrorism problem. This has virtually criminalized the beliefs of over a billion people in the minds of many in the West, possibly leading us further down the path to even worse conflict.

Western hawks like to focus on the enemy's citations of religious scripture as though they are occurring in a complete vacuum. This is a convenient way for them to demonize the enemy as completely irrational while directing attention away from the severe human deprivation caused by America's recent wars — the context in which the most radical ideologies have thrived and spread. It should be easy to understand why Iraqis, for example, many of whom have nothing left after all these years of war except their faith, might believe Biblical forces are at work after so

---

[68] Adam Curtis, *The Power of Nightmares: The Rise of the Politics of Fear*, "Part 1: Baby Its Cold Outside," YouTube video, 59:23, televised by the BBC in 2004, posted by Adam Curtis Documentary, May 20, 2016, https://www.youtube.com/watch?v=dTg4qnyUGxg.

[69] Myriam Francois-Cerrah, "Islamic State Wants to Divide the World into Jihadists and Crusaders," *Telegraph*, November 18, 2015, http://www.telegraph.co.uk/news/worldnews/islamic-state/12002726/The-grey-zone-How-Isis-wants-to-divide-the-world-into-Muslims-and-crusaders.html.

[70] Alex Nowrasteh, "Muslim Assimilation: Demographics, Education, Income, and Opinions of Violence," CATO at Liberty, August 24, 2016, https://www.cato.org/blog/muslim-assimilation-demographic-education-income-opinions-violence; Philip Giraldi, "Hating the Haters," Unz Review, January 13, 2015, http://www.unz.com/pgiraldi/hating-the-haters/; Michael Hirsh, "Inside the FBI's Secret Muslim Network," Politico, March 24, 2016, http://www.politico.com/magazine/story/2016/03/fbi-muslim-outreach-terrorism-213765.

[71] Juan Cole, "Sharpening Contradictions: Why al-Qaeda Attacked Satirists in Paris," Informed Comment, January 7, 2015, https://www.juancole.com/2015/01/sharpening-contradictions-satirists.html.

many have died and so much of their society has been distorted or destroyed. Certainly, apocalyptic Christian doctrines got a boost in attention in the United States after the calamity of September 11th.[72]

When attacks in the West occur, we always hear the refrain from hawks, "Where are the moderate Muslims denouncing this terrorism?" Yet, when Muslim leaders do denounce violence and terrorism,[73] the major television media mostly ignore it, helping perpetuate the idea that terrorist violence has broad support among Muslims, when, in fact, it does not.

If leaders of the Western nations are truly attempting to initiate a new Enlightenment era of democratic values in the Arab and Muslim worlds, as they claim,[74] perhaps trying to live by our highest principles and leading by example — promoting natural, individual rights and self-government in the free market of ideas — might be a more effective strategy than the current policy of propping up some of the world's most repressive governments, while launching invasions and carrying out regime change operations against others. So far, these methods have only led to massive casualties, sectarian civil war and a return to fundamentalism by people who very well might otherwise have been much more receptive to the more positive aspects of our ideas and traditions.

---

[72] Nancy Gibbs, "The Bible and the Apocalypse," *Time*, June 23, 2002, http://content.time.com/time/press_releases/article/0,8599,265363,00.html.

[73] Heraa Hashmi, comp., "Worldwide Muslims Condemn List," https://muslimscondemn.com/ or https://docs.google.com/spreadsheets/d/1e8BjMW36CMNc4-qc9UNQku0blstZSzp5FMtkdlavqzc/edit#gid=0; Arwa Mahdawi, "The 712-page Google Doc That Proves Muslims Do Condemn Terrorism," *Guardian*, March 26, 2017, https://www.theguardian.com/world/shortcuts/2017/mar/26/muslims-condemn-terrorism-stats; Ben Kentish, "25,000 Muslims Just Came Together to Condemn Extremism," *Independent*, October 14, 2016, http://www.independent.co.uk/news/world/muslims-come-together-condemn-terrorism-extremism-canada-ahmadiyya-a7361941.html; Harriet Sherwood and Helen Pidd, "UK Muslim Leaders Condemn 'Cowardly' London Attack," *Guardian,* March 23, 2017, https://www.theguardian.com/uk-news/2017/mar/23/uk-muslim-leaders-condemn-cowardly-london-attack; Heather Timmons, "Muslims Around the World Condemn Terrorism After the Paris Attacks," Quartz, November 14, 2015, https://qz.com/550104/muslims-around-the-world-condemn-terrorism-after-the-paris-attacks/; Mary Kate Cary, "Pressing a Muslim Reformation: You Wouldn't Know It from the Press but Moderate Muslims Do Denounce Terrorism," *U.S. News and World Report*, December 18, 2015, https://www.usnews.com/news/the-report/articles/2015-12-18/yes-moderate-muslims-do-denounce-terrorism-though-the-media-ignores-it; Erica Pishdadian, "Paris Terrorist Attacks: Muslims, Iranian and Arab Leaders Condemn ISIS Violence in France," International Business Times, November, 14 2015, http://www.ibtimes.com/paris-terrorist-attacks-muslims-iranian-arab-leaders-condemn-isis-violence-france-2184848; "Where Are the Muslim voices?" American Muslim, accessed May 16, 2017, http://webcache.googleusercontent.com/search?q=cache:PFoqOfnA6IcJ:www.theamericanmuslim.org/files/voices.ppt+&cd=1&hl=en&ct=clnk&gl=us; Caroline Mortimer, "70,000 Indian Muslim Clerics Issue Fatwa Against ISIS, the Taliban, Al-Qaeda and Other Terror Groups," *Independent*, December 10, 2015, http://www.independent.co.uk/news/world/asia/70000-indian-muslim-clerics-issue-fatwa-against-isis-the-taliban-al-qaida-and-other-terror-groups-a6768191.html; Lauren Markoe, "Muslim Scholars Tell Islamic State: You Don't Understand Islam," *Sojourners*, September 24, 2014, https://sojo.net/articles/muslim-scholars-tell-islamic-state-you-don-t-understand-islam; Esposito and Mogahed, *Who Speaks for Islam?*

[74] George W. Bush, "Inaugural Address," 41 Weekly Comp. Pres. Doc. 74 (January 20, 2005).

The Suicide Bombers

After the September 11th attacks, professor Robert Pape at the University of Chicago decided to study Islam to discover what it was about the religion that led people to commit suicide terrorism. He candidly admits he was shocked to find out that his premise was incorrect. Instead, his research showed suicide attacks are a reaction to foreign occupation. Pape found evidence of such attacks on civilians and soldiers in many far-flung places and throughout recorded history, with no tie to Islam whatsoever. Examples range from the use of knives and swords by the Jewish Sicarii, or "dagger men," in resistance against the Roman occupation of antiquity,[75] to the Shinto[76] and Buddhist[77] Japanese kamikaze pilots' attacks on the U.S. Navy in World War II, to the fierce Hindu-atheist-Marxist Tamil Tigers of Sri Lanka, who, for two decades before 2003, were the "world leaders" in the use of suicide terrorist tactics against their Buddhist, Sinhalese enemies.[78]

Pape, his graduate students and staff created a database of every suicide attacker on earth since 1980.[79] His work has shown that rather than representing psychopathic and irrational murder, like that of serial killers, or a species of "egoistic" or "fatalistic" suicide, such as that of a successful businessman jumping out of a window after a deal goes terribly wrong or a person with severe depression who has given up on life, suicide attack tactics are instead based on "altruistic" motives and sound "strategic logic" in war.[80] Yet, egoistic suicide continues to be the model used by Western terrorism experts to explain suicide terrorism. The bombers are losers, they say — young, poor, uneducated, hopeless and full of rage. Having

---

[75] Pape, *Dying to Win*, 33-34; Paul Christian, "Who Were the Sicarii?" *Meridian Magazine*, June 7, 2004, http://ldsmag.com/article-1-4364/; "Martyrdom and Murder," *Economist*, January 8, 2004, http://www.economist.com/node/2329785.

[76] Bruce Wallace, "They've Outlived the Stigma," *Los Angeles Times*, September 25, 2004, http://articles.latimes.com/2004/sep/25/world/fg-kamikaze25/3.

[77] Christopher Harding, "Into Nothingness," Aeon, November 10, 2014, https://aeon.co/essays/the-zen-ideas-that-propelled-japan-s-young-kamikaze-pilots; Pape, *Dying to Win*, 35-36.

[78] Pape, *Dying to Win*, 139-154; Iselin Frydenlund, "The Secular Suicide Bomber," PRIO Network, April 7, 2015, http://blogs.prio.org/2015/04/the-secular-suicide-bomber/; Robert Pape, interviewed by Lynn Neary, "Tamil Tigers: Suicide Bombing Innovators," NPR News, May 21, 2009, http://www.npr.org/templates/story/story.php?storyId=104391493; Amy Waldman, "Masters of Suicide Bombing: Tamil Guerrillas of Sri Lanka," *New York Times*, January 14, 2003, http://www.nytimes.com/2003/01/14/world/masters-of-suicide-bombing-tamil-guerrillas-of-sri-lanka.html.

[79] Chicago Project on Security and Terrorism, "Suicide Attack Database."

[80] Robert A. Pape, "The Strategic Logic of Suicide Terrorism," *American Political Science Review* 97, no. 3 (August 2003), http://www.columbia.edu/itc/journalism/stille/Politics%20Fall%202007/readings%20weeks%206-7/Strategic%20Logic%20of%20Suicide%20Missions.pdf; Pape, *Dying to Win*, 176.

nothing to live for, they murder innocent people because evil Wahhabist Salafists brainwash them and promise them virgins in heaven as a reward.[81]

According to Pape, this model must be scrapped. Suicide bombers are typically middle or upper middle class, well-educated, successful, socially connected people who know exactly what they are doing. Pape and his researchers found that the single most significant factor in determining whether someone would commit an act of suicide terrorism was the presence of foreign combat forces on the attacker's territory. For the perceived greater good, they sacrifice their own lives to kill others as part of a strategic campaign aimed at the target population to coerce the removal of foreign troops from their land.[82]

Of course, there are other important variables involved that determine whether a society will tolerate their young men and women going to such extremes. These include the degree of difference between the cultures of the occupiers and occupied, and the strength of the resultant belief that the occupying force intends to change the society being occupied in fundamental ways.[83] When the Americans — predominantly white, black and Hispanic, as well as Christian[84] — occupied primarily Arab and Muslim Iraq, they openly stated their intention to completely reorder Iraqi culture and society. In response, resistance began immediately, including the use of suicide attacks, which had never been seen before in Iraq. In contrast, in western Sudan, where all sides of the conflict are Arab and Sunni Muslim,[85] a massive war that killed at least 200,000 people[86] raged at the same time, yet there were no reported suicide attacks at all.[87]

According to Pape's research, another significant factor determining whether groups will resort to suicide terrorism is a credible belief among those inflicting the attacks that it will succeed in changing the behavior of their target government or population, either frightening them into retreat or baiting them into full-scale conflict.[88] As Pape explains, democracies like Spain, which withdrew from the second Iraq war due to popular

[81] Adam Lankford, "Ron Paul Is Wrong About 9/11, Studies Show," Huffington Post, September 19, 2011, http://www.huffingtonpost.com/dr-adam-lankford/ron-paul-9-11_b_969112.html; "Robert A. Pape and Adam Lankford," Scott Horton Show, radio archive, September 21, 2011, https://scotthorton.org/interviews/antiwar-radio-robert-a-pape-and-adam-lankford/.

[82] Pape, Dying to Win, 4, 21, 27, 42.

[83] Pape, "It's the Occupation, Stupid."

[84] David Segal and Mady Wechsler Segal, "America's Military Population," Population Bulletin 59, no. 4 (2004), http://www.prb.org/Source/ACF1396.pdf.

[85] Heba Aly, "Sudanese: 'What Arab-African Rift?'," Christian Science Monitor, August 22, 2008, http://www.csmonitor.com/World/Africa/2008/0822/p06s01-woaf.html.

[86] "UN: 100,000 More Dead in Darfur Than Reported," CNN, April 22, 2008, http://www.cnn.com/2008/WORLD/africa/04/22/darfur.holmes/index.html.

[87] Chicago Project on Security and Terrorism, "Suicide Attack Database."

[88] Pape, Dying to Win, 349.

demand after the Madrid attacks of 2004, are much more likely to be targets of suicide terrorist attacks than governments like that of China, which represses Taliban- and al Qaeda-tied Muslim Uighurs in the Xinjiang Province, but whose Communist Politburo remains unimpressed and unmoved in reaction to the civilian deaths caused by terrorist attacks, thus disincentivizing them.

The Shi'ite militia Hezbollah waged a campaign of suicide attacks against Israel and their allies for 16 years before Israel finally withdrew from Lebanon in 2000. As soon as they did, the attacks stopped. In fact, according to Pape's database, the last one was in 1999.[89]

The Palestinians, on the other hand, remain subjugated under Israeli military rule in the West Bank and Gaza Strip. The third Palestinian uprising, or "Knife Intifada," which began in 2015, is reminiscent of the Jewish Zealots' war against the Romans millennia before. This new insurgency is currently being waged by unorganized young people and has replaced old Hamas-style organized bombing campaigns with individual attacks on occupation soldiers and civilian colonists.[90] The idea that the largely westernized, millennial youth waging these suicide attacks are motivated by some "radical" and fundamentalist belief in Islam, rather than the outright military occupation and colonization of the West Bank and East Jerusalem — where they live — is so plainly false that hardly anyone tries to push it anymore.[91] Instead, we are told, the Palestinians just hate; that's all. Well, you see, they teach their kids to hate Jews, and then they simply hate, because that's just how they are. So what are the Israelis supposed to do, not defend themselves?[92]

The bin Ladenite war against the United States is no different, whether it is the old "core al Qaeda" of the 1990s and early 2000s; al Qaeda in Iraq,

[89] Chicago Project on Security and Terrorism, "Suicide Attack Database"; Pape, "It's the Occupation, Stupid."

[90] Peter Beaumont, "Israel-Palestine: Outlook Bleak as Wave of Violence Passes Six-Month Mark," *Guardian,* March 31, 2016, https://www.theguardian.com/world/2016/mar/31/israel-palestine-violence-knife-attacks-west-bank-gaza.

[91] Avi Issacharoff, "'Lone Wolf Intifada' is Not Driven by Religion, and for Now It Seems to be Waning," *Times of Israel,* April 2, 2016, http://www.timesofisrael.com/lone-wolf-intifada-is-not-driven-by-religion-and-for-now-it-seems-to-be-waning/; Shlomi Eldar, "This is Not Your Father's Intifada," al-Monitor, January 27, 2016, http://www.al-monitor.com/pulse/en/originals/2016/01/west-bank-palestinian-youth-shahid-second-intifada-idf.html; Jodi Rudoren, "Leaderless Palestinian Youth, Inspired by Social Media, Drive Rise in Violence in Israel," *New York Times,* October 13, 2015, https://www.nytimes.com/2015/10/14/world/middleeast/leaderless-palestinian-youth-inspired-by-social-media-drive-a-rise-in-violence.html.

[92] "Gaza Kids Put on Play About Stabbing, Killing Israelis," *Times of Israel,* April 27, 2016, http://www.timesofisrael.com/gaza-kids-put-on-play-about-stabbing-killing-israelis/; Jodi Rudoren and Rami Nazzal, "Palestinian Anger in Jerusalem and West Bank Gets a Violent Soundtrack," *New York Times,* October 22, 2015, https://www.nytimes.com/2015/10/23/world/middleeast/palestinians-israel-stabbings-shootings.html.

Syria or Yemen; or the Islamic State today. Their motive to attack America begins with American intervention in the Middle East. Bin Laden, Scheuer wrote, was "out to drastically alter U.S. and Western policies toward the Islamic world, not necessarily to destroy America, much less its freedoms and liberties." He was a "practical warrior, not an apocalyptic terrorist in search of Armageddon."[93]

Cynthia Storer, a former CIA analyst during the Bill Clinton and George W. Bush eras, confirms the agency's "framework" for what drives people to commit acts of terrorism is not religion-based at all, but is instead political and "absolutely universal." Terrorism is not about Islam; it is about virtually powerless people reacting — striking back — against governments they perceive to be oppressing them, governments they have cause to believe can never be reformed peacefully. It is a government's violent reactions against rising challenges to its power that drive radicals to commit acts of terrorism. These then provoke new government reactions against the terrorists, which inevitably hurt more innocent civilians, thereby creating more terrorists.[94]

Some reports from major media outlets now concede that, for example, CIA drone strikes in Yemen have created a bigger al Qaeda problem there than the one we had before the U.S. started bombing in the first place. Yet they insist on framing the issue around the mostly unstated presumption that September 11, 2001, was the start of this all, even if they find the government's tactics and strategy since then to be slightly deficient in certain cases.[95] But how dishonest is that? TV news anchors and big-name newspaper reporters must remember Osama bin Laden's threats and terrorist attacks in the 1990s. They have memories of George H. W. Bush's first Iraq war and the subsequent United Nations sanctions crisis. Apparently, they just do not want to admit the truth to the people.

Millions of American men and women have joined, and continue to join, the U.S. military to go and fight and risk their lives mostly because of one big attack on our country 15 years ago. Is it really that hard to imagine

[93] Scheuer, *Imperial Hubris*, xvii.

[94] Storer, *Scott Horton Show*, March 13, 2017.

[95] Ibrahim Mothana, "How Drones Help Al Qaeda," *New York Times*, June 13, 2012, http://www.nytimes.com/2012/06/14/opinion/how-drones-help-al-qaeda.html; Nic Robertson, "In Swat Valley, US Drone Strikes Radicalizing a New Generation," CNN, April 15, 2013, http://www.cnn.com/2013/04/14/world/asia/pakistan-swat-valley-school/index.html; Hassan Abbas, "How Drones Create More Terrorists," *Atlantic*, August 23, 2013, http://www.theatlantic.com/international/archive/2013/08/how-drones-create-more-terrorists/278743/; Vivian Salama, "Death from Above: How American Drone Strikes Are Devastating Yemen," *Rolling Stone*, April 14, 2014, http://www.rollingstone.com/politics/news/death-from-above-how-american-drone-strikes-are-devastating-yemen-20140414; Bill Briggs, "Study: US Drone Strikes More Likely to Kill Civilians Than US Jet Fire," NBC News, July 2, 2013, http://www.nbcnews.com/news/investigations/study-us-drone-strikes-more-likely-kill-civilians-us-jet-v19254842.

the lengths they might go to had they been born in the Arab world instead, under permanent, American-sponsored despotism, military occupation and war?

The U.S. government is lucky the residents of the Middle East are mostly Arabs and Muslims, and that most Americans know virtually nothing about the region, religion, language or people.[96] Like the Japanese imperialists and the Russian, Chinese, Korean and Vietnamese Communist enemies of previous times, they are quite alien to the majority of Americans. It is therefore all too easy for the government to make a good lie stick when it comes to misrepresenting the nature of the crisis we are in. This is especially true because the U.S. government, which most Americans personally identify with, has instigated the conflict through acts the population has largely supported.

What's to Hate About U.S. Foreign Policy?

Since World War II, the U.S. government has maintained a world empire.[97] At first, this was justified as a defense against communism, a "containment policy" against Soviet and Chinese expansionism.[98] But since the end of the bi-polar world of the U.S.-Soviet Cold War 25 years ago,[99] the military now unabashedly refers to its global posture as "full-spectrum dominance."[100] Neoconservative and "realist" think tankers like to call it "benevolent global hegemony"[101] or "primacy."[102] Today the Pentagon maintains over 800 bases around the world in more than 135

---

[96] Michael Lipka, "Muslims and Islam: Key Findings in the US and Around the World," Pew Research, February 27, 2017, http://www.pewresearch.org/fact-tank/2017/02/27/muslims-and-islam-key-findings-in-the-u-s-and-around-the-world/.

[97] Chalmers Johnson, *Nemesis: The Last Days of the American Republic* (New York: Metropolitan, 2008); Paul Wolfowitz et al., "1992 Defense Planning Guidance," Office of the Secretary of Defense, February 1992, http://nsarchive.gwu.edu/nukevault/ebb245/doc03_extract_nytedit.pdf.

[98] [George F. Kennan], "The Sources of Soviet Conduct," *Foreign Affairs*, July 1947, https://www.foreignaffairs.com/articles/russian-federation/1947-07-01/sources-soviet-conduct; James S. Lay, "A Report to the National Security Council - NSC 68," President's Secretary's File, Truman Papers, April 12, 1950, https://www.trumanlibrary.org/whistlestop/study_collections/coldwar/documents/pdf/10-1.pdf.

[99] Charles Krauthammer, "The Unipolar Moment," *Foreign Affairs*, February 1991, https://www.foreignaffairs.com/articles/1991-02-01/unipolar-moment.

[100] Jim Garamone, "Joint Vision 2020 Emphasizes Full-spectrum Dominance," American Forces Press Service, June 2, 2000, http://archive.defense.gov/news/newsarticle.aspx?id=45289.

[101] William Kristol and Robert Kagan, "Toward a Neo-Reaganite Foreign Policy," *Foreign Affairs*, July/August 1996, https://www.foreignaffairs.com/articles/1996-07-01/toward-neo-reaganite-foreign-policy.

[102] Zbigniew Brzezinski, *The Grand Chessboard: American Primacy and Its Geostrategic Imperatives* (Lebanon, IN: Basic, 1997).

countries,[103] counts all the rest of the world's most powerful nations in Europe and Asia as its close allies or satellites,[104] outmatches Russia[105] and China[106] — its only "near-peer competitors" — in terms of conventional military power by orders of magnitude and dominates every ocean and sea on the planet with its unprecedented naval force.[107]

Rather than following the model of outright colonialism set by European empires of earlier times, America has opted for a unique system of dominance comprised of a global network of military bases,[108] periodic coups[109] and behind the scenes maneuvering.[110] But it is, nevertheless, the most powerful and influential empire the world has ever known, with political, military, economic and even cultural dominance in almost every part of the planet.[111] The world follows America's lead, or else.[112] And it is clear that the United States' military empire in the Middle East significantly predates the terrorists' war against the American people.

In April 2016, retired army colonel, academic historian and conservative war critic, Andrew Bacevich, published *America's War for the Greater Middle East: A Military History*. His account necessarily begins long before September 11, 2001. As Bacevich explains, America's mission in the region has never really been to "fight them over there so we don't have to fight them here," but instead, in the words of the policymakers themselves, to achieve and maintain global dominance.[113] Terrorism? Well, that's just a minor side effect — "a small price to pay for being a superpower," as policy planners for the Joint Chiefs of Staff at the Pentagon were repeatedly heard to say by a "very senior" special operations commander in the 1990s.[114] Fighting against terrorism then

[103] David Vine, *Base Nation: How U.S. Military Bases Abroad Harm America and the World* (New York: Metropolitan, 2015).

[104] NATO.int.

[105] Jonathan Masters, "How Strong is the Russian Military?" *Newsweek*, December 12, 2014, http://www.newsweek.com/how-strong-russian-military-291366.

[106] David Axe, "Why China is Far from Ready to Meet the US on a Global Battlefront," Reuters, June 22, 2015, http://blogs.reuters.com/great-debate/2015/06/21/why-china-is-far-from-ready-to-meet-the-u-s-on-a-global-battlefront/.

[107] "US Navy," GlobalSecurity.org, http://www.globalsecurity.org/military/agency/navy/.

[108] Vine, *Base Nation*.

[109] Stephen Kinzer, *Overthrow: America's Century of Regime Change from Hawaii to Iraq* (New York: Times, 2006).

[110] John Perkins, *Confessions of an Economic Hit Man* (Oakland: Berrett-Koehler, 2004).

[111] Chalmers Johnson, *The Sorrows of Empire: Militarism, Secrecy, and the End of the Republic* (New York: Metropolitan, 2004).

[112] William Blum, "Overthrowing Other People's Governments: The Master List," February 2013, https://williamblum.org/essays/read/overthrowing-other-peoples-governments-the-master-list.

[113] Andrew J. Bacevich, *America's War for the Greater Middle East: A Military History* (New York: Random House, 2016).

[114] Richard H. Schultz Jr., "Showstoppers: Nine Reasons Why We Never Sent Our Special Operations Forces After Al Qaeda Before 9/11," *Weekly Standard*, January 26, 2004,

becomes a convenient cover for the further escalation of the kinds of interventionist policies that created the terrorism problem in the first place.

This was the dynamic bin Laden was betting on — that the American government was looking for and willing to exploit any excuse to expand its Middle Eastern empire, and that in doing so, it would sow the seeds of its own demise. This, all while helping to prepare the field for the growth of an eventual bin Ladenite Islamist state to dominate the region in the future.

As veteran intelligence beat reporter James Bamford explained, bin Laden's partner,

> Ayman al-Zawahiri argued that al Qaeda should bring the war to "the distant enemy" in order to provoke the Americans to strike back and "personally wage the battle against Muslims." It was that battle that bin Laden and Zawahiri wanted to spark [with their attacks on U.S. targets]. As they made clear in their declaration of war "against Jews and Crusaders," they believed that the United States and Israel had been waging war against Muslims for decades. Now their hope was to draw Americans into a desert Vietnam, with bin Laden in the role of North Vietnamese president Ho Chi Minh.[115]

Ronald Reagan's Arab-Afghan Holy Warriors

This "Vietnam trap" bin Laden was planning for the United States was not so original a concept. In fact, it is how Osama bin Laden ended up in Afghanistan in the first place. President Jimmy Carter's National Security Advisor, Zbigniew Brzezinski, boasted that when the Soviet Union invaded Afghanistan on December 24, 1979, he sent a memo to the boss: "We now have the opportunity of giving to the USSR its Vietnam war."[116]

By 1979, "Vietnam" had already become a shorthand term for bloody, no-win, far-flung quagmire that breaks the military and treasury and causes terrible disruptions to society back home. Badly burned by the experience, the American people were even said by the political establishment to have come down with the lamented "Vietnam Syndrome" — such a severe reluctance to engage in any further overseas military conflicts that it

---

http://www.weeklystandard.com/showstoppers/article/4846.

[115] James Bamford, *A Pretext for War: 9/11, Iraq, and the Abuse of America's Intelligence Agencies* (New York: Doubleday, 2004), 210-211.

[116] "The Brzezinski Interview with *Le Nouvel Observateur*," trans. William Blum and David N. Gibbs, interview conducted January 15-21, 1998, posted by David N. Gibbs to the University of Arizona website, http://dgibbs.faculty.arizona.edu/brzezinski_interview.

amounted to a form of illness.[117] If such a disaster had been inflicted on the American people by previous administrations, the thinking went, perhaps rather than "containing" communism, the U.S. could instead provoke it into over-expansion to inflict similar "self"-destruction on the Soviets. As Brzezinski and former CIA officials like Robert Gates have boasted, Carter signed a finding on July 3, 1979, authorizing the beginning of covert CIA aid to the Afghan mujahideen, in order to provoke the very invasion by the Soviets that Carter later claimed necessitated U.S. intervention there.[118]

Foreign correspondent Eric Margolis, who covered the 1980s Afghan war extensively, is dubious that U.S. covert intervention is what made the difference in the Soviet decision to invade, pointing out that the Americans involved had an interest in inflating their own role in events. According to Margolis, the Soviets saw a crisis coming anyway. The USSR's favored warlords had gotten so diverted and out of control torturing and murdering people and fomenting civil war that the Kremlin feared the survival of the entire Kabul regime was at risk.[119] Famed Soviet dissident Andrei Sakharov agrees with Margolis, writing that Afghan President Hafizullah Amin's independent and destructive policies made him unacceptable to Moscow. The KGB murdered him immediately after invading the country.[120] Regardless, first the Carter and then the Reagan administrations, along with their Saudi and Pakistani allies, lent massive financial and material support to the mujahideen resistance fighters. These included Afghans as well as the "International Islamic Brigades," comprised of thousands of so-called "Arab-Afghans"[121] from across the Middle East who were sent by their governments to fight a holy war against the Communists' invasion of Muslim land. The U.S. eventually even provided advanced, guided, shoulder-fired, surface-to-air "Stinger" missiles, which helped the Afghan resistance to level the fight against the

---

[117] Ronald Reagan, "Veterans of Foreign Wars Convention Speech, 'Peace: Restoring the Margin of Safety,'" delivered in Chicago, Illinois, August 18, 1980, https://reaganlibrary.archives.gov/archives/reference/8.18.80.html.

[118] Steve Coll, *Ghost Wars: The Secret History of the CIA, Afghanistan, and bin Laden, from the Soviet Invasion to September 10, 2001* (London: Penguin, 2004), 46; Robert Gates, *From the Shadows: The Ultimate Insider's Story of Five Presidents and How They Won the Cold War* (New York: Simon & Schuster, 1996), 146.

[119] Eric S. Margolis, *War at the Top of the World: The Struggle for Afghanistan, Kashmir and Tibet* (Oxford: Routledge), 17.

[120] Andrei Sakharov, "Afghanistan, Gorky, and an Open Letter to Leonid Brezhnev, 1980," in *The Case for Withdrawal from Afghanistan*, ed. Nick Turse, (New York: Verso, 2010), 17.

[121] Steve Galster, "Afghanistan: The Making of US Policy, 1973-1990," National Security Archive, October 9, 2001, http://nsarchive.gwu.edu/NSAEBB/NSAEBB57/essay.html; Steve Coll, *Ghost Wars*; George Crile, *Charlie Wilson's War: The Extraordinary Story of the Largest Covert Operation in History* (New York: Atlantic Monthly, 2003).

attack helicopters of the technologically sophisticated Soviet air forces.[122] President Reagan met and had his picture taken with mujahideen leaders in the White House's Oval Office.[123] Hollywood even released the movie *Rambo III* in 1988 to explain the supposedly covert, but widely known, operation to the American people. In the film, the protagonist's mentor, Colonel Trautman, baits his KGB captor:

> There won't be a [Soviet] victory. Every day, your war machines lose ground to a bunch of poorly armed, poorly equipped freedom fighters. The fact is that you underestimated your competition. If you'd studied your history, you'd know that these people have never given up to anyone. They'd rather die than be slaves to an invading army. You can't defeat a people like that. We tried; we already had our Vietnam! Now you're going to have yours.

Sylvester Stallone's John Rambo, and therefore all right-thinking American patriots, revered the mujahideen for their dedication to their religious beliefs and heroic, selfless bravery in defending their land and people from foreign invasion.[124]

The mujahideen did deserve some credit. Communism was slowly falling apart due to the simple laws of economics,[125] but the CIA, Saudis, Pakistanis and mujahideen — mostly the Afghans, but also the Arab and other foreign fighters — did help to destabilize and further bankrupt the ramshackle Soviet empire,[126] setting it up to be finished off completely by the oil price crash of the late 1980s.[127] At least that was what the Reagan Republicans[128] and, more importantly, the Arab-Afghan mujahideen believed; with faith in God and a few trusty AK-47s, they had brought down the mighty USSR, one of the most powerful empires in history.[129]

---

[122] Michael M. Phillips, "Launching the Missile That Made History," *Wall Street Journal*, October 1, 2011, http://www.wsj.com/articles/SB10001424052970204138204576598851109446780; Ernest May and Philip Zelikow, "Politics of a Covert Action: The US, the Mujahideen, and the Stinger Missile," Harvard Kennedy School of Government, November 9, 1999.

[123] "Reagan Meets Afghan Rebels," *New York Times*, June 17, 1986, http://www.nytimes.com/1986/06/17/world/reagan-meets-afghan-rebels.html.

[124] Sylvester Stallone, David Morrell and Sheldon Lettich, *Rambo III*, directed by Peter MacDonald (1988; Vancouver: Lions Gate, 2004), DVD.

[125] Ludwig von Mises, *Socialism: An Economic and Sociological Analysis*, 2nd ed. (Indianapolis: Liberty Fund, 2010).

[126] John Mueller, *Overblown: How Politicians and the Terrorism Industry Inflate National Security Threats, and Why We Believe Them* (New York: Free, 2009), 83-85.

[127] Rafael Reuveny and Aseem Prakash, "The Afghanistan War and the Breakdown of the Soviet Union," *Review of International Studies* 25 (1999): 693-708, http://faculty.washington.edu/aseem/afganwar.pdf.

[128] Lee Edwards, "Ronald Reagan and the Fall of Communism," Heritage Foundation, January 27, 2010, http://www.heritage.org/research/lecture/ronald-reagan-and-the-fall-of-communism.

[129] "Bin Laden: Goal Is to Bankrupt US," CNN, November 1, 2004, http://www.cnn.com/2004/WORLD/meast/11/01/binladen.tape/; Alan Cullison, "Inside Al

Abdullah Yusuf Azzam was one of the principal ideological and administrative leaders of the recruitment drive for the Arab effort to support the Afghan jihad and leader of the "Afghanistan Services Bureau" that would later become Osama bin Laden's al Qaeda. In 1986, Margolis met with Azzam in Pakistan. He told Margolis, "When we have finished driving the Soviet imperialists from Afghanistan, we mujahideen will then go and drive the American imperialists from Arabia, and then liberate Palestine."[130]

At first, Margolis was baffled. He had only ever heard pro-Soviet communists call America an "empire." The U.S. was helping Saudi Arabia and Pakistan to support Azzam and his men in their war for freedom against the USSR. How could he say such a thing? But later it became clear to Margolis what Azzam meant: the "Carter Doctrine" of permanent U.S. supremacy in the Persian Gulf — announced in response to the USSR's invasion of Afghanistan — already had America's military presence spreading throughout the Arabian Peninsula. In fact, the United States had maintained a base at Manama, Bahrain since 1944[131] and at Dhahran, Saudi Arabia, between 1948 and 1962.[132] As part of the Carter Doctrine, the Reagan administration had begun to expand the military's presence further in the 1980s, beginning with an air force base at Thumrait, Oman, in 1981. The build-up continued in Saudi Arabia as the U.S. slowly took over and expanded Saudi military bases in a process they called "overbuilding and overstocking." This was a fig-leaf for the presence of American forces, equipment and contractors at what were ostensibly still Saudi bases.[133] Seventy more permanent bases were later added in Kuwait, Qatar, Oman, and the United Arab Emirates to join those in Saudi Arabia and Bahrain as the U.S. prepared to wage the first Iraq war in 1990–1991. With all the new U.S. arms came scores of new American contractors and military advisers to go with them.[134] The rapidly increasing U.S. presence in the Arabian Peninsula created severe resentment. As Professor Pape has emphasized, to the population of Saudi Arabia, and especially the bin Ladenites, these state borders are meaningless; they view Arabia as one

Qaeda's Hard Drive," *Atlantic*, September 2004, http://www.theatlantic.com/magazine/archive/2004/09/inside-al-qaeda-s-hard-drive/303428/.
[130] Eric Margolis, "Bin Laden and Me: Freedom Fighters, Terrorists, and History," *Toronto Sun*, September 28, 2008, http://www.commondreams.org/views/2008/09/28/bin-laden-and-me.
[131] John K. Cooley, "US Presence in Persian Gulf: A History," ABC News, March 13, 2002, http://abcnews.go.com/International/story?id=81402.
[132] "King Abdulaziz Air Base," GobalSecurity.org, http://www.globalsecurity.org/military/world//gulf/abdulaziz-ab.htm.
[133] Steve Coll, *The Bin Ladens: An Arabian Family in the American Century* (London: Penguin, 2008), 246.
[134] Richard Clarke, *Against All Enemies: Inside America's War on Terror* (New York: Free, 2004), 39, 60-61.

holy peninsula, just as the 50 states of the United States are considered one country by Americans.[135]

Azzam was not just blowing smoke back in 1986; he was already pivoting his followers toward a new enemy just as America was getting its Middle East project into full gear.

The New Order

When the bankrupt Soviet empire withdrew from Afghanistan in 1989[136] and completely disintegrated[137] two years later, Washington's war hawks, far from taking the lesson they had just helped to inflict to heart, saw only an opportunity to extend their power and influence. As the incisive comedian and social critic, George Carlin, said in his 1992 HBO special, "We just couldn't wait for that Cold War to be over, could we? Couldn't wait for the Cold War to be over so we can go and play with our toys in the sand! — go and play with our toys in the sand!"[138]

And so, the hawks found a reason. When Iraq invaded its smaller neighbor Kuwait in the summer of 1990, the U.S. launched Operation Desert Storm, a short and seemingly easy war[139] to drive Saddam Hussein's forces back out early the next year. Once Kuwait's king, Jaber Al-Ahmad Al-Sabah, had been restored to his throne, President George Bush Sr. exclaimed, "It's a proud day for America. By God, we've kicked the Vietnam Syndrome once and for all!"[140]

Dick Cheney, who had been secretary of defense under President George Bush Sr. during the first Iraq war, explained in a 2014 interview with then-*Weekly Standard* editor William Kristol that in order to finally "close the deal" with Saudi King Fahd to allow the U.S. to build and occupy massive bases in the Saudi Desert, he had agreed to the King's condition that the soldiers and airmen would be removed as soon as Iraq was driven from Kuwait and the alleged threat of an Iraqi invasion of Saudi

---

[135] Pape, *Dying to Win*, 82.

[136] "Soviet Withdrawal from Afghanistan," *Tass*, February 15, 2016, http://tass.com/world/856745.

[137] Francis X. Clines, "Gorbachev, Last Soviet Leader, Resigns; US Recognizes Republics' Independence," *New York Times*, December 25, 1991,
http://www.nytimes.com/learning/general/onthisday/big/1225.html#article.

[138] George Carlin, *Jammin' in New York*, directed by Rocco Urbisci, filmed at Paramount Theater, Madison Square Garden, New York, aired on HBO, 1992, https://georgecarlin.com/shop/jammin-new-york/.

[139] George H. W. Bush, "Transcript of President Bush's Address on End of the Gulf War," delivered to a joint session of Congress, *New York Times*, March 7, 1991,
http://www.nytimes.com/1991/03/07/us/after-war-president-transcript-president-bush-s-address-end-gulf-war.html.

[140] "President George H. W. Bush Remarks to the American Legislative Exchange Council," March 1, 1991, http://www.presidency.ucsb.edu/ws/?pid=19351.

Arabia[141] had been thwarted.[142]

But U.S. forces did not leave. Once the first Iraq war was over, new excuses for permanent occupation presented themselves. During the war to expel Iraqi forces from Kuwait, Bush Sr. had released a radio message over Voice of America[143] and the military dropped leaflets over Iraqi army units, as well as civilian populations, encouraging the Shi'ite Arabs and the Kurds to rise up and overthrow the primarily Sunni Arab-backed dictatorship of Saddam Hussein. This led them to believe the U.S. would back their efforts.[144] Not only did Bush then refuse to do so, but under the terms of Iraq's surrender in the war, the U.S. agreed to allow Hussein to keep his attack helicopters and use them to slaughter his opponents.[145] According to journalist Barry Lando, the U.S. eventually even outright intervened on Saddam's side, landing American helicopters on a highway to Baghdad to block an Iraqi army division that was marching on the capital to remove him.[146]

This was the Great Stab in the Back in the Desert of 1991. As Iraq analyst Joel Wing wrote, the Bush Sr. administration really did want either a military coup or a popular uprising in which the Shi'ites and Kurds would overthrow Saddam Hussein. But his war council suddenly changed their minds when they realized the presence of Iranian-backed militias among the resistance meant they were about to reverse the entire Reagan-era effort to contain the results of the 1979 Shi'ite revolution in Iran by backing Saddam Hussein's Iraq in the 1980s Iran-Iraq war. Bush Sr. quickly turned right around and betrayed the uprising instead.[147]

---

141 Jean Heller, "Public Doesn't Get Picture with Gulf Satellite Photos," *St. Petersburg Times* [Florida], January 6, 1991, https://scotthorton.org/fairuse/public-doesnt-get-picture-with-gulf-satellite-photos/; Scott Peterson, "In War, Some Facts Less Factual," *Christian Science Monitor*, September 6, 2002, http://www.csmonitor.com/2002/0906/p01s02-wosc.html.

142 "Vice President Dick Cheney: Personal Reflections on his Public Life," interviewed by Bill Kristol, *Conversations with Kristol*, October 12, 2014, http://conversationswithbillkristol.org/video/dick-cheney/.

143 "Bush Statement at Raytheon; Excerpts from 2 Statements by Bush on Iraq's Proposal for Ending Conflict," *New York Times*, February 16, 1991, http://nytimes.com/1991/02/16/world/war-gulf-bush-statement-excerpts-2-statements-bush-iraq-s-proposal-for-ending.html.

144 Micah Zenko, "Who Is to Blame for the Doomed Iraqi Uprisings of 1991?," *National Interest*, March 7, 2016, http://nationalinterest.org/blog/the-buzz/behind-the-doomed-iraqi-uprisings-1991-15425.

145 Patrick E. Tyler, "After the War: Bush Aims Rebuke at Schwarzkopf for Truce Remark," *New York Times*, March 28, 1991, http://www.nytimes.com/1991/03/28/world/after-the-war-bush-aims-rebuke-at-schwarzkopf-for-truce-remark.html.

146 Barry M. Lando, *Web of Deceit: The History of Western Complicity in Iraq, from Churchill to Kennedy to George W. Bush* (New York: Other, 2007), 173-174; Barry Lando, interviewed by the author, *Scott Horton Show*, radio archive, January 15, 2015, https://scotthorton.org/interviews/11515-barry-lando/.

147 Joel Wing, "When the US Helped Start a Rebellion in Iraq That It Didn't Want," Musings on Iraq, March 21, 2016, http://musingsoniraq.blogspot.com/2016/03/when-us-helped-start-rebellion-in-iraq.html.

As a result, tens of thousands of Shi'ite Arabs and Kurds were slaughtered.[148] The U.S., France and Britain then announced permanent "no-fly zones" of allied air patrols in the far north and south of Iraq in the name of grounding Iraqi air forces to secure those they had just sacrificed.[149] They further proclaimed that the international economic sanctions policy imposed before the war would remain in place until the U.S. agreed that all conditions of the ceasefire had been satisfied. And so, the bases in Saudi stayed.

Osama Turns on Us

The U.S. and UN coalition's war, coupled with America's decision to stay in Arabia and maintain a war footing against Iraq, was not without broader consequences. Osama bin Laden, the wealthy son of a powerful Saudi construction magnate who had contributed large sums of money and equipment to the 1980s war effort in Afghanistan and had been wounded in battle against Communist forces there, was incensed that the Americans had received the Saudi king's writ to force Saddam Hussein's army out of Kuwait. Bin Laden had attempted to volunteer his men for the cause. He was even more enraged by the expanded and indefinite presence of "crusader" U.S. combat forces during and after the war on what he considered to be the holy territory of the Arabian Peninsula. The Arab-Afghan mujahideen, the U.S. government's once-friendly, even heroic, "freedom fighter" allies from the great anti-Soviet holy war of the 1980s, had become the enemies of the American people. With the Soviet invaders gone from Afghanistan, they were now determined to drive U.S. combat forces from the Arabian Peninsula by any means necessary.[150]

The danger inherent in sending thousands of young men from Arab countries to fight the Soviets in Afghanistan had been obvious to many at the time. As Egyptian preacher Abu Hamza explained to journalist Andrew Cockburn, this policy "was meant to actually divert people from the problems in their own country." It was "like a pressure-cooker vent. If you keep [the cooker] all sealed up, it will blow up in your face, so you

[148] "Endless Torment: The 1991 Uprising in Iraq and Its Aftermath," Human Rights Watch, June 1992, https://www.hrw.org/reports/1992/Iraq926.htm.

[149] Michael R. Gordon, "British, French and US Agree to Hit Iraqi Aircraft in the South," *New York Times*, August 19, 1992, http://www.nytimes.com/1992/08/19/world/british-french-and-us-agree-to-hit-iraqi-aircraft-in-the-south.html.

[150] Steve Coll, *Ghost Wars*, 222-223; Abdel Bari Atwan, "Why bin Laden Was Radicalized," CNN, May 17, 2011, http://www.cnn.com/2011/OPINION/05/17/osama.bin.laden.al.qaeda/; Clarke, *Against All Enemies*, 59; Lisa Beyer, "The Most Wanted Man in the World," *Time*, September 24, 2001, http://content.time.com/time/magazine/article/0,9171,1000871,00.html; Atwan, *The Secret History of al Qaeda*, 45-46.

have to design a vent, and this Afghan jihad was the vent."

However, as Cockburn further explained,

> [soon] the sponsoring governments began to recognize a flaw in the scheme: the vent was two-way. I heard this point most vividly expressed in 1994, at a dinner party on a yacht cruising down the Nile. The wealthy host had deemed it safer to be waterborne owing to a vigorous terror campaign by Egyptian jihadists. At the party, this defensive tactic elicited a vehement comment from Osama El-Baz, a senior security adviser to Hosni Mubarak. "It's all the fault of those stupid bastards at the CIA," he said, as the lights of Cairo drifted by. "They trained these people, kept them in being [even] after the Russians left, and now we get this."[151]

The actions of George H. W. Bush's successor just made matters that much worse.

Iraq War 1½: The Bill Clinton Years

Soon after coming into power, the Bill Clinton administration adopted a program of "dual containment" of both Iraq and Iran.[152] This was done presumably to replace the policy of arming both sides against each other in battle, as the U.S. had done during the Iran-Iraq war of the 1980s.[153] However, this containment following the first Iraq war relied on a sanctions regime that amounted to a full-scale global economic embargo against Iraq and ended up killing almost as many people as had died during the entire Iran-Iraq war. What the dual containment policy really meant was no peace could be reached. No end to the Cold War against Iran or the "warm" one against Iraq would be possible for the remainder of the twentieth century — and beyond. The U.S. would also need to keep all their new bases in Arabia to do the containing. The war George H. W. Bush had sworn would "not be another Vietnam"[154] continued, albeit mostly from the Treasury Department in Washington and 30,000 feet in the sky over Iraq.

---

[151] Andrew Cockburn, "A Special Relationship," *Harper's Magazine*, January 2016, http://harpers.org/archive/2016/01/a-special-relationship.

[152] Barbara Conry, "America's Misguided Policy of Dual Containment in the Persian Gulf," Cato Institute, November 10, 1994, https://object.cato.org/sites/cato.org/files/pubs/pdf/fpb033.pdf.

[153] Seymour M. Hersh, "US Secretly Gave Aid to Iraq Early in Its War Against Iran," *New York Times*, January 26, 1992, http://www.nytimes.com/1992/01/26/world/us-secretly-gave-aid-to-iraq-early-in-its-war-against-iran.html; Lawrence E. Walsh, "Final Report of the Independent Council for Iran/Contra Matters, Volume I: Investigations and Prosecutions," United States Court of Appeals for the District of Columbia Circuit, August 4, 1993, https://fas.org/irp/offdocs/walsh/.

[154] George H. W. Bush, "Address to the Nation Announcing Allied Military Action in the Persian Gulf," American Presidency Project, January 16, 1991, http://presidency.ucsb.edu/ws/?pid=19222.

Americans think of the Bill Clinton years as a time of peace. His wars, and news of them, mostly stayed far from home. But as journalist Jeremy Scahill has reported, during Clinton's presidency, the U.S. Air Force bombed Iraq an average of three to four times per week.[155] The American people were told each of these bombings represented an attempted radar lock by Iraqi ground stations, an act of "aggression" against U.S. pilots flying over a foreign nation. However, according to the *New York Times*, after 1998, radar and other military installations were deemed legitimate targets of self-defense, "even when they presented no direct threat."[156] Not one U.S. plane was ever hit, much less shot down, by Iraqi forces during the entire decade after the first Iraq war. However, hundreds of innocent civilians the U.S. was supposedly protecting were killed in these bombings.[157]

The 1990s United Nations blockade was an even more tragic story. The United States forced a global sanctions regime on Iraq, which completely destroyed what was left of the Iraqi economy after Iraq War I. The U.S., which had been happy to look the other way when Hussein was importing "dual use" items to manufacture chemical and biological weapons to use against Iran a few years before,[158] now, in addition to banning Iraqi oil sales, was forbidding the importation of "possible dual use" spare parts for repairing delivery trucks and the country's electrical grid. Even chlorine for disinfecting civilian water supplies was banned under the pretense that the Iraqis must only want it to make banned chemical weapons.[159] Basic medicines that were cheap and plentiful elsewhere in the world became impossible to obtain. Malnutrition was widespread. There were deadly epidemics of cholera and typhoid. It was a ruthless economic war against all Iraqi men, women and children.[160] The American people, diverted by euphemisms such as "sanctions" in place of "blockade" and comparisons to the full-scale air and tank war that had just been waged, may not have

---

[155] Jeremy Scahill, "No Fly Zones over Iraq," CounterPunch, December 4, 2002, http://www.counterpunch.org/2002/12/04/no-fly-zones-over-iraq/; Jeremy Scahill, interviewed by the author, *Scott Horton Show,* radio archive, May 20, 2009, https://scotthorton.org/interviews/antiwar-radio-jeremy-sachill/.

[156] Douglas Jehl, "Saudis Admit Restricting US Warplanes in Iraq," *New York Times*, March 22, 1999, http://www.nytimes.com/1999/03/22/world/saudis-admit-restricting-us-warplanes-in-iraq.html.

[157] Scahill, "No Fly Zones over Iraq."

[158] Christopher Dickey, "How Saddam Happened," *Newsweek*, September 22, 2002, http://www.newsweek.com/how-saddam-happened-144919; Margolis, *War at the Top of the World*, 85; Shane Harris and Matthew M. Aid, "CIA Files Prove America Helped Saddam as He Gassed Iran," August 26, 2013, *Foreign Policy*, http://foreignpolicy.com/2013/08/26/exclusive-cia-files-prove-america-helped-saddam-as-he-gassed-iran/.

[159] Joy Gordon, "Sanctions as Siege Warfare," *Nation*, March 4, 1999, https://www.thenation.com/article/sanctions-siege-warfare/.

[160] "Iraq Sanctions: Humanitarian Implications and Options for the Future," Global Policy Forum, August 6, 2002, https://www.globalpolicy.org/component/content/article/170-sanctions/41947.html.

realized the new status quo was a permanent, global trade embargo that was starving and strangling the entire civilian population of the country.[161] Any doubts they may have had were apparently sufficiently smothered in political partisanship, racism and nationalism. Study after study conducted throughout the 1990s, including those by the U.S. Air Force,[162] Harvard University and the United Nations,[163] as well as in journals ranging from the *New England Journal of Medicine*[164] to the UK's *Lancet*,[165] showed the unbearable suffering of the Iraqi population. But this only proved the success of the program. Civilian deaths were a prime feature, not a bug, of the sanctions policy. As Pentagon officials explained to the *Washington Post*, "People say, 'You didn't recognize that [bombing civilian infrastructure] was going to have an effect on water or sewage[?]' Well, what were we trying to do with sanctions — help out the Iraqi people? No. What we were doing with the attacks on infrastructure was to accelerate the effect of the sanctions." And, "Big picture, we wanted to let people know, 'Get rid of this guy and we'll be more than happy to assist in rebuilding. We're not going to tolerate Saddam Hussein or his regime. Fix that, and we'll [allow you to] fix your electricity.'"[166]

Finally, in 1996, the United Nations Oil for Food program was introduced. But it was far too little, too late for hundreds of thousands of people. According to the UN, as many as a million people died of this deprivation, more than half of them children, in what Americans called "peacetime."[167]

Two UN officials overseeing the sanctions, Denis Halliday[168] and Hans

---

[161] Les Roberts, interviewed by the author, *Scott Horton Show*, radio archive, March 8, 2011, https://scotthorton.org/interviews/antiwar-radio-les-roberts/.

[162] Randy T. Odle, "UN Sanctions Against Iraq, Their Effects and Their Future," Air War College, April 1997, http://www.au.af.mil/au/awc/awcgate/awc/97-144.pdf.

[163] Barbara Crossette, "Iraq Sanctions Kill Children, U.N. Reports," *New York Times*, December 1, 1995, http://www.nytimes.com/1995/12/01/world/iraq-sanctions-kill-children-un-reports.html.

[164] Harvard Study Team, "The Effect of the Gulf Crisis on the Children of Iraq," *New England Journal of Medicine* 325 (1991): 977-980. http://www.nejm.org/doi/full/10.1056/NEJM199109263251330#t=article.

[165] Mohamed M. Ali and Iqbal H. Shah, "Sanctions and Childhood Mortality in Iraq," *Lancet* 335, no. 9218 (2000): 1851-1857. http://www.thelancet.com/journals/lancet/article/PIIS0140-6736(00)02289-3/abstract.

[166] Barton Gellman, "Allied Air War Struck Broadly in Iraq," *Washington Post*, June 23, 1991, https://www.washingtonpost.com/archive/politics/1991/06/23/allied-air-war-struck-broadly-in-iraq/e469877b-b1c1-44a9-bfe7-084da4e38e41/?utm_term=.2a3bb80ce23f.

[167] Barbara Crossette, "Iraq Sanctions Kill Children, UN Reports," *New York Times*, December 1, 1995, http://www.nytimes.com/1995/12/01/world/iraq-sanctions-kill-children-un-reports.html; "Special Report: United Nations' Food & Agriculture Organization and World Food Program Food Supply and Nutrition Assessment Mission to Iraq," Food and Agriculture Organization of the United Nations, October 3, 1997, http://www.fao.org/docrep/004/W6519e/W6519e00.htm.

[168] Mark Siegal, "Former UN Official Says Sanctions Against Iraq Amount to 'Genocide,'" *Cornell Chronicle*, September 30, 1999, http://www.news.cornell.edu/stories/1999/09/former-un-official-says-sanctions-against-iraq-amount-genocide.

von Sponeck,[169] resigned in disgust at the devastation they had helped to cause.

It was common knowledge in foreign policy circles during this period that despite the strict rules governing the Oil for Food program, Hussein's regime was diverting the profits from the oil sales for its own needs. Saddam was "spending it all on his palaces," as the saying went at the time. The Iraqi people's suffering was not being alleviated. Yet this was seen only as another useful talking point for the effort to demonize the dictator. The idea of lifting the embargo on the Iraqi people and figuring out a better way to proceed was apparently never seriously considered. Journalist Rod Nordland perfectly summed up the conventional wisdom in Washington when he wrote in 2000:

> [N]o one in Washington believes Saddam has given up his ambition to build weapons of mass destruction. The former boss of the UN weapons inspectors, Richard Butler, told Israel's Knesset last week that the Iraqis have the expertise to build a nuclear weapon within a year, provided they could get the raw materials. Ending the sanctions would give Saddam vastly increased oil revenues and freedom from import controls, making it easier for him to buy the nuclear supplies he needs. Because of that, the current ugly stalemate — half war, half peace — may drag on indefinitely. There seems to be little relief in sight for Saddam's long-suffering people.[170]

In *Invisible War: The United States and the Iraq Sanctions*, author Joy Gordon explained there was nothing anyone could do to end the blockade. The sanctions were indefinite without a new resolution to repeal them, which was impossible due to the veto power of the United States on the UN Security Council.[171]

The 1990s was also an era of endless UN weapons inspections under the terms of the ceasefire at the end of the war. These were done under the pretense of ridding Saddam Hussein's Iraq of the chemical weapons the U.S. and its allies had given him — and that he had used against the Iranians with U.S. assistance and against the Iraqi Kurds without the slightest hint of opposition — only a decade before.[172] The fact that these weapons were virtually all destroyed by the end of 1991,[173] and that the

---

[169] "UN Sanctions Rebel Resigns," BBC News, February 14, 2000, http://news.bbc.co.uk/2/hi/middle_east/642189.stm.

[170] Rod Nordland, "Saddam's Long Shadow," *Newsweek*, July 30, 2000, http://www.newsweek.com/saddams-long-shadow-161483.

[171] Joy Gordon, *Invisible War: The United States and the Iraq Sanctions* (Cambridge, MA: Harvard University Press, 2010), 44.

[172] Harris and Aid, "CIA Files Prove America Helped Saddam as He Gassed Iran"; Margolis, *War at the Top of the World*, 85; Dickey, "How Saddam Happened."

[173] "DCI Special Advisor Report on Iraq's WMD," CIA, September 30, 2004,

UN inspectors were completely satisfied of this fact by the end of 1995,[174] had no apparent effect on the massive global sanctions regime other than to change its goal from pretended arms control to outright regime change.

When the United Nations Special Commission on Iraq was ready to declare the country free of weapons of mass destruction in 1997, it was preempted by Clinton's secretary of state, Madeleine Albright, who announced that no matter what, the sanctions regime would persist until the people of Iraq overthrew Saddam Hussein.[175] The fact that the Iraqi people were starving, dying and getting weaker under the sanctions in relation to their formerly U.S.-supported government, and the fact that the U.S. had encouraged and then betrayed the Iraqi majority when they had tried to overthrow Saddam Hussein during the 1991 uprising, seemed to mean nothing to the Clinton government. Nor was there any reason, beyond wishful thinking, to believe that there would be a revolt within the Ba'ath Party or the military. A 1996 coup attempt by the CIA and their British counterparts in MI-6 ended in disaster.[176]

When asked about the 500,000 children who had reportedly been deprived to death as a result of the embargo, Secretary Albright infamously told CBS News, "We think the price is worth it" — worth it, to continue this ruinous policy even though it was officially based on a plain absurdity. This number represented more children, as her interlocutor put it, "than died at [the nuclear bombing of] Hiroshima," in World War II.[177] Albright has since repeatedly apologized for saying what she did in such a crude manner, but has still not been asked whether she is sorry for actually enforcing the policy that killed so many innocent people and enraged so many new enemies. She has certainly not volunteered to do so.[178]

As a senior official in the George W. Bush administration later surprisingly admitted,

https://www.cia.gov/library/reports/general-reports-1/iraq_wmd_2004.

[174] Scott Ritter, interviewed by the author, *Scott Horton Show,* radio archive, February 5, 2005, https://scotthorton.org/interviews/february-5-2005-hour-2-scott-ritter/; "Transcript of Part One of Correspondent Brent Sadler's Exclusive Interview with Hussein Kamel," CNN, September 21, 1995, http://www.cnn.com/WORLD/9509/iraq_defector/kamel_transcript/.

[175] Andrew Cockburn, interviewed by author, *Scott Horton Show,* radio archive, April 18, 2007, http://scotthorton.org/interviews/2007/04/18/antiwar-radio-andrew-cockburn-pt2/; Madeleine K. Albright, "Policy Speech on Iraq," March 26, 1997, http://www.womenspeecharchive.org/women/profile/speech/index.cfm?ProfileID=110&SpeechID=472.

[176] Patrick Cockburn, "Iraqi Officers Pay Dear for West's Coup Fiasco," *Independent,* February 17, 1998, http://www.independent.co.uk/news/iraqi-officers-pay-dear-for-wests-coup-fiasco-1145298.html; Jenifer Mattos, "Coup Attempt Against Saddam Fails," *Time,* July 12, 1996, http://content.time.com/time/nation/article/0,8599,6902,00.html.

[177] "Secretary of State Madeleine Albright Interview," Leslie Stahl, *60 Minutes,* CBS News, originally aired May 12, 1996, YouTube video, 0:53, https://www.youtube.com/watch?v=omnskeu-puE.

[178] "Democracy Now! Confronts Madeleine Albright on Iraq Sanctions: Was It Worth the Price?," interviewed by Amy Goodman, *Democracy Now!,* November 30, 2004, https://www.democracynow.org/2004/7/30/democracy_now_confronts_madeline_albright_on.

[F]atwas from Osama ... cited the effects of sanctions on Iraqi children and the presence of U.S. troops as a sacrilege that justified his jihad. In a real sense, September 11 was part of the cost of containing Saddam. No containment, no U.S. troops in Saudi Arabia. No U.S. troops there, then bin Laden might still be redecorating mosques and boring friends with stories of his mujahideen days in the Khyber Pass.[179]

Deputy Secretary of Defense Paul Wolfowitz later even cited the necessity of removing U.S. combat forces stationed in Saudi Arabia as one of the benefits of invading Iraq:

There are a lot of things that are different now [that the U.S. occupies Iraq], and one that has gone by almost unnoticed — but it's huge — is that ... we can now remove almost all of our forces from Saudi Arabia. Their presence there over the last 12 years has been a source of enormous difficulty for a friendly government. It's been a huge recruiting device for al Qaeda. In fact, if you look at bin Laden, one of his principle grievances was the presence of so-called crusader forces on the holy land, Mecca and Medina. I think just lifting that burden from the Saudis is itself going to open the door to other positive things. I don't want to speak in messianic terms. It's not going to change things overnight, but it's a huge improvement.[180]

And in fact, as soon as the U.S. invaded Iraq in the spring of 2003, they began to close the major airbases remaining in Saudi Arabia.[181] The *New York Times* explained at the time, this was because,

The drastically reduced American profile could simplify the government's position among Saudis who espouse Osama bin Laden's contention that the American military foothold was an affront to the kingdom's sovereignty. For years, the American presence not far from Islam's two holiest sites, at Mecca and Medina, has provided al Qaeda with an important rallying cry.[182]

---

[179] Walter Russell Mead, "The Revolutionary," *Esquire*, October 28, 2004, http://archive.esquire.com/issue/20041101, cited by Jon Schwarz in "Why Do So Many Americans Fear Muslims? Decades of Denial About America's Role in the World," Intercept, February 18, 2017, https://theintercept.com/2017/02/18/why-do-so-many-americans-fear-muslims-decades-of-denial-about-americas-role-in-the-world/.

[180] "Deputy Secretary of Defense Paul Wolfowitz Interview with Sam Tannenhaus," *Vanity Fair*, posted at US Department of Defense website, May 9, 2003, http://archive.defense.gov/Transcripts/Transcript.aspx?TranscriptID=2594.

[181] Eric Schmitt, "Rumsfeld Says US Will Cut Forces in Gulf," *New York Times*, April 29, 2003, http://www.nytimes.com/2003/04/29/world/aftereffects-military-presence-rumsfeld-says-us-will-cut-forces-in-gulf.html.

[182] Don van Natta Jr., "Last American Combat Troops Quit Saudi Arabia," *New York Times*, September 22, 2003, http://www.nytimes.com/2003/09/22/world/the-struggle-for-iraq-last-american-combat-troops-quit-saudi-arabia.html.

The Far Enemy

In the 1990s, Dr. Ayman al Zawahiri, a former surgeon who was one of the leaders of Egyptian Islamic Jihad, began to merge his group with bin Laden's group. They agreed that the local revolutions they would someday like to wage, particularly against the regimes in Egypt and Arabia and ultimately leading to the creation of a new Islamic caliphate, would be impossible as long as the powerful American military was there to support the governments of its client states.[183] The "far enemy" would have to be driven out of the region first.[184] "We must move the battle to the enemy's grounds to burn the hands of those who ignite fire in our own countries." The "only language understood by the West," Zawahiri said, was "maximum casualties."[185]

Their strategy was fairly simple, as bin Laden and Zawahiri repeatedly explained. They wanted to replicate their success against the Soviet Union by provoking America into invading the region outright, to bog the U.S. military down and bleed its treasury dry, ultimately forcing complete collapse and withdrawal from the Middle East.[186]

Some of their colleagues had already started attacking. In 1990, the groups that were then beginning to merge into what we now call al Qaeda assassinated the radical rabbi Meir Kahane in New York City, for his support of Israeli expansion in the West Bank.[187] This was followed by the targeting of U.S. marines in the botched Yemen hotel bombings of 1992. The CIA was aware of Osama bin Laden's role in the attempted Yemen attacks by April of 1993.[188]

Next was the first hit on the World Trade Center with another — thankfully botched — bombing in February 1993, which killed six people, but could have been much worse. The bombers failed in their attempt to topple one tower over into the other, which, at midday, could have

---

[183] Ayman al-Zawahiri, "Knights Under the Prophet's Banner," *Ash-Sharq al-'Awsat*, December 2001, https://azelin.files.wordpress.com/2010/11/ayman-al-zawahiri-knights-under-the-prophets-banner-second-edition.pdf; Atwan, *Secret History*, 82-84.

[184] Fawaz A. Gerges, *The Far Enemy: Why Jihad Went Global*, 2nd ed., (Cambridge: Cambridge University Press, 2009).

[185] Andrew Higgins and Alan Cullison, "Saga of Dr. Zawahiri Sheds Light on the Roots of al Qaeda Terror," *Wall Street Journal*, July 2, 2002, http://www.wsj.com/articles/SB1025558570331929960.

[186] Osama bin Laden, "Declaration of War Against the Americans Occupying the Land of the Two Holy Places," PBS, August 1996.

[187] Peter Lance, "First Blood: Was Meir Kahane's Murder al Qaeda's Earliest Attack on US Soil?," *Tablet*, http://www.tabletmag.com/jewish-news-and-politics/44243/first-blood; Peter Lance, *1,000 Years for Revenge: International Terrorism and the FBI—the Untold Story* (New York: William Morrow, 2004), 33-37.

[188] Peter Bergen, *Holy War Inc.: Inside the Secret World of Osama Bin Laden* (New York: Free, 2001), 176.

instantly killed tens of thousands of people.[189] The ringleader of the plot, "the blind Sheikh," Omar Abdel Rahman of Egyptian Islamic Jihad, had been allowed into the country only with the assistance of CIA officials who considered him an old friend from the 1980s Afghan jihad.[190] The terrorists' conspiracy could have been thwarted entirely, as the FBI had an undercover informant inside the plot in a position to create a fake bomb with inert explosives. But the FBI supervisor, Carson Dunbar, refused to cooperate with his agents' efforts, leading the informant, Ahmed Salem, to bail out of the operation. Salem was then replaced by the ultimate bomb maker, Abdul Basit, better known as Ramzi Yousef. No one at either agency was held accountable.[191]

A thorough review of Yousef's statements fails to uncover a single claim that his intent was to convert Americans to his religion or kill anyone who failed to do so. Nor was any plot to subjugate American culture under conservative Sharia law revealed.[192] At Yousef's eventual sentencing hearing, the convict went into an extended tirade about America's "terrorist" foreign policy, support for Israel and blockade against Iraq. The federal judge, Kevin Duffy, then completely ignored Yousef's statement and instead refuted only what the government had claimed about his motives: "You weren't seeking conversions. The only thing you wanted to do was to cause death. Your God is not Allah. You worship death and destruction."[193]

Next came the thwarted plots against the Lincoln and Holland Tunnels and United Nations headquarters in New York.[194] Then followed a string of attacks planned by Ramzi Yousef in the Philippines in 1995, where he fled after the 1993 World Trade Center attack.[195] After an accidental fire

---

[189] "World Trade Center Truck Bombing," GlobalSecurity.org, http://www.globalsecurity.org/security/profiles/world_trade_center_truck_bombing.htm.

[190] Douglas Jehl, "CIA Officers Played Role in Sheik Visas," New York Times, July 22, 1993, http://www.nytimes.com/1993/07/22/nyregion/cia-officers-played-role-in-sheik-visas.html.

[191] Alison Mitchell, "Official Recalls Delay in Using Informer," New York Times, July 16, 1993, http://www.nytimes.com/1993/07/16/nyregion/official-recalls-delay-in-using-informer.html; Ralph Blumenthal, "Tapes Depict Proposal to Thwart Bomb Used in Trade Center Blast," New York Times, October 28, 1993, http://www.nytimes.com/1993/10/28/nyregion/tapes-depict-proposal-to-thwart-bomb-used-in-trade-center-blast.html; Lance, 1,000 Years for Revenge, 7-123.

[192] Alison Mitchell, "Letter Explained Motive in Bombing, Officials Now Say," New York Times, March 28, 1993, http://www.nytimes.com/1993/03/28/nyregion/letter-explained-motive-in-bombing-officials-now-say.html.

[193] "Excerpts from Statements in Court," New York Times, January 9, 1998, http://www.nytimes.com/1998/01/09/nyregion/excerpts-from-statements-in-court.html.

[194] John J. Goldman and Robert L. Jackson, "Eight Suspects Seized in Plot to Bomb U.N., Other N.Y. Targets," Los Angeles Times, June 25, 1993, http://articles.latimes.com/1993-06-25/news/mn-7023_1_trade-center.

[195] "Terrorists Plotted to Blow Up 11 US Jumbo Jets," Los Angeles Times, reprinted in Baltimore Sun, May 28, 1995, http://articles.baltimoresun.com/1995-05-28/news/1995148047_1_bojinka-philippines-plot.

at their Philippines apartment, Ramzi Yousef and his partners Wali Khan Amin Shah and Abdul Hakim Murad fled, but when Shah and Murad returned in an attempt to collect important materials, they were captured, along with a laptop computer of Yousef's. The computer revealed plans to assassinate Pope John Paul II and President Bill Clinton on their scheduled trips to the Philippines, as well as a plan called Bojinka, which was a scheme to time bomb 10 or more airliners over the Pacific Ocean. A test run of this failed to destroy the plane, but did kill the Japanese businessman underneath whose seat Yousef had planted a small bomb. There was also a plot said to have been thought up originally by Murad to hijack airliners and crash them into multiple targets on both U.S. coasts — the "planes operation," which later became the September 11th plot in the hands of Yousef's uncle, Khalid Sheikh Mohammed.[196]

Then came the Saudi National Guard training center bombings in 1995, which killed five Americans,[197] and the Khobar Towers attack near Dhahran, Saudi Arabia, in 1996, which killed 19 U.S. airmen in their barracks. For political reasons, the U.S. decided to blame the Khobar attack on "Iranian-backed Saudi Hezbollah," thus letting the guilty escape blame and, even worse, depriving the American people of an obvious and important truth: never mind America's bought and paid-for princes who rule these countries, there are deadly serious people there who want U.S. military forces off their land. It was later shown that the Khobar Towers attack was almost certainly orchestrated by Osama bin Laden and Khalid Sheikh Mohammed of al Qaeda.[198] Bin Laden himself took credit for the attack to Abdel Bari Atwan, Palestinian-British editor of the newspaper *Al-Quds al-Arabi* in London.[199]

On August 7, 1998, in Nairobi, Kenya, and Dar es Salaam, Tanzania, al Qaeda struck again with devastating dual truck bomb attacks against the U.S. embassies there, killing hundreds of people.[200] Atwan later wrote, "Al Qaeda explained that these cities had been chosen because they each housed a large U.S. military presence and because both the Kenyan and Tanzanian governments backed U.S. aggression against Iraq and had close

---

[196] Lance, *1,000 Years for Revenge*, 216, 233-244, 254-261.

[197] "Ambassador: Car Bomb Destroyed Military Building," CNN, November 13, 1995, http://www.cnn.com/WORLD/9511/saudi_blast/11am/.

[198] Gareth Porter, "Who Bombed Khobar Towers? Anatomy of a Crooked Terrorism Investigation," Truthout, September 1, 2015, http://www.truth-out.org/news/item/32589-who-bombed-khobar-towers-anatomy-of-a-crooked-terrorism-investigation; "William Perry: US Eyed Iran Attack After Bombing," UPI, June 6, 2007, http://www.upi.com/Business_News/Security-Industry/2007/06/06/Perry-US-eyed-Iran-attack-after-bombing/UPI-70451181161509/; Wayne Barrett, "Rudy's Ties to a Terror Sheikh," *Village Voice*, November 20, 2007, http://www.villagevoice.com/news/rudys-ties-to-a-terror-sheikh-6424129.

[199] Abdel Bari Atwan, *The Secret History of al Qaeda*, 36-37, 54, 168-169.

[200] "Attacks on US Embassies in Kenya and Tanzania," GlobalSecurity.org, http://www.globalsecurity.org/security/ops/98emb.htm.

links with Israel." Bill Clinton's government retaliated with Tomahawk cruise missile strikes on bin Laden's Afghan training camps, but bin Laden survived, having left two days before.[201]

The African embassy attacks were followed up by the thwarted "millennium attack" on Los Angeles International Airport in 1999,[202] a failed attack on the navy ship *USS The Sullivans* in January of 2000,[203] a foiled plot against the Radisson Hotel in Amman, Jordan,[204] and finally, the rubber-dinghy bomb attack on the *USS Cole* at port in Aden, Yemen, which killed 17 sailors in October of that year.[205]

During the growing al Qaeda war against America during the 1990s, the Clinton administration apparently still believed the mujahideen could be useful in achieving other foreign policy goals. While bin Laden had also claimed to target America for its tacit support for Russia, China, Uzbekistan and India in their violent suppression of Muslims,[206] the U.S. covertly favored al Qaeda's allies in Chechnya in their fight with Russia;[207] the Uighurs against China;[208] mujahideen affiliates and allies in Bosnia in the mid-nineties,[209] where September 11th ringleader Khalid Sheikh

---

[201] Atwan, *Secret History*, 55.

[202] Lisa Myers, "Foiling Millennium Attack Was Mostly Luck," NBC News, April 29, 2004, http://www.nbcnews.com/id/4864792/ns/nbc_nightly_news_with_brian_williams/t/foiling-millennium-attack-was-mostly-luck/.

[203] "Failed *USS The Sullivans* Bombing," GobalSecurity.org, http://www.globalsecurity.org/security/profiles/failed_uss_the_sullivans_bombing.htm.

[204] Clarke, *Against All Enemies*, 205.

[205] "USS Cole Bombing," GlobalSecurity.org, http://www.globalsecurity.org/security/profiles/uss_cole_bombing.htm.

[206] Scheuer, *Imperial Hubris*, 212; Osama bin Laden, *Messages to the World*, 140.

[207] Coleen Rowley, "Chechen Terrorists and the Neocons," Consortium News, April 19, 2013, https://consortiumnews.com/2013/04/19/chechen-terrorists-and-the-neocons/; Kevin Cirilli, "Chechen Rebels' Ties to Al Qaeda, Osama bin Laden," Politico, April 19, 2013, http://www.politico.com/story/2013/04/chechnya-primer-090326; John Laughland, "The Chechens' American Friends," *Guardian*, September 8, 2004, https://www.theguardian.com/world/2004/sep/08/usa.russia.

[208] Margolis, *War at the Top of the World*, 69; Eric Margolis, interviewed by the author, *Scott Horton Show*, radio archive, June 25, 2007, https://scotthorton.org/interviews/antiwar-radio-eric-margolis/.

[209] John R. Schindler, *Unholy Terror: Bosnia, Al-Qaeda, and the Rise of Global Jihad* (Minneapolis: Zenith, 2007); Brendan O'Neill, "How We Trained al-Qaeda," *Spectator*, September 13, 2003, http://archive.spectator.co.uk/article/13th-september-2003/31/how-we-trained-al-qaeda; Cees Wiebes, "Srebrenica: a 'Safe' Area, Appendix II, Intelligence and the War in Bosnia 1992-1995: The Role of the Intelligence and Security Services," NIOD Netherlands Institute for War Documentation, http://bit.ly/1wA321n; John Pomfret, "Bosnia's Muslims Dodged Embargo," *Washington Post*, September 22 1996, http://www.washingtonpost.com/wp-srv/inatl/longterm/bosvote/front.htm; Craig Pyes et al., "Bosnia Seen as Hospitable Base and Sanctuary for Terrorists," *Los Angeles Times*, October 7, 2001, http://articles.latimes.com/2001/oct/07/news/mn-54505/2; "Clinton-Approved Iranian Arms Transfers Help Turn Bosnia into Militant Islamic Base," Republican Policy Committee Report, Congressional Press Release, US Congress, January 16, 1997, http://www.globalresearch.ca/articles/DCH109A.html.

Mohammed earned his stripes;[210] as well as the al Qaeda-tied Kosovo Liberation Army of jihadists and gangsters in the Kosovo War of 1999.[211] In both the Bosnia and Kosovo wars, the U.S. supported al Qaeda's friends who were fighting against the Russian-aligned Serbs. All this was taking place despite Clinton's declaration that terrorism was "the enemy of our generation," one against which "we must prevail."[212]

Clinton's chief Balkans negotiator, Richard Holbrooke, later told the *Los Angeles Times*, "I think the [Bosnian] Muslims wouldn't have survived without" this help from the Arab mujahideen veterans of the 1980s Afghan war.[213] After September 11th, Clinton and some of his congressional allies were incredulous that al Qaeda would attack the U.S. after America had sided with Muslims in the Balkan wars.[214]

But why should the Democrats have expected a bunch of professional terrorists to be impressed by these efforts on their behalf? None of the rest of America's Mideast policies had changed, and al Qaeda's war against the U.S. had only continued to grow during that time. Clinton had helped to further build up jihadist forces, but he had failed to buy them off.

In 1998, Brzezinski, who had recommended so much of the U.S. policy towards the mujahideen, gave an infamous interview to the magazine *Le Nouvel Observateur*. When asked whether he had any regrets about the rise of the Taliban fundamentalist regime, which had taken hold of much of Afghanistan in 1996, in the wake of the Americans' efforts on behalf of the mujahideen in the 1980s — and, implicitly, its sheltering of international anti-Western terrorists such as Osama bin Laden — Brzezinski replied:

---

[210] Brendan O'Neill, "The Bosnian Connection," *New Statesman*, August 2, 2004, http://www.newstatesman.com/node/160271; Terry McDermott, "The Mastermind: Khalid Sheikh Mohammed and the Making of 9/11," *New Yorker*, September 13, 2010, http://www.newyorker.com/magazine/2010/09/13/the-mastermind.

[211] James Bovard, "When the Spoils of War Are Human Organs," *Washington Times*, August 4, 2014, http://www.washingtontimes.com/news/2014/aug/4/bovard-when-the-spoils-of-war-are-human-organs/; US Senate Republican Policy Committee, "The Kosovo Liberation Army: Does Clinton Policy Support Group with Terror, Drug Ties? From 'Terrorists' to 'Partners,'" Federation of American Scientists, March 31, 1999, https://fas.org/irp/world/para/docs/fr033199.htm; Brendan O'Neill, "How We Trained al-Qaeda."

[212] Bill Clinton, "Remarks on American Security in a Changing World at George Washington University," 32 Weekly Comp. Pres. Doc. 1404 (August 5, 1996).

[213] Craig Pyes et al., "Bosnia Seen as Hospitable Base and Sanctuary for Terrorists."

[214] "Bill Clinton Goes 'On the Record,'" interviewed by Greta Van Susteren, Fox News, June 7, 2005, http://www.foxnews.com/story/2005/06/07/bill-clinton-goes-on-record.html; Tom Lantos, "The Outlook for the Independence of Kosova: Hearing," House Foreign Affairs Committee, April 17, 2007, p. 16, http://bit.ly/2n75d9m; Brad Sherman, *Proceedings and Debates of the 107th Congress Congressional Record*, vol. 147, September 21, 2001, http://bit.ly/2maefBi.

What is most important to the history of the world? The Taliban or the collapse of the Soviet empire? Some stirred-up Muslims or the liberation of Central Europe and the end of the Cold War?[215]

In the same year, Republican Senator Orrin Hatch of Utah, who also supported the effort to back the mujahideen in the 1980s, told NBC News' Robert Windrem that even considering the growing list of al Qaeda attacks against the United States, "It was worth it."

"Those were very important, pivotal matters that played an important role in the downfall of the Soviet Union," he said. Hatch seemed to assume that the USSR would not have fallen otherwise, and that the innocent people killed by the rising generation of terrorists, their survivors and the millions of victims of the eventual wars justified by their deaths would share his same value judgment on the issue.[216]

During all this time leading up to the September 11th attacks on New York and Washington, D.C., the Clinton administration was thankfully too bogged down in the president's personal and domestic political scandals to react for the worse.[217] However, while Clinton did not take the bait and invade Afghanistan, neither did he reconsider the policies motivating al Qaeda nor confront the enemy he had provoked[218] — other than his 1998 cruise missile attacks on a few mostly empty Afghan training camps and the essential al-Shifa antibiotics factory in Sudan, a move that was based on completely false claims that it was a chemical weapons plant. These actions helped to make a folk hero out of bin Laden and disrupted the TV news cycle for a couple of days, but accomplished little else[219] beyond killing thousands of people deprived of the vital medicines the Sudanese factory had provided.[220]

---

[215] "The Brzezinski Interview," *Le Nouvel Observateur.*

[216] Michael Moran, "Bin Laden Comes Home to Roost: His CIA Ties Are Only the Beginning of a Woeful Story," NBC News, August 24, 1998, http://www.nbcnews.com/id/3340101/t/bin-laden-comes-home-roost/.

[217] Peter Baker, "Senate Launches Impeachment Trial; Rules Still Debated," *Washington Post,* January 7, 1999, http://www.washingtonpost.com/wp-srv/politics/special/clinton/stories/update010799.htm.

[218] Duncan Gardham and Iain Hollingshead, "The Bin Laden Hunter: Ex-CIA Man Had Bin Laden In His Sights 10 Times," *Daily Telegraph,* May 21, 2011, http://www.telegraph.co.uk/news/worldnews/asia/pakistan/8527515/The-bin-Laden-hunter-ex-CIA-man-had-bin-Laden-in-his-sights-10-times.html; Dan Good, "Bill Clinton, Hours Before 9/11 Attacks: 'I Could Have Killed' Osama bin Laden," ABC News, August 1, 2014, http://abcnews.go.com/US/bill-clinton-hours-911-attacks-killed-osama-bin/story?id=24801422; Michael Scheuer, interviewed by the author, *Scott Horton Show,* radio archive, March 22, 2007, https://scotthorton.org/interviews/antiwar-radio-michael-scheuer/; Michael Scheuer, interviewed by the author, *Scott Horton Show,* radio archive, September 2, 2010, https://scotthorton.org/interviews/antiwar-radio-michael-scheuer-9/.

[219] Daniel Pearl, "In Sudan Bombing, 'Evidence' Depends on Who Is Viewing It," *Wall Street Journal,* October 28, 1998, http://www.wsj.com/articles/SB909467144320930000.

[220] Jonathan Belke, "Year Later, US Attack on Factory Still Hurts Sudan," *Boston Globe,* August 22,

But then, finally, came the attacks of September 11, 2001.

For a population completely distracted by stock market bubbles, tabloid-style news and syndicated *Seinfeld* reruns during the "peacetime" years of Bill Clinton, and which largely looked on the new millennium as another beautiful "morning in America," with politics under the new George W. Bush administration seen as not much more than a slight distraction until that point,[221] the broadcast images of the hijack attack could not have been more misleading: the planes came straight out of the clear blue sky — just like in the cliché. A stunned population did not know what to make of it. This was "blowback" as properly defined — consequences of secret or unknown foreign policies, which catch the population off guard and leave them open to false interpretations about the nature of the conflict.[222]

American hawks have often cited bin Laden's taunts that U.S. withdrawal after the Beirut truck bomb attack on U.S. marines in 1983 and the disastrous "Black Hawk Down" events in Somalia in 1993 proved America was a paper tiger that could easily be scared into withdrawal from the region with just a few more similar attacks.[223] They concluded that America needed to "go big" this time instead.[224] Bin Laden may well have understood that forcing America to retreat from its overall policy of dominance in the region was a far different matter than chasing the military out of minor missions in places like Lebanon and Somalia. Or perhaps the strategy of scaring the U.S. off with foreign "pinprick" attacks had already been deemed to have failed. Either way, the attacks of September 11th, which killed nearly 3,000 people, but could have killed many thousands more, were clearly designed to provoke[225] — to give the

1999, http://www.hartford-hwp.com/archives/33/183.html.

[221] "Bush Actually President, Nation Suddenly Realizes," *Onion* (satire), March 31, 2001, http://www.theonion.com/article/bush-actually-president-nation-suddenly-realizes-315.

[222] Chalmers Johnson, "Blowback," *Nation*, September 27, 2001, https://www.thenation.com/article/blowback/; James Risen, "Oh, What a Fine Plot We Hatched. (And Here's What to Do the Next Time)," *New York Times*, June 18, 2000, http://www.nytimes.com/2000/06/18/weekinreview/word-for-word-abc-s-coups-oh-what-fine-plot-we-hatched-here-s-what-next-time.html; Donald Wilber, "Appendix E. Military Critique — Lessons Learned from TPAJAX re Military Planning Aspect of Coup d'Etat," in "CIA Clandestine Service History, Overthrow of Premier Mossadeq of Iran, November 1952-August 1953," CIA, March 1954, http://nsarchive.gwu.edu/NSAEBB/ciacase/EXL.pdf; Johnson, *Blowback*, 8.

[223] Osama bin Laden, "In His Own Words," *New York Times*, August 23, 1998, http://nytimes.com/1998/08/23/weekinreview/the-world-osama-bin-laden-in-his-own-words.html.

[224] Jack Kelly, "Bin Laden Finds Out US Is No Paper Tiger," *Toledo Blade*, November 25, 2001, http://www.toledoblade.com/Opinion/2001/11/25/Bin-Laden-finds-out-U-S-is-no-paper-tiger.html; Susan Page, "Why Clinton Failed to Stop bin Laden," *USA Today*, November 12, 2001, http://usatoday30.usatoday.com/news/attack/2001/11/12/clinton-usatcov.htm; Peter Bergen, "9/11: Osama bin Laden's Spectacular Miscalculation," CNN, September 7, 2016, http://www.cnn.com/2016/09/08/opinions/september-11-al-qaeda-spectacular-miscalculation-bergen/index.html.

[225] Grenier, *88 Days to Kandahar*, 4-5.

U.S. government reason to launch a full-scale war in Afghanistan and beyond. Only the U.S. government, manipulated into overreacting — really, given an opportunity to take advantage of a horrible situation — could accomplish this tiny group of terrorists' seemingly impossible goals. These included ending American dominance of the Middle East through imperial overstretch and self-destruction, along with the further radicalization of the region, destabilization of U.S.-supported dictatorships and a vast increase in the terrorists' own power and influence over the future. By attacking New York and Washington, al Qaeda succeeded in making America, in the words of ex-CIA analyst Scheuer, its "indispensable ally" in their scheme.[226]

But government and TV said America had been attacked because it had been an inward-looking "sleeping giant" as the Terror Juggernaut was closing in, provoked and emboldened by American weakness and isolationist indifference, and that the government would have to begin to take a much more activist approach to world affairs now that everything had changed.

Just as the enemy had planned.

In 2010, *Rolling Stone* magazine published an interview with one of Osama bin Laden's sons, Omar.

> My father's dream was to bring the Americans to Afghanistan. He would do the same thing he did to the Russians. I was surprised the Americans took the bait. I so much respected the mentality of President Clinton. He was the one who was smart. When my father attacked his places, he sent a few cruise missiles to my father's training camp. He didn't get my father, but after all the war in Afghanistan, they still don't have my father. They have spent hundreds of billions. Better for America to keep the money for its economy. In Clinton's time, America was very, very smart. Not like a bull that runs after the red scarf.
>
> I was in Afghanistan when Bush was elected. My father was so happy. This is the kind of President he needs — one who will attack and spend money and break the country. I'm sure my father wanted [Sen. John] McCain more than Obama [in the 2008 election]. McCain has the same mentality as Bush.[227]

---

[226] Scheuer, *Imperial Hubris*, p. i; Michael Scheuer, interviewed by the author, *Scott Horton Show*, radio archive, October 22, 2005, http://scotthorton.org/interviews/2005/10/22/october-22-2005-hour-1-michael-scheuer/; Michael Scheuer, *Scott Horton Show*, March 22, 2007, https://scotthorton.org/interviews/antiwar-radio-michael-scheuer/; Michael Scheuer, *Scott Horton Show*, radio archive, May 18, 2007, http://scotthorton.org/interviews/2007/05/19/antiwar-radio-michael-scheuer-2/.

[227] Guy Lawson, "Osama's Prodigal Son: The Dark, Twisted Journey of Omar bin Laden," *Rolling Stone*, January 20, 2010, http://www.rollingstone.com/politics/news/osamas-prodigal-son-20100120.

This may be a naïve view of Clinton and Obama, but the point remains that the more the Americans want to fight in their enemy's part of the world in the short term, the better it helps to achieve Osama bin Laden's goals in the long term.

The reporter asked Omar bin Laden if he thought his father would launch any more attacks in the United States. He replied, "I don't think so. He doesn't need to. As soon as America went to Afghanistan his plan worked. He's already won."

Chapter Two: Invasion

"All that we have to do is to send two mujahideen to the furthest point east to raise a piece of cloth on which is written al Qaeda, in order to make generals race there to cause America to suffer human, economic and political losses without their achieving anything of note other than some benefits for their private corporations. This is in addition to our having experience in using guerrilla warfare and the war of attrition to fight tyrannical superpowers, as we, alongside the mujahideen, bled Russia for 10 years, until it went bankrupt and was forced to withdraw in defeat. ... So we are continuing this policy of bleeding America to the point of bankruptcy." — Osama bin Laden, October 2004

"We're angry, but we're not stupid." — George W. Bush, September 2001

Unnecessary War

Even after the September 11, 2001, attacks on New York and Washington, there still never needed to be a War on Terrorism or invasion of Afghanistan.

The Taliban government of Afghanistan, which harbored Osama bin Laden and al Qaeda, had played no role in the September 11th attacks and sought no war with the United States. Tipped off by Uzbek jihadis about an impending strike on the U.S., the Taliban had even sent their Foreign Minister, Wakil Ahmed Muttawakil, to attempt to warn the American embassy in Peshawar, Pakistan, and the United Nations in July of 2001, though there is no evidence the Taliban knew of the specifics of the September 11th plot. Muttawakil's warnings were ignored.[1] Mullah Omar, the spiritual and political leader of Afghanistan's Taliban government, along with much of the Taliban leadership, had been trying to get rid of the troublesome Saudi since bin Laden had returned to Afghanistan in 1996, and had been especially outraged by his fatwas and interviews with foreign media. Part of the problem was that after surviving the U.S. Tomahawk cruise missile strikes launched in retaliation for al Qaeda's bombing of the two embassies in east Africa in 1998, bin Laden's status was raised in the minds of the Afghan population, making him that much more difficult for the new regime to sacrifice, though certain of their leaders continued to try.[2]

As the *Washington Post* reported on October 29, 2001, U.S. officials had met with the Taliban at least 20 times after the 1998 African embassy bombings to discuss Osama bin Laden's extradition. The talks continued, according to the *Post*, "until just days before" the September 11th attacks. After the U.S. threatened in early 1999 to hold the Taliban responsible for any future act of terrorism attributable to bin Laden, the regime had started working much harder to get rid of him. One representative even invited the U.S. to assassinate bin Laden in order to solve the problem.[3]

---

[1] Kate Clark, "Revealed: The Taliban Minister, the US Envoy and the Warning of September 11 That Was Ignored," *Independent*, September 6, 2002,
http://www.independent.co.uk/news/world/politics/revealed-the-taliban-minister-the-us-envoy-and-the-warning-of-september-11-that-was-ignored-131426.html.

[2] Alex Strick van Linschoten and Felix Kuehn, *An Enemy We Created: The Myth of the Taliban-Al Qaeda Merger in Afghanistan* (Oxford: Oxford University Press, 2012), 152-153; Ahmed Rashid, *Taliban: Militant Islam, Oil and Fundamentalism in Central Asia* (New Haven, CT: Yale University Press, 2010), 75; Gareth Porter, "Taliban Regime Pressed on Anti-US Terror," Inter Press Service, February 11, 2010, http://www.ipsnews.net/2010/02/afghanistan-taliban-regime-pressed-bin-laden-on-anti-us-terror/; Esposito and Mogahed, *Who Speaks for Islam? What a Billion Muslims Really Think*.

[3] Alan Cullison and Andrew Higgins, "A Once-Stormy Terror Alliance Was Solidified by Cruise Missiles," *Wall Street Journal*, August 2, 2002,
http://www.wsj.com/articles/SB1028236160532452080; K.M. Johnson, "Osama bin Laden: Taliban

While some believed the Taliban were simply stalling for time and never truly meant to hand bin Laden over, former CIA station chief Milton Bearden, who ran the covert Afghan war in the 1980s, told the *Post*, "We never heard what they were trying to say. We had no common language. Ours was, 'Give up bin Laden.' They were saying, 'Do something to help us give him up.' … Every time the Afghans said, 'He's lost again,' they are saying something. They are saying, 'He's no longer under our protection.' They thought they were signaling us subtly, and we don't do signals. … I have no doubts they wanted to get rid of him. He was a pain in the neck."[4]

Noting the "segregated relationship" between the Taliban government and their Saudi and Egyptian al Qaeda guests, including differences in Taliban leader Mullah Omar and al Qaeda leader bin Laden's schools of Islamic thought and their vastly different political priorities, as well as the history of distance and personal animosity between the two, the scholars Strick van Linschoten and Felix Kuehn wrote the two "were from different worlds, with different beliefs, different customs, different agendas, and — until the September 11th attacks — different paths for the future. The evidence by no means shows a joint agenda or any interest on bin Laden's part in sharing operational details with the Taliban."[5]

Three months before the September 11th attacks, United Press International editor at large Arnaud de Borchgrave interviewed Taliban leader Mullah Omar. Omar denounced bin Laden's fatwas against the United States as "null and void" since, Omar said, "bin Laden is not entitled to issue fatwas as he did not complete the mandatory 12 years of Koranic studies to qualify for the position of mufti." Mullah Omar told de Borchgrave he had "offered the United States and the United Nations to place international monitors to observe him pending the resolution of the [African embassy bombings] case, but so far we have received no reply." According to de Borchgrave, Mullah Omar had called bin Laden a "chicken bone stuck in his throat, that he can't swallow or spit out."[6]

Omar was clearly seething with resentment that the radical Osama bin Laden was endangering the Taliban's fledgling regime, which had not even finished taking control of the entire country.[7] And while his proposed plan for an international tribunal for bin Laden might not have fit U.S. desires

Spokesman Seeks New Proposal for Resolving Bin Laden Problem," State Department Document, November 28, 1998,
http://nsarchive.gwu.edu/NSAEBB/NSAEBB343/osama_bin_laden_file08.pdf.

[4] David B. Ottaway and Joe Stephens, "Diplomats Met with Taliban on Bin Laden," *Washington Post*, October 29, 2001, https://www.washingtonpost.com/archive/politics/2001/10/29/diplomats-met-with-taliban-on-bin-laden/15c446d3-0c6e-4429-b8f3-9896951fc444/.

[5] Van Linschoten and Kuehn, *An Enemy We Created*, 170.

[6] Arnaud de Borchgrave, "Mullah Omar: bin Laden — 'Null and void,'" June 14, 2001, UPI, http://www.upi.com/Mullah-Omar-bin-Laden-Null-and-void/70171008031323/.

[7] Grenier, *88 Days to Kandahar*, 61, 62.

perfectly, it would have been better than the reality of bin Laden's escape from accountability for another decade.

Once the attack on New York and Washington, D.C., took place and the United States threatened war, Taliban leaders again showed their willingness to negotiate the handover of bin Laden in an attempt to avoid the coming conflict. Their conditions quickly changed from stubborn-but-reasonable to virtually non-existent. They first demanded proof of bin Laden's guilt be provided,[8] and then only that he would be turned over to the Organization of the Islamic Conference (OIC), a group of 56 Muslim nations,[9] which, in practice, could have been Bahrain, Jordan, Egypt, Malaysia or another U.S.-friendly government, any of which would have extradited him to America immediately. When the U.S. refused these seemingly modest terms, the Taliban offered to turn bin Laden over to the government of Pakistan, again offering a solution that was no impediment to the U.S.'s ability to take custody within days, but which provided just the smallest amount of face-saving for the Taliban regime, bound as they were by their traditional "Pashtunwali" honor code, which demands full protection for guests. This offer was reportedly ruined by Pakistani dictator General Pervez Musharraf over the very thin excuse that Pakistan would be unable to guarantee bin Laden's safety while he awaited trial.[10] Finally, just a few days after the U.S. bombing of Afghanistan began in early October, the Taliban promised to hand bin Laden over to *any* country other than the United States and without seeing evidence of his guilt.[11] This was still not good enough to stave off the invasion. As the *Guardian* reported on October 16, 2001:

> For the first time, the Taliban offered to hand over bin Laden for trial in a country other than the U.S. without asking to see evidence first in return for a halt to the bombing, a source close to Pakistan's military leadership said.

---

[8] "White House Says 'No' to Taliban Demand for Proof," CBC News, September 21, 2001, http://www.cbc.ca/news/world/white-house-says-no-to-taliban-demand-for-proof-1.257637.

[9] Gareth Porter, "US Refusal of 2001 Taliban Offer Gave bin Laden a Free Pass," Inter Press Service, May 3, 2011, http://www.ipsnews.net/2011/05/us-refusal-of-2001-taliban-offer-gave-bin-laden-a-free-pass/.

[10] Patrick Bishop, "Pakistan Blocks bin Laden Trial," *Telegraph*, October 4, 2001, http://www.telegraph.co.uk/news/worldnews/asia/afghanistan/1358464/Pakistan-blocks-bin-Laden-trial.html.

[11] "US Rejects New Taliban Offer," ABC News, October 14, 2001, http://abcnews.go.com/International/story?id=80482&page=1; Kathy Gannon, "Bush Rejects Taliban Bin Laden Offer," *Washington Post*, October 14, 2001, http://www.washingtonpost.com/wp-srv/aponline/20011014/aponline135016_000.htm; Rory McCarthy, "New Offer on Bin Laden," *Guardian*, October 16, 2001, http://www.guardian.co.uk/world/2001/oct/17/afghanistan.terrorism11; Anand Gopal, interviewed by the author, *Scott Horton Show*, radio archive, October 15, 2014, http://scotthorton.org/interviews/2014/10/15/101514-anand-gopal/.

But U.S. officials appear to have dismissed the proposal and are instead hoping to engineer a split within the Taliban leadership.

The offer was brought by Mullah Wakil Ahmed Muttawakil, the Taliban foreign minister and a man who is often regarded as a more moderate figure in the regime. He met officials from the CIA and Pakistan's ISI intelligence directorate in Islamabad on Monday. ... [U]ntil now the Taliban regime has consistently said it has not seen any convincing evidence to implicate the Saudi dissident in any crime.

"Now they have agreed to hand him over to a third country without the evidence being presented in advance," the source close to the military said. ... The U.S. administration has not publicly supported the idea of a trial for Bin Laden outside America and appears intent on removing from power the Taliban leader Mullah Mohammed Omar and the hardliners in the regime.[12]

"When I said no negotiations, I meant no negotiations," President Bush declared.[13] Americans wanted revenge. The U.S. government wanted war.

The Trap

As Mullah Omar and the Taliban chose to sacrifice their regime and, indeed, their country by not doing everything they could to ditch bin Laden and al Qaeda at the nearest CIA station, the U.S. made a comparable mistake in choosing to lash out militarily instead of doing everything they could to get bin Laden peacefully — to short circuit his ultimate plan. The U.S. attack on Afghanistan was almost exactly what bin Laden had expected and plotted, though perhaps he had underestimated the amount of damage the CIA and air force would be able to inflict in such a short amount of time.

Wall Street Journal reporter Alan Cullison obtained two al Qaeda computers in Kabul just two weeks after the attacks of September 11, 2001. One of them contained a treasure trove of al Qaeda documents and correspondence. He was unable to examine the other before handing it over to U.S. intelligence officers. In a 2004 article for the *Atlantic*, Cullison quotes from a letter found on the first computer, which bin Laden had written to Mullah Omar and the Taliban leadership, pleading with them to try to understand why he had provoked such an assault. Just wait, he told

[12] McCarthy, "New Offer on Bin Laden."

[13] Elizabeth Bumiller, "President Rejects Offer by Taliban for Negotiations," *New York Times*, October 15, 2001, http://www.nytimes.com/2001/10/15/world/nation-challenged-president-president-rejects-offer-taliban-for-negotiations.html.

them, in ten years the U.S. will be bogged down, burnt out, bankrupt, and helpless just like the USSR before them. Sucking up a bit to Mullah Omar in an apparent attempt to stay in his good graces in the face of the American aerial onslaught against the regime's forces, bin Laden explained that Plan A was that the U.S. would turn and withdraw as it had done previously after taking losses in Beirut and Somalia, but that Plan B — the provocation of the U.S. into a long and fruitless war that would end up leading to the same end, only even more painfully for America — would be just as good or better for them in the long term. Bin Laden wrote:

> We treasure your message, which confirms your generous, heroic position in defending Islam and in standing up to the symbols of infidelity of this time.

> I would like to emphasize the major impact of your statements on the Islamic world. Nothing harms America more than receiving your strong response to its positions and statements. Thus it is very important that the Emirate respond to every threat or demand from America ... with demands that America put an end to its support of Israel, and that U.S. forces withdraw from Saudi Arabia. ... Their threat to invade Afghanistan should be countered by a threat on your part that America will not be able to dream of security until Muslims experience it as reality in Palestine and Afghanistan.

> Keep in mind that America is currently facing two contradictory problems:

> a) If it refrains from responding to jihad operations, its prestige will collapse, thus forcing it to withdraw its troops abroad and restrict itself to U.S. internal affairs. This will transform it from a major power to a third-rate power, similar to Russia.

> b) On the other hand, a campaign against Afghanistan will impose great long-term economic burdens, leading to further economic collapse, which will force America, God willing, to resort to the former Soviet Union's only option: withdrawal from Afghanistan, disintegration, and contraction. ...

> We ask God to grant the Muslim Afghan nation, under your leadership, victory over the American infidels, just as He singled this nation out with the honor of defeating the Communist infidels.

In February of 2002, Vice Admiral Thomas R. Wilson, the director of the Defense Intelligence Agency, testified to the U.S. Senate Committee on Intelligence, "The strategic intent [of the September 11th attacks] was to deliver a blow that would force the U.S. to either alter its Middle East policies, or goad America into a 'disproportionate response' that would trigger an apocalyptic confrontation between Islam and the West."[14]

This illustrates how U.S. policy plays into the hands of our enemies. Having painted themselves into a corner, the Americans end up losing either way, whether they get the message and withdraw from the region immediately or if they take the bait, invade and stay until the occupation becomes financially unsustainable. Bin Laden's letter also demonstrates the depravity of al Qaeda — to wish to recreate the devastation of the 1980s Soviet war in Afghanistan, where perhaps a million innocent people were killed,[15] as a means to freeing the Arabian Peninsula from American dominance. In fact, bin Laden had previously told Atwan he "greatly regretted" the fact that President Bill Clinton withdrew U.S. forces from Somalia after the "Black Hawk Down" incident of 1993. Though bin Laden later cited this withdrawal as proof America was ultimately a weak adversary, at the time, just two years after the first Iraq war, the al Qaeda leader claimed he sought to bog down the U.S. in a "war of attrition" there. The innocent Somalis who were to end up caught in the crossfire were of no apparent concern to bin Laden any more than were the tens of thousands of Afghans killed in the U.S. war since 2001.[16]

The *Journal*'s Cullison elaborated on what he'd learned from his deep dive into the al Qaeda leadership's thought processes, debates, structure and plans:

> Perhaps one of the most important insights to emerge from the computer is that 9/11 sprang not so much from al Qaeda's strengths as from its weaknesses. The computer did not reveal any links to Iraq or any other deep-pocketed government; amid the group's penury, the members fell to bitter infighting. The blow against the United States was meant to put an end to the internal rivalries, which are manifest in vitriolic memos between Kabul and cells abroad. Al Qaeda's leaders worried about a military response from the United States, but in such a response they spied opportunity: they had fought the Soviet Union in Afghanistan, and they fondly remembered that war as a galvanizing experience, an event that roused the indifferent of the Arab world to fight and win against a technologically superior Western infidel. The jihadis expected the United States, like the Soviet Union, to be a clumsy opponent. Afghanistan would again become a slowly filling graveyard for the imperial ambitions of a superpower.

---

[14] Thomas R. Wilson, "September 11, 2001: Attack on America Statement Before the Senate Select Committee on Intelligence," Defense Intelligence Agency, February 6, 2002, http://avalon.law.yale.edu/sept11/wilson_001.asp.

[15] Alan Taylor, "The Soviet War in Afghanistan, 1979 - 1989," *Atlantic*, August 4, 2014, https://www.theatlantic.com/photo/2014/08/the-soviet-war-in-afghanistan-1979-1989/100786/.

[16] Atwan, *The Secret History of al Qaeda*, 49.

Like the early Russian anarchists who wrote some of the most persuasive tracts on the uses of terror, al Qaeda understood that its attacks would not lead to a quick collapse of the great powers. Rather, its aim was to tempt the powers to strike back in a way that would create sympathy for the terrorists. Al Qaeda has so far gained little from the ground war in Afghanistan; the conflict in Iraq, closer to the center of the Arab world, is potentially more fruitful. As Arab resentment against the United States spreads, al Qaeda may look less like a tightly knit terror group and more like a mass movement. And as the group develops synergy in working with other groups branded by the United States as enemies (in Iraq, … Kashmir, the Mindanao Peninsula, and Chechnya, to name a few places), one wonders if the United States is indeed playing the role written for it on the computer.[17]

Unlimited War

For the sake of argument, assuming the false premises that the U.S. must never "negotiate with evil" and absolutely had to go to war against al Qaeda in Afghanistan after the September 11th attacks were true, Congress made a terrible error when they went along with almost all of the Bush administration's suggested language for their Authorization to Use Military Force (AUMF).[18] Though many in Congress who voted for it may have believed they were voting to authorize the invasion of Afghanistan, this ultimately open-ended resolution has served as the legal basis for at least six separate, unrelated interventions in the decade and a half since.[19]

As soon as President George W. Bush delivered his statement from the Oval Office on the night of the September 11th attacks, the die was cast. The first premise of the war, boldly stated early in the president's address was false: "These acts of mass murder were intended to frighten our nation into chaos and retreat. But they have failed; our country is strong." With matador bin Laden's red cape waved, the American bull would now charge headlong into catastrophe. "Our military is powerful, and it's prepared." There was no mention of al Qaeda, even though the government already

---

[17] Alan Cullison, "Inside Al Qaeda's Hard Drive."

[18] Authorization for Use of Military Force, Pub. L. No. 107-40, 155 Stat. 224 (2001), https://www.congress.gov/107/plaws/publ40/PLAW-107publ40.pdf; Tom Daschle, "Power We Didn't Grant," *Washington Post*, December 23, 2005, http://www.washingtonpost.com/wp-dyn/content/article/2005/12/22/AR2005122201101.html.

[19] Gregory D. Johnsen, "60 Words and a War Without End: The Untold Story of the Most Dangerous Sentence in US History," Buzzfeed News, January 16, 2014, https://www.buzzfeed.com/gregorydjohnsen/60-words-and-a-war-without-end-the-untold-story-of-the-most.

knew who had been responsible for the attack.[20] The closest Bush came to defining the enemy in his original statement was an attempt to conflate the guilty with the Taliban government of Afghanistan, "We will make no distinction between the terrorists who committed these acts and those who harbor them."[21]

In his speech to Congress nine days after the attack, Bush declared war on "terrorism," a mandate so broad it could include the targeting of almost any violent political group on earth. Now, we were told, *everything had changed*. It was to be a "new era" of war to "end evil" on earth. And now we know for a fact why the administration framed the conflict the way they did: The president and his men had already decided, the very day of the attack, that they would be launching a project far greater than a mere hunt for the leaders of the group which was responsible. The Terror War would, like the Cold War with the old Soviet Union, serve as a larger framework for numerous smaller wars. "There are thousands of these terrorists in more than 60 countries," Bush lied. "Our war on terror begins with al Qaeda, but it does not end there. It will not end until every terrorist group of global reach has been found, stopped and defeated."[22]

In fact, before the sun had gone down on the evening of the 11th and anyone could even be certain the attacks were completely over, Secretary of Defense Donald Rumsfeld was already telling his staff to plan for war against Iraq. Undersecretary of Defense for Intelligence Stephen Cambone took notes:

> Hard to get good case. Need to move swiftly. Near term target needs — go massive — sweep it all up, things related and not. … Best info fast. Judge whether good enough [to] hit SH [Saddam Hussein] at same time — not only UBL [Osama bin Laden]. Tasks. [Pentagon General Counsel] Jim Haynes to talk with PW [Deputy Secretary of Defense Paul Wolfowitz], for additional support [for] connection with UBL.[23]

Over at the White House, Richard Clarke, the head of counterterrorism, was doing everything he could to keep the focus on Osama bin Laden in Afghanistan, forcefully debunking Deputy Secretary of Defense Paul Wolfowitz's immediate conflation of bin Laden's group with the government of Iraq. Wolfowitz had long associated himself with the journalistic quackery of author Laurie Mylroie, who blamed Iraq for

---

[20] Bob Woodward, *Bush at War* (New York: Simon & Schuster, 2002), 4.

[21] George W. Bush, "Address to the Nation on the Terrorist Attacks," 37 Weekly Comp. Pres. Doc. 1301 (September 11, 2001).

[22] George W. Bush, "Address Before a Joint Session of the Congress on the United States Response to the Terrorist Attacks of September 11," 37 Weekly Comp. Pres. Doc. 1347 (September 20, 2001).

[23] Joel Roberts, "Plans for Iraq Attack Began On 9/11," CBS News, September 4, 2002, http://www.cbsnews.com/news/plans-for-iraq-attack-began-on-9-11/; Image of document, PBS.org, https://pbs.twimg.com/media/CsGCPwLWAAAI8tw.jpg.

secretly orchestrating the entire al Qaeda war against the U.S., blaming Saddam Hussein for the first World Trade Center bombing in 1993, as well as the shooting outside CIA headquarters later that year, which in reality was a lone wolf attack tied to neither,[24] the 1995 Oklahoma City Bombing[25] and all the al Qaeda strikes overseas in the years since.[26] The CIA, FBI and the rest of the government had dismissed her ravings,[27] which all hung on the provably false claim that al Qaeda operative Ramzi Yousef was actually an Iraqi secret police agent who had stolen Yousef's identity.[28] For Wolfowitz, neoconservative leader Richard Perle and a few of their fellow travelers, though, it was the ultimate case of confirmation bias, if not simply lying in the pursuit of other agendas.[29]

Retired U.S. Army General Wesley Clark, the former commander of NATO forces in Europe, later told the story of going to the Pentagon shortly after the September 11th attacks and seeing a memo that had been drawn up by Secretary of Defense Donald Rumsfeld's staff. The memo included a list of seven countries to be the subject of U.S. regime-change policies in the new War on Terrorism: Iraq, Syria, Lebanon, Libya, Somalia, Sudan and Iran.[30] None of the governments of these countries supported al Qaeda or threatened the United States.

Those guilty of organizing the deadly September 11th attacks and their secret base in Afghanistan? A side issue, too remote to make an effective demonstration of American power and resolve. As Rumsfeld complained, there were "no good targets" there.[31]

Some of Bush's advisers reportedly were so intent on launching a war against the "better" target of Iraq in the days immediately after the attacks

---

[24] "Prosecutor: US Mideast Policy Motivated CIA Shooting," CNN, November 5, 1997, http://edition.cnn.com/US/9711/05/cia.shooting/; "'Iraq Bombing Angered Kasi,' Jury Is Told," *Los Angeles Times*, November 6, 1997, http://articles.latimes.com/1997/nov/06/news/mn-50861.

[25] Peter Bergen, "Armchair Provocateur: Reading Laurie Mylroie, the Neocons' Favorite Conspiracy Theorist," *Washington Monthly*, December 2003, https://www.unz.org/Pub/WashingtonMonthly-2003dec-00027.

[26] Clarke, *Against All Enemies*, 30, 32, 95, 231-233, 237; Laurie Mylroie, "Who is Ramzi Yousef? And Why It Matters," *National Interest*, Winter 1995/96, https://fas.org/irp/world/iraq/956-tni.htm; Laurie Mylroie and Judith Miller, *Study of Revenge: Saddam Hussein's Unfinished War Against America* (Washington, D. C.: AEI, 2000); Laurie Mylroie, *The War Against America: Saddam Hussein and the World Trade Center Attacks; A Study of Revenge,* 2nd rev. ed., (New York: Harper Paperbacks, 2001).

[27] Andrew C. McCarthy, "Still Willfully Blind After All These Years," *National Review*, April 30, 2008, http://www.nationalreview.com/article/224339/still-willfully-blind-after-all-these-years-andrew-c-mccarthy

[28] Michael Isikoff, "Terror Watch: The Enemy Within," *Newsweek*, April 20, 2004, http://www.newsweek.com/terror-watch-enemy-within-124865.

[29] Peter Bergen, "Armchair Provocateur."

[30] "Gen. Wesley Clark Weighs Presidential Bid," interview by Amy Goodman, *Democracy Now!*, March 2, 2007, https://democracynow.org/2007/3/2/gen_wesley_clark_weighs_presidential_bid.

[31] Andrea Stone, "Ex-aide: Bush Ignored Terror Threat," *USA Today*, March 20, 2004, http://usatoday30.usatoday.com/news/washington/2004-03-20-clarke_x.htm.

that they actually wanted to start launching strikes against Saddam Hussein's government right away — before, or at least simultaneously with, the assault against the guilty al Qaeda members hiding in Afghanistan.[32] When British Prime Minister Tony Blair arrived to discuss the war a week after the attack, the talk was so centered on Iraq he felt it necessary to lecture Bush, "[D]on't get distracted; the priorities [are] al-Qaeda, Afghanistan, the Taliban."[33]

Republican Representative Ron Paul of Texas proposed an authorization far more limited in scope, which would have allowed attacks only against al Qaeda and those fighting directly for them. The whole operation might have been over by Christmas 2001 had the mission been defined more narrowly — and focused on the actual enemy. As Dr. Paul wisely explained to the House of Representatives at the time, his more limited authorization would

> resolve one of the most vexing problems facing the country: how do we obtain retribution against the perpetrators of the attacks without inflicting massive damage on the Middle East which could drive moderate Arabs into an allegiance with bin Laden and other terrorists? This is because using [this resolution] shows the people of the region that we are serious when we say our quarrel is not with them but with Osama bin Laden and all others who would dare commit terrorist acts against the United States.[34]

The congressman's argument fell on deaf ears. Instead, the much broader authorization was passed, the war was expanded and bin Laden was able to live free for nearly another decade after the September 11th attacks before finally being put down. His partner, Ayman al Zawahiri, was still at large and directing al Qaeda in 2017.[35]

The administration's plans were so grandiose they had already lost sight of their original target and changed the September 11th attacks from a reason to defend Americans to an excuse to launch new wars. It is likely

[32] Lawrence Wilkerson, email message to author, April 8, 2017; Andy McSmith, "Chilcot Report: The Inside Story of How Tony Blair Led Britain to War in Iraq," *Independent*, July 4, 2016, http://www.independent.co.uk/news/uk/politics/chilcot-report-iraq-war-inquiry-tony-blair-george-bush-us-uk-what-happened-a7119761.html.

[33] Bryan Burrough et al., "The Path to War," *Vanity Fair*, December 19, 2008, http://www.vanityfair.com/news/2004/05/path-to-war200405.

[34] Ron Paul, "Air Piracy Reprisal and Capture Act 2001," remarks delivered before the United States House of Representatives, October 10, 2001, http://avalon.law.yale.edu/sept11/speech_ron_paul_1010.asp; September 11 Marque and Reprisal Act of 2001, H.Res. 3076, 107th Cong. (2001), https://www.govtrack.us/congress/bills/107/hr3076/text.

[35] Philip Issa, "Al Qaeda Leader Tells Fighters to Prepare for Long Syria War," *Chicago Tribune*, April 24, 2017, http://www.chicagotribune.com/news/nationworld/ct-al-qaida-syria-war-20170424-story.html.

that for this reason more than any other, the U.S. stuck with the "light and fast" Rumsfeld Doctrine in the initial invasion of Afghanistan, which consisted mostly of embedding CIA officers and a handful of special operations forces with the "Northern Alliance" of Afghan warlords, who at that moment had been on the eve of their defeat at the hands of the Taliban, cornered in parts of the far northwest of the country.[36] But with American spies on the ground with laser designators directing U.S. B-52 heavy bombers against Taliban targets, it was not long before the regime had given up the cities and headed for the hills.

America's Most Wanted

Bob Woodward, *Washington Post* reporter and author of the semi-official history of the decision-making during that time, *Bush at War*, wrote that even though the CIA was suggesting an attempt to split the Taliban away from al Qaeda, the leadership of Mullah Omar or both, Secretary Rumsfeld was insistent on including Taliban military targets in his initial set lists to avoid the appearance of "pounding sand" in a war in which the actual enemy, al Qaeda, had virtually no fixed targets to attack. National Security Advisor Condoleezza Rice and others in the government predicted that once the war started and they were attacked together, some factions of the Taliban would rally together with al Qaeda in response, making any exploitable distinctions moot.[37] And though the Taliban had tried one last offer to surrender al Qaeda after the bombing started, when Bush still refused to negotiate, "any possibility of a deal pretty much evaporated after that," according to journalist Anand Gopal.[38]

When the National Security Council met at the White House on Tuesday, September 25, two weeks after the attacks and more than a week before the bombing of Afghanistan had even begun, "the president spoke first," declaring, "'We can't define the success or failure in terms of capturing UBL.'" Secretary of Defense Donald Rumsfeld agreed, saying, "We ought to have a broad beginning and an ending. It ought to focus on al Qaeda — it shouldn't focus on UBL ... It's not over if we get his head on a platter. And the failure to get his head on a platter is not failure." Combining an almost perfectly satirical take on the incentives of bureaucratic expansion with the preconceived plan to take the war to Iraq, Rumsfeld went on to suggest, "As part of the war on terrorism, should we be getting something going in another area, other than Afghanistan, so

[36] Elise Labot, "US Gives $43 Million to Afghanistan," CNN, May 17, 2001, http://www.cnn.com/2001/US/05/17/us.afghanistan.aid/.

[37] Woodward, *Bush at War*, 123-128.

[38] Gopal, *Scott Horton Show*, October 15, 2014.

that success or failure and progress isn't measured just by Afghanistan?"[39]

Woodward dryly, perhaps entirely without irony, notes that on the day after the attack, "Rumsfeld worried that a coalition built around the goal of taking out al Qaeda would fall apart once they succeeded in that mission, making it more difficult to continue the war on terrorism elsewhere." In other words, if the U.S.A. won by defeating the enemy, the war would be over. So, to avoid that problem, they would have to be far more ambiguous about just who was to be included as enemy targets in the war.[40]

The president was clearly of the same mind. A month later, on October 11, with the bombing campaign just a few days old, Bush reiterated to the assembled Principals Committee of the National Security Council: "If we don't get UBL, it doesn't mean it's a failure." He declared the objective was simply the overthrow of the Taliban and "UBL killed, captured or on the run," a phrase that was so "loose," as Woodward observed, that "it had already been achieved."[41]

Woodward also showed how this attitude affected the administration's decision making. Incredibly, in all the conversation and debate at the highest levels of the Bush government at the start of the war, as the CIA was getting their mission going, no one bothered to ask just where exactly in Afghanistan the Arab fighters were — especially the few hundred associates of Osama bin Laden who could truly be counted as members of al Qaeda. Even though the Bush government had already decided to destroy the Taliban regime, one might think they still would have focused their actual efforts on al Qaeda first. Instead, nearly two months were spent taking the city of Mazar-e-Sharif, in the far north near the Uzbekistan border, and the capital city of Kabul from the Taliban.[42]

In *Jawbreaker: The Attack on Bin Laden and Al-Qaeda: A Personal Account by the CIA's Key Field Commander*, CIA officer Gary Berntsen, the second on-scene commander in charge of the early stages of the invasion, explained that the orders from Central Command (CENTCOM) Commander General Tommy Franks were specific: U.S. intelligence and military forces were to focus on assisting Northern Alliance warlord General Rashid Dostum in his attempts to take the cities of Mazar-e-Sharif, Kunduz and Taloqan in the Afghan north and northwest first, and only then begin the attack against the Arab Brigade of alleged al Qaeda fighters on the Shomali Plain north of the capital city of Kabul.[43] It makes

---

[39] Woodward, *Bush at War*, 121-137.

[40] Ibid., 48.

[41] Ibid., 227-229.

[42] Ibid., 293-311.

[43] Berntsen and Pezzullo, *Jawbreaker*, 90-91.

perfect sense that these were Dostum's priorities, but why America's? Franks explained they wanted to set up a land link to Uzbekistan as soon as possible. But what for? Uzbekistan was as far as could be from where the action should have been — bin Laden's so-called "lion's den" hideout at Tora Bora in eastern Afghanistan, near the city of Jalalabad. U.S. Army Rangers already controlled the Bagram air base on the eastern edge of the Shomali Plain. How could Franks have decided to prioritize targets hundreds of miles away when the Rangers were already where they needed to be to take on the first group of Arab fighters? While the Arab Brigade fighting alongside the Taliban on the Shomali Plain were not truly members of bin Laden's group,[44] it seems reasonable to expect U.S. forces to have acted, at that point, as though any group of armed Arab fighters serving the Taliban would be with al Qaeda, especially since intelligence locating bin Laden and his men at Tora Bora was apparently not acquired until November 25.[45] What made no sense was Central Command's insistence on running the wrong way and fighting indigenous forces in the far north and northwest of the country.

As Berntsen wrote, the mission given to him by the administration was to "defeat the Taliban," with the "added responsibility" of hunting down bin Laden "and destroying what we could of his terrorist organization."[46] Washington clearly had their priorities mixed up. It may not have been too late even to use the Taliban *against* al Qaeda. One Taliban commander on the Shomali Plain wanted to surrender his entire group to the CIA and Northern Alliance. At Berntsen's direction, he willingly executed 20 Arab fighters under his command, presumed by the Americans to be true al Qaeda members, before surrendering with over 700 more of his men the following day — a clear sign of the Taliban's willingness to sacrifice their Arab-Afghan allies to survive. Even if these Taliban leaders could not be induced to help hunt down bin Laden and the core al Qaeda group, they could have at least been ignored until the real enemy had been located and captured or killed.[47]

However, whatever the motivation, the decision made to focus on hiring local warlords to fight the Taliban regime, instead of focusing on finding Osama bin Laden and his al Qaeda allies as quickly as possible, provided enough time for many in bin Laden's core group, those most responsible for the deadly attack on the United States, to make a run for the border — east toward Pakistan.

In December 2001, the CIA, Army Delta Force and their Northern

---

[44] Storer, *Scott Horton Show*, March 13, 2017.

[45] Berntsen and Pezzullo, *Jawbreaker*, 249.

[46] Ibid., 100.

[47] Ibid., 159-160.

Alliance allies finally tracked down and cornered al Qaeda at Tora Bora in the White Mountains of eastern Afghanistan. This was where the plan to outsource America's fight to the Northern Alliance and other associated warlords proved to be a disaster. Warlord Hajji Zaman later laughed that he had taken millions in cash from the CIA and then helped escort Osama bin Laden and his friends across the border anyway.[48] "Eastern Alliance" warlord and the CIA's former favorite asset[49] from the 1980s war, Gulbuddin Hekmatyar of the Hizb-e-Islami group, later took credit for helping with the escape as well.[50] Bin Laden's partner Ayman al Zawahiri admitted in a video released in 2006 that U.S. forces had pinned down what was left of al Qaeda to an area of only one square kilometer. They had been facing certain defeat, but, he bragged, the Americans had refused to take the necessary risk to finish the job.[51] Gen. Franks denied multiple requests to reinforce the CIA and their Northern and Eastern Alliance allies at Tora Bora with marines or Rangers. According to the *New York Times*, then-Marine Corps General, now secretary of defense under Donald Trump, James Mattis had 4,000 marines ready to go only miles away and asked for permission to get into the fight where his men could have been used to seal off the border, but "the general was turned down." It was "a week or so" later that Osama bin Laden escaped.[52]

Berntsen later complained that he had asked repeatedly for Army Rangers to back up the agency paramilitaries and Delta Force operators fighting at Tora Bora. "I'd sent my request for 800 U.S. Army Rangers and was still waiting for a response. I repeated to anyone at headquarters who would listen: We need Rangers now! The opportunity to get bin Laden and his men is slipping away!!" [emphasis in original] Again, the request was denied.[53]

Berntsen was sent home in the middle of the ongoing battle of Tora Bora in mid-December.[54] He later wrote in *Jawbreaker* that he just could not understand why the generals and politicians were so reluctant to send troops. Days and weeks had gone by with Berntsen and his men repeatedly requesting, even begging, for reinforcements over and over again.[55]

[48] Anand Gopal, *No Good Men Among the Living: America, the Taliban, and the War through Afghan Eyes* (New York: Metropolitan, 2014), 147-148.

[49] Coll, *Ghost Wars*, 120.

[50] "Afghan Warlord Says He Helped Bin Laden Escape," Reuters, January 11, 2007, http://www.reuters.com/article/us-pakistan-binladen-idUSISL33869920070111.

[51] Stephen Ulph, "Al-Zawahiri's New Video Calls on Muslims to Support the Mujahideen," *Terrorism Focus*, vol. 3 iss. 15, April 18, 2006.

[52] Mary Anne Weaver, "Lost at Tora Bora," *New York Times Magazine*, September 11, 2005, http://www.nytimes.com/2005/09/11/magazine/lost-at-tora-bora.html.

[53] Berntsen and Pezzullo, *Jawbreaker*, 290.

[54] Ibid., 297-298.

[55] Ibid., 277, 306.

Gen. Franks later took responsibility for the failure to capture bin Laden, telling Congress he had been certain Pakistan had deployed enough soldiers from the Pakistani Frontier Corps on their side of the border to capture the terrorists the CIA, Delta Force and air force had chased right into their supposed net.[56] However, military satellite photos reportedly showed at the time that the Pakistani troops had not arrived and "seemed unlikely to appear soon," according to journalist Ron Suskind.[57] The Pakistanis did catch about 130 al Qaeda fighters who escaped from Tora Bora, but these apparently included none of the leadership, who crossed the border a day or two later.[58] Franks was certainly responsible for choosing to rely on the Pakistani troops, but the decision making went much higher up the chain than that. Berntsen's boss, Henry Crumpton, the head of the Afghan war for the CIA, who himself had repeatedly asked Franks for marines, personally briefed President Bush and Vice President Cheney, saying the Afghan militias were "definitely not" up to the job while pleading for reinforcements, to no avail.[59]

At the time bin Laden and Zawahiri escaped in mid-December 2001, there were less than 200 core al Qaeda members left.[60] The Arab Brigade foot soldiers fighting for the Taliban on the Shomali Plain north of Kabul are often cited as belonging to al Qaeda to inflate their strength, but they did not survive the U.S. Air Force onslaught in any case.[61]

If the Bush government had sent the marines after al Qaeda at Tora Bora, they could have captured or killed them in short order. But, would the American people have cared about all the claims that Iraqi dictator Saddam Hussein was working with Osama bin Laden if bin Laden was already dead and the war was over, justice done, mission accomplished? Who would have supported the indefinite occupation of Afghanistan if al Qaeda's leaders had already been killed?

The Bush administration's explanations for why they were unable to prevent bin Laden's escape never really seemed to add up. They claimed that they, too, were frustrated he and his few dozen surviving cohorts had escaped over the border into Pakistan. The unstated implication seemed to be that as far as the U.S. was concerned, the border was a magical, semipermeable forcefield that would allow fleeing Arab terrorists through, but never Delta Force operators, Rangers or marching marines chasing

---

[56] Ibid., 314-315.

[57] Ron Suskind, *The One Percent Doctrine: Deep Inside America's Pursuit of Its Enemies Since 9/11* (New York: Simon & Schuster, 2006), 58-59.

[58] Grenier, *88 Days*, 290.

[59] Ibid., 58.

[60] Berntsen and Pezzullo, *Jawbreaker*, 307-308.

[61] Woodward, *Bush at War*, 123; Berntsen and Pezzullo, *Jawbreaker*, 168-169.

after them.[62] But why should it have been a problem to send a small expeditionary force into an allied nation in hot pursuit of enemy terrorists who had orchestrated a massive attack that killed almost 3,000 American civilians? The administration said it just could not be done. They were afraid of upsetting local Afghan tribes if they had added enough Rangers or infantry to make the attempt. "The reality was, if we put our troops in there, we would inevitably end up fighting Afghan villagers — creating bad will at a sensitive time — which was the last thing we wanted to do," Lt. Gen. Mike DeLong, a deputy to Franks at Central Command, wrote in *Inside CentCom*.[63] But why would they be afraid of that? Could they not explain to the elders that they come in peace, hunting one particular, 6½-foot Arab in a brown robe and a few dozen of his friends, and could they please be so kind as to point in the right direction? If not, could the Delta Force not have called in airstrikes against those locals rallying to bin Laden's defense whether on the Afghan or Pakistani side of the border? Assistant Secretary of State Richard Armitage had already instructed the Pakistani government in Islamabad that failure to cooperate with the American invasion of Afghanistan would lead to their being bombed "back to the stone age."[64] By this time, according to former CIA Islamabad station chief Robert Grenier, "Not only were [the Pakistanis] supplying basing rights and support to U.S. military operations, but ISI was providing everything we asked for in terms of on-ground investigations and intelligence cooperation." In fact, Grenier had already worked out a plan for communication with local Pakistani army forces to prevent friendly fire accidents in case the U.S. did end up following al Qaeda members across the border.[65] Instead, it was like a car chase scene out of an old movie where bank robbers make it past the state line and the local cops must come to a screeching halt and stomp on their hats. This restriction was because of fear, not of objections by America's allies in the Pakistani state, but of what some local tribesmen might say? To this day, in major media, the conventional wisdom just seems to almost go without saying: once Osama bin Laden and friends "slipped" across the Pakistani border, that was simply the end of even the possibility of pursuit.[66]

---

[62] United States Senate Committee on Foreign Relations, "Tora Bora Revisited: How We Failed to Get Bin Laden and Why It Matters Today," report to members of the Committee on Foreign Relations, United States Senate, November 30, 2009, https://www.gpo.gov/fdsys/pkg/CPRT-111SPRT53709/html/CPRT-111SPRT53709.htm.

[63] Mike DeLong and Noah Lukeman, *Inside CentCom: The Unvarnished Truth About the Wars in Afghanistan and Iraq* (Washington, DC: Regnery, 2004), 57.

[64] "US Threatened to Bomb Pakistan, says Musharraf," *Daily Telegraph*, September 22, 2006, http://www.telegraph.co.uk/news/worldnews/1529561/US-threatened-to-bomb-Pakistan-says-Musharraf.html.

[65] Grenier, *88 Days*, 271, 289.

[66] Berntsen and Pezzullo, *Jawbreaker*, 308; Susan Glasser, "The Battle of Tora Bora: Secrets, Money,

Well, that was all beside the point anyway, DeLong later told Inter Press Service, deploying a spectacular straw-man argument, because "there weren't enough [marines] to police 1,500 kilometers of border." But nobody ever said they needed to do that. Fifteen hundred kilometers is approximately 932 miles, more than 60 percent of the entire length of the Afghan-Pakistan border from Iran to China — nearly equivalent to the distance between Houston and Chicago. It was the area just adjacent to Tora Bora, in the very south-western part of Nangarhar Province, that was at issue.[67]

This was the job these men had believed they were signing up for in the first place: if they were to put their lives on the line in battle, it was to "bring justice" to those who actually attack and kill Americans. Instead, as of mid-summer 2017, more than 2,400 U.S. soldiers and marines have been killed in Afghanistan, along with more than 1,000 allied NATO soldiers,[68] fighting tribesmen so landlocked out in the Afghan wilderness they have never even heard of the September 11th attacks that supposedly justify the occupation of their country[69] — not to mention the thousands of Pakistanis who have also been killed in the fighting that has dragged on in that nation as well.[70]

Numerous military and CIA men involved in the assault later made the same complaint. In 2008, a Delta Force commander named Thomas Greer, using the pseudonym "Dalton Fury,"[71] told CBS News' *60 Minutes*[72] that there was no doubt bin Laden was there at Tora Bora, and even after al Qaeda had escaped, Delta Force was ready and raring to take off chasing them, with multiple plans for cornering fleeing al Qaeda members in the valleys of western Pakistan in the first days following their escape. Twice

---

Mistrust," *Washington Post*, February 9, 2002, https://www.washingtonpost.com/world/the-battle-of-tora-bora-secrets-money-mistrust/2011/05/05/AFpB3L2F_story.html; Annie Lawrey, "How Osama bin Laden Escaped," *Foreign Policy*, December 11, 2009, http://foreignpolicy.com/2009/12/11/how-osama-bin-laden-escaped-2/; Peter Bergen, "The Account of How We Nearly Caught Osama bin Laden in 2001," *New Republic*, December 29, 2009, https://newrepublic.com/article/72086/the-battle-tora-bora; Gordon Corera, "Bin Laden's Tora Bora Escape, Just Months After 9/11," BBC News, July 21, 2011, http://www.bbc.com/news/world-us-canada-14190032; "Assault on Tora Bora," *Frontline*, PBS, September 8, 2002, http://pbs.org/wgbh/pages/frontline/shows/campaign/ground/torabora.html.

[67] Gareth Porter, "Bush Had No Plan to Catch Bin Laden After 9/11," Inter Press Service, September 29, 2008, http://www.ipsnews.net/2008/09/politics-us-bush-had-no-plan-to-catch-bin-laden-after-9-11/.

[68] Operation Enduring Freedom, ICasualties.org, http://icasualties.org/oef/.

[69] Paul Tait, "Few Afghans Know Reason for War, New Study Shows," Reuters, November 19, 2010, http://www.reuters.com/article/us-afghanistan-report-idUSTRE6AI2OX20101119.

[70] "Drone Strikes in Pakistan," The Bureau of Investigative Journalism, retrieved July 7, 2017, https://thebureauinvestigates.com/projects/drone-war/pakistan

[71] Dalton Fury [Thomas Greer], *Kill Bin Laden: A Delta Force Commander's Account of the Hunt for the World's Most Wanted Man* (New York: St. Martin's, 2009).

[72] "Elite Officer Recalls Bin Laden Hunt," *60 Minutes*, CBS News, October 2, 2008, http://www.cbsnews.com/news/elite-officer-recalls-bin-laden-hunt/.

their plans were thwarted by higher-ups, and they were continually let down by the local Afghan warlords upon whom they had been left to rely. Greer later told U.S. Senate Foreign Relations Committee staff, "I definitely think it was worth the risk to the force to assault Tora Bora for Osama bin Laden. What other target out there ... could be more important to our nation's struggle in the Global War on Terror?"[73] Despite all the arguments that there were not enough troops available to reinforce the CIA and Delta operators there, it has been shown there were plenty of Rangers available for exactly the kind of "block and sweep" operation called for in such situations,[74] not to mention Gen. Mattis's 4,000 marines.

Average Americans might have wondered where were the paratroopers? Was putting Osama bin Laden's "head in a box," as CIA Counter-terrorism Chief Cofer Black put it,[75] or his body on trial, as the law would have it,[76] not the focus of this mission? The Defense Department claimed that any large deployment of ground forces would result in a mandate to stay forever, bogged down in the mountains, occupying and building a nation, but they made the claim without explanation as to why that would be the case.[77] Could they not deploy enough troops to catch al Qaeda and then pull them right back out again? And why would they need to take the war to the Taliban near the capital city if the goal was bin Laden and his remaining al Qaeda members at Tora Bora? The U.S. had enough resources to fight the Taliban regime, but not the al Qaeda group that had attacked our country? This nonsensical reasoning, combined with the thin excuse of being worried about angering some random Pakistani tribesmen were they to chase al Qaeda across the border, was a strong indication it was just that — an excuse for a policy decision made to call off the hunt for Osama bin Laden and his cohorts after the regime change in Kabul was accomplished, in favor of attacking other, more "doable" targets in Iraq, as Deputy Defense Secretary Wolfowitz had so eloquently put it.[78]

President Bush, whose government had already publicly changed the focus of the war to Saddam Hussein's Iraq, was questioned by a reporter at a news conference on March 13, 2002:

---

[73] US Senate Committee on Foreign Relations, "Tora Bora Revisited."

[74] Peter John Paul Krause, "The Last Good Chance: A Reassessment of US Operations at Tora Bora," *Security Studies* 17 (2008): 644–684; Annie Lowrey, "How Osama bin Laden Escaped."

[75] "'Bring Me the Head of Bin Laden,'" BBC News, May 4, 2005, http://news.bbc.co.uk/2/hi/americas/4511943.stm.

[76] Acts of Terrorism Transcending National Boundaries, 18 U.S. Code § 2332b (2012).

[77] Woodward, *Bush at War*, 83.

[78] Ibid.

Question: Mr. President, in your speeches now you rarely talk [about] or mention Osama bin Laden. Why is that? Also, can you tell the American people if you have any more information, if you know if he is dead or alive? Final part — deep in your heart, don't you truly believe that until you find out if he is dead or alive, you won't really eliminate the threat of —

Bush: Deep in my heart I know the man is on the run if he's alive at all. Who knows if he's hiding in some cave or not; we haven't heard from him in a long time. And the idea of focusing on one person is — really indicates to me people don't understand the scope of the mission.

Terror is bigger than one person. And he's just — he's a person who's now been marginalized. His network, his host government has been destroyed. He's the ultimate parasite who found weakness, exploited it, and met his match. He is — as I mentioned in my speech, I do mention the fact that this is a fellow who is willing to commit youngsters to their death and he, himself, tries to hide — if, in fact, he's hiding at all.

So I don't know where he is. You know, I just don't spend that much time on him, Kelly, to be honest with you. I'm more worried about making sure that our soldiers are well-supplied; that the strategy is clear; that the coalition is strong; that when we find enemy [Taliban] bunched up like we did in Shahikot Mountains, that the military has all the support it needs to go in and do the job, which they did.

And there will be other battles in Afghanistan. There's going to be other struggles like Shahikot, and I'm just as confident about the outcome of those future battles as I was about Shahikot, where our soldiers are performing brilliantly. We're tough, we're strong, they're well-equipped. We have a good strategy. We are showing the world we know how to fight a guerrilla war with conventional means.

Question: But don't you believe that the threat that bin Laden posed won't truly be eliminated until he is found either dead or alive?

Bush: Well, as I say, we haven't heard much from him. And I wouldn't necessarily say he's at the center of any command structure. And, again, I don't know where he is. I — I'll repeat what I said. I truly am not that concerned about him. I know he is on the run. I was concerned about him when he had taken over a country. I was concerned about the fact that he was basically running Afghanistan and calling the shots for the Taliban.

But once we set out the policy and started executing the plan, he became — we shoved him out more and more on the margins. He has no place to train his al Qaeda killers anymore. And if we — excuse me for a minute — and if we find a training camp, we'll take care of it. Either we will or our friends will.[79]

Though it is impossible to know for certain what U.S. political leaders were thinking at the time, the president could hardly have been clearer about his intent in this statement. The hunt for the chief perpetrator of the September 11th attacks had been canceled. It had only been six months. Bush, who later admitted to Bob Woodward that he "was not on point" and did not "feel that sense of urgency" to focus on bin Laden or al Qaeda in his eight months on the job as president before September 11th[80] — in fact, he had ignored *forty* Presidential Daily Briefs from the CIA mentioning al Qaeda before the attacks[81] — had already changed the subject entirely. The bad guys were long gone, but the war would continue, in Afghanistan and beyond.

After bin Laden and his associates escaped, Americans were told Operation Enduring Freedom must endure or al Qaeda would return and again use Afghanistan as a base to stage terrorist attacks against the United States "homeland," as we have been instructed to refer to our country in this new era. Other than building schools for little children, this Afghanistan as "safe-haven" myth must be the most bankrupt excuse for a military occupation ever invented. The few dozen core al Qaeda members who survived the initial air force bombing campaign fled Afghanistan by the end of 2001. They were a virtual non-factor in the war against the Taliban regime and at no point did they have major influence in the insurgency against the occupation that grew up in later years. If any ever did come back it would not matter. Afghanistan is exile. Afghanistan is as far as someone could ever get from anywhere. It provides no special access to any target in the West whatsoever — in fact, just the opposite.

The September 11th hijackers, none of whom were Afghans, gained entry to the United States under regular tourist and student visas.[82] The terrorists launched the attack from Massachusetts, Virginia and New Jersey. They had planned them in Malaysia, Germany, Spain, Florida and Maryland. The only thing about Afghanistan that benefits our enemies is its distance made it somewhat difficult for the U.S. to hit back against targets there, but there were no targets left in Afghanistan to bomb by 2002. Al Qaeda's surviving members had fled to the neighboring state of Pakistan, an American ally.

[79] George W. Bush, "The President's News Conference," 38 Weekly Comp. Pres. Doc. 407 (March 13, 2002), https://georgewbush-whitehouse.archives.gov/news/releases/2002/03/20020313-8.html.
[80] Woodward, *Bush at War*, 39.
[81] Clarke, *Against All Enemies*, 1.
[82] Martha Raddatz, "State Dept. Lapses Aided 9/11 Hijackers," ABC News, October 23, 2002, http://abcnews.go.com/WNT/story?id=130051.

Most of them decided to spread from Pakistan to other parts of the region, planning further attacks in Yemen, Saudi Arabia and Qatar. Those left hiding in Pakistan would try to set an example for others in the region to follow, changing, former FBI counter-terrorism officer Ali Soufan said, from "Chief Operators" to "Chief Motivators" for others seeking to join the war against America.[83]

It would be almost impossible to overstate the lengths to which the Bush[84] and Obama[85] governments went to push this ridiculous safe-haven myth, arguing, in effect, that America could *never* leave Afghanistan because of the possibility things would get worse if they did: the Afghan state would fail, and then when the Taliban regained power it would be guaranteed that they would allow al Qaeda to return as well.

In the early years of the war, it was common to hear the two terms al Qaeda and the Taliban used interchangeably as the government worked hard to conflate Osama bin Laden's group with Mullah Omar's government. Again, there were less than 200 members of al Qaeda who ever escaped to Pakistan who could potentially come back to Afghanistan, and many of them have since either been arrested by police and spies,[86] gone back home to pick up the revolution there,[87] or were later killed in

---

[83] Ali Soufan, *The Black Banners: The Inside Story of 9/11 and the War Against al-Qaeda* (New York: W. W. Norton, 2011), 346-348.

[84] George W. Bush, "Remarks in a Discussion on Education in Springfield, Ohio ," 40 Weekly Comp. Pres. Doc. 2152 (September 27, 2004); George W. Bush and Hamid Karzai, "The President's News Conference with President Hamid Karzai of Afghanistan," 41 Weekly Comp. Pres. Doc. 857 (May 23, 2005); George W. Bush, "Transcript: President Bush's Speech in Atlanta," *Washington Post*, September 7, 2006, http://www.washingtonpost.com/wp-dyn/content/article/2006/09/07/AR2006090700697.html; George W. Bush, "Remarks to the American Enterprise Institute for Public Policy Research," 43 Weekly Comp. Pres. Doc. 165 (February 15, 2007); George W. Bush, "The President's News Conference with President Hamid Karzai of Afghanistan in Kabul, Afghanistan," 44 Weekly Comp. Pres. Doc. 1534 (December 15, 2008).

[85] Barack Obama, "Remarks at the United States Military Academy at West Point, New York," DCPD-200900962 (December 1, 2009); Ben Feller, "Obama in Afghanistan: No Terror 'Safe Haven,'" *Press Democrat*, December 3, 2010, http://www.pressdemocrat.com/news/2254353-181/obama-in-afghanistan-no-terror?gallery=2359627&artslide=0; Barack Obama, "Address to the Nation on the Drawdown of United States Military Personnel in Afghanistan," DCPD-201100463 (June 22, 2011); Cora Currier and Blair Hickman, "Where Obama and Romney Stand on the War in Afghanistan," ProPublica, September 24, 2012, https://www.propublica.org/article/where-obama-and-romney-stand-on-the-war-in-afghanistan; David Jackson, "Obama Makes Surprise Visit to Afghanistan," *USA Today*, May 25, 2014, http://www.usatoday.com/story/news/2014/05/25/obama-afghanistan-memorial-day-visit/9568209/; Barack Obama, "Remarks on United States Military Strategy in Afghanistan and an Exchange with Reporters ," DCPD-201500726 (October 15, 2015); Barack Obama, "Remarks on United States Military Strategy in Afghanistan," DCPD-201600400 (July 6, 2016).

[86] "Top al-Qaeda Leaders Captured or Killed on Pakistani Soil," *News International*, May 3, 2011, https://www.thenews.com.pk/archive/print/298864-top-al-qaeda-leaders-captured-or-killed-on-pakistani-soil.

[87] Soufan, *The Black Banners*, 346-348.

the CIA's drone war in Pakistan.[88] Iran had worked with the United States to quickly arrest any Arabs who had crossed their border during the initial invasion and deport them back to their home countries.[89] To justify continuing the mission, the U.S. government encouraged this confusion and invoked the safe-haven myth to cover up the fact that, though a handful of al Qaeda's leaders had escaped, America had already won the war. This small group of terrorists who had never managed to control their own county or district, much less province or nation-state, were already dead, imprisoned or had been driven out of the country, into further exile.

A limited mission, focused on Osama bin Laden and his few hundred men, could have been over by the end of 2001. While this has been considered to be an extreme position since that time, at this point even Gary Berntsen has admitted this is likely true. "The war could have been over pretty quickly," he told reporter Michael Hirsh in 2016, lamenting Bush's refusal to allow the Rangers and marines to reinforce the CIA and Delta Force at Tora Bora. "We could have had the entire al Qaeda command structure had we done that. Also, the terrorism that metastasized into Pakistan might not have happened. It's impossible to prove any of this. It's a what-if. But, sadly, we lost the opportunity."[90]

General Anthony Zinni, a former Commander of Central Command agrees. Al Qaeda, in 2001, "was a band of maybe a thousand radicals. Yet we created an investment in this that was on a level of what we do for existential threats. Obviously, we were traumatized by 9/11. I don't mean to play that down. But this was not communism or fascism."[91]

The Law

On the afternoon of September 11, 2001, Vice President Dick Cheney and his attorney and friend David Addington decided the old indict-and-prosecute model of dealing with terrorism must end. The attack was to be treated not as a crime, but as an act of war — an act demanding war, "a new kind of war," in response.[92] To wage this new kind of war, the

---

[88] Stephen Tankel, "Going Native: The Pakistanization of al Qaeda," War on the Rocks, October 22, 2013, https://warontherocks.com/2013/10/going-native-the-regionalization-of-al-qaeda/; David Sanger and Eric Schmitt, "US Weighs Taliban Strike into Pakistan," New York Times, March 18, 2009,
http://query.nytimes.com/gst/fullpage.html?res=9C04E1DC1F39F93BA25750C0A96F9C8B63.
[89] "Iran Gave US Help on Al Qaeda After 9/11," CBS News, October 7, 2008,
http://www.cbsnews.com/news/iran-gave-us-help-on-al-qaeda-after-9-11/.
[90] Michael Hirsh, "An Anniversary of Shame," Politico, September 11, 2016,
http://www.politico.com/magazine/story/2016/09/9-11-15-years-anniversary-of-shame-214239.
[91] Ibid.
[92] John Barry et al., "The Roots of Torture," Newsweek, May 24, 2004,

administration would need a new legal theory, what they called "the New Paradigm."[93] The doctrine stated that under the constitution's "Commander in Chief" clause, in the new era of the "Global War on Terrorism," President Bush's authority could override any rule, law, treaty or even any other part of the constitution, under his mandate to protect the country. This pretended legal theory was all-important to Cheney and Addington. Part of the reason for the creation of the ensuing lawless torture and spying programs in the war was simply to prove they could cross this constitutional line, and, in fact, move it, and that no one could do anything about it.[94] As journalist Charlie Savage wrote,

> [A]s far as the executive branch was concerned, the modest boundaries on Bush's wartime authority that Congress had tried to impose in its September 14 resolution were meaningless. Congress may have thought it was granting the president limited wartime powers after 9/11, but the Bush-Cheney administration decided in secret that it wielded unlimited wartime powers. "We think it beyond question," [Deputy Assistant U.S. Attorney General in the Office of Legal Counsel at the Department of Justice John] Yoo concluded, that Congress cannot "place any limits on the President's determinations as to any terrorist threat, the amount of military force to be used in response, or the method, timing, and nature of the response. These decisions, under our Constitution, are for the President alone to make." …

> The Bush-Cheney team argued statutes and treaties that restrict what the military and other security forces can do are unconstitutional; because of the new and improved Unitary Executive Theory, only the commander in chief could decide how the executive branch should go about defending America. …

> In case an interrogator was ever prosecuted for violating the anti-torture law, Yoo laid out page after page of legal defenses he could mount to get the charges dismissed. And should someone balk at this strained interpretation of the law, Yoo offered his usual trump card: Applying the anti-torture law to interrogations authorized by the president would be unconstitutional, since only the commander in chief could set standards for questioning enemy combatants.[95]

---

http://www.newsweek.com/roots-torture-128007.

[93] Jane Mayer, "The Hidden Power: The Legal Mind Behind the White House's War on Terror," *New Yorker*, July 3, 2006, http://www.newyorker.com/magazine/2006/07/03/the-hidden-power.

[94] Charlie Savage, "Hail to the Chief," *Boston Globe*, November 26, 2006, http://archive.boston.com/news/globe/ideas/articles/2006/11/26/hail_to_the_chief/; Jack Goldsmith, *The Terror Presidency: Law and Judgment Inside the Bush Administration*, reprint ed. (New York: W. W. Norton, 2009).

[95] Charlie Savage, *Takeover: The Return of the Imperial Presidency and the Subversion of American Democracy*,

"The entire world is a battlefield," the administration claimed. The old rule of law would have to make way for new authority in the name of the permanent emergency. The administration even maintained in court that, hypothetically, a "little old lady" in neutral Switzerland could be abducted and held by the CIA or military without due process over an allegation she had mistakenly donated to the wrong Palestinian charity.[96]

The administration's lawyers set about writing their infamous memos[97] to justify vastly expanded presidential authority and suspend mandates that U.S. forces abide by the now "obsolete" and "quaint" Geneva Conventions and their prohibitions against war crimes. The lawyers at first used a spurious interpretation of the law as an excuse to claim that, despite the fact the United States and the government of Afghanistan under the Taliban were both signatories to the Conventions, they did not apply to the Taliban, even though they were a national government, since they were in the middle of a civil war, and so amounted only to a "failed state." Though Bush ended up deciding Geneva did apply to the Taliban, but not al Qaeda, he maneuvered around its restrictions by declaring that because they were a religious group and did not all have matching uniforms, alleged Taliban fighters were to be considered terrorists and "unlawful enemy combatants," rather than prisoners of war.[98] This allowed the U.S. to hold them in custody under an entirely new system of ad-hoc procedures, including brutalization and indefinite detention at Guantánamo Bay prison halfway around the world in Cuba. Under the Obama government, the designation "unlawful enemy combatant" was changed to "unprivileged enemy belligerent," but the premise remained virtually the same.[99]

Torture itself was redefined by President Bush's lawyers to mean inflicted pain on a captive at least equivalent to "organ failure." One memo, anticipating eventual deaths in custody at the hands of CIA interrogators, preemptively excused these future killings as necessary to prevent greater harm. As journalist James Bovard wrote, "The Justice Department stressed that even intentionally killing people during an interrogation might be okay."[100]

---

reprint ed. (New York: Back Bay, 2008) 121-122, 124, 155-156.

[96] Jennifer K. Elsea, "Enemy Combatant Detainees: Habeus Corpus Challenges in Federal Court," Congressional Research Service, https://fas.org/sgp/crs/natsec/RL33180.pdf.

[97] "Torturing Democracy, Key Documents," National Security Archive at George Washington University, http://nsarchive.gwu.edu/torturingdemocracy/documents/theme.html.

[98] George W. Bush, "Memorandum to National Security Council Principles' Committee," February 7, 2002, http://www.pegc.us/archive/White_House/bush_memo_20020207_ed.pdf; Mayer, "The Hidden Power."

[99] Joanne Mariner, "A First Look at the Military Commissions Act of 2009, Part One," FindLaw, November 4, 2009, http://supreme.findlaw.com/legal-commentary/a-first-look-at-the-military-commissions-act-of-2009-part-one.html.

[100] James Bovard, *Attention Deficit Democracy* (New York: Palgrave MacMillan, 2005), 115-116.

The Office of Legal Counsel lawyers wrote,

> The *necessity defense* may prove especially relevant in the current circumstances.

> First, the defense is not limited to certain types of harms. Therefore, the harm inflicted by necessity may include intentional homicide, so long as the harm avoided is greater (i.e., preventing more deaths).[101]

This later became known as the "Golden Ticket," better even than a get-out-of-jail-free card. Combined with court rulings protecting "state secrets," this memo has amounted to total impunity, even after it was retracted, since CIA torturers were presumably acting in "good faith" under the protection of the memo at the time of their crimes.[102] And this is despite the historical record, which shows the torture regime had begun many months before the memo's August 2002 date.[103]

It should have made no difference whether the Taliban had signed the Geneva Conventions or not. The U.S. government's ratification is meant to restrict its behavior regardless of who the enemy is.[104] And the United States Constitution and federal laws and military orders[105] had already banned the torture of prisoners of war long before the international treaties, which codified the same norms worldwide, were implemented. This is not to say the CIA and U.S. forces never used torture in previous conflicts, only that they were clearly breaking the law when they did.[106]

The order had gone out to the CIA and military alike that the Taliban

---

[101] "Memorandum for Alberto R. Gonzales Counsel to the President: Standards of Conduct for Interrogation Under U.S.C. 2340-2340A," Office of the Assistant Attorney General, August 1, 2002, https://www.justice.gov/sites/default/files/olc/legacy/2010/08/05/memo-gonzales-aug2002.pdf; "Memos from George W. Bush's Justice Department's Office of Legal Counsel," National Security Archive at George Washington University, http://nsarchive.gwu.edu/torturingdemocracy/documents/theme.html.

[102] "Statement of Attorney General Eric Holder on Closure of Investigation into the Interrogation of Certain Detainees," United States Department of Justice, August 30, 2012, https://www.justice.gov/opa/pr/statement-attorney-general-eric-holder-closure-investigation-interrogation-certain-detainees.

[103] Andy Worthington, "CIA Torture Began in Afghanistan 8 Months Before DoJ Approval," April 27, 2009, http://www.andyworthington.co.uk/2009/04/27/cia-torture-began-in-afghanistan-8-months-before-doj-approval/.

[104] Jean Pictet, ed., *Commentary on the Geneva Conventions of August 12, 1949*, vol. I, 1952, https://www.icrc.org/en/publication/0203-commentary-geneva-conventions-12-august-1949-volume-I.

[105] Robert A. Nowlan, *The American Presidents, Washington to Tyler* (Jefferson, NC: McFarland, 2012), 43.

[106] Barbara Myers, "The Secret Origins of the CIA's Torture Program and the Forgotten Man Who Tried to Expose It," *Nation*, June 1, 2015, https://www.thenation.com/article/secret-origins-cias-torture-program-and-forgotten-man-who-tried-expose-it/; James LeMoyne, "Testifying to Torture," *New York Times*, June 5, 1988, http://www.nytimes.com/1988/06/05/magazine/testifying-to-torture.html.

and their al Qaeda allies were outside of the protection of the laws of war: "The rules are 'Grab whom you must. Do what you want.'"[107] Thousands of innocents, Taliban foot soldiers and insurgent fighters would be treated the same as al Qaeda terrorists: denied prisoner-of-war status, degraded, dehumanized and tortured. Methods included beatings; shackling captives in medieval-style, unnatural "stress positions" for hours or days — including hanging them from their wrists from ceilings, walls and cell doors; severe temperature manipulation; prolonged sleep deprivation; mock executions; and being held so long they had no choice but to urinate and defecate on themselves.

The CIA quickly established a network of lawless, "black site" prisons[108] in places including Thailand,[109] Morocco,[110] Poland,[111] Romania,[112] the island base at Diego Garcia in the Indian Ocean,[113] and even on navy ships on the high seas, all of which remained hidden for years.[114]

The CIA proved that torture works very well for getting blatant lies out of their captives. They brutally tortured a British citizen named Binyam Mohamed, including slicing his genitals with a razor blade, until he made up a story accusing American al Qaeda member Jose Padilla of plotting to attack the U.S. with a radioactive "dirty bomb."[115] Ibn al-Shaykh al-Libi, an al Qaeda member captured in Afghanistan, was tortured into claiming

---

[107] Seymour M. Hersh, "The Gray Zone: How a Secret Pentagon Program Came to Abu Ghraib," *New Yorker*, May 24, 2004, http://www.newyorker.com/magazine/2004/05/24/the-gray-zone.

[108] Dana Priest, "CIA Holds Terror Suspects in Secret Prisons," *Washington Post*, January 2, 2005, http://www.washingtonpost.com/wp-dyn/content/linkset/2006/04/17/LI2006041700530.html.

[109] Sheri Fink et al., "CIA Torture Detailed in Newly Disclosed Documents," *New York Times*, January 19, 2017, https://www.nytimes.com/2017/01/19/us/politics/cia-torture.html.

[110] David Rose, "Tortured Reasoning," *Vanity Fair*, December 2008, http://www.vanityfair.com/magazine/2008/12/torture200812.

[111] Nick Hawton, "Hunt for CIA 'Black Site' in Poland," BBC News, December 28, 2006, http://news.bbc.co.uk/2/hi/europe/6212843.stm, Larisa Alexandrovna and David Dastych, "Soviet-era Compound in Northern Poland was Site of Secret CIA Interrogation, Detentions," RawStory.com, March 7, 2007, http://www.rawstory.com/news/2007/Sovietera_compound_in_Poland_was_site_0307.html.

[112] Gordon Corera, "CIA 'Secret Prison' Found in Romania," BBC News, December 8, 2011, http://www.bbc.com/news/world-europe-16093106.

[113] Adam Zagorin, "US Used UK Isle for Interrogations," *Time*, July 31, 2008, http://content.time.com/time/world/article/0,8599,1828469,00.html.

[114] Duncan Campbell and Richard Norton-Taylor, "US Accused of Holding Terror Suspects on Prison Ships," *Guardian*, June 2, 2008, https://www.theguardian.com/world/2008/jun/02/usa.humanrights.

[115] David Rose, "How MI5 Colluded in My Torture," *Mail on Sunday*, March 8, 2009, http://www.dailymail.co.uk/news/article-1160238/How-MI5-colluded-torture-Binyam-Mohamed-claims-British-agents-fed-Moroccan-torturers-questions--world-exclusive.html; William Glaberson, "Questioning 'Dirty Bomb' Plot, Judge Orders US to Yield Papers on Detainee," *New York Times*, October 30, 2008, http://www.nytimes.com/2008/10/31/us/31gitmo.html; Rose, "Tortured Reasoning."

the group had been trained in the manufacture of chemical weapons by the government of Iraq.[116] September 11th ringleader, Khalid Sheikh Mohammed,[117] and a man named Abu Zubaydah[118] — who, the CIA later admitted, was not even truly a member of al Qaeda[119] — were both tortured by the agency into inventing numerous fantastic stories about anti-American terrorist plots,[120] with Zubaydah adding to the false accusations against Iraq.[121] These stories provided the basis for numerous "Orange Alert" announcements from the Office, later the Department, of Homeland Security, which helped to increase the overall climate of fear of terrorism, and especially of the threat of Saddam Hussein's regime, in the run-up to the invasion of Iraq in 2003.[122]

The CIA also continued their "extraordinary rendition" program, begun in the Clinton years,[123] which simply meant kidnapping people and sending them either back to their home countries or to a friendly regime like that of Hosni Mubarak, then-dictator of Egypt, to be tortured or murdered.[124] Former CIA officer Robert Baer once explained how the

[116] Dana Priest, "Al Qaeda-Iraq Link Recanted," *Washington Post*, August 1, 2004, http://www.washingtonpost.com/wp-dyn/articles/A30909-2004Jul31.html; Peter Finn, "Detainee Who Gave False Iraq Data Dies in Prison in Libya," *Washington Post*, May 12, 2009, http://www.washingtonpost.com/wp-dyn/content/article/2009/05/11/AR2009051103412.html; Andy Worthington, "New Revelations About the Torture of Ibn al-Shaykh al-Libi," June 18, 2009, http://www.andyworthington.co.uk/2009/06/18/world-exclusive-new-revelations-about-the-torture-of-ibn-al-shaykh-al-libi/; Michael Isikoff and Mark Hosenball, "Al-Libi's Tall Tales," *Newsweek*, November 10, 2005, https://web.archive.org/web/20051126201544/http://www.msnbc.msn.com/id/9991919/site/newsweek/.

[117] Dexter Filkins, "Khalid Sheikh Mohammed and the CIA," *New Yorker*, December 31, 2014, http://www.newyorker.com/news/news-desk/khalid-sheikh-mohammed-cia.

[118] David Sleight, "CIA Cables Document Agency's Torture of Abu Zubaydah," ProPublica, February 22, 2017, https://www.propublica.org/article/cia-cables-document-black-site-torture-of-abu-zubaydah.

[119] Helen Duffy, "The CIA Tortured Abu Zubaydah, My Client. Now Charge Him or Let Him Go," *Guardian*, December 15, 2014, https://www.theguardian.com/commentisfree/2014/dec/15/cia-tortured-abu-zubaydah-guantanamo-bay-trial-senate-report; US Senate Select Committee on Intelligence, "Committee Study of the Central Intelligence Agency's Detention and Interrogation Program," December 3, 2014, p. 410, https://www.amnestyusa.org/pdfs/sscistudy1.pdf.

[120] Marcy Wheeler, "KSM Had the CIA Believing in Black Muslim Convert Jihadist Arsonists in Montana for 3 Months," Emptywheel, December 15, 2014, https://www.emptywheel.net/2014/12/15/ksm-had-the-cia-believing-in-black-muslim-jihadist-converts-in-montana-for-3-months/.

[121] Rose, "Tortured Reasoning."

[122] Jonathan S. Landay, "Abusive Tactics Used to Seek Iraq-al Qaeda Link," McClatchy Newspapers, April 21, 2009, http://www.mcclatchydc.com/news/nation-world/world/article24535114.html; "NY Terror Alert Came from Bin Laden Aide," *USA Today*, May 23, 2002, https://usatoday30.usatoday.com/news/nation/2002/05/23/ny-alert.htm; "Profile: Khalid Shaikh Mohammed," Fox News, March 1, 2003, http://www.foxnews.com/story/2003/03/01/profile-khalid-shaikh-mohammed.html.

[123] Clarke, *Against All Enemies*, 143-144; Stephen Grey, "Five Facts and Five Fictions About CIA Rendition," *Frontline*, PBS, November 4, 2007, http://www.pbs.org/frontlineworld/stories/rendition701/updates/updates.html.

[124] Jane Mayer, "Outsourcing Torture: The Secret History of America's 'Extraordinary Rendition'

rendition program worked: "If you want a serious interrogation, you send a prisoner to Jordan. If you want them to be tortured, you send them to Syria. If you want someone to disappear — never to see them again — you send them to Egypt."[125]

The CIA was responsible for torturing at least five men to death. One of them, Gul Rahman, was frozen to death at the "Salt Pit" torture dungeon, code-named "COBALT," outside Kabul.[126] According to Secretary of State Colin Powell's former chief of staff, Army Col. Lawrence Wilkerson, at least 100 individuals in Afghanistan and Iraq died in military custody with at least 25 of them classified by military investigators as "homicides." Wilkerson testified to Congress on June 18, 2008, "Last time I checked it was 108 [deaths in custody], and the total number that were declared homicides by the military services, or by the CIA, or others doing investigations, CID [United States Army Criminal Investigation Command], and so forth — was 25, 26, 27."[127] The Associated Press later corroborated Wilkerson's claim of 108 deaths based on its compilation of statistics from sources in the various military branches.[128]

Bagram Air Base, north of Kabul, also contained a torture prison, made famous in the Alex Gibney documentary, *Taxi to the Dark Side*,[129] about the murder of an innocent young Afghan cab driver, Dilawar of Yakubi, at the hands of members of the U.S. Army. Canadian child-torture victim, and later Guantánamo "war crimes" convict, Omar Khadr's treatment at Bagram paints a clear enough picture of the worst sort of sadism. American forces indulged their September 11th revenge lust in inhuman brutality against their captives with no restraint — including against an innocent[130] 15-year-old boy. His attorney later described Khadr being "forced to stand in crucifix position until he soiled himself. ... His hair

---

Program," *New Yorker*, February 14, 2005,
http://www.newyorker.com/magazine/2005/02/14/outsourcing-torture.

[125] Stephen Grey, "America's Gulag," *New Statesman*, May 17, 2004,
http://www.newstatesman.com/node/159775.

[126] Jason Leopold, "Barbaric Conditions That Led to a Detainee's Death Are Laid Bare in CIA Reports," *Vice*, June 14, 2016, https://news.vice.com/article/cia-black-site-conditions-that-led-to-detainee-death-laid-bare-by-report.

[127] From the Department of Justice to Guantánamo Bay: Administration Lawyers and Administration Interrogation Rules Part II: Hearing Before the Subcommittee on the Constitution, Civil Rights and Civil Liberties, 110 Congress (2008), https://fas.org/irp/congress/2008_hr/gtmo-pt2.pdf.

[128] Ayaz Nanji, "108 Died in US Custody," CBS News, March 16, 2005,
http://www.cbsnews.com/news/report-108-died-in-us-custody/.

[129] *Taxi to the Dark Side*, directed by Alex Gibney, (2008; Velocity/Thinkfilm).

[130] Omar el Akkad, "Khadr Couldn't Have Thrown Grenade That Killed US Soldier: Defense Lawyer," *Globe and Mail*, December 12, 2008,
http://www.theglobeandmail.com/news/world/khadr-couldnt-have-thrown-grenade-that-killed-us-soldier-defence-lawyer/article20391135/.

was then used as a mop to clean it up." His torturers threatened him with being raped to death. Thousands more military captives, virtually none having anything to do with the attacks on the United States, fared just as bad or worse than Khadr did.[131]

From the beginning, the Salt Pit and Bagram prisons were filled with the innocent and insignificant. CIA officer Gary Berntsen set the tone early in the war when he told his subordinates not to bother trying to differentiate between the enemy and simple bystanders:

> We're in Afghanistan, not a U.S. court of law. There will be no presumption of innocence until proven guilty here. If we encounter Arabs, Chechens, Chinese Uigars, Muslims from Burma or non-Afghans, they're not businessmen or aid workers. They're the enemy until proven otherwise, and the burden of proof is on them.[132]

U.S. agents were also duped and used by the Northern Alliance and other warlords against local enemies, many of whom were not members of the Taliban government or tied to their movement in any way. American soldiers and spies with no background knowledge of the country, languages, customs, tribes, factions or history just started handing out cash in exchange for "intelligence." Old grudges, large bounties and wild rumors were enough to get completely innocent people raided, arrested, tortured, imprisoned and killed.

The military prison at Guantánamo Bay, Cuba, which was established under the theory that the U.S. Constitution could not apply there,[133] was soon filled with nearly 800 men, almost all of whom were simply goat herders and Taliban foot soldiers, and none of whom had anything to do with the September 11th plot, with the exception of Mohammed Mana Ahmed al-Qahtani, who was an actual September 11th co-conspirator, meant to be the twentieth hijacker, but who had been denied entry to the U.S. in August 2001. Al-Qahtani had been captured on the battlefield in Afghanistan and brought to Guantánamo before anyone had figured out who he was.[134] According to Judge Susan J. Crawford, who was appointed

---

[131] Jeff Tietz, "The Unending Torture of Omar Khadr," *Rolling Stone*, August 24, 2006, http://www.rollingstone.com/politics/news/the-unending-torture-of-omar-khadr-20060824; Carol Rosenberg, "Interrogator Says Khadr Was Told He'd Likely Be Raped in US," *Miami Herald*, May 6, 2010, http://www.mcclatchydc.com/news/nation-world/world/article24581992.html; Dennis Edney, interviewed by the author, *Scott Horton Show*, radio archive, February 4, 2015, http://scotthorton.org/interviews/2015/02/04/2415-dennis-edney/.

[132] Berntsen and Pezzullo, *Jawbreaker*, 207.

[133] Scott Packard, "How Guantanamo Bay Became the Place the US Keeps Detainees," *Atlantic*, September 4, 2013, https://www.theatlantic.com/national/archive/2013/09/how-guantanamo-bay-became-the-place-the-us-keeps-detainees/279308/.

[134] Schmidt, Susan, and Dan Eggen, "Man Refused Entry May Have Been 9/11 Plotter," *Washington Post*, January 21, 2004, https://www.washingtonpost.com/archive/politics/2004/01/21/man-refused-entry-may-have-been-911-plotter/72cf8177-12ed-4acb-a6c4-0187bd1e5a4c/.

Convening Authority of Military Commissions by the Bush administration, al Qahtani was tortured so badly, she refused to refer his case for prosecution.[135]

Otherwise, they filled Guantánamo Bay with almost 800 nobodies. Many of the training camps and foreign fighters in Afghanistan at the time of the invasion had been there for the training of local jihad movements across the Central Asian "-stans," China and the disputed region of Kashmir, between Pakistan and India.[136] But anyone who happened to be foreign — especially Arab — and in Afghanistan in 2001 or 2002 was considered part of al Qaeda until proven otherwise, and perhaps not even then. The same went for those who, just like in the old totalitarian Soviet Union, simply failed to inform on their neighbors first when the Americans came around looking for enemies to fight. To this day, there is an entire category of prisoners at Guantánamo that prosecutors have admitted they lack the evidence to try, even in the rigged Guantánamo Bay military court system, who they will never release.[137] Other than Qahtani, none of these include any real al Qaeda members, who were not even brought to Guantánamo from their CIA "black site" prisons until 2006.[138] By that time, the George W. Bush administration was seeing its grand assertions of power begin to be eroded by the Supreme Court[139] and had decided to start sending the vast majority of the 700-plus captives being held at Guantánamo back home.[140]

The military had a terrible information problem.[141] Soldiers doing the sweeps and arrests across Afghanistan were depending on the men and women later in the process to sort out the guilty from the innocent, while those further up the chain assumed they were only being sent men who were already determined to have done something wrong. In reality, any captives of discernible al Qaeda intelligence value had already been handed

[135] Bob Woodward, "Guantánamo Detainee Was Tortured, Says Official Overseeing Military Trials," *Washington Post*, January 14, 2009, http://www.washingtonpost.com/wp-dyn/content/article/2009/01/13/AR2009011303372.html.

[136] Eric Margolis, *American Raj: Liberation or Domination? Resolving the Conflict Between the West and the Muslim World* (Toronto: Key Porter, 2008), 202.

[137] Ed Pilkington, "US Government Identifies Men on Guantánamo 'Indefinite Detainee' List," *Guardian*, June 17, 2013, https://www.theguardian.com/world/2013/jun/17/us-identifies-guantanamo-bay-detainees.

[138] Jonathan Karl, "'High-Value' Detainees Transferred to Guantanamo," ABC News, September 6, 2006, http://abcnews.go.com/International/story?id=2400470.

[139] Rasul v. Bush 542 U.S. 466 (2004), https://www.law.cornell.edu/supct/html/03-334.ZO.html; Hamdan v. Rumsfeld 548 U.S. 557 (2006), https://www.law.cornell.edu/supremecourt/text/05-184; Boumediene v. Bush 553 U.S. 723 (2008), https://www.law.cornell.edu/supremecourt/text/06-1195.

[140] Andy Worthington, *The Guantánamo Files: The Stories of the 774 Detainees in America's Illegal Prison* (London: Pluto, 2007).

[141] Friedrich A. Hayek, "The Use of Knowledge in Society," *American Economic Review* 35, no. 4. (1945): 519-30, http://www.econlib.org/library/Essays/hykKnw1.html.

over to the CIA, with the army getting the rest.[142]

A 2002 CIA study "concluded that a substantial number of the [Guantánamo] detainees appeared to be low-level militants, aspiring holy warriors who had rushed to Afghanistan to defend the Taliban, or simply innocents in the wrong place at the wrong time."[143] The Guantánamo prison amounted to a very effective public relations stunt, which made it seem to Americans as though there were legions of terrorist enemies out there. The Bush government claimed all the captives being held at Guantánamo were "the worst of the worst."[144] Chairman of the Joint Chiefs of Staff General Richard Myers claimed, "These are people who would gnaw through hydraulic lines at the back of a C-17 to bring it down."[145] Prison officials and staff were being fed the same line as the American people and were expecting 10-foot tall comic book terrorist bogeymen by the time the first planeloads arrived.[146]

Years later, the *New York Times* admitted that "contrary to the repeated assertions of senior administration officials, none of the detainees at the United States Naval Base at Guantánamo Bay ranked as leaders or senior operatives of al Qaeda. ... [O]nly a relative handful — some put the number at about a dozen, others more than two dozen — were sworn [al] Qaeda members or other militants able to elucidate the organization's inner workings." This was out of more than 770 men held there.

> [A]lmost immediately, questions began to emerge — in Afghanistan, at Guantánamo and eventually in Washington — about the pedigrees of some of the men and why they had been selected to go to Cuba. ...
>
> Officials of the Department of Defense now acknowledge that the military's initial screening of the prisoners for possible shipment to Guantánamo was flawed. It was not until hundreds of detainees had arrived here that the classified criteria even referred directly to the threat that they might represent, military officials said.
>
> But some clues were obvious. Some of the detainees were elderly or infirm. One of those was Faiz Muhammad, a genial old man with a long wispy beard whom interrogators nicknamed "Al Qaeda Claus." Another, who was able to make the trip only after extensive medical

[142] Lawrence Wilkerson, interviewed by the author, *Scott Horton Show*, radio archive, July 2, 2010, https://scotthorton.org/interviews/antiwar-radio-lawrence-wilkerson-3/.

[143] Tim Golden and Don Van Natta Jr., "US Said to Overstate Value of Guantánamo Detainees," *New York Times*, June 21, 2004, http://www.nytimes.com/learning/students/pop/articles/21GITM.html.

[144] Ibid.

[145] "Shackled Detainees Arrive in Guantanamo," CNN, January 11, 2002, http://edition.cnn.com/2002/WORLD/asiapcf/central/01/11/ret.detainee.transfer/index.html.

[146] Brandon Neely, interviewed by the author, *Scott Horton Show*, radio archive, November 1, 2011, http://scotthorton.org/interviews/2011/11/01/antiwar-radio-brandon-neely-2/.

care from Army doctors in Afghanistan, quickly became known as "Half-Dead Bob."[147]

Others were there as a simple case of mistaken identity. For example, Abdul Zahir spent 14 years in miserable captivity, away from his family in Afghanistan, before the government finally admitted he was the wrong man. Zahir had been a translator for the Taliban, and not the al Qaeda member of the same name. The evidence against him was a cache of "chemical and biological agents," which, the government confessed more than a decade later, turned out to be containers of salt, sugar and petroleum jelly. His lawyer, U.S. Air Force Lt. Col Sterling Thomas, later argued that the assessment 14 years later that the suspect was "probably misidentified" was the "strongest indictment" of detention procedures anyone could need. Even now, the fact that the accusations against Zahir have finally been dismissed may only mean he will join the other score or so who have been cleared for release and yet still remain captives at Guantánamo Bay.[148]

As Col. Wilkerson explained, it was Northern Alliance warlords like Gen. Rashid Dostum who took most of the prisoners in the initial stages of the war, with the addition of only a few who had been grabbed by American CIA paramilitaries or military special operations forces. The military knew almost immediately they had been stuck with a bunch of nobodies. From the beginning, 80–85 percent had "nil" intelligence value about the Taliban, much less Osama bin Laden. Furthermore, many of the captives had been rounded up in sweeps of villages, or had been sold to the U.S. for bounties of $5,000 by Afghan warlords with agendas, or were just regular men who were simply the victims of those willing to unleash the American Superpower on their neighbor down the road due to grievances having nothing to do with political matters at all.[149] But President Bush's memo of February 7, 2002,[150] which denied the application of the Geneva Conventions to al Qaeda and in large part to the Taliban, also canceled the old method of determining who had been captured, known as the Status Review Tribunal. The U.S. military already

[147] Golden and Van Natta Jr., "US Said to Overstate Value of Guantánamo Detainees."

[148] "Abdul Zahir, Mistakenly Detained by US for 14 Years, Cleared for Release from Guantánamo Bay," Gitmo Watch, July 20, 2016, http://www.gitmowatch.com/press-release/; Britain Eakin, "'Wrong Guy' Who Spent 14 Years in Gitmo Gets Transfer Hearing," Graver News, June 11, 2016, https://gravernews.com/wrong-guy-who-spent-14-years-in-gitmo-gets-transfer-hearing/; Sterling Thomas, interviewed by the author, *Scott Horton Show*, radio archive, July 21, 2016, https://scotthorton.org/interviews/72116-sterling-thomas/.

[149] Lawrence Wilkerson, interviewed by the author, *Scott Horton Show*, radio archive, March 27, 2009, http://scotthorton.org/interviews/2009/03/27/antiwar-radio-lawrence-wilkerson-2/.

[150] George W. Bush, "Humane Treatment of al Qaeda and Taliban Detainees," White House Memorandum, February 7, 2002, http://www.washingtonpost.com/wp-srv/nation/documents/020702bush.pdf.

knew how to vet their prisoners to determine who was a prisoner of war, civilian, spy, guerrilla, etc., and how the law applied to each. However, Wilkerson explained, with the old rules canceled, the pressure was on to just hurry, get some bodies and put them on a plane. Though high-level officials soon realized their mistake, they continued to characterize the entire population of Guantánamo as the world's most dangerous terrorists to the American people, even as they quietly moved to start repatriation as quickly as possible.

The ad-hoc court system set up at Guantánamo — and then, later, even the congressionally mandated system — has been so bad that, so far, a total of seven prosecutors have resigned rather than participate in such a corrupt system any longer.[151] The "convictions" have been a world-wide laughing stock. Osama bin Laden's cook[152] and his sometimes-driver[153] were convicted of "war crimes." David Hicks, an Australian fighter for the Taliban, pleaded guilty to "war crimes," but then was released for time served on the condition that he promised not to describe his torture and "embarrass" the United States. After the commissions that convicted him were disbanded by President Obama and replaced with different ones, Hicks told the story and eventually wrote a book about it.[154]

Despite the fact that malaria is not a prevalent disease in Afghanistan or Cuba, where it is seldom seen,[155] inmates were given treatment-level, as opposed to prophylactic-level, doses of the dangerous anti-malaria drug mefloquine, or Lariam. This could cause severe, bad LSD trip-type reactions and lasting harm among the inmates. Journalists Jason Leopold and Jeffrey Kaye wrote, "Since its introduction, [mefloquine] has been

---

[151] Peter Finn, "Guantánamo Prosecutor Quits, Says Evidence Was Withheld," *Washington Post*, September 25, 2008, http://www.washingtonpost.com/wp-dyn/content/article/2008/09/24/AR2008092402101.html.

[152] Jane Sutton, "Bin Laden's Cook Gets 14-year Sentence," Reuters, August 11, 2010, http://www.reuters.com/article/us-guantanamo-sudan-idUSTRE67A3HO20100811.

[153] "Bin Laden's Driver Convicted of Terror Charges," ABC News, August 6, 2008, http://abcnews.go.com/TheLaw/story?id=5525131.

[154] "David Hicks Gives Graphic Account of Torture at Guantánamo," *Independent Australia*, May 23, 2001, https://independentaustralia.net/article-display/david-hicks-gives-graphic-account-of-torture-at-guantanamo,3424; David Hicks, *Guantánamo: My Journey* (New York: Random House, 2012); Jason Leopold, "David Hicks: One of Guantánamo Bay's First Detainees Breaks His Silence," Truthout, February 15, 2011, http://www.truth-out.org/news/item/258:exclusive-one-of-guantanamo-bays-first-detainees-breaks-his-silence; Jason Leopold, "My Tortured Journey with Former Guantánamo Detainee David Hicks," Truthout, February 16, 2011, http://www.truth-out.org/news/item/45:my-tortured-journey-with-former-guantanamo-detainee-david-hicks.

[155] "Health Information for Travelers to Cuba," Centers for Disease Control and Prevention, https://wwwnc.cdc.gov/travel/destinations/clinician/none/cuba; William Winkenwerder Jr., "Department of Defense Memo to John M. McHugh, Chairman, Subcommittee on Military Personnel," Truthout, September 13, 2002, http://www.truth-out.org/archive/files/memo-2.pdf; Mario J. Penton and Caridad Cruz, "Nearly a Dozen People Diagnosed with Malaria Are Hospitalized in Cienfuegos," *Miami Herald*, January 10, 2017, http://www.miamiherald.com/news/nation-world/world/americas/cuba/article125685704.html.

directly linked to serious adverse effects, including depression, anxiety, panic attacks, confusion, hallucinations, bizarre dreams, nausea, vomiting, sores and homicidal and suicidal thoughts."[156] The manufacturers themselves warn these symptoms "have been reported to continue long after mefloquine has been stopped." They add, "mefloquine should not be taken for prophylaxis in patients with active depression or with a recent history of depression, generalized anxiety disorder, psychosis, or schizophrenia or other major psychiatric disorders."[157]

Yet, as Leopold and Kaye report,

> The drug was administered to Guantánamo detainees without regard for their medical or psychological history, despite its considerable risk of exacerbating pre-existing conditions. Mefloquine is also known to have serious side effects among individuals under treatment for depression or other serious mental health disorders, which numerous detainees were said to have been treated for, according to their attorneys and published reports.

> In 2002, when the prison was established and mefloquine first administered, there were dozens of suicide attempts at Guantánamo. That same year, the DoD [Department of Defense] stopped reporting attempted suicides.

Though the military had claimed that this was all medically necessary, they did not give these medicines to U.S. troops or the many contractors working at the base, many coming from malaria-prone parts of the world. U.S. Army doctor Remington Nevin, author of an article on the subject in the medical journal, *Tropical Medicine and International Health*,[158] and Army Sgt. Joseph Hickman, who wrote a book investigating the deaths of three detainees on his watch at Guantánamo, have both suggested that these treatment-level doses of mefloquine were administered to the prisoners there at least in part due to the medicine's "adverse effects" — as an element of the military's abusive interrogation program.[159]

---

[156] Jason Leopold and Jeffrey Kaye, "Controversial Drug Given to All Guantanamo Detainees Akin to 'Pharmacologic Waterboarding,'" Truthout, December 1, 2010, http://www.truth-out.org/news/item/253:exclusive-controversial-drug-given-to-all-guantanamo-detainees-akin-to-pharmacologic-waterboarding.

[157] "Roche: Lariam Brand of Mefloquine Hydrochloride," US Food and Drug Administration, https://www.accessdata.fda.gov/drugsatfda_docs/label/2009/019591s026s028lbl.pdf.

[158] RL Nevin, "Mass Administration of the Antimalarial Drug Mefloquine to Guantánamo Detainees: A Critical Analysis," Tropical Medicine & International Health 17 (August 2010): 1281-1288, https://www.ncbi.nlm.nih.gov/labs/articles/22882560/.

[159] Jeffrey Kaye, "New Book: Antimalarial Drugs Part of Secret Program to Torture Detainees at Guantanamo," Shadow Proof, April 5, 2015, https://shadowproof.com/2015/04/05/new-book-antimalaria-drugs-part-of-secret-program-to-torture-detainees-at-guantanamo/; Joseph Hickman, *Murder at Camp Delta: A Staff Sergeant's Pursuit of the Truth About Guantánamo Bay* (New York: Simon and Schuster, 2015).

Many of the captives were subjected to brutal torture far beyond the forced taking of drugs. Later investigations revealed scenes from meetings at Guantánamo Bay straight out of the films *Dr. Strangelove* or the George Lucas dystopian science-fiction classic *THX 1138*, where even mid-level prison staff participated in coming up with new ideas for how to torture the inmates, including copying what they saw on the Fox TV show *24*,[160] which itself had been developed for the express purpose, according to its creator, of helping to normalize the new torture regime in the minds of the American people.[161] At least three Guantánamo prisoners have committed suicide, out of hundreds of attempts overall.[162] In June 2006, at least three more were killed in CIA custody at the secret Camp No, or Penny Lane, site nearby. These apparent murders were covered-up and claimed by the army to have been suicides. No one has ever been held accountable.[163]

After navy general counsel Alberto Mora objected to the illegality of the military's torture program at Guantánamo in 2004,[164] the very worst of the torture there stopped. However, captives were still subject to sleep and sensory deprivation, the playing of the most horrible music[165] on full volume, verbal humiliation and, especially, isolation, to create a sense of hopeless futility on the part of the prisoners. Kaye later showed that a modified version of the "frequent-flier program" at Guantánamo, which involved the near-constant movement of prisoners from cell to cell to prevent them from gaining any sense of stability, remained in place for

---

[160] Philippe Sands, "The Green Light," *Vanity Fair*, May 2008, http://www.vanityfair.com/news/2008/05/guantanamo200805.

[161] Jane Mayer, "Whatever It Takes," *New Yorker*, February 19, 2007, http://www.newyorker.com/magazine/2007/02/19/whatever-it-takes.

[162] Mark P. Denbeaux et al., "June 10th Suicides at Guantánamo: Government Words and Deeds Compared," University School of Law, August 21, 2006, https://law.shu.edu/publications/guantanamoReports/guantanamo_report_june_suicides_8_21_06.pdf.

[163] Mark P. Denbeaux et al., "Uncovering the Cover Ups: Death in Camp Delta," *Seton Hall Law School, Public Law & Legal Theory Research Paper Series,* Paper No. 2437423, May 17, 2014, Revised: June 19, 2014, https://papers.ssrn.com/sol3/papers.cfm?abstract_id=2437423; The Other Scott Horton, (no relation to the author), "The Guantánamo 'Suicides,'" *Harper's*, March 2010, http://harpers.org/archive/2010/03/the-guantanamo-suicides/; The Other Scott Horton, (no relation to the author), "The Guantánamo 'Suicides,' Revisited," *Harper's*, June 2014, http://harpers.org/archive/2014/06/the-guantanamo-suicides-revisited/; The Other Scott Horton (no relation to the author), interviewed by the author, *Scott Horton Show*, radio archive, January 19, 2010, https://scotthorton.org/interviews/antiwar-radio-scott-horton-20/; Jeffrey Kaye, "Deconstructing the Campaign to Malign Award-Winning Article on Guantánamo 'Suicides,'" Truthout, June 1, 2011, http://www.truth-out.org/news/item/1381:deconstructing-the-campaign-to-malign-awardwinning-article-on-guantanamo-suicides; Hickman, *Murder At Camp Delta*; Denbeaux et al., "June 10th Suicides at Guantánamo."

[164] Alberto J. Mora, "The Mora Memo," United States Department of the Navy, July 7, 2004, http://www.newyorker.com/images/pdf/2006/02/27/moramemo.pdf.

[165] "James Hetfield Is 'Honored' Metallica's Music Was Used by US Military to 'Help Us Stay Safe,'" Blabbermouth, March 3, 2017, http://www.blabbermouth.net/news/james-hetfield-is-honored-metallica-music-was-used-by-us-military-to-help-us-stay-safe/.

years after 2004.[166] All this was in addition to the torture of simply being held indefinitely without charge or trial for years on end. Whatever "enhanced interrogation techniques" the CIA was still using at the secret Penny Lane black site in a separate part of the base remains unknown.[167]

When President Barack Obama came to power in 2009, he announced — contrary to the "take care" clause of the U.S. Constitution's Article II, which declares the president "shall" enforce the law[168] — his administration's Department of Justice would "look forwards, not backwards" when it came to lawbreaking in the previous administration's torture program.[169] Obama turned a blind eye to any crimes committed by the CIA or the military under the torture program other than one preliminary investigation into the deaths of two captives, Manadel al-Jamadi, who was killed by CIA officers in Abu Ghraib prison in Iraq, and Rahman — an investigation which was quickly resolved in favor of the CIA.[170]

Apparently as a reaction to Obama's claims that he was going to close the prison, the abuse worsened. The Immediate Reaction Force raid teams began escalating their beatings of inmates in their cells under the guise of searches and cell transfers.[171] The hunger strike that was launched in reaction to the new wave of oppression was dealt with severely. Captives were force-fed Ensure, a liquid food substitute, through thick rubber hoses jammed up their noses, sometimes still covered with the previous victims' blood and snot.[172] Through these brutal methods, along with increased isolation of the inmates in solitary confinement, the widespread hunger strike was broken,[173] and the media's attention was lost.

[166] Jeffrey Kaye, "New DoD Report Details Nightmare Leading to Gitmo Detainee's Death," Shadow Proof, June 29, 2013, https://shadowproof.com/2013/06/29/new-dod-report-details-nightmare-leading-to-gitmo-detainees-death/.

[167] Adam Goldman and Matt Apuzzo, "CIA Turned Guantánamo Bay Inmates into Double Agents, Ex-Officials Claim," Yahoo! News, November 26, 2013, https://www.yahoo.com/news/penny-lane-gitmos-other-secret-cia-facility-050929062--politics.html.

[168] US Const. art. II, § III, https://www.archives.gov/founding-docs/constitution-transcript.

[169] Josh Gerstein and Mike Allen, "Obama Muddles Torture Message," NBC7 (San Diego), http://www.nbcsandiego.com/news/archive/Obama_muddles_torture_message.html.

[170] Eric Holder, "Statement of Attorney General Eric Holder on Closure of Investigation into the Interrogation of Certain Detainees," United States Department of Justice, August 30, 2012, https://www.justice.gov/opa/pr/statement-attorney-general-eric-holder-closure-investigation-interrogation-certain-detainees.

[171] Jeremy Scahill, "Little Known Military Thug Squad Still Brutalizing Prisoners at Gitmo Under Obama," Alternet, May 14, 2009, http://www.alternet.org/story/140022/little_known_military_thug_squad_still_brutalizing_prisoners_at_gitmo_under_obama.

[172] Kent Sepkowitz, "The Writhing, Miserable Reality of Force Feeding at Guantánamo Bay," Daily Beast, May 2, 2013, http://www.thedailybeast.com/articles/2013/05/02/the-writhing-miserable-reality-of-force-feeding-at-guant-namo-bay.html.

[173] Charlie Savage, "Guantánamo Hunger Strike Is Largely Over, US Says," New York Times, September 23, 2013, http://www.nytimes.com/2013/09/24/us/guantanamo-hunger-strike-largely-over-us-says.html.

During the Obama years, the Bagram Air Base prison became a substitute black site for alleged jihadis and terrorists from all over the world. It did not matter whether they had ever been to Afghanistan before in their lives.[174] The Democrats adopted the same legal theories the previous administration had tried to invoke in the case of the prison at Guantánamo Bay, to hide their prisoners from the law with simple geography and secrecy. By then, Senator John McCain had shepherded the Detainee Treatment Act of 2005 through the U.S. Senate, reinstituting the Army Field Manual's procedures for handling detainees, but with two loopholes — compromises agreed to by the Bush-Cheney administration. The first was the new law would not apply to the Central Intelligence Agency,[175] the second was the Army Field Manual would itself be rewritten with a new Appendix M that would continue to allow the military's use of sleep deprivation, temperature manipulation and other "lesser" tortures to continue.[176] When Obama became president, with a wink and a nudge he signed an executive order mandating the CIA and Defense Department both follow the newly rewritten manual, rather than pre-existing law, which should still have banned the abuses in the new manual, regardless.[177]

By the end of the Obama years, even the most mainstream journalists had to admit that the whole Guantánamo project amounted to a hoax. Based on newly revealed documents prepared by the military for the Periodic Review Board, Carol Rosenberg of the *Miami Herald* wrote, "The 'Dirty 30' probably weren't all Osama bin Laden bodyguards after all. The 'Karachi 6' weren't a cell of bombers plotting attacks in Pakistan for al-Qaeda. An Afghan man captured 14 years ago as a suspected chemical weapons maker was confused for somebody else." As Rosenberg notes, some of these men, who were tortured and held without trial for years,

---

[174] Daphne Eviatar, "Detained and Denied in Afghanistan," Human Rights First, 2011, https://www.humanrightsfirst.org/wp-content/uploads/pdf/Detained-Denied-in-Afghanistan.pdf; The Other Scott Horton (no relation to the author), "Obama's Secret Afghan Prisons," *Harper's*, January 29, 2010, http://harpers.org/blog/2010/01/obamas-secret-afghan-prisons/.

[175] R. Jeffrey Smith and Josh White, "Cheney Plan Exempts CIA from Bill Barring Abuse of Detainees," *Washington Post*, October 25, 2005, http://www.washingtonpost.com/wp-dyn/content/article/2005/10/24/AR2005102402051.html.

[176] Jeffrey Kaye, "How the US Army's Field Manual Codified Torture -- and Still Does," Alternet, January 6, 2009, http://www.alternet.org/story/117807/how_the_u.s._army%27s_field_manual _codified_torture_--_and_still_does; Eric Schmitt, "New Army Rules May Snarl Talks with McCain on Detainee Issue," *New York Times*, December 14, 2005, http://www.nytimes.com/2005/12/14/politics/new-army-rules-may-snarl-talks-with-mccain-on-detainee-issue.html; *FM-2-22.3 (FM 34-52) Human Intelligence Collector Operations*, Department of the Army, September 2006, https://fas.org/irp/doddir/army/fm2-22-3.pdf.

[177] From the Department of Justice to Guantanamo Bay: Administration Lawyers and Administration Interrogation Rules Part 1: Hearing before the Subcommittee on the Constitution, Civil Rights, and Civil Liberties, 110 Congress. (2008) (Congressional Testimony of Marjorie Cohn on Torture Policy), https://www.gpo.gov/fdsys/pkg/CHRG-110hhrg42212/html/CHRG-110hhrg42212.htm.

had been seized only for wearing a Casio brand wristwatch, which was the same brand as that used by Ramzi Yousef in the test-run bombings of a movie theater and the Philippine Airlines 747 in 1995.[178] "Everybody's drinking the Kool-Aid. You see conspiracies everywhere," an intelligence analyst from Guantánamo confessed to Rosenberg in 2016. "The intelligence unit was 'picking up on one or two [ultimately unimportant or untrue] things and holding on to it tightly like it was gospel.'"[179]

There is reason to believe that torture is in part responsible for our modern terrorism problem in the first place. In fact, two of the most notorious terrorists of the modern era, bin Laden's partner and current al Qaeda leader, Ayman al Zawahiri,[180] and Abu Musab al Zarqawi,[181] the founder and, for a time, leader of al Qaeda in Iraq, were subjected to brutal torture by U.S. allies Egypt and Jordan before becoming the butchers the world would later find them to be. This was very likely true of Abu Bakr al Baghdadi, leader of ISIS, as well. The U.S. Army now concedes Baghdadi was held at the infamous Abu Ghraib prison in Iraq during the same time frame that the published photos of the U.S.'s torture victims there were taken.[182]

According to Tony Camerino, the formerly pseudonymous "Matthew Alexander," author of *How to Break a Terrorist: The U.S. Interrogators Who Used Brains, Not Brutality, to Take Down the Deadliest Man in Iraq*, the torture depicted in photographs from Abu Ghraib prison in the second Iraq war and the hoods and orange jumpsuits from the pictures of the prison at Guantánamo Bay have helped only to expand the ranks of local insurgencies and international terrorist groups alike. Camerino says torture was the single greatest reason cited by Iraqis and foreign fighters for why they joined up to fight the Americans during Iraq War II.[183] By abandoning the pretense of American values and instead embracing torture as a

---

[178] Lance, *1,000 Years for Revenge*, 236-244, 254-261.

[179] Carol Rosenberg, "New Guantánamo Intelligence Upends Old 'Worst of the Worst' Myths," *Miami Herald*, October 7, 2016, http://www.military.com/daily-news/2016/10/07/new-guantanamo-intelligence-upends-old-worst-worst-myths.html.

[180] Wright, *The Looming Tower*, 55.

[181] Gerges, *The Far Enemy*, 256.

[182] Joshua Eaton, "US Military Now Says ISIS Leader Was Held in Notorious Abu Ghraib Prison," Intercept, August 25, 2016, https://theintercept.com/2016/08/25/u-s-military-now-says-isis-leader-was-held-in-notorious-abu-ghraib-prison/.

[183] Matthew Alexander, "I'm Still Tortured by What I Saw in Iraq," *Washington Post*, November 30, 2008, http://www.washingtonpost.com/wp-dyn/content/article/2008/11/28/AR2008112802242.html; Tony Camerino [Matthew Alexander] and John R. Bruning, *How to Break a Terrorist: The U.S. Interrogators Who Used Brains, Not Brutality, to Take Down the Deadliest Man in Iraq* (New York: Free, 2008); Tony Camerino [Matthew Alexander], interviewed by the author, *Scott Horton Show*, radio archive, December 3, 2008, https://scotthorton.org/interviews/antiwar-radio-matthew-alexander/; Tony Camerino [Matthew Alexander], interviewed by the author, *Scott Horton Show*, radio archive, January 9, 2015, https://scotthorton.org/interviews/10915-tony-camerino/.

national policy in the name of acting "tough" to protect the population, the U.S. government has increased the danger by helping to create a whole new generation of bin Ladenites.

As the *Atlantic* pointed out in 2013,

> Guantánamo Bay has often been the focus of jihadist media and propaganda. Just recently, the *Islamic Emirate of Afghanistan* — the mouthpiece of the Taliban — put out a statement calling attention to the ongoing hunger strike at Guantánamo Bay. ... In 2010, al Qaeda in the Arabian Peninsula (AQAP) released the first issue of *Inspire*, their English language recruitment magazine. ... The plight of prisoners at Guantánamo Bay has been featured prominently in several issues. In the 2010 inaugural issue of *Inspire*, an essay by Osama bin Laden mentions "the crimes at Abu Ghraib and Guantánamo . . . which shook the conscience of humanity." Tellingly, bin Laden points out that "there has been no mentionable change" at Guantánamo and the prison is noted again later in the issue. ...

> The essays of Abu Sufyan al-Azdi and Uthman al-Gamidi, two former detainees who returned to AQAP upon their release, call new individuals to join the jihad, whether at home or abroad. In Issue 7, Yahya Ibrahim notes that Guantánamo Bay "exposed the West for what it really is" and "showed the world the American understanding of human rights."[184]

David Rhode, a *New York Times* reporter who was captured and held by the Taliban for more than half a year, later wrote:

> [S]ome of the consequences of Washington's anti-terrorism policies had galvanized the Taliban. Commanders fixated on the deaths of Afghan, Iraqi and Palestinian civilians in military airstrikes, as well as the American detention of Muslim prisoners who had been held for years without being charged. America, Europe and Israel preached democracy, human rights and impartial justice to the Muslim world, they said, but failed to follow those principles themselves.[185]

The Bush administration believed that they were teaching the enemy a lesson about dominance and strength and why they better learn to submit to the will of American power,[186] when in fact their brutal mistreatment of

---

[184] Thérèse Postel, "How Guantanamo Bay's Existence Helps Al-Qaeda Recruit More Terrorists," *Atlantic*, April 12, 2013, https://www.theatlantic.com/international/archive/2013/04/how-guantanamo-bays-existence-helps-al-qaeda-recruit-more-terrorists/274956/.

[185] David Rhode, "7 Months, 10 Days in Captivity," *New York Times*, October 17, 2009, http://www.nytimes.com/2009/10/18/world/asia/18hostage.html.

[186] Seymour M. Hersh, "The Gray Zone: How a Secret Pentagon Program Came to Abu Ghraib," *New Yorker*, May 24, 2004, http://www.newyorker.com/magazine/2004/05/24/the-gray-zone; Brian Whitaker, "Its Best Use Is as a Doorstop," *Guardian*, May 24, 2004,

local Afghans belied the U.S.'s promises of charity, goodwill and high-minded motivations for the occupation, and helped drive resistance to the American military presence instead.[187]

Karzai and the Warlords

At the start of the Afghan war, Secretary of Defense Donald Rumsfeld was so singularly focused on using the September 11th attacks as a pretense for launching a war in Iraq that there was one positive side to his strategy: after allowing bin Laden to escape, he wanted to get out. Just as wiser heads had advised the Soviet war cabinet not to invade Afghanistan in 1979,[188] he had argued that trying to nation-build in a war-torn tribal society would be impossible and they should pull the military out almost immediately. It turns out that Rumsfeld was right about at least this one "known known," not that he stood by it for long. Tens of thousands of soldiers would arrive soon enough — just not soon enough to catch bin Laden or his partner Ayman al Zawahiri.[189] They would instead be used for just the kind of nation-building project the defense secretary had been trying to avoid, shoring up the new government's allies and attacking its enemies in a state of permanent war.

America's new Afghan partner, the Northern Alliance, was in large measure simply a coalition of those who had served the Soviet Communists during the 1980s war,[190] including their leader, the former CIA favorite Ahmad Shah Massoud, who, it turns out, had been a KGB-owned double agent all along.[191] Massoud was assassinated in an al Qaeda suicide bombing two days before the September 11th attacks, presumably so his unifying force would be removed from the equation when the Americans came to retaliate.[192] In fact, the timing of the killing of Massoud may have been partially coincidental, as the bombers had been delayed for some time in their attempt to arrange the meeting that led to Massoud's

---

https://www.theguardian.com/world/2004/may/24/worlddispatch.usa.

[187] For more on the CIA and military torture programs in Afghanistan, Iraq, Guantánamo Bay and various black sites under both the Bush and Obama administrations, see Appendix III.

[188] Alexander Lyakhovsky, *The Tragedy and Valor of Afghan* (Moscow: GPI Iskon, 1995), 109-112. Excerpt available at the National Security Archive, http://nsarchive.gwu.edu/NSAEBB/NSAEBB396/docs/Lyakhovsky,%20Decision%20to%20send%20troops%20into%20Afghanistan.pdf; Eric Margolis, email message to the author, October 24, 2016.

[189] Woodward, *Bush at War*, 190, 276.

[190] Van Linschoten and Kuehn, *An Enemy We Created*, 206.

[191] Margolis, *War at the Top of the World*, 53-55.

[192] Alan Cullison and Andrew Higgins, "Forgotten Computer Reveals Thinking Behind Four Years of al Qaeda Doings," *Wall Street Journal*, December 31, 2001, http://www.wsj.com/articles/SB100975171479902000.

death.[193] In the end, it did not matter much since Massoud's allied warlords soon came together around U.S. forces and new, U.S.-installed interim president Hamid Karzai.[194]

If it is true, as Aldous Huxley said, that "the means employed determine the nature of the ends produced,"[195] then the Americans' decision to bring together the last of the Afghan Communists still resisting the Taliban in order to form the new government guaranteed only further destruction. Abdul Rashid Dostum, an ethnic Uzbek warlord, had been a general in the puppet army serving the Kremlin and fighting against the mujahideen in the 1980s.[196] Since America had now switched sides in the fight, the CIA recruited and paid him, and had him working closely with U.S. Special Forces when he massacred at least hundreds, possibly thousands, of Taliban prisoners who were being held in large metal shipping containers at Dasht-i-Leili in November 2001. Dostum's men opened fire on the containers with automatic rifles, killing many with bullets and drowning the rest in their blood.[197] Such was the beginning of America's rehabilitation of Afghanistan's Communist butchers. Dostum was named deputy defense minister in December 2001, was promoted to army chief of staff in 2010 and is currently the vice president of Afghanistan.[198] In July 2016, Human Rights Watch (HRW) accused Dostum and his militias of committing numerous war crimes, including massacres of unarmed civilian Pashtun tribesmen. HRW's Patricia Gossman demanded criminal prosecution by the government in Kabul, remarking at the time, "The killings in Faryab [Province] are the latest in a

---

[193] "Massood Murder Plotters Convicted," BBC News, May 17, 2005, http://news.bbc.co.uk/2/hi/south_asia/4555633.stm.

[194] Mark Oliver, "The New Afghan Administration," *Guardian*, December 5, 2001, https://www.theguardian.com/world/2001/dec/05/qanda.markoliver; "Who Are the Northern Alliance?," BBC News, November 13, 2001, http://news.bbc.co.uk/2/hi/south_asia/1652187.stm.

[195] Aldous Huxley, *Ends and Means: An Inquiry into the Nature of Ideals and into the Methods Employed for Their Realization* (New York: Harper Brothers, 1937), 10.

[196] Patrick Cockburn, "Rashid Dostum: The Treacherous General," *Independent*, November 30, 2001, http://www.independent.co.uk/news/people/profiles/rashid-dostum-the-treacherous-general-9224857.html.

[197] "State Department FOIA Release to Physicians for Human Rights Regarding Dasht-e-Leili Massacre," Wikileaks, https://file.wikileaks.org/file/dasht-e-leili-afghanistan-massacre-foia-2002-2008.pdf; John Barry, "The Death Convoy of Afghanistan," *Newsweek*, August 25, 2002, http://www.newsweek.com/death-convoy-afghanistan-144273; Amy Goodman, "Afghan Massacre: Eyewitnesses Testify US Troops Complicit in Massacre of Up to 3,000 Taliban POWs," *Democracy Now!*, May 23, 2003, https://www.democracynow.org/2003/5/23/afghan_massacre_the_convoy_of_death; "The Dasht-e-Leili Massacre of Taliban Prisoners of War, US FOIA, part I, 2002-2008," Wikileaks, July 22, 2009, https://wikileaks.org/wiki/The_Dasht-e-Leili_Massacre_of_Taliban_prisoners_of_war,_US_FOIA,_part_I,_2002-2008; *Afghan Massacre: The Convoy of Death*, directed by Jamie Doran, 2002, http://topdocumentaryfilms.com/afghan-massacre/.

[198] Mujib Mashal and Fahim Abed, "Afghan Vice President Seen Abducting Rival," *New York Times*, November 27, 2016, https://www.nytimes.com/2016/11/27/world/asia/afghan-vice-president-is-accused-of-assaulting-rival-and-taking-him-hostage.html.

long record of atrocities by Dostum's militia forces. The fact that these forces, and Vice-President Dostum himself, have never been held accountable, has undermined security in northern Afghanistan."[199] The Afghan vice president's maintenance of his own private army throughout the Bush and Obama years tells us much about how he got the position in the first place, and that neither the Afghan National Army (ANA) or the United States had the motive or ability to force him to disband or integrate his forces. His impunity solidified, for years Dostum murdered civilians in the name of fighting the Taliban before finally being forced to at least temporarily leave the country in the summer of 2017 after being credibly accused of ordering the kidnapping and rape of a former provincial governor.[200]

President Karzai, a longtime CIA asset, expatriate oil company lobbyist and protégé of powerful neoconservative foreign policy mandarin, Zalmay Khalilzad, was installed as interim president in the capital city of Kabul by American forces in December 2001,[201] after their first choice, Abdul Haq, rushed too far ahead of the battle lines and was caught and hanged by the retreating Taliban.[202] Karzai swore he would simply be a placeholder until nation-wide presidential elections could be held, and that he would not even be running. When elections were finally held in 2004, Karzai did run and win, though the election was a farce, with widespread fraud and intimidation tactics employed by the U.S.,[203] as well as Karzai's thugs. As the BBC reported at the time, villagers were beaten and told, "Vote Karzai or we'll burn your house down."[204] Karzai's presidency quickly became a joke, however, and he became known as "the mayor of Kabul,"[205] since he and his government had so little influence over what was happening in the rest of the country, the newly christened "Islamic Republic of Afghanistan."[206] The Taliban was gone, but the project to attempt to build

---

[199] "Afghanistan: Forces Linked to Vice President Terrorize Villagers," Human Rights Watch, July 31, 2016, https://www.hrw.org/news/2016/07/31/afghanistan-forces-linked-vice-president-terrorize-villagers.

[200] Sune Engel Rasmussen, "Vice-President Leaves Afghanistan Amid Torture and Rape Claims," *Guardian*, May 19, 2017, https://www.theguardian.com/world/2017/may/19/vice-president-leaves-afghanistan-amid-torture-and-claims.

[201] Woodword, *Bush at War*, 314.

[202] Margolis, *American Raj*, 207; Berntsen and Pezzullo, *Jawbreaker*, 81.

[203] Paul Watson, "US Hand Seen in Afghan Election," *Los Angeles Times*, September 23, 2004, http://articles.latimes.com/2004/sep/23/world/fg-meddle23.

[204] Crispin Thorold, "Vote Threat to Afghan Tribesmen," BBC News, September 24, 2004, http://news.bbc.co.uk/2/hi/south_asia/3687276.stm.

[205] Henry Schuster, "Kabul Comes Undone," CNN, June 1, 2006, http://edition.cnn.com/2006/WORLD/asiapcf/06/01/schuster.column/index.html.

[206] Constitution of the Islamic Republic of Afghanistan, ratified January 26, 2004, http://www.diplomatie.gouv.fr/en/IMG/pdf/The_Constitution_of_the_Islamic_Republic_of_Afghanistan.pdf.

a government powerful enough to maintain control over the entire country, and keep them out, was just beginning.

In Afghanistan, the Pashtun (or Pathan) tribes represent a strong plurality of approximately forty percent of the population, while the Tajiks, Hazaras, Uzbeks, Turks and other ethnic groups make up the rest.[207] Previous estimates had the Pashtuns at as much as sixty percent of the population.[208] The different groups tend to be geographically separate from each other as well, with the Pashtun tribes dominating in the south and east of the country, and divided by the old British-drawn border with neighboring Pakistan, known as the Durand Line.[209] For the most part, the other ethnic groups share the rest of the country, though there are some Pashtun populations in the north of the country, in Kunduz, for example. These divisions became much starker during the many years of the war with the Russians and the following civil war. Though Karzai was himself a Pashtun of the Popalzai tribe, and the son of a powerful tribal leader from Kandahar Province who was assassinated in Pakistan in 1999,[210] observers were quick to point out that hardly proved the Pashtun population would have representation in the new government.[211] America sided with the ethnic minority coalition and built the officer corps of the Afghan National Army almost exclusively from Tajik tribal ranks.[212] And though the U.S. had attempted to institute quotas when it came to army recruitment, ANA abuses and a growing Pashtun refusal to participate in the army guilty of abusing them became a self-reinforcing spiral, observed Chris Mason, a member of the Afghanistan Inter-agency Operations Group from 2003 to 2005. This had the potential of leading to full-fledged ethnic civil war.[213] In the southern part of the country, efforts have focused

---

[207] US State Department, "Afghanistan," Country Studies, http://countrystudies.us/afghanistan/38.htm; Nancy Hopkins, ed., "Afghanistan in 2012: A Survey of the Afghan People," Asia Foundation, http://www.asiafoundation.org/resources/pdfs/Surveybook2012web1.pdf.

[208] Zaman Stanizai, "From Identity Crisis to Identity in Crisis in Afghanistan," Pacifica Graduate Institute, December 16, 2009, http://www.mei.edu/content/identity-crisis-identity-crisis-afghanistan.

[209] See fully detailed ethnic and religious maps of the region and of Afghanistan at http://foolserrand.us/maps or see Dr. Michael R. Izady's complete collection at http://gulf2000.columbia.edu/maps.shtml.

[210] "Abdul Ahad Karzai, 77, Afghan Official, Dies," *Washington Post*, July 25, 1999, https://www.washingtonpost.com/archive/local/1999/07/25/abdul-ahad-karzai-77-afghan-official-dies/a86fc24b-b473-41a8-904d-dcc54d07d2e3/?utm_term=.5328c5b285c7.

[211] Brendan O'Neill, "When Nation-Building Destroys," Spiked, April 4, 2002, http://www.spiked-online.com/newsite/article/10709.

[212] Heidi Vogt, "Ethnic Divisions Plague Afghan Army," NBC News, July 28, 2010, http://www.nbcnews.com/id/38432732/ns/world_news-south_and_central_asia/t/afghan-army-struggles-ethnic-divisions/.

[213] Gareth Porter, "Tajik Grip on Afghan Army Signals New Ethnic War," Inter Press Service, November 28, 2009, http://www.ipsnews.net/2009/11/politics-tajik-grip-on-afghan-army-signals-

on the creation of a mostly Pashtun division of the Afghan National Police, which has only empowered the kind of men who more properly belong in jail themselves. The criminality of the men the U.S. has been installing as police and other officials since the early years of the war has been a major contributing factor in driving civilians into the insurgency.[214]

The first premise of the entire U.S.-UN-NATO-NGO coalition occupation and nation-building project in Afghanistan centered on the creation of a strong central government in Kabul. This necessarily meant the creation of a government of the leaders of the ethnic groups that control the capital city at the expense of the plurality Pashtun tribes. But the Westerners involved almost universally favor strong central government at home and cannot seem to understand that attempting to create one in Afghanistan is only a prescription for more violence waged both in defiance of or for control over the central state apparatus.

It is easy to understand how the U.S. government and American people have been able to convince themselves that authoritarian, theocratic goons like the Taliban, representing a throwback to ignorant and medieval barbarism, must be the worst thing that ever happened to the people of Afghanistan. Surely, whatever it is our government is doing over there to fight them must, then, be for the best. Who could argue for the Taliban? Good question. The answer is many of the people of Afghanistan, who had accepted their rule in the first place as relief from the tyranny and corruption of the warlords who had fought over the country after the withdrawal of the Soviets in 1989. The Russians had killed so many Pashtun tribal leaders that their systems of power were almost completely broken, leaving the population helpless before vile criminal militias and gangs, and leading to a situation where their religious leadership was virtually forced to step in.[215] The Taliban's rise to authority began in the mid-1990s when they were encouraged by the people of Kandahar Province to take power to stop kidnappers and rapists of women and young girls and boys and to outlaw these practices.[216] The Taliban — literally, "students" — were mostly young Afghans, raised in Pakistani refugee camps, and recruited by Mullah Omar and other Pashtun veterans of the old U.S.-backed jihad against the Soviets to defeat the various factions whose criminality and civil wars were tearing the country apart.

new-ethnic-war/.

[214] Danny Singh, "The Afghan National Police: A Study on Corruption and Clientelism," Security Sector Reform Resource Center, November 3, 2015, http://www.tandfonline.com/doi/full/10.1080/14678802.2014.963391; Gareth Porter, "Afghanistan: Child Rapist Police Return Behind US, UK Troops," Inter Press Service, July 29, 2009, http://www.ipsnews.net/2009/07/afghanistan-child-rapist-police-return-behind-us-uk-troops/.

[215] Gopal, No Good Men Among the Living, 79-82.

[216] Margolis, American Raj, 197; Rashid, Taliban, 25; van Linschoten and Kuehn, An Enemy We Created, 114-115.

The Pakistani- and Saudi-supported Taliban were cruel and oppressive, but they were not corrupt. Their religious rule was considered by the Pashtuns, and possibly even a majority of Afghans, to be peaceful compared to the endless violence of warlords from both sides of the 1980s Soviet war, such as Massoud, Dostum, General Mohammed Fahim, Gulbuddin Hekmatyar and others. The Taliban abolished the vast majority of organized crime and gangs, disarmed and disbanded the separate warring militias and shot criminals, providing real safety — at least from private actors. This does not mean that they necessarily had legitimate "popular sovereignty" in the Western sense. The Taliban took power by force, and many people were certainly oppressed under their rule, which was enforced ruthlessly, even murderously. This was especially true in the capital of Kabul, and in the north where their strictures and dictates were far less welcome than out in the Pashtun-dominated countryside where their movement had originated. Initially, however, Taliban forces were even welcomed into the multi-ethnic, and relatively sophisticated capital city, if only they would drive out the brutal thieves and warlords of Massoud's army.[217] As Anand Gopal has written, the Taliban "were never an alien force. Rather, they were as Afghan as kebabs or the Hindu Kush — a fact that U.S. soldiers would learn the hard way."[218]

When the Russians offered to provide weapons and aid to the government in Kabul in 2015,[219] it should have served as a stark reminder of whose side the U.S. took in Afghanistan when it invaded in 2001, and why it is necessary for foreign governments like the former Soviet Union or the United States to help keep them in power. The Taliban have a reputation for brutal authoritarianism from their years in power between 1996 and 2001, as well as since their revival in 2004, and yet a major portion of the Afghan population still seem to prefer their rule to the corrupt warlords the U.S. has foisted on the country in their place.[220]

In destroying the Taliban, the American military overthrew the only real, popular locus of Pashtun power in the country and replaced it with warlords and criminals who would not have had the strength or popular support they would need to gain it otherwise.[221] Aside from the obvious

[217] Rashid, *Taliban*, 49-51.

[218] Gopal, *No Good Men*, 82.

[219] Franz-Stefan Gady, "Russia to Sell Modern Attack Helicopters to Afghanistan," Diplomat, October 9, 2015, http://thediplomat.com/2015/10/russia-to-sell-modern-attack-helicopters-to-afghanistan/; Frud Bezhan, "Afghanistan's Dostum Turns to Old Ally Russia for Help," Radio Free Europe/Radio Liberty, October 7, 2015, https://www.rferl.org/a/afghanistan-russia-dostum-seeks-military-help/27293696.html.

[220] Bob Woodward, *Obama's Wars* (New York: Simon & Schuster, 2010), 243.

[221] "'Just Don't Call It a Militia': Impunity, Militias, and the 'Afghan Local Police,'" Human Rights Watch, September 12, 2011, https://www.hrw.org/report/2011/09/12/just-dont-call-it-militia/impunity-militias-and-afghan-local-police; Julius Cavendish, "After the US Pulls Out, Will

divisions along general ethnic and religious lines, Afghanistan is also fractured upon far narrower tribal, clan and family divisions.[222] It is not only that the representatives that the Pashtun population suffers under are criminals, but that they are from a small set of politically connected families, tribes and clans who fight with other Pashtuns and exploit their hold on state police power to deprive and abuse outsiders and competitors. The only political representation or security force many are left with is the Taliban or their insurgent allies, the Haqqani Network.[223]

Even with U.S. military support, the state America built in Kabul will never be able to truly control the whole country. Attempts by American and international forces to create new, democratic alternatives to tribal and religious power, particularly in the predominantly Pashtun areas, have never amounted to much.[224] Instead, the U.S. and the local population seem destined to remain stuck between the warlords and the Taliban.

Even in the north of the country, the Tajik, Uzbek, Hazara and other ethnic, tribal, and political factions have their own problems. Without the Taliban serving as a common enemy, their coalition will surely come apart. Considering the history of the Afghan civil wars of the 1990s, with repeated back-stabbing and changing of allies by warlords of every description,[225] it seems that regardless of the state of the Taliban-based insurgency outside the capital city, there is a decent chance that without the U.S. military there to continue propping up its power, the factions that currently make up the state will turn against each other, and the "National Unity Government" in Kabul will come crashing down. This, then, could lead to new rounds of violence over the form of, and control over, the next regime.

The experts in Washington, D.C., would argue that this is why U.S. forces cannot leave. If withdrawal is almost certain to lead to increased violence in the short term, then America must stay, and the war there must continue until the Afghans have finally adopted our peaceful, democratic ways of settling their differences.[226] How cynical to suggest we should just

CIA Rely More on Afghan Mercenaries?," *Christian Science Monitor*, November 16, 2011, http://www.csmonitor.com/World/Asia-South-Central/2011/1116/After-the-US-pulls-out-will-CIA-rely-more-on-Afghan-mercenaries.

[222] Isaac Kfir, "The Role of the Pashtuns in Understanding the Afghan Crisis," *Perspectives on Terrorism*, Vol 3, No 4 (2009), http://www.terrorismanalysts.com/pt/index.php/pot/article/view/81/html.

[223] Gopal, *No Good Men*, 118-131; Gareth Porter, "Afghanistan: Child Rapist Police Return Behind US, UK Troops," Inter Press Service, July 29, 2009, http://www.ipsnews.net/2009/07/afghanistan-child-rapist-police-return-behind-us-uk-troops/.

[224] Matthieu Aikins and Anand Gopal, "The Ghost Polls of Afghanistan," *Harper's*, April 7, 2014, http://harpers.org/blog/2014/04/the-ghost-polls-of-afghanistan/; Gopal, *No Good Men*, 151-168.

[225] Steve Coll, *Ghost Wars*, 262-263, 282.

[226] Christopher D. Kolenda, "Focused Engagement: A New Way Forward in Afghanistan," Center for a New American Security, February 21, 2017,

abandon Afghanistan again, leaving its people in the lurch! But it has been American experts' violence in Afghanistan, especially over the last decade and a half, that has distorted local power relationships there so badly as to virtually guarantee such backlash when the U.S. finally does withdraw, whether it does so now or years from now.

The occupation of Afghanistan is and has been destined for disaster. Even if one accepts the argument that the U.S. absolutely had to invade the country and knock off the Taliban after the September 11th attacks, it is clear that if the Afghan people were ever to have had a chance to create a sustainable political future for themselves without the Taliban — and without the warlords the Taliban had taken power from in the first place — they needed to work out the alternative for themselves. Instead, the U.S. has intervened all over, picking winners and losers based on bad or scarce information, making political compromises with terrible criminals, and sowing the seeds of future distortions of power. The U.S. has backed warlords and heroin kingpins and, like a chapter out of Joseph Heller's *Catch-22*, has even been paying the Taliban enemy tens of millions of dollars in protection fees — taxes — to be allowed to transport needed fuel, equipment and other supplies across the massive nation in order to fight against them. The insurgents use this money to buy weapons from corrupt officers in the U.S.-supplied Afghan National Army, which they then use to fight the occupation in return.[227]

The U.S.A. is bogged down half a world away in the legendary "Graveyard of Empires" — a country the size of Texas; with mountains like Colorado and deserts like California; landlocked in the center of Eurasia; fighting tribesmen who could not be tamed by the Macedonian, British or Soviet military occupations — giving itself another "Vietnam," when at the end of the day there is no reason to believe this war could ever be any more successful than that one. Meanwhile, our only actual enemies laugh at America's wanton self-destruction.[228]

The military may be able to maintain the status quo for the near term. Changing generals in charge for the eighteenth[229] time is not likely to make

https://www.cnas.org/publications/reports/focused-engagement; "Afghan Government Could Collapse After NATO Pullout, Report Warns," *Telegraph*, October 8, 2012, http://www.telegraph.co.uk/news/worldnews/asia/afghanistan/9593194/Afghan-government-could-collapse-after-Nato-pullout-report-warns.html; Ryan Browne, "Top US General: 'Shortfall of a Few Thousand' Troops in Afghanistan," CNN, February 9, 2017, http://cnn.com/2017/02/09/politics/afghanistan-us-troops-shortfall-general-nicholson/index.html.

[227] Gopal, *No Good Men*, 206; *The Wikileaks Files*, [Reference ID AFG20071109n1067], https://wikileaks.org/afg/event/2007/11/AFG20071109n1067.html, p. 388; C. J. Chivers, "Arms Sent by US May Be Falling into Taliban Hands," *New York Times*, May 19, 2009, http://www.nytimes.com/2009/05/20/world/asia/20ammo.html.

[228] Osama bin Laden, "Full Transcript of bin Laden's Speech," Al-Jazeera, November 1, 2004, http://www.aljazeera.com/archive/2004/11/200849163336457223.html.

[229] List of ISAF-Resolute Support Commanders, NATO, http://www.rs.nato.int/history.html; Tom

much difference one way or the other. But there does not seem to be a way for the U.S. to slowly unwind their Afghan intervention or create a soft landing for those whose power they have inflated. As a result, U.S. forces are in an "impossible" position: they can never declare victory, therefore they can never leave. However, the political pressure to stay forever to stave off the inevitable is all coming from Washington, D.C., and the Pentagon. The American people would probably be happy to hear our part of war there was finally over either way.[230]

From a personal or humanitarian perspective, of course, we all would like to see the Taliban fade away. But in terms of protecting the United States and American people from future attacks, the military's mission in Afghanistan is pointless, while attempts to pacify the Pashtun population and attempts to force them to submit to the rule of the government in Kabul and its foreign accomplices have already proven impossible.

Bowman, "Next Afghan War Commander to Re-Evaluate US Response," NPR News, January 28, 2016, http://npr.org/2016/01/28/464744453/next-afghan-war-commander-to-re-evaluate-u-s-response.

[230] "CNN Poll: Afghanistan War Arguably Most Unpopular in US History," CNN Political Unit, December 30, 2013, http://politicalticker.blogs.cnn.com/2013/12/30/cnn-poll-afghanistan-war-most-unpopular-in-u-s-history/; Frank Newport, "More Americans Now View Afghanistan War as a Mistake," Gallup, February 19, 2014, http://www.gallup.com/poll/167471/americans-view-afghanistan-war-mistake.aspx.

Chapter Three: The Long War

"A long war lies ahead." — General John Abizaid, July 2004

"It was not a good thing the last time — when the Soviet Union left, the United States did not stay by the Afghan people. This time the Afghan people could be certain that they'll have friends and partners for a long time to come." — Secretary of State Condoleezza Rice, March 2005

Empire

So what is the war about?

Dominance — not of the people of Afghanistan so much as of the Eurasian landmass itself.

From the beginning of the occupation of Afghanistan, limiting the power of the neighboring states became a primary concern. As Woodward writes, "[Secretary of State Colin] Powell and the State Department argued that ... they needed a strong central government [allied with America] so Afghanistan did not, yet again, become a great power game in which all [other] interested parties would try to carve out territory or spheres of influence."[1]

An important part of the Washington consensus about why the U.S. must never leave is the widespread belief among Washington, D.C., experts and the American public that one of the reasons September 11th happened was because America had casually abandoned poor Afghanistan after the Soviets had withdrawn and Operation Cyclone, the CIA's mission of support for the mujahideen in the 1980s, had wound down. We should have never left, they said. The U.S. should have made a permanent commitment to occupying, rebuilding and creating a modern, Western European, liberal, democratic nation-state there as soon as the Soviet Union pulled out in 1989. Then Afghanistan would have been our friend, and the September 11th attacks would never have taken place. Unfortunately, America's callous neglect led to the rise of all the problems there, but we would never make that mistake again.[2]

But the truth is the Americans never left after the 1980s war — not really. Pakistani journalist Ahmed Rashid coined the term "the new Great Game" in 1997 to describe the competition among the regional and global powers over the control of oil and natural gas pipeline routes out of the Central Asian Caspian Basin. The United States had been a major player in this contest, and, according to Rashid, the Clinton administration had gone along with Saudi and Pakistani support for the rise of the Taliban beginning in the mid-1990s in the hopes of winning a contract to build an oil pipeline from Turkmenistan through Afghanistan and on to the port of Karachi in Pakistan. Therefore, not only did the U.S. support the Taliban's rise, they even favored the prospect of the Taliban's military victory over the Northern Alliance and consolidation of power over all of Afghanistan toward that end, rather than a negotiated settlement and

---

[1] Woodward, *Bush at War*, 321.

[2] Astri Suhrke, *When More is Less: The International Project in Afghanistan* (Oxford: Oxford University Press, 2011), 20.

necessary division of power. For example, U.S. officials were pleased when the Taliban seized the ancient city of Herat in far western Afghanistan in 1995. And when they sacked the capital of Kabul in 1996, an American diplomat told Rashid it would be great if the Taliban went ahead and conquered the whole country. "The Taliban will probably develop like the Saudis did. There will be Aramco, pipelines, an emir, no parliament and lots of Sharia law. We can live with that." Another high-ranking diplomat admitted, "The U.S. acquiesced in supporting the Taliban because of our links to the Pakistan and Saudi governments who backed them. But we no longer do so and we have told them categorically that we need a settlement."[3]

According to U.S. foreign policy grand strategists such as Zbigniew Brzezinski, who drew from the ideas of British imperial thinker Halford Mackinder, the global naval power of the U.S. and UK must be complemented by domination of Eastern Europe, the "heartland" of the "world island," otherwise it would naturally be dominated by the Russians. In his 1997 book, *The Grand Chessboard: American Primacy and Its Geostrategic Imperatives*, Brzezinski cited the Mackinder mantra as the basis of all modern geopolitical thinking:

> Who rules East Europe commands the Heartland;
> Who rules the Heartland commands the World Island;
> Who rules the World Island commands the World.

But to dominate the heartland, he argued, one must control the "pivot area" of Central Asia, including Afghanistan. With the Soviet Union out of the way, America was ready to embrace world empire on a level never seen before:

> Geopolitics has moved from the regional to the global dimension, with preponderance over the entire Eurasian continent serving as the central basis for global primacy. The United States, a non-Eurasian power, now enjoys international primacy, with its power directly deployed on three peripheries of the Eurasian continent, from which it exercises a powerful influence on the states occupying the Eurasian hinterland. But it is on the globe's most important playing field — Eurasia — that a potential rival to America might at some point arise. Thus, focusing on the key players and properly assessing the terrain has to be the point of departure for the formulation of American geostrategy for the long-term management of America's Eurasian geopolitical interests. ...

> To put it in a terminology that harkens back to a more brutal age of ancient empires, the three grand imperatives of imperial geostrategy

---

[3] Rashid, *Taliban*, 5-6, 168-180.

are to prevent collusion and maintain security dependence among the vassals, to keep tributaries pliant and protected, and to keep the barbarians from coming together.

In other words, we are supposed to believe that if societies on the other side of the planet are working together then it must be at our expense and that this must be prevented at any cost. Furthermore, we are apparently meant to take it as an article of faith that American political dominance in Eastern Europe — presuming the propriety of such a project on its own terms — is somehow dependent on similar dominance in Central Asia. Perhaps these things would be true in some sense if we were all navel-gazing naval strategists or pandering politicians for a living. Unfortunately for us, they are the ones who write the doctrines the rest of the country is forced to follow.[4]

Sheila Heslin, an energy expert from the Clinton White House's National Security Council, explained at the time, "U.S. policy was to promote the rapid development of Caspian energy... We did so specifically to promote the independence of these oil-rich countries, to in essence break Russia's monopoly control over the transportation of oil from that region, and frankly, to promote Western energy security through diversification of supply."[5] The California company Unocal finally gave up their pipeline quest after the cruise missile attack on Afghan training camps launched in retaliation for al Qaeda's African embassy attacks and the collapse of oil prices in the late 1990s.[6]

Aid to Afghanistan's Taliban government had continued even in the early months of the first George W. Bush administration in 2001[7] because the Taliban were still considered a check against Iran and a potential weapon against China and the former-Soviet "-stans."[8]

It is not that the current occupation is about someday building the pipeline after all, only that the story of America's neglect of Afghanistan between the Soviet war and the American one is a dangerous myth. The U.S. did intervene in that country in the Bill Clinton years, and it was to help our Saudi and Pakistani allies support the rise of the Taliban in order to advance U.S. interests, not to try to save the people from it.

Now that the U.S. occupies Afghanistan, blatant imperial exploitation continues to surface from time to time as a rationalization for America's

---

[4] Brzezinski, *The Grand Chessboard*, 38-40; David Gordon, "The Hegemonic Imperative," review of *The Grand Chessboard: American Primacy and Its Geostrategic Imperatives*, by Zbigniew Brzezinski, *Mises Review* 4, No. 4 (Winter 1998).

[5] Sheila Heslin, Testimony before the US Senate, September 17, 1997, cited in Rashid, *Taliban,* 174.

[6] Rashid, *Taliban,* 175.

[7] Elise Labott, "US Gives $43 Million to Afghanistan," CNN, May 17, 2001, http://edition.cnn.com/2001/US/05/17/us.afghanistan.aid/.

[8] Margolis, *American Raj*, 202-203.

permanent presence, though at best the U.S. may be able to limit other nations' access to resources and trade routes there. When the success of the later Obama-era troop "surge" of 2009-2012 began to be publicly doubted, U.S. Army Gen. David Petraeus held up mineral wealth as a rationale for the continued occupation. There are nearly a trillion dollars' worth of minerals in Afghanistan, the *New York Times* reported in 2010. "Pentagon officials and American geologists" had discovered "huge veins of iron, copper, cobalt, gold and critical industrial metals like lithium."

"There is stunning potential here," Petraeus said. "There are a lot of ifs, of course, but I think potentially it is hugely significant." We cannot pull our military out now, you see. If we do, Chinese businessmen may come armed with investment capital and develop these resources instead of us — and that would be catastrophic.[9] In reality, none but the most daring "adventure capitalists" from the East or West will put money into Afghan mining due to the endlessly unstable security situation and lack of infrastructure.[10] Did the generals really think the American public would be impressed by such arguments? That the U.S. Army should militarily occupy a country in the heart of Eurasia indefinitely because a few American companies might be able to make some money mining lithium there someday? Apparently.

Just as destructive as imperial, geostrategic power plays and gold digging is the evil of everyday bureaucratic politics. By 2004, America's post-September 11th war in Afghanistan became a team-building exercise for the entire U.S.-European NATO military alliance.[11] The occupation was its first major project after the war against Serbia in 1999 and was widely perceived as a test of the "cohesiveness of the alliance."[12]

In 2003, Marine Corps General Jim Jones, the supreme allied commander of NATO forces in Europe, along with other NATO-oriented interests within the Pentagon, lobbied Secretary Rumsfeld to turn over the military mission there to NATO's command.[13] Rumsfeld still wanted to avoid a large military commitment to Afghanistan. But under pressure to do something about the increasing violence in the country, he decided to go ahead and let NATO take over the mission and send European troops to pick up the slack.[14]

---

[9] James Risen, "US Identifies Vast Mineral Riches in Afghanistan," *New York Times*, June 13, 2010, http://www.nytimes.com/2010/06/14/world/asia/14minerals.html.

[10] James Bandler, "J.P. Morgan's Hunt for Afghan Gold," *Forbes*, May 11, 2011, http://fortune.com/2011/05/11/j-p-morgans-hunt-for-afghan-gold/.

[11] Suhrke, *When More is Less*, 11.

[12] Paul Gallis, "NATO in Afghanistan: A Test of the Transatlantic Alliance," Defense Technical Information Center, August 22, 2006, http://www.dtic.mil/dtic/tr/fulltext/u2/a461360.pdf.

[13] Gareth Porter, "How Afghanistan Became a War for NATO," Inter Press Service, January 3, 2011, http://www.ipsnews.net/2011/01/how-afghanistan-became-a-war-for-nato/.

[14] David Rohde and David Sanger, "How a 'Good War' in Afghanistan Went Bad," *New York Times*,

As journalist Gareth Porter pointed out,[15] Jones was quite open about his priorities, telling the American Forces Press Service that after the dissolution of the Soviet Union and their Warsaw Pact alliance, "NATO was in limbo for a bit." But after the September 11th attacks, America's NATO allies had a new "unifying anchor point" for the alliance and the bureaucracy itself. However, Jones admitted, the difficult task of "doing better" at "defining why NATO is as useful to our citizens on both sides of the Atlantic" still remained.[16] Then-Lieutenant General Karl Eikenberry also acknowledged to Congress that "the long view of the Afghanistan campaign is that it is a means to continue the transformation of the alliance."[17] Author Astri Suhrke identified a dangerous "rhetoric trap" where dire claims were made repeatedly that the future existence of the NATO alliance rested on victory in Afghanistan. Gen. Jones's claim that "if we don't succeed here, organizations like NATO, by association the European Union, and the United Nations might be relegated to the dustbin of history,"[18] framed a hopeless and impossible task as absolutely essential, even though the reasoning behind this assertion was never explained. NATO — the North Atlantic Treaty Organization — is supposed to be a defensive alliance for Western Europe and North America. It could just as easily be argued that its diversion off onto a side-project of nation-building in Afghanistan endangers, rather than secures, its existence.[19] Regardless, there seems to be little reason to think that these fears are appropriate. Despite all of NATO's failures in Afghanistan, alliance membership growth[20] and U.S. military expansion into Eastern Europe[21] continue on as before.

But America and Western Europe's military alliance bureaucracy was prepared to "help" the people of Afghanistan, no matter how hard they resisted, in order to make sure to justify its own continuing existence. If there was a silver lining in all this it was that European politicians and commanders had put so many restrictions on the use of their forces in the country that the amount of further harm they could do was more limited

---

August 12, 2007, http://www.nytimes.com/2007/08/12/world/asia/12afghan.html.

[15] Gareth Porter, "How Afghanistan Became a War for NATO."

[16] Jim Garamone, "NATO, EUCOM Transforming for New Threats," American Forces Press Service, August 26, 2011, http://www.eucom.mil/media-library/article/21430/NATO-EUCOM-transforming-new-threats.

[17] Gareth Porter, "How Afghanistan Became a War for NATO."

[18] Woodward, *Obama's Wars*, 127.

[19] Suhrke, *When More is Less*, 11.

[20] Associated Press, "Montenegro Ratifies NATO Membership in Historic Shift to Western Alliance," *Guardian,* April 28, 2017, https://www.theguardian.com/world/2017/apr/28/montenegro-ratifies-nato-membership-in-historic-shift-to-western-alliance.

[21] Elizabeth Palmer, "With Volunteers and US Tanks, Estonia Tells Russia It's 'Ready to Fight,'" CBS News, March 2, 2017, http://www.cbsnews.com/news/estonia-russia-nato-us-troops-volunteer-civilian-estonian-defense-league/.

than it otherwise could have been.[22]

A major exception to this was the ill-fated British mission to shore up central government authority in the southern Helmand Province. More than 7,000 of their soldiers fought the Taliban to a standstill between 2005 and 2009 when the first U.S. marines were sent in to reinforce them. Yet the UK never controlled more of the province than their own bases, the capital of Lashkar Gah, the town of Sangin and whatever small village or valley they were invading at any given time.[23]

The military bases of empire also become projects in search of justifications. As a Senate Foreign Relations Committee report noted in 1970, "Once an American overseas base is established it takes on a life of its own. Original missions may become outdated but new missions are developed, not only with the intention of keeping the facility going, but often to actually enlarge it. Within the government departments most directly concerned — State and Defense — we found little initiative to reduce or eliminate any of these overseas facilities."[24]

Former Cold War theoretician turned critic of American empire Chalmers Johnson observed, "The Pentagon tries to prevent local populations from reclaiming or otherwise exerting their rights over these long-established bases (as in the cases of the Puerto Rican movement to get the navy off Vieques Island, which it used largely for target practice, and of the Oldnawan movement [in Okinawa] to get the marines and air force to go home — or at least go elsewhere). It also works hard to think of ways to reestablish the right to bases from which the United States has withdrawn or been expelled (in places like the Philippines, Taiwan, Greece, and Spain)."[25] While the Bagram air base may ultimately be worthless to the American people, to the military, it is an "enduring counter-terrorism platform," which must be preserved at all costs.[26]

---

[22] Craig S. Smith, "NATO Runs Short of Troops to Expand Afghan Peacekeeping," *New York Times*, September 18, 2004, http://www.nytimes.com/2004/09/18/world/asia/nato-runs-short-of-troops-to-expand-afghan-peacekeeping.html; C. J. Chivers, "Dutch Soldiers Stress Restraint in Afghanistan," *New York Times*, April 6, 2007,
http://www.nytimes.com/2007/04/06/world/asia/06afghan.html.

[23] Ann Scott Tyson, "British Troops, Taliban in a Tug of War over Afghan Province," *Washington Post*, March 30, 2008, http://www.washingtonpost.com/wp-dyn/content/article/2008/03/29/AR2008032902033.html.

[24] US Senate Subcommittee on Security Agreements and Commitments Abroad, Committee on Foreign Relations, December 21, 1970; cited by Chalmers Johnson in, *Sorrows of Empire: Militarism, Secrecy and the End of the Republic*, (New York: Metropolitan), p. 151, cited in "US Military Bases and Empire," *Monthly Review* 53, no. 10 (March 2002), https://monthlyreview.org/2002/03/01/u-s-military-bases-and-empire/.

[25] Chalmers Johnson, *Sorrows of Empire: Militarism, Secrecy and the End of the Republic*, (New York; Metropolitan, 2004), 151-152.

[26] Kevin Baron, "Afghanistan Needs 'Thousands' More Troops, US General Says," Defense One, February 9, 2017, http://www.defenseone.com/threats/2017/02/afghanistan-needs-thousands-more-troops-us-general-says-stunning-assessment/135280/.

As America's military power in the region grew in relation to rivals Iran, Russia and China, it became that much more difficult to make the decision to leave. Yet the presence of these bases makes violent conflict with these states, the latter two of which are armed with nuclear weapons, that much more likely, and, therefore, only serve to endanger the American people, if not the careers of the officers in charge of administering the new bases.

Finally, and perhaps above all, is the ever-present issue of "the real Great Game": arms sales and control of the defense budget. Not that the U.S. government needed much persuasion beyond bin Laden's minions' attacks to justify diving headlong into the Afghan quagmire, but then came legions of New York- and Washington, D.C.-based pressure groups subsidized by American tax dollars that had been laundered through defense firms like Lockheed, Northrup Grumman, Raytheon and General Dynamics. These companies recycle a small fraction of the money they make from weapons contracts in the form of donations to think tanks and institutions full of "experts" from the "foreign policy community," who then write up endless "studies," rationalizations and justifications for staying the course in the War on Terror. Millions of dollars are also spent on directly lobbying Congress to support these policies, which keep the arms manufacturers in business.[27]

This is beyond the proverbial lobbyist-bureaucrat "conflict of interest" or "revolving door." It is the "Iron Triangle," or "Deep State," of military and intelligence officers, arms manufacturers and the congressmen, lobbyists and public relations flacks who keep the whole project going — the very same post-World War II National Security State, or "Military Industrial Complex," that President Dwight D. Eisenhower helped to construct and then belatedly warned us about,[28] and that has never been

---

[27] Sam Stein, "Top Defense Contractors Spent $27 Million Lobbying at Time of Afghan Surge Announcement," Huffington Post, March 23, 2010, http://www.huffingtonpost.com/2010/01/21/top-defense-contractors-s_n_431542.html; Jeremy Scahill, "Bipartisan Mercs? Blackwater Hires Powerful Democratic Lobbyist," Nation, May 14, 2010, https://www.thenation.com/article/bipartisan-mercs-blackwater-hires-powerful-democratic-lobbyist; C. Wright Mills, The Power Elite (Oxford: Oxford University Press, 2000); William D. Hartung, Prophets of War: Lockheed Martin and the Making of the Military-Industrial Complex (New York: Nation, 2012); Nick Turse, The Complex: How the Military Invades Our Everyday Lives (New York: Metropolitan, 2009); James Carroll, House of War: The Pentagon and the Disastrous Rise of American Power (Boston: Mariner, 2007); Tom Engelhardt, ed., Shadow Government: Surveillance, Secret Wars, and a Global Security State in a Single-Superpower World (Chicago: Haymarket, 2014); Michael J. Glennon, National Security and Double Government (Oxford: Oxford University Press, 2014); Mike Lofgren, The Deep State: The Fall of the Constitution and the Rise of a Shadow Government (London: Penguin, 2016); Dana Priest and William M. Arkin, Top Secret America: The Rise of the New American Security State (Boston: Little, Brown, 2011); William M. Arkin, American Coup: How a Terrified Government Is Destroying the Constitution (Boston: Little, Brown, 2013); Tim Shorrock, Spies for Hire: The Secret World of Intelligence Outsourcing (New York: Simon & Schuster, 2009); Richard Cummings, "Lockheed Stock and Two Smoking Barrels," Playboy, January 16, 2007, http://www.corpwatch.org/article.php?id=14307.

[28] Dwight D. Eisenhower, "The Chance for Peace," or "Cross of Iron," delivered before the American Society of Newspaper Editors, April 16, 1953,

tamed in all the decades since. It seems the national security bureaucracy replaced much of America's constitutional form of government at some point long past.[29] Their priorities now vastly outweigh those of the civilian population, just as Eisenhower had cautioned. The necessity of emergency has been their mandate to maintain power,[30] and it appears that they will never let it go.

None of these things really have anything to do with helping the people of Afghanistan or even securing true American national defense interests there. Instead, the economics of politics create a conspiracy of a thousand separate interests and motives, none of them significant enough to justify the policy on their own, yet they somehow add up to a bureaucratic inertia that has thus far proven impossible to restrain.

Missed Chances for Peace

The sad truth is that even if one accepts the case for an initial invasion, and even a small, indefinite U.S. and NATO occupation, and believes in the legitimacy of all the other rationalizations for the mission in Afghanistan since it began, there was still no need to fight a long-term war against a Taliban-based insurgency. As Anand Gopal reported, when their regime was falling in late 2001 and early 2002, many of its most important leaders were prepared to surrender on the terms set forth by America and the new Karzai regime. They sent a letter to Karzai accepting the legitimacy of the new Afghan government as well as his legitimacy as Afghanistan's interim ruler, explaining they had the full permission of Mullah Omar to surrender. The Taliban also agreed to turn in their weapons, including all their hidden caches around the country and had even taken the further initiative to withdraw from Kandahar City in the Afghan south, leaving it to coalition forces. As Gopal wrote,

> The main request of the Taliban officials in this group was to be given immunity from arrest in exchange for agreeing to abstain from political life. At this juncture, these leading Taliban members (as well as the rank and file) did not appear to view the government and its foreign backers as necessitating a 1980s-type jihad. Some members even saw the new government as Islamic and legitimate. Indeed, Mullah

---

http://www.informationclearinghouse.info/article9743.htm; Transcript of President Dwight D. Eisenhower's Farewell Address, January 17, 1961,
https://www.ourdocuments.gov/doc.php?doc=90&page=transcript.
[29] The National Security Act of 1947. Pub. L. No. 80-253 (1947),
http://global.oup.com/us/companion.websites/9780195385168/resources/chapter10/nsa/nsa.pdf.
[30] William F. Buckley, "The Party and the Deep Blue Sea," *Commonweal*, January 1952, pp. 391-392,
http://www.unz.org/Pub/Commonweal-1952jan25-00391.

Obaidullah and other former Taliban officials even surrendered to Afghan authorities in early 2002. But Karzai and other government officials ignored the overtures — largely due to pressures from the United States and the Northern Alliance, the Taliban's erstwhile enemy. … Widespread intimidation and harassment of these former Taliban ensued. Sympathetic figures in the government told Jalaluddin Haqqani and others in the group that they should flee the country, for they would not be safe in Afghanistan. So the men eventually vanished across the border into Pakistan's Baluchistan province. Many of the signatories of the letter were to become leading figures in the insurgency.

The widespread torture, murder, extortion and other abuses of former Taliban members left behind in Kandahar Province by the new U.S.-installed authorities quickly turned these acquiescent, defeated opponents into permanent insurgent enemies. Even Mullah Akhtar Muhammad Mansour, who later became the leader of the Taliban for a time after Mullah Omar died, "had accepted the new government and was living at home," Gopal wrote. "But the violent drive against former Taliban by [the new government in Kandahar Province] and U.S. Special Forces led Mansour to realize it would be a mistake to stay in Afghanistan. 'He said that this government wouldn't let him live in peace,' recalled lawmaker Ahmad Shah Achekzai, who had met him during that time. 'It wasn't a surprise to us when he finally fled to Pakistan and rejoined the Taliban.'"

For the first three years of the occupation, virtually the entire leadership of the Taliban movement, less Mullah Omar himself, tried to find a way to negotiate their return to Afghanistan in peace. Each time, a "lack of political will by the central government in Kabul and opposition from some sections of the U.S. leadership meant that such approaches were ultimately ignored." The Pentagon and CIA saw the Taliban as an enemy on equal par with al Qaeda and thought these Taliban leaders should be captured and brought to Guantánamo. But the obvious proof they were not intractable jihadists was demonstrated by their attempt to capitulate to U.S. forces. Only after continued targeting did they decide they had no option but to take up arms in resistance.[31]

Gopal elaborates on this tragedy in *No Good Men Among the Living: America, the Taliban, and the War through Afghan Eyes*. In 2002, after two months of U.S. bombing,

> [and with his] back to the wall, Mullah Omar drew up a letter to Hamid Karzai, acknowledging [his] selection as interim president. The letter also granted Omar's ministers, deputies, and aides the right to

---

[31] Anand Gopal, "Missed Opportunities in Kandahar," *Foreign Policy*, November 10, 2010, http://foreignpolicy.com/2010/11/10/missed-opportunities-in-kandahar/.

surrender and formalized the handover of his vehicles, books, and other possessions to tribal elders.

On December 5, a Taliban delegation arrived at the U.S. special forces camp north of Kandahar City to officially relinquish power. According to a participant, Karzai was asked that he allow Mullah Omar to "live in dignity" in exchange for his quiescence. The delegation members which included Defense Minister Mullah Obaidullah, Omar's trusted aide Tayeb Agha, and other key leaders, pledged to retire from politics and return to their home villages. Crucially, they also agreed that their movement would surrender arms, effectively ensuring that the Taliban could no longer function as a military entity. There would be no jihad, no resistance from the Taliban to the new order — even as leaders of al Qaeda were escaping to Pakistan to continue their holy war. The difference between the two groups may have never been so apparent, but as Washington declared victory, they passed largely unnoticed.[32]

In January of 2002, Taliban Foreign Minister Mullah Muttawakil, who had tried to warn the U.S. of the impending September 11th attacks, surrendered, just as the former finance minister, Agha Jan Mutassim, was publicly announcing the Taliban's abandonment of any effort to regroup and its support for the new Karzai government. It was, "in effect," Gopal explained, "the entire Taliban cabinet; key military commanders and important governors; diplomats; and top officials who had worked with Mullah Omar. The avalanche of surrenders knew no bounds of ideology; leaders of the notorious whip-wielding religious police were among the earliest to defect."[33]

According to Dutch journalist Bette Dam, Taliban leader Mullah Omar, after approving his fellows' letter of surrender, simply went home. The Americans were convinced Omar remained the leader of the Taliban in its insurgency. They made him "far, far bigger as an enemy than [they] should have," as Omar, Dam said, "hardly was active" after 2001. But the U.S. government was insistent on seeing Osama bin Laden and Mullah Omar as one and the same, as explained to Dam by the U.S. ambassador at the dawn of the war. Echoing Gopal's earlier analysis, Dam noted that, even on the face of it, this was clearly not true as evidenced by the Taliban's refusal to join bin Laden's international jihad against the U.S. and its allies in the first place, preferring "revolution in one country" and attempting to try to conserve the power they had already gained until al Qaeda got them into such trouble with the American superpower.[34]

---

[32] Gopal, *No Good Men*, 47.

[33] Ibid., 104-105.

[34] Bette Dam, interviewed by the author, *Scott Horton Show*, radio archive, August 24, 2016, http://scotthorton.org/interviews/82416-bette-dam/.

Alex Strick Van Linschoten and Felix Kuehn's *An Enemy We Created: The Myth of the Taliban-Al Qaeda Merger in Afghanistan* is the most exhaustive study to date on the question of the relationship between al Qaeda and the Taliban. They wrote that Omar had personally instructed Osama bin Laden that while he was a guest in Afghanistan he needed to be patient and respect the fact that the Taliban's doctrine was centered on victory in Afghanistan, rather than revolution across the region. One of Omar's associates had conveyed this position to the U.S. before September 11th as well.[35]

Bin Laden had refused to pledge allegiance to Mullah Omar. Instead, he sent a proxy so it would remain deniable that he ever had personally sworn loyalty to the Afghan leader when bin Laden's plan brought the weight of the U.S. military down upon Omar's regime.[36]

In Dam's view, one of the greatest deficiencies of the occupation was in failing to find the willingness to ask honest questions of the motives of the resistance. Afghanistan is not split by "radical Islam" and ideology, but "families, clans and tribes," and they often switch sides. Afghans "see Westerners as a tool, to use for their personal gains — to survive" in a desperate state of permanent war, extreme poverty and instability. Why does the president or a certain governor send U.S. forces here or there? To settle personal, family and tribal disputes the Americans can never understand. "[Locals] here say, 'It's the Taliban!' because they know how to speak your language." Dam has seen it "again and again" through the years: "American troops fly into a place like Helmand or Herat [Provinces] for 5 or 6 months at a time and say, 'Where is the Taliban?!' And the tribal leaders just manipulate them," using U.S. and allied forces to settle local scores. By always choosing to see each conflict as a fight between good guys and bad guys, the U.S. creates self-defeating policies and makes new enemies they have to deal with later.[37]

At the end of 2002, seeing no end in sight to U.S. and associated warlords' continued harassment, persecution and exclusion from participation in the new Afghan system, the remnants of the Taliban government began to re-form as the "Quetta Shura," named for their refuge, the southern Pakistani city of Quetta, and began their long, slow march back to power.[38]

---

[35] Van Linschoten and Kuehn, *An Enemy We Created*, 140-41, 155.

[36] Vahid Brown, "Bin Ladin's Dubious Pledge to Mullah Omar," West Point Counter Terrorism Center, January 13, 2010, https://www.ctc.usma.edu/posts/the-facade-of-allegiance-bin-ladin%E2%80%99s-dubious-pledge-to-mullah-omar.

[37] Dam, *Scott Horton Show*, August 24, 2016.

[38] Gopal, *No Good Men*, 195-196.

It's the Occupation

The implementation of backward policies by the U.S. that then lead to worse conflict has been a consistent theme throughout the history of the Afghan insurgency. First is the simple fact of the military occupation of Afghanistan by America and its Western allies, with their completely different cultures, ethnicities and predominant religion. Secondly, Western leaders have boldly and repeatedly announced their intentions to change the form of Afghanistan's government and their people's entire way of life. These are circumstances that would drive any state in America or anywhere else in the world to rise up in armed insurrection. But in case after case, we have Afghans, such as Jalaluddin Haqqani and various Taliban leaders, who were resigned to the occupation and the new government, who tried to deal and negotiate with it and the Americans, and who were targeted anyway, and then driven into the arms of the insurgency. Would anyone deny the Taliban is a religious movement? Of course not. It is their entire identity. But their religion is not why they fight. The fact is they are simply men, and virtually all men of any culture, if given half a chance, would fight back against a foreign army occupying their country, no matter what claims the invaders had made about being there to help. Additionally, as Eric Margolis has explained, the Pashtuns are a traditional warrior culture and "had defeated all previous foreign invaders since the fourth century BC. The Pashtun would fight on for another century, if necessary, or even two, until they were free of foreign occupation and able to resume their favored pastime, feuding among themselves."[39] The ancient tribal Pashtunwali honor code, which far predates Islam, mandates this. To deny or ignore this is a disservice to the truth and to the American people as well. Despite the narrative the government, media and military continually tell us and each other, U.S. troops are not seen by Afghans as a benevolent force, creating a new grass-roots democratic system for the people to use to secure the blessings of liberty, but as invading imperial enemies to be resisted. The term *insurgency* itself implies reaction and resistance against a greater, dominating power.

None of this is to say the insurgency is itself an honorable enterprise. Their terrorist attacks on civilian targets and massacres of prisoners discredit them, qualifying them as war criminals. But Americans commit war crimes as well. And as Chris Sands, Afghan correspondent for the *National*, observed, when civilians are killed by the Taliban in Kandahar, locals still blame the [U.S.-supported] government instead of the Taliban, who are "rarely the subject of people's fury" in such circumstances.[40]

---

[39] Margolis, *American Raj*, 218.

[40] Chris Sands, "Chaos Central," in *The Case for Withdrawal from Afghanistan*, ed. Nick Turse, (New

In the Vietnam War, the "wise men" of America's foreign policy establishment had created a consensus and consent for their war by claiming the Vietnamese fought us because they're communists. The Soviet Union and the Maoist Chinese would have knocked all the dominoes down until the Reds ruled all of Southeast Asia if we did not stop them in Vietnam.[41] And, it was decided, anyone fighting on that side was fighting for the same agenda, too. It did not matter that the Vietnamese had a proud and ancient history of resistance to all foreign invaders, including multiple successful defensive wars against China.[42] It did not matter that the implementation of the "Clear, Hold, Build" counterinsurgency strategy, in the form of the "Strategic Hamlet Program" beginning as early as 1962, complete with "resettlement and control measures" for the local population, was driving, rather than diminishing, the South Vietnamese insurgency.[43] All that mattered was that everyone of importance in the foreign policy communities in New York and Washington, D.C., wanted to avoid seeming weak on communism.[44] Interestingly, in a manner similar to the Taliban years later, the Viet Minh, the South Vietnamese Communist leadership, had been acquiescent to the South Vietnamese government and American power. But in the late 1950s, South Vietnamese President Ngo Dinh Diem pursued them ruthlessly, driving them to violent resistance in the first place.[45] American policymakers' refusal to base their policy on the reality of Vietnamese nationalist resistance against the American invasion helped to lead the U.S. deeper into that quagmire for years before it finally withdrew.

The resistance in Afghanistan is no different. They fight because they have been invaded, occupied and targeted by a foreign army. Their reaction would be no different if they were Catholics, Taoists or Buddhists; Russians, Filipinos or Brazilians.

Even still, for the first couple of years after the initial fighting was over

---

York: Verso, 2010), 64-70.

[41] Gareth Porter, *Perils of Dominance: Imbalance of Power and the Road to War in Vietnam* (Oakland: University of California Press, 2006), 229-258.

[42] Alexander Woodside, *Vietnam and the Chinese Model: A Comparative Study of Nguyen and Ch'ing Civil Government in the First Half of the Nineteenth Century* (Cambridge, MA: Harvard University Press, 1971), 19-21; Michael Sullivan, "Ask the Vietnamese About War, and They Think China, Not the US," Morning Edition, NPR News, May 1, 2015, http://www.npr.org/sections/parallels/2015/05/01/402572349/ask-the-vietnamese-about-war-and-they-think-china-not-the-u-s.

[43] "The Strategic Hamlet Program, 1961-1963," *Pentagon Papers*, Gravel Edition, Volume 2, (Boston: Beacon, 1971), 128-159. https://www.mtholyoke.edu/acad/intrel/pentagon2/pent4.htm.

[44] Edward G. Lansdale, "Vietnam: Do We Understand Revolution?," *Foreign Affairs*, October 1964, https://www.foreignaffairs.com/articles/vietnam/1964-10-01/viet-nam-do-we-understand-revolution; Samuel P. Huntington, "The Bases of Accommodation," *Foreign Affairs*, July 1968, https://www.foreignaffairs.com/articles/vietnam/1968-07-01/bases-accommodation.

[45] Gareth Porter, *Vietnam: The Politics of Bureaucratic Socialism*, (Ithica, NY: Cornell University Press, 1993) 17-18.

and the Taliban and al Qaeda had fled, the American soldiers and marines occupying the country were mostly sitting around feeling stranded and bored with no enemies to fight. So, just like the larger terror war, writ small, they set out to make new ones.[46]

It took a while for things to get bad enough to make it worse. People of all different tribal and ethnic groupings were happy to see the end of Taliban rule. The U.S. had the run of the place. But instead of being light and fast and knocking the enemy's lights out and leaving, the occupation grew and grew. As former Army Ranger Rory Fanning explained, "The Taliban had surrendered a few months before I arrived in Afghanistan in late 2002, but that wasn't good enough for our politicians back home and the generals giving the orders. Our job was to draw people back into the fight."[47]

In addition to the Taliban, the Haqqani Network, headed by Mawlawi Jalaluddin Haqqani, has been a huge problem for the U.S. and Afghan government over the past decade. It is allied with, and almost equal in power to, the Taliban itself. As Gopal explained years later, America's war with the Haqqani Network "could [also] have gone so differently" at the beginning of the war. Al Qaeda was dead or had fled. The Taliban had given up the fight and were trying to negotiate with the new government.

> Tens of thousands of U.S. forces, however, had arrived on Afghan soil, post-9/11, with one objective: to wage a war on terror. ...
>
> [T]he U.S. would prosecute that war even though there was no enemy to fight. To understand how America's battle in Afghanistan went so wrong for so long, a (hidden) history lesson is in order. In those early years after 2001, driven by the idée fixe that the world was rigidly divided into terrorist and non-terrorist camps, Washington allied with Afghan warlords and strongmen. Their enemies became ours, and through faulty intelligence, their feuds became repackaged as "counter-terrorism." The story of Jalaluddin Haqqani, who turned from America's potential ally into its greatest foe, is the paradigmatic case of how the war on terror created the very enemies it sought to eradicate.

Soon after the invasion, the U.S. made a surrender offer to the CIA's old mujahideen ally that included a stint in jail, which Haqqani refused. In retaliation, the U.S. not only bombed his house, killing a family member, but also a school Haqqani had built for the poor — a strike which killed

---

[46] Van Linschoten and Kuehn, *An Enemy We Created*, 262-263.

[47] Rory Fanning, "Talking to the Young in a World That Will Never Truly Be 'Postwar,'" TomDispatch, April 7, 2016, http://www.tomdispatch.com/blog/176125/tomgram%3A _rory_fanning,_talking_to_the_young_in_a_world_that_will_never_truly_be_%22 postwar%22.

34 people, "almost all children," Gopal reported. Though Haqqani wished to negotiate his surrender, the U.S. had instead decided to ally with another warlord, Pacha Khan Zadran, or "PKZ," who promised to defeat Haqqani for the Americans. Gopal continues:

> On December 20, 2001, the American-backed Hamid Karzai was preparing for his inauguration as interim president of Afghanistan. Nearly 100 of Loya Paktia's[48] leading tribal elders set out that afternoon in a convoy for Kabul to congratulate Karzai and declare their loyalty, a gesture that would go far in legitimizing his rule among the country's border population. From Pakistan, Haqqani sent family members, close friends, and political allies to participate in the motorcade — an olive branch to the new government. ...

> Near sunset, [the convoy] reached a hilltop and was forced to stop: PKZ and hundreds of his armed men were blocking the road. Malek Sardar, an elder from Haqqani's tribe, approached him. "He was demanding that the elders should accept him as leader of Loya Paktia," Sardar told me. "He wanted our thumb prints and signatures right then and there." Sardar promised to return after the inauguration to discuss the matter, but PKZ would not budge, so the convoy backed up and headed off to find a different route to Kabul.

> On his satellite phone, Sardar called officials in the Afghan capital and at the U.S. consulate in Peshawar, Pakistan, looking for help, but he was too late. PKZ, who had the ear of key American military figures, had informed them that a "Haqqani-al Qaeda" cavalcade was making its way toward Kabul. Shortly thereafter, amid deafening explosions, cars started bursting into flames. "We could see lights in the sky, fire everywhere. People were screaming and we ran," Sardar said. The Americans were bombing the convoy. The attacks would continue for hours. As Sardar and others took cover in a pair of nearby villages, planes circled back and struck both locations, destroying nearly 20 homes and killing dozens of inhabitants. In all, 50 people, including many prominent tribal elders, died in the assault. ...

> Later, a tribal commission set up to investigate the massacre determined that PKZ had fed the Americans "intelligence" that Qale Niazi was a Haqqani stronghold. According to a United Nations investigation, 52 people had died: 17 men, 10 women, and 25 children.

Haqqani and his men went into hiding in Pakistan's tribal provinces. But in 2002 Haqqani tried again to make peace, sending his brother Ibrahim Omari and many of his fighters to Afghanistan to pledge allegiance to the new government. They went to work for the CIA in "anti-

---

[48] Loya Paktia is a region of Eastern Afghanistan that includes Paktia, Paktika and Khost Provinces.

terrorist" militias known as "Counterterrorism Pursuit Teams," but were soon betrayed by the military, who, acting on behalf of their favored warlord, PKZ, arrested and tortured Omari and his men at the Bagram Air Base prison. The U.S. government had finally succeeded in making a deadly enemy out of another of their holy-warrior, freedom-fighter heroes of earlier times. Haqqani's son Sirajuddin now controls the group, which, as a part of the anti-U.S. insurgency, has killed at least hundreds of civilians and Western and Afghan troops in the years since these opportunities were wasted. In 2009, a Jordanian double-agent working for the Haqqanis killed seven and wounded six CIA officers and contractors in a suicide bombing at Camp Chapman, near the city of Khost,[49] leading to further escalation of the U.S. war against this former CIA asset and unnecessary enemy in the following years.[50]

Afghan warlord Gul Agha Shirzai, who took over and prepared Bagram Airfield for the U.S. at the beginning of the war, became the biggest mobster around, with his own Blackwater-type mercenary force and large interests in the opium industry. But again, by April 2002, when the bulk of U.S. military forces arrived at Bagram, al Qaeda was already long gone, and the Taliban had completely abandoned the field. There were no enemies left to fight, and yet, U.S. forces had "a clear political mandate: defeat terrorism."

> Eager to survive and prosper, [Shirzai] and his commanders followed the logic of the American presence to its obvious conclusion. They would create enemies where there were none, exploiting the perverse incentive mechanism that the Americans — without even realizing it — had put in place. Shirzai's enemies became America's enemies, his battles its battles. His personal feuds and jealousies were repackaged as "counter-terrorism," his business interests as Washington's.

In one case, Shirzai falsely accused a local tribal elder named Hajji Burget Khan of having ties to terrorists, leading to a massive, violent raid on his village which led to the deaths of a few people, including Khan, and permanent resentment against the American invaders, who believed they were "fighting terrorism" and keeping America safe. Gopal concluded, "In the years to come thousands would be killed on all sides, but it was the memory of Hajji Burget Khan's murder that the villagers would never relinquish."[51]

---

[49] Elizabeth Gould and Paul Fitzgerald, *Crossing Zero: The AfPak War at the Turning Point of American Empire* (San Francisco: City Lights, 2011), 133-135.

[50] Anand Gopal, "How the US Created the Afghan War — and Then Lost It," TomDispatch, April 29, 2014, http://www.tomdispatch.com/post/175837/tomgram%3A_anand_gopal,_how_to_lose _a_war_that_wasn't_there.

[51] Gopal, *No Good Men*, 107-112.

Elsewhere, Gopal wrote:

> The killing of Hajji Burget Khan is often cited as the single most important destabilizing factor in Maiwand district and other Ishaqzai [tribal] areas. Three Taliban commanders from the region ... all mentioned the killing as one of the main factors that led them to join the insurgency. Afghan government officials concede that it had disastrous effects in the area.[52]

Jan Muhammad Khan (JMK) was another warlord, also a murderer, dope dealer, child rapist and good friend and fellow tribesman of President Hamid Karzai. Though the local population hated and feared his tyranny, Karzai appointed JMK to be governor of Uruzgan Province. There was a battle going on in Uruzgan, a struggle for dominance between JMK and Karzai's Popalzai tribes and the Ghilzai tribes. JMK completely exploited U.S. troops, using them to slaughter his enemies in the previous provincial administration, men who had always opposed the Taliban and had supported the new U.S.-backed government. He even came up with missions for U.S. troops to go out to "fight drugs," while in fact just sending them to kill or otherwise neutralize his Ghilzai black market business competition and to keep heroin prices artificially high. America's disastrous relationship with JMK serves as just one example of the impossibility of the U.S. ever being in the position to understand who is who in Afghanistan or make good choices about whom to support or target. As Gopal demonstrates, anti-Taliban and pro-American tribal leaders, politicians and officials have repeatedly been shot, rounded up and tortured — many have even ended up in Guantánamo Bay.

In the north, there are also horrible warlords, but there have been far fewer U.S. troops for them to use as tools against each other, so ceasefires have mostly reigned. It was the abuse of innocents at the hands of U.S. soldiers being used by the likes of Shirzai and JMK that drove the rise of the resistance in the early years.[53]

Girls' Schools and Nation Building

With the growing military occupation came a growing list of new responsibilities to fulfill. It became the mission of America and the NATO alliance not to "fight terror," but to spread democracy, create a parliament, liberate and educate oppressed women and girls, abolish poppy farming and build a whole new physical infrastructure of roads and buildings — a

---

[52] Anand Gopal, "Coalition Violence in Southern Afghanistan," *Foreign Policy*, November 17, 2010, http://foreignpolicy.com/2010/11/17/coalition-violence-in-southern-afghanistan/.
[53] Gopal, *No Good Men*, 118-131, 203.

new nation. The State Department, Non-Governmental Organizations (NGOs) and contractors of every kind established themselves in Kabul. An entirely new NATO bureaucracy — the International Security Assistance Force (ISAF), known to American G.I.s as "I Suck At Fighting" or "In Sandals And Flip-flops"[54] — was established in Kabul. All of these entities were certain their presence was necessary to bring Afghan society into the brave, new future. Neighborhoods of mansions grew up all around the capital of this poorest of countries as various special interests cashed in, and an entire corrupt culture of decadence established itself in the country — especially Kabul, where politicians and power brokers built their giant houses[55] and where drugs,[56] indentured servitude,[57] prostitution (including of children)[58] and graft thrived. Since then, Afghanistan has consistently ranked near the worst in the world in terms of corruption.[59]

Americans were, frankly, drunk on revenge and hubris. Despite all reason, they allowed themselves to be convinced there was nothing that could not be accomplished by U.S. soldiers and marines, up to and including "ending tyranny in our world." They were all such brave and heroic idols, so full of valor and honor and freedom, that there was nothing on earth that could stand in their way.[60] These were all just feelings, propaganda slogans chanted and repeated to achieve a consensus to go forward, for one thing, with the impossible plan of remaking one of the most primitive and warlike societies on the planet — one that, due in part to U.S. intervention in the first place, had already been at war for 30 years. This nation-building task was to be accomplished by NATO Eurocrats and American teenagers and twenty-somethings with automatic

---

[54] Michael Hastings, "The Runaway General," *Rolling Stone*, June 22, 2010, http://www.rollingstone.com/politics/news/the-runaway-general-20100622.

[55] Karin Brulliard, "Affluent Afghans Make Their Homes in Opulent 'Poppy Palaces,'" *Washington Post*, June 6, 2010, http://www.washingtonpost.com/wp-dyn/content/article/2010/06/05/AR2010060502872.html.

[56] Matthieu Aikins, "Afghanistan: The Making of a Narco State," *Rolling Stone*, December 4, 2014, http://www.rollingstone.com/politics/news/afghanistan-the-making-of-a-narco-state-20141204.

[57] Jessica Shulberg, "The American Government Is Funding Human Trafficking," *New Republic*, November 14, 2014, https://newrepublic.com/article/120269/contractors-violate-us-zero-tolerance-policy-human-trafficking.

[58] John Nova Lomax, "WikiLeaks: Texas Company Helped Pimp Little Boys to Stoned Afghan Cops," *Houston Press*, December 7, 2010, http://www.houstonpress.com/news/wikileaks-texas-company-helped-pimp-little-boys-to-stoned-afghan-cops-6718414.

[59] "Corruption Perceptions Index, National Integrity System's Assessment, Afghanistan, 2015," Transparency International, http://www.transparency.org/research/cpi/overview; Rod Nordland and Jawad Sukhanyar, "US-Backed Effort to Fight Afghan Corruption Is a Near-Total Failure, Audit Finds," *New York Times*, September 27, 2016, https://www.nytimes.com/2016/09/28/world/asia/afghanistan-corruption-financial-disclosure.html.

[60] George W. Bush, "Inaugural Address."

rifles who were, essentially, expected to just will it to happen. The fact that this made no sense whatsoever was beside the point. Obvious truth no longer mattered. "Everything changed," they said. "United we stand" was the popular slogan on TV. "You're either with us, or you are with the terrorists." And since the decisions of "us" were being made by our political leaders, the role of the American people was said to be to love and support their policies, or, in the famous words of Bill O'Reilly, formerly of Fox News, "Shut up."

Since the beginning of the occupation, the American people have been subjected to an endless barrage of propaganda about helping the people of Afghanistan. Entire legions of both honest and cynical do-gooders have spun endless tales of all the great things they are attempting to do for the Afghan people. First Lady Laura Bush contributed greatly to the theme that the U.S. was in Afghanistan on a permanent nation-building mission in her radio address of November 18, 2001, in which she vowed the War on Terrorism would also be "a fight for the rights and dignity of women" in Afghanistan and promised that the U.S. and its allies were going to liberate them, not just from the oppression of Taliban rule, but from that of their cultural traditions as well, soon adding elementary school photo opportunities and visits with women in Kabul to reinforce her message.[61] Though it may seem well-intentioned and innocuous, this was actually throwing down the gauntlet and defining the goals of the war so broadly that it could never be won, and so could never be allowed to end. This was especially true considering that the Northern Alliance were horrible oppressors of women themselves and that among the Pashtuns, the Taliban's Islamist law was actually often more liberal than the ancient Pashtunwali code and tribal customs, including on the all-important question of the right of women to own property.[62] There is no doubt that quality of life for many has improved in terms of access to roads, electricity, schools and other basic services in the bigger cities compared to life under the Taliban. And it is true that many well-intentioned people have spent much effort trying to help the Afghan people.[63] But if this is truly the purpose of America's mission there, then why is it, experienced Central Asia reporter Eric Margolis asks, that the U.S. says virtually nothing about the oppression of women in Tajikistan, India and Saudi Arabia, where traditions are not much different? It must be because protecting women's rights as a reason for occupation is really just public relations for the rubes, he concludes.[64]

---

[61] James Gerstenzang and Lisa Getter, "Laura Bush Addresses State of Afghan Women," *Los Angeles Times*, November 18, 2001, http://articles.latimes.com/2001/nov/18/news/mn-5602.

[62] Gopal, *No Good Men*, 173.

[63] Skateistan, skateboards for Afghan kids, https://skateistan.org/.

[64] Margolis, *War at the Top of the World*, 67-68.

Some international aid workers recognize that from a certain point of view, they are the accomplices of those who wage wars they themselves would never approve of, simply due to the fact that the militaries involved count on the presence of NGOs and aid workers to help mitigate the worst of the deprivation their violence causes. Bill Kelsey, a relief pilot who delivered aid to Afghanistan at the beginning of the war, explains that he and others like him are simply trying to do the right thing, and to also represent America well, yet he struggles with the ethical dilemma many people in the aid industry all face — namely, the degree to which they are "co-dependent" with the warriors whose policies they seek to ameliorate. Additionally, these groups must often channel funds and supplies to the worst actors in violent conflicts in the name of neutrality. In many cases, food aid that is meant to feed starving civilians goes instead to soldiers, prolonging the conflicts that lead to the deprivation in the first place. Even when the food is not taken directly by soldiers, relief for civilians still frees up extra food for the soldiers that would not otherwise be available.[65]

After "major combat operations have ended," and "civilian control" kicks in, the distortions of power are just as bad. It makes no sense for foreigners to build a more powerful government and military than the locals could afford to keep even if they wanted to. Afghanistan's entire gross domestic product is less than twenty billion dollars per year.[66] The U.S. spends more than four billion dollars per year just on maintaining the Afghan National Army.[67] According to the Special Inspector General for Afghanistan Reconstruction (SIGAR), while President Obama requested more than four billion dollars for Afghan security forces for the fiscal year 2017, the Afghan government "planned to contribute only $336 million in 2016, approximately 17% of [the Afghan government's] total estimated domestic revenues for that year, to cover the expenses of its Ministry of Interior (including all police forces) and Ministry of Defense (including the army)." In effect, the American policy amounts to either a plan to stay forever to prop up the endlessly dependent Afghan state or a plan for its eventual collapse.

Occupation forces focused on impossible projects like poppy

---

[65] Bill Kelsey, interviewed by the author, *Scott Horton Show,* radio archive, March 24, 2007, http://scotthorton.org/interviews/2007/03/24/antiwar-radio-bill-kelsey/; Andrew Anthony, "Does Humanitarian Aid Prolong Wars?," *Guardian,* April 24, 2010, https://www.theguardian.com/society/2010/apr/25/humanitarian-aid-war-linda-polman.

[66] "Afghanistan GDP," Trading Economics, http://www.tradingeconomics.com/afghanistan/gdp; "South Asia: Afghanistan," CIA World Factbook, https://www.cia.gov/library/publications/the-world-factbook/geos/af.html.

[67] "High-Risk List," Special Inspector General for Afghanistan Reconstruction, January 2017, https://www.sigar.mil/pdf/spotlight/2017_High-Risk_List.pdf; Yochi J. Dreazen, "The US Spends $14K per Afghan Troop Per Year, but Each Earns $1,872," *Atlantic,* April 16, 2012, http://www.theatlantic.com/international/archive/2012/04/the-us-spends-14k-per-afghan-troop-per-year-but-each-earns-1-872/255934/.

eradication, while simultaneously depending on criminals and warlords —
including heroin dealers — to serve as governors and policemen across
the country, further increasing corruption and exacerbating the insurgency
in response.[68]

An "Afghan-owned" system imposed from the outside can never be a
good fit, even assuming the goodwill and expertise of the foreigners doing
the implementing, because as long as the government is dependent on easy
outside revenue, they will not do the work of creating the security
necessary for real wealth to be created. Thus, America is creating a "rentier
state" in Afghanistan, as journalist Astri Suhrke wrote,[69] though a modified
version. Rather than exploiting Afghanistan's natural resources, the
government administrators and NGOs are extracting all their wealth from
Western taxpayers as the money comes *in* to this desperately poor country.
Just the same, the U.S. and its allies are building a boom town, destined to
be a future ghost town, in the heart of the capital city. And since the money
is almost entirely coming from outside the country, especially for the cost
of the national army and police, it makes the government accountable only
to its foreign financiers rather than the people they supposedly serve. (Not
that taxation was ever a guarantee of representation).

In one of the poorest countries in the world, there have been attempts
by NATO governments and NGOs to indulge in all sorts of projects that
could never be maintained without endless amounts of money from
Western governments, beginning with the road system, but also including
the courts, government-run agricultural and mining projects, drug wars,
civilian air industry, dams, farms, expensive hospitals, office parks,
buildings and technological projects, and on and on and on.

SIGAR reported in January 2017, "Much of the more than $115 billion
the United States has committed to Afghanistan reconstruction projects
and programs risks being wasted because the Afghans cannot sustain the
investment — financially or functionally — without massive, continued
donor [nation] support. ... Donors were expected to finance
approximately 69% of Afghanistan's $6.5 billion ... national budget [in
2016]." The inspectors cite a World Bank report stating that Afghanistan's
"aid dependence will continue beyond 2030."[70]

---

[68] Scott Baldauf, "Afghanistan's New Jihad Targets Poppy Production," *Christian Science Monitor*, May
16, 2005, http://www.csmonitor.com/2005/0516/p07s01-wosc.html; Gareth Porter, "Afghanistan:
US, NATO Forces Rely on Warlords for Security," Inter Press Service, October 29, 2009,
http://www.ipsnews.net/2009/10/afghanistan-us-nato-forces-rely-on-warlords-for-security/;
Abagail Hall, "America Risks Losing the War on Terror in Afghanistan Unless it Legalizes the
Opium Trade," Quartz, December 9, 2016, http://qz.com/859268/americas-failed-war-on-drugs-
in-afghanistan-is-threatening-to-doom-its-war-on-terror-as-well/.

[69] Suhrke, *When More is Less*, 15-17.

[70] "Navigating Risk and Uncertainty in Afghanistan," World Bank, Brussels Conference on
Afghanistan, October 4–5, 2016, cited in "High-Risk List," Special Inspector General for

Furthermore, U.S. and allied aid fails to achieve lasting benefits to the Afghan economy because so much of the money goes to the foreign contractors hired to do the work that the money does not trickle down into the local economy. The Afghan people never have a chance to build new businesses to fulfill the needs of their fellow citizens. Despite the billions of dollars poured into the Afghan economy, regular people see virtually none of it.

As the *Independent's* Middle East correspondent, Patrick Cockburn, explained in 2010, widespread hunger remained an issue even in Kabul, the capital city and heart of the occupation — military and civilian — where the most money was being spent. Aid money arrives in massive amounts, he explained, but is then diverted through the numerous organizations, each of them taking their cut along the way. Aid money can help people in limited circumstances, of course, but no amount of it can ever really act as investment capital for the kind of industries that can generate real wealth for the people until peace and long-term stability are achieved.[71]

As one SIGAR report stated,

> [C]ontracting represents a high risk to the success of Afghanistan reconstruction. The usual difficulties of contract management are magnified and aggravated by Afghanistan's remoteness, active insurgency, widespread corruption, limited ministerial capability, difficulties in collecting and verifying data, and other issues. ... SIGAR has found that challenges in Afghanistan are so widespread that sometimes there is an assumption that if you throw enough money or people at a problem, the status quo will improve. In other words, implementers sometimes think their initial objective need not be precise, because the intervention will surely do some good somewhere.[72]

In many cases, SIGAR concedes, the U.S. ends up "channeling material resources to insurgent groups."

> Surveys and anecdotal evidence indicate that corrupt officials at all levels of government victimized and alienated the Afghan population. Substantial U.S. funds found their way to insurgent groups, some portion of which was due to corruption. Corruption also undermined faith in the international reconstruction effort. The Afghan public witnessed limited oversight of lucrative reconstruction projects by the

---

Afghanistan Reconstruction, January 2017, https://www.sigar.mil/pdf/spotlight/2017_High-Risk_List.pdf.

[71] Patrick Cockburn, interviewed by the author, *Scott Horton Show*, radio archive, December 20, 2010, http://scotthorton.org/interviews/antiwar-radio-patrick-cockburn-16/.

[72] "High-Risk List," SIGAR.

military and aid community, leading to bribery, fraud, extortion, and nepotism, as well as the empowerment of abusive warlords and their militias.[73]

As Suhrke points out, it has been in the interest of all the U.S. and international bureaucracies at the UN and NATO to try to prove they could rebuild Afghanistan in America's image. The same dynamic played out in Vietnam two generations before. For the State Department, the Pentagon, aid agencies and NGOs, Afghanistan is an enormous "experiment," one with all the perverse economic incentives involved in virtually all levels of bureaucracy and contracting. Except in Afghanistan it is an experiment being run with far more money, far less accountability and far greater consequences than the average government program. And since nothing is ever really accomplished in this war, the answer continues to be to "invest" more in similar projects in the hope that one day it will finally all pay off. In business, this is known as "throwing good money after bad." In the private sector, eventual bankruptcy serves as the ultimate check on those stuck believing, despite all evidence, that success is just around the corner. But in government work, with the taxpayers and bondholders footing the bill, this kind of continual failure can go on, seemingly forever.[74]

Corruption in Afghanistan remains at historic levels. It is not just the $43 million gas station.[75] America has spent more than $100 billion on Afghan reconstruction. In early 2017, SIGAR released a report explaining that, "[a]djusted for inflation, the $115 billion in U.S. appropriations provided to reconstruct Afghanistan exceeds the funds committed to the Marshall Plan, the U.S. aid program that, between 1948 and 1952, helped 16 West European countries recover in the aftermath of World War II." The reconstruction effort remains "tenuous and incomplete," SIGAR says. "Much of the reconstruction mission is at risk."[76] Previously, in April 2016, SIGAR issued a report admitting they had no way to verify if any of the more than $759 million they had distributed in the name of education in the country over the past decade and a half had made any difference whatsoever.[77] Stories of State Department, U.S. Agency for International

---

[73] "Corruption in Conflict: Lessons Learned from the US Experience with Corruption in Afghanistan," Special Inspector General for Afghanistan Reconstruction, September 2016, https://www.sigar.mil/interactive-reports/corruption-in-conflict/lessons.html.

[74] Suhrke, *When More is Less*, 1-8.

[75] Cassandra Vinograd, "US Spent $43 Million on Afghanistan Gas Station," NBC News, November 2, 2015, http://www.nbcnews.com/news/world/u-s-spent-43-million-afghanistan-gas-station-sigar-report-n454036.

[76] "High-Risk List," SIGAR.

[77] "Primary and Secondary Education in Afghanistan: Comprehensive Assessments Needed to Determine the Progress and Effectiveness of over $759 Million in DOD, State, and USAID Programs," Special Inspector General for Afghanistan Reconstruction, April 2016,

Development (USAID) and Pentagon contractors charging millions of dollars to deliver worthless school buildings with no electricity or plumbing, in the middle of nowhere, for "ghost students" who either never existed or were too far away to attend, are legion.[78] Yet, the money just keeps coming.[79] Afghanistan is consistently ranked among the most corrupt countries in the world.[80] The money comes in from the U.S. and other Western governments, zigzags through Afghanistan's various slush funds and lands in corrupt officials' private bank accounts in the Persian Gulf.[81] Provincial Reconstruction Teams, sent hither and yon to disperse U.S. aid to the Afghan people over the years, have been only a model of corruption and inefficiency, doling out money to the connected and accomplishing nothing for the people. There has been virtually no accountability for the completion of projects or for criminal fraud and abuse of aid money.[82]

Another SIGAR report, from September 2016, revealed U.S. sponsored efforts to crack down on official corruption by leaders of the National Unity Government were "a near-total failure." The "High Office of Oversight" was completely unable to enforce their demands for disclosures by the highest Afghan officials, much less hold them accountable for their various embezzling schemes.[83]

https://www.sigar.mil/pdf/audits/SIGAR-16-32-AR.pdf.

[78] Steve Rennie, "Afghan Enrollment Claims Fail to Make Grade; School Numbers Don't Add Up," *Winnipeg Free Press*, February 10, 2011, http://www.winnipegfreepress.com/breakingnews/afghan-enrolment-claims-fail-to-make-grade-school-numbers-dont-add-up-115705699.html; Heath Druzin, "Report: Contractors Were Paid Millions but Afghan School Remains Dangerous, Unfinished," *Stars and Stripes*, July 18, 2013, https://www.stripes.com/news/report-contractors-were-paid-millions-but-afghan-school-remains-dangerous-unfinished-1.230953; Megan McCloskey et al., "Behold: How the US Blew $17 Billion in Afghanistan," ProPublica, December 18, 2015, https://www.pri.org/stories/2015-12-18/behold-american-taxpayer-what-happened-nearly-half-billion-your-dollars; Azmat Khan, "Ghost Students, Ghost Teachers, Ghost Schools," BuzzFeed News, July 9, 2015, https://www.buzzfeed.com/azmatkhan/the-big-lie-that-helped-justify-americas-war-in-afghanistan.

[79] Cheryl Benard, "Expensive and Useless: America's Botched Afghanistan Aid," *National Interest*, June 7, 2016, http://nationalinterest.org/feature/expensive-useless-americas-botched-afghanistan-aid-16491?.

[80] Joel Brinkley, "Money Pit: The Monstrous Failure of US Aid to Afghanistan," *World Affairs Journal*, January/February 2013, http://www.worldaffairsjournal.org/article/money-pit-monstrous-failure-us-aid-afghanistan; Marguerite Ward, "Afghanistan is on the Brink After US Invests $100 Billion," CNBC, February 3, 2016, http://www.cnbc.com/2016/02/03/afghanistan-is-on-the-brink-after-us-invests-100-billion.html.

[81] Andrew Higgins, "Officials Puzzle Over Millions of Dollars Leaving Afghanistan by Plane for Dubai," *Washington Post*, February 25, 2010, http://www.washingtonpost.com/wp-dyn/content/article/2010/02/24/AR2010022404914.html; Michael Isikoff, "Run on Afghan Bank's Deposits Reported," NBC News, September 2, 2010, http://www.nbcnews.com/id/38976292/ns/world_news-south_and_central_asia/t/run-afghan-banks-deposits-reported/.

[82] Nordland and Sukhanyar, "US-Backed Effort to Fight Afghan Corruption."

[83] "Afghanistan's High Office of Oversight: Personal Asset Declarations of High Ranking Afghan Government Officials Are Not Consistently Registered and Verified," Office of Special Projects,

A 2011 *Wall Street Journal* investigation revealed massive corruption at the U.S.-supported Dawood National Military Hospital in Kabul, including systemic abuse and neglect of wounded soldiers and policemen who could not afford to bribe the doctors and nurses to take care of them and so were instead left to die of their wounds or starve to death. These problems persisted for years after the U.S. Army first took note of them in 2006. The Afghan National Army general in charge was a common criminal who during his tenure stole tens of millions of dollars' worth of drugs and medical supplies while extorting patients for the slightest bit of actual medical care.[84] Two witnesses later accused the American general in charge of the U.S. training mission in Afghanistan, Lt. Gen. William B. Caldwell, of attempting to thwart the opening of an investigation by the Department of Defense inspector general due to concerns that it would make President Obama and the Democrats look bad if the scandal became public in the months before the mid-term congressional elections of 2010.[85]

The U.S. and Afghan governments built a massive and extremely expensive power plant near Kabul that was completely redundant with existing facilities and nearly useless. They also spent hundreds of millions of dollars on diesel generators for Kandahar City, which the local government could never afford to run itself in the long term. But don't worry, the army said, these generators were only meant as a temporary "bridging solution" until the new hydroelectric Kajak Dam in the neighboring Helmand Province could be finished.[86] It never was.[87] Like a Chinese "ghost city," these projects are built based on political connections and considerations rather than economic necessity, and they fail for the same reason.[88]

Special Inspector General for Afghanistan Reconstruction, September 19, 2016, https://www.sigar.mil/pdf/special%20projects/SIGAR-16-60-SP.pdf.

[84] Maria Abi-Habib, "At Afghan Military Hospital, Graft and Deadly Neglect," *Wall Street Journal*, September 3, 2011, http://www.wsj.com/articles/SB10001424053111904480904576496703389391710.

[85] Gareth Porter, "General's Defense on Afghan Scandal Ducks Key Evidence," Inter Press Service, September 13, 2012, http://www.ipsnews.net/2012/09/generals-defence-on-afghan-scandal-ducks-key-evidence/.

[86] Rajiv Chandrasekaran, "US Construction Projects in Afghanistan Challenged by Inspector General's Report," *Washington Post*, July 30, 2012, https://www.washingtonpost.com/world/national-security/us-construction-projects-in-afghanistan-challenged-by-inspector-generals-report/2012/07/29/gJQAZuLSJX_story.html.

[87] Ben Brody, "USAID's $500 Million Dam Project Circling the Drain in Afghanistan," Global Post, August 8, 2014, https://www.pri.org/stories/2014-08-08/usaid-s-500-million-dam-project-circling-drain-afghanistan; Megan Rose, "Afghanistan Waste Exhibit A: Kajaki Dam, More Than $300M Spent and Still Not Done," ProPublica, January 19, 2016, https://www.propublica.org/article/afghanistan-waste-kajaki-dam-more-than-300-million-spent-still-not-done.

[88] Pratap Chatergee, "Paying Off the Warlords," in *The Case for Withdrawal from Afghanistan,* edited by Nick Turse, (New York: Verso, 2010), 82-86.

In October of 2016, SIGAR released an audit of the military and USAID's "investment" in Afghanistan's road system. They found that "since 2002, USAID and DOD have spent approximately $2.8 billion to construct and repair Afghanistan's road infrastructure, and perform capacity-building activities." According to Afghan officials — the Americans are unable to travel to see the sites for themselves due to the "security situation" — 20 percent of the roads the U.S. has built have been "destroyed" while the other 80 percent "continue to deteriorate." The report continued, "USAID estimated that unless maintained, it would cost about $8.3 billion to replace Afghanistan's road infrastructure, and estimated that 54 percent of Afghanistan's road infrastructure suffered from poor maintenance and required rehabilitation beyond simple repairs." Though they only have the authority or ability to review a small part of the money wasted in Afghanistan, SIGAR's quarterly reports have become a historical catalog of the U.S. government's failures there.[89]

The constant mantra of the NGOs, military, State Department officials, politicians, academics and policy experts has been that the U.S. and its allies should have done and given more sooner and should be doing more now and always. In their eyes, the original "light footprint" of the U.S. Army after the toppling of the Taliban was the war chiefs' biggest mistake. To the interventionists, the return of the Taliban is the result of a failure to do enough nation building, rather than a response to the increasing numbers of hostile foreign combat troops and international intervention in Afghan affairs. Their solution? More troops and more nation-building.[90]

Injun Country

According to military theorist Robert Kaplan, virtually the entire so-called Muslim World should be considered "Injun Country,"[91] analogous to the American Old West where our heroes had free rein and the natives could either bow to our civilized ways or die. But instead of "Injuns,"

---

[89] "Afghanistan's Road Infrastructure: Sustainment Challenges and Lack of Repairs Put US Investment at Risk," Special Inspector General for Afghanistan Reconstruction, October 29, 2016, https://sigar.mil/pdf/audits/SIGAR-17-11-AR.pdf; Megan McCloskey et al., "We Blew $17 Billion in Afghanistan. How Would You Have Spent It?," ProPublica, December 17, 2015, https://projects.propublica.org/graphics/afghan, Special Inspector General for Afghanistan Reconstruction Quarterly Reports, https://www.sigar.mil/quarterlyreports/index.aspx?SSR=6.

[90] Suhrke, *When More is Less*, 12-13.

[91] Robert Kaplan, *Imperial Grunts: On the Ground with the American Military, from Mongolia to the Philippines to Iraq and Beyond* (New York: Random House, 2005), 4; Andrew J. Bacevich, "Robert Kaplan: Empire Without Apologies," *Nation*, September 8, 2005, https://www.thenation.com/article/robert-kaplan-empire-without-apologies/.

America's pretend cowboys had new and ever-increasing enemies in the form of "the Taliban," which had changed from the name of an actual group and one-time government to a simple slander term for anyone who attacked or violently resisted American forces in the country, whether they had the slightest thing to do with Mullah Omar's old regime or not.

By 2004, some actual Taliban leaders had returned to the southern Helmand Province and had begun organizing violent resistance there. Secretary of Defense Rumsfeld released a memo conflating al Qaeda and the Taliban while also complaining that his department had no "metrics" for how well the military was doing or what kind of progress they were making in what was now turning out to be a "long, hard slog."[92] In the spring of 2004, Rumsfeld doubled U.S. troop levels there to 20,000.[93]

Starting in 2005, the insurgency genuinely started making a comeback, riding local resentment against the escalating American and allied occupation. It was also around this time that the Taliban began using suicide attack tactics imported from bin Ladenite fighters involved with the Sunni-based insurgency in the then-ongoing second Iraq war. As Patrick Cockburn wrote, "The presence of foreign troops in support of a hated local faction and corrupt and violent Afghan security forces meant that America, Britain and others were provoking the insurrection they were supposedly trying to suppress." A former Pakistani army colonel, himself a Pashtun, told Cockburn that "hatred of all foreigners" was "at the center of Pashtun culture," and that their war of resistance against the occupation would never end.[94] The Taliban started creating a shadow court system to compete with the new government in predominantly Pashtun areas of the country, while the Bush administration canceled scheduled troop withdrawals in response to the growing violence.[95] As McClatchy Newspapers reported, "Afghanistan has become Iraq on a slow burn. Five years after they were ousted, the Taliban are back in force, their ranks renewed by a new generation of diehards. Violence, opium trafficking, ethnic tensions, corruption and political anarchy are all worse than they've been at any time since the U.S.-led intervention in 2001."[96]

---

[92] "Rumsfeld's War on Terror Memo," *USA Today*, October 16, 2003,
http://usatoday30.usatoday.com/news/washington/executive/rumsfeld-memo.htm.

[93] Associated Press, "A Timeline of US Troop Levels in Afghanistan Since 2001," *Military Times*, July 6, 2016, http://www.militarytimes.com/story/military/2016/07/06/timeline-us-troop-levels-afghanistan-since-2001/86755782/; "Bush Announces New Steps to Aid Afghanistan," Voice of America News, June 19, 2004, http://learningenglish.voanews.com/a/a-23-a-2004-06-19-1-1-83118837/122275.html.

[94] Patrick Cockburn, *The Age of Jihad: Islamic State and the Great War for the Middle East* (New York: Verso, 2016), 183-184.

[95] Jonathan Landay, "4 US Troops Killed in Afghanistan as Insurgents Step Up Attacks," McClatchy, August 21, 2005, http://www.mcclatchydc.com/latest-news/article24448462.html.

[96] Jonathan Landay, "Five Years into Afghanistan, US Confronts Taliban's Comeback," McClatchy, October 1, 2006, http://www.mcclatchydc.com/latest-news/article24458476.html.

Complaints in the U.S. media invariably focused on the alleged lack of resources devoted to the Afghan occupation — both for the military and for civilian nation-building efforts, particularly in the Pashtun-dominated south. But increased intervention would only lead to worse consequences, rather than stabilizing the situation.

This was because, as journalist Jean MacKenzie explained after living in and reporting from Afghanistan for more than five years, Afghans saw very little difference between the U.S. occupation and the Soviet one of the 1980s. The average Afghan did not feel respected by U.S. troops or believe the American soldiers were there to help them, so their insurgency simply escalated in response to each new American increase in a perpetual cycle of violence.[97]

In 2004, U.S. generals and military theorists started referring to the "Long War" in Afghanistan and the larger "arc of crisis" in Central Asia. As the *Guardian* explained, a Pentagon report released by Joint Chiefs Chairman Peter Pace

> set out a plan for prosecuting what the Pentagon describes ... as "The Long War," which replaces the "War on Terror." The Long War represents more than just a linguistic shift: it reflects the ongoing development of U.S. strategic thinking since the September 11 attacks. Looking beyond the Iraq and Afghan battlefields, U.S. commanders envisage a war unlimited in time and space against global Islamist extremism. "The struggle ... may well be fought in dozens of other countries simultaneously and for many years to come," the report says. The emphasis switches from large-scale, conventional military operations, such as the 2003 invasion of Iraq, towards a rapid deployment of highly mobile, often covert, counter-terrorist forces.

> Among specific measures proposed are: an increase in special operations forces by 15%; an extra 3,700 personnel in psychological operations and civil affairs units — an increase of 33%; nearly double the number of unmanned aerial drones; the conversion of submarine-launched Trident nuclear missiles for use in conventional strikes; new close-to-shore, high-speed naval capabilities; special teams trained to detect and render safe nuclear weapons quickly anywhere in the world; and a new long-range bomber force.

> The Pentagon does not pinpoint the countries it sees as future areas of operations but they will stretch beyond the Middle East to the Horn of Africa, north Africa, central and southeast Asia and the northern Caucasus.

---

[97] Jean McKenzie, interviewed by the author, *Scott Horton Show,* radio archive, September 9, 2009, https://scotthorton.org/interviews/antiwar-radio-jean-mackenzie-2/.

> The Cold War dominated the world from 1946 to 1991: the Long War could determine the shape of the world for decades to come.[98]

That's why America needs all those nuclear submarines 25 years after the fall of the Soviet Union: to fight tribesmen armed with homemade landmines and AK-47s.

The next escalation of U.S. combat forces in Afghanistan, the so-called "phase three" increase of troop numbers in the south in 2006, "appears to have helped motivate many to side with the insurgency at the time," van Linschoten and Kuehn wrote in *An Enemy We Created*. "In many parts of the country — nowhere more than in Helmand which was officially under the lead of British forces — individuals joined up in reaction to what was perceived by many as a 'settling of scores' dating back to the Anglo-Afghan wars, and the Taliban capitalized on a feeling of disappointment and disenfranchisement of the general population."[99]

In 2007, the Bush administration admitted their 2006 escalation had not worked, but they decided another just might do the trick. Secretary of State Condoleezza Rice traveled to Brussels to pressure America's NATO allies to escalate their efforts in the country and increase aid to the Karzai regime. "Everyone talks about the Taliban military offensive this spring," Kurt D. Volker, a senior State Department official working on NATO's Afghanistan policy, told the *Washington Post*. "We should be the ones taking the offensive if there is an offensive to be done. ... It needs to be across the board. It's not just a military issue; it's a comprehensive issue — development, counter-narcotics, reconstruction and military." A different senior official predicted to the *Post* that U.S. troops would have a "bloody year in the south" and still faced the problems of "corruption, opium production, and lack of roads and other infrastructure."[100] Surely, just a few more tens of billions of dollars and a few more military missions would straighten all of that out.

It was apparently considered irrelevant that all of the al Qaeda attacks during this timeframe took place outside of Afghanistan.[101] The number of Taliban attacks were, however, on the rise, and there was no denying the occupation was failing. But the conventional wisdom endured: the U.S. just had not done enough. The *New York Times* recounted officials' complaints:

---

[98] Simon Tisdall and Ewen MacAskill, "America's Long War," *Guardian*, February 15, 2006, https://www.theguardian.com/world/2006/feb/15/politics.usa1.

[99] Van Linschoten and Kuehn, *An Enemy We Created*, 272-279.

[100] Michael Abramowitz, "Bush Plans New Focus on Afghan Recovery," *Washington Post*, January 25, 2007, http://washingtonpost.com/wp-dyn/content/article/2007/01/24/AR2007012401877.html.

[101] Van Linschoten and Kuehn, *An Enemy We Created*, 263-264.

"I said from the get-go that we didn't have enough money and we didn't have enough soldiers," said Robert P. Finn, who was the ambassador in 2002 and 2003. "I'm saying the same thing six years later."

Zalmay Khalilzad, who was the next ambassador and is now the American ambassador to the United Nations, said, "I do think that state-building and nation-building, we came to that reluctantly," adding that "I think more could have been done earlier on these issues."

And Ronald E. Neumann, who replaced Mr. Khalilzad in Kabul, said, "The idea that we could just hunt terrorists and we didn't have to do nation-building, and we could just leave it alone, that was a large mistake."[102]

More money, more troops, more aid, more time. It's just not enough; it's never enough — but surely just one more escalation *will* be enough. Or maybe two.

By 2007 and 2008, Afghanistan was in chaos, with massive resentment building against the U.S., allies and the government they had installed. This was not just from the Pashtun tribes who bore the brunt of American war efforts there, but also from Hazaras, Sikhs and other minorities in the north.[103] U.S. troops' job was often reduced to "drawing fire" — to be the "bullet sponge" as they tried to coax their elusive enemies out into the daylight.[104]

America and NATO's paradoxical support for the Taliban by way of protection money paid to them to allow the transport of supplies to stranded Western troops had, by this point, gotten way out of hand.[105] The military was paying hundreds of millions of dollars to various insurgent groups, including the Taliban and corrupt government officials, as extortion fees for protection, turning the war into a parody of itself as the insurgency channeled those resources right back into the fight against the occupation. The U.S. military was not only paying the Taliban to leave them alone, but sometimes would even hire Taliban vehicles to ride escort for ISAF's supply trucks, with one driving in front, one behind. Hamid Wardak, son of the Afghan defense minister at the time, ran a company which specialized in hiring Taliban fighters to provide protection for American supply vehicles. He even set up a firm in Washington so that he

---

[102] David Rohde and David Sanger, "How a 'Good War' in Afghanistan Went Bad," *New York Times*, August 12, 2007.

[103] Sands, *The Case for Withdrawal from Afghanistan.*

[104] C. J. Chivers, "G.I.'s in Remote Afghan Post Have Weary Job, Drawing Fire," *New York Times*, November 9, 2008, http://www.nytimes.com/2008/11/10/world/asia/10outpost.html.

[105] Gopal, *No Good Men*, 275.

could lobby for prolonging the war and his profits.[106] There is a certain logic to it, as long as you are willing to abandon all reason to entertain it.[107]

Pakistan and the Taliban

In the early years after the September 11, 2001, attacks, the Pakistani national police helped the FBI and CIA arrest dozens of al Qaeda operatives,[108] including some of the conspirators behind the attack. Among these were Ramzi bin al Shibh, a friend of lead hijacker Mohammed Atta and alleged coordinator of the attack, and Khalid Sheikh Mohammed, alleged commander of the group and uncle of Ramzi Yousef, the 1993 World Trade Center bomber. Both men had bragged of their role in the plot to al Jazeera's Yosri Fouda.[109]

But matters were much more complicated when it came to the connections between the Pakistani military and their spy agency, Inter-Service Intelligence (ISI), and escaped leaders of the Taliban. In fact, as investigative reporter Seymour Hersh discovered, the U.S. even acquiesced to Pakistani demands to let their air force evacuate some Afghan Taliban leaders from the country in the early days of the war due to the fact that some Pakistani military and intelligence officers were embedded with them.[110] This was just the beginning of a new chapter in America's twisted relationship with long-time ally Pakistan. They were helping the U.S. fight its al Qaeda enemies inside their own country, while at the same time continuing to back America's enemies in Afghanistan — the Afghan Taliban, Hizb-e-Islami and the Haqqani network — including providing safe-haven for them on the Pakistani side of the border.[111]

This has led to a situation somewhat like what the U.S. faced in trying

[106] Aram Roston, "Afghan Lobby Scam: Has a Major Military Contractor in Afghanistan Created an Astroturf Organization to Promote Long-term US Engagement?," *Nation*, December 22, 2009, https://www.thenation.com/article/afghan-lobby-scam/.

[107] Turse, ed., *The Case for Withdrawal from Afghanistan*, 88, 92; Aram Roston, "How the US Funds the Taliban," *Nation*, November 11, 2009, https://www.thenation.com/article/how-us-funds-taliban/.

[108] "Top al-Qaeda Leaders Captured or Killed on Pakistani Soil," *News International*, May 3, 2011, https://www.thenews.com.pk/archive/print/298864-top-al-qaeda-leaders-captured-or-killed-on-pakistani-soil.

[109] Yosri Fouda, "Top Secret - The Road to September 11," al Jazeera, September 11, 2002, YouTube video, 41:08, https://www.youtube.com/watch?v=NVV91uhfMcM; Giles Tremlett, "Al-Qaeda Leaders Say Nuclear Power Stations Were Original Targets," *Guardian*, September 8, 2002, https://www.theguardian.com/world/2002/sep/09/september11.afghanistan.

[110] Seymour Hersh, "The Getaway," *New Yorker*, January 28, 2002, http://www.newyorker.com/magazine/2002/01/28/the-getaway-2.

[111] "Pakistan Continues to Be Safe Haven for Terrorists: Pentagon Report Says Haqqani Network Biggest Threat," First Post, December 17, 2016, http://www.firstpost.com/world/pakistan-continues-to-be-safe-haven-for-terrorists-pentagon-report-says-haqqani-network-biggest-threat-3160764.html.

to defeat South Vietnamese Vietcong insurgents who had sanctuary across the border in Laos and Cambodia in the Vietnam war. The governments of those countries were powerless to stop the Vietcong, no matter their alliances with the United States. All they could do was "allow" the secret invasions and air wars waged against them by the Americans to make up for that fact.[112]

But what could explain such treachery as our friends, the Pakistanis, providing aid and comfort to the U.S.'s enemies on their territory when their ability to crush them was nowhere near as constrained? The answer is simple: the Pakistani military considers Afghanistan to be their backyard and "strategic depth" safe-zone for retreat in the event of a full-scale — even nuclear — war with their rival to the east, India.[113] India and Pakistan have been fierce opponents since being partitioned by the British Empire after World War II. They have fought four wars since then, and both are armed with nuclear weapons. The Indian-occupied region of Kashmir remains a major source of tension and possible conflict between the two countries. Keeping friendly forces in power in Afghanistan, therefore, has been the highest-level priority of the Pakistani military for decades.[114] Meanwhile, the U.S. not only supports India's allies in Afghanistan among the old Northern Alliance, but has promoted the signing of security pacts that provide for the training of thousands of Afghan soldiers by India,[115] and has encouraged the Indians to buy Russian attack helicopters and other weapons for the Afghan National Army.[116] This is in part because the U.S. wishes to please the Indian government, which it sees as an important ally in America's larger strategic interest in "containing" India's neighbor to their northeast, China.[117] From the perspective of the Pakistani

---

[112] George Wright, "Declassified Files Portray Lon Nol as 'Shaken' Man," *Cambodia Daily*, January 20, 2017, https://www.cambodiadaily.com/morenews/declassified-files-portray-lon-nol-as-shaken-man-123761/.

[113] Barbara Elias, ed., "Pakistan: 'The Taliban's Godfather'?," National Security Archive at George Washington University, http://nsarchive.gwu.edu/NSAEBB/NSAEBB227/; Khalid Masood Khan, "The Strategic Depth Concept," *Nation* (Pakistan), October 16, 2015, http://nation.com.pk/columns/16-Oct-2015/the-strategic-depth-concept.

[114] Margolis, *American Raj*, 198.

[115] Tom Wright and Margherita Stancati, "Karzai Sets Closer Ties with India on Visit," *Wall Street Journal*, October 5, 2011, http://www.wsj.com/articles/SB10001424052970203791904576610923980017098.

[116] Franz-Stefan Gady, "US General Asks India for More Military Assistance in Afghanistan," Diplomat, August 14, 2016, http://thediplomat.com/2016/08/us-general-asks-india-for-more-military-assistance-in-afghanistan/; Franz-Stefan Gady, "India Delivers 4th Combat Helicopter to Afghanistan," Diplomat, December 1, 2016, http://thediplomat.com/2016/12/india-delivers-4th-combat-helicopter-to-afghanistan/; Michael Kugelman, "The Most Important Arms Deal You Never Heard Of," War on the Rocks, December 22, 2015, https://warontherocks.com/2015/12/the-most-important-arms-deal-youve-never-heard-of/; James Mackenzie and Sanjeev Miglani, "Afghanistan Turns to India for Military Helicopters, Likely to Rile Pakistan," Reuters, November 6, 2015, http://in.reuters.com/article/india-afghanistan-idINKCN0SV0E620151106.

[117] Conn Hallinan, "A Global Nuclear Winter: Avoiding the Unthinkable in India and Pakistan,"

government, it is intolerable that India's allies would ever be able to truly establish a monopoly of force in Afghanistan, and so they see it as necessary to continue to support their friends and ideological cousins, the Afghan Taliban and broader Pashtun insurgency, to prevent it from happening. This was the reason Pakistan had backed the Taliban's rise to power in the 1990s in the first place. The ISI began renewing support for the Taliban as early as 2003, though the U.S. did not start keeping track of it until 2007.[118]

So, the U.S. was bribing one ally to back another ally, forcing a third ally to back our own and our first ally's enemies, which required the U.S. to turn to the first ally for help against the third, and then around again. This has continued for more than a dozen years. In fact, the reality is even more convoluted than this. Our other allies, the Saudi royals, have continued to finance the Taliban resistance against the U.S. all along as well, since the Taliban serves as a check on the power of Afghanistan's ethnic Hazaras, who are Shi'ites aligned with Saudi Arabia's nemesis, Iran.[119]

While the Bush administration was slow to catch on to the dynamics at play, there is no question the Obama administration understood a major part of the problem with the Taliban insurgency was in Pakistan. His government tried to re-title the entire conflict the "Af-Pak war" to emphasize the point. It is also clear that Obama and his government understood that Pakistan's major motivation for their backing of the Afghan Taliban and Haqqani Network was the Afghan National Army's alliance with India.[120] However, the Obama administration continued the policy of bringing India in as an ally of the Afghan government anyway. When the CIA escalated the drone war in Pakistan, it was primarily against al Qaeda and Pakistani Taliban, a.k.a. Tehrik-i-Taliban, targets way up in Waziristan and the Northwest Tribal Territories. The war against the Pakistani faction of the Taliban, a separate group from the Afghan Taliban, was mostly done as a payoff to the Pakistani government for allowing strikes against the last few members of the original al Qaeda group still hiding with them there. The leaders of the Afghan Taliban, on the other hand, stayed safe in Quetta, in Pakistan's southwest, far from where the Predator and Reaper drone wars were being fought. It was explained to the new president by Director of National Intelligence Mike McConnell,

Foreign Policy in Focus, December 8, 2016, http://fpif.org/global-nuclear-winter-avoiding-unthinkable-india-pakistan/.

[118] Patrick Cockburn, *Chaos and Caliphate: Jihadis and the West in the Struggle for the Middle East* (New York: OR Books, 2016), 182-183.

[119] Carlotta Gall, "Saudis Bankroll Taliban, Even as King Officially Supports Afghan Government," *New York Times*, December 6, 2016, http://www.nytimes.com/2016/12/06/world/asia/saudi-arabia-afghanistan.html.

[120] Woodward, *Obama's Wars*, 216.

just days after being sworn in, that Quetta was off limits due to the high population density.[121] Though the CIA had created "Counter-terrorism Pursuit Teams" for the purposes of secretly crossing the border into Pakistan, they never had any successes against the actual Afghan Taliban leadership there,[122] only limited results against rank and file Taliban and Haqqani network fighters.[123]

The Americans were also limited in their ability to pressure the Pakistanis to back down from this policy since the U.S. had become almost completely dependent on the ability to ship military supplies hundreds of miles through Pakistan from the Port of Karachi, all the way through the Khyber Pass and into Afghanistan. By 2011, approximately 80 percent of U.S. supplies for the "surge" escalation were transported through this route.[124] After U.S. helicopters attacked and killed 28 of their soldiers at two border posts in an alleged case of accidental friendly fire, the Pakistanis allowed some militant attacks on allied convoys and shut down the route for almost all of 2012,[125] forcing the U.S. to depend more on the northern route through Russia.[126] Apparently the Pakistanis did not need to do this more than once to prove their point about the limits of U.S. influence to the Obama administration.[127]

There were other factors that also prevented the U.S. from leaning too hard on the Pakistani government for providing support to the Afghan Taliban and Haqqani Network. The Obama administration needed Pakistani cooperation to wage the drone war, and they were also afraid of further destabilizing a government which possessed nuclear weapons in a country full of extremists of all descriptions.[128]

As Patrick Cockburn stated:

---

[121] Ibid., 7-8.

[122] Mark Mazzetti, "CIA Takes on Bigger and Riskier Role on Front Lines," *New York Times*, December 31, 2009, http://www.nytimes.com/2010/01/01/world/asia/01khost.html.

[123] Gareth Porter, "Pakistan Drone Story Ignored Military Opposition to Strikes," Inter Press Service, October 25, 2013, http://www.ipsnews.net/2013/10/pakistan-drone-story-ignored-military-opposition-to-strikes/.

[124] Ahmed Rashid, *Pakistan on the Brink: The Future of America, Pakistan and Afghanistan*, (New York: Penguin, 2012), 167-168.

[125] Christian Parenti, "With Friends Like These: On Pakistan," *Nation*, April 30, 2013, https://www.thenation.com/article/friends-these-pakistan/.

[126] Richard Norton-Taylor et al., "Convoy Attacks Trigger Race to Open New Afghan Supply Lines," *Guardian*, December 9, 2008, https://www.theguardian.com/world/2008/dec/09/afghanistan-nato-supply-routes/.

[127] Peter Bergen, "Trump's Emerging Plan for Afghanistan Breaks with Obama Approach," CNN, June 21, 2017, http://www.cnn.com/2017/06/21/opinions/trump-plan-for-afghanistan-breaks-with-obama-approach-bergen/index.html.

[128] Karl Eikenberry, "The Limits of Counterinsurgency Doctrine in Afghanistan," *Foreign Affairs*, September/October 2013, https://www.foreignaffairs.com/articles/afghanistan/2013-08-12/limits-counterinsurgency-doctrine-afghanistan.

An American success in Afghanistan was impossible once the Pakistani Army had decided to give full backing to a return of the Taliban. The U.S. faced the same strategic weakness as the Soviet army during its Afghan campaign. However many setbacks the anti-Soviet mujahideen or the anti-American Taliban suffered, they could always retreat across the 1,600-mile long border with Pakistan to rest, reorganize and reequip. President Barack Obama was told during his first days in office that the heart of the military problems facing the U.S. in Afghanistan lay in Pakistan, but Washington could never work out an effective way of dealing with it.[129]

It is clear that America's "best" people did have some understanding of the incentives and pressures the various neighboring states and powers faced and the position in which they had put the Pakistanis. Zbigniew Brzezinski explained in the late 1990s that America's interest was in supporting the China-Pakistan-Taliban alliance in Afghanistan to keep the Indians, Russians and Iranians out.[130] Since 2001, the U.S. has been fighting for the exact opposite ends. Is it that Brzezinski had America's interests upside down in 1997 or that everyone in power since then has been fighting for the wrong side? In either case, the U.S. has seemed to ignore its own previously demonstrated understanding of the situation and continued to insist that it is essential to enlist the Indians' help to prop up the Kabul government in the short term, while inevitably leading to worse Pakistani and Pashtun reactions against them in the long run.

Korengal

For the American public, Afghanistan, overshadowed by events in Iraq and across the Middle East, soon became a forgotten war, much like the Korean War had been eclipsed by the even more destructive invasion of Vietnam. Once the thrill of taking revenge for the September 11th attacks had worn off, American television and newspaper audiences lost interest in the war, and the media lost interest in covering it beyond hyping a few publicity stunts at the holidays, which left the story to be told through other means.

Journalist Sebastian Junger produced the famous documentaries *Restrepo* (2010) and *Korengal* (2014) about U.S. Army forces stationed in the Korengal Valley — "the Valley of Death" — in far eastern Afghanistan, which highlight the absolute waste of life and property the war in Afghanistan represents.[131]

---

[129] Cockburn, *Chaos and Caliphate*, 203.

[130] Brzezinski, *The Grand Chessboard*, 139, 149, 187.

[131] Sebastian Junger and Tim Hetherington, *Restrepo*, (New York: Virgil Films and Entertainment,

The conflict in the Korengal Valley began in 2002 when the U.S. took bad advice from a timber baron who needed to get a local tribal leader and some competing businessmen out of his way. Misinformed that the local tribe was made up of "Taliban terrorists," the U.S. betrayed the compliant tribal elder, shipped him off to Guantánamo and then bombed and killed the timber baron's business competitors. "Soon, one village after another turned to open insurrection."[132]

Most of the people of Korengal did not even really know what Afghanistan was, much less the United States. They simply lived in the little world of their home valleys and villages. And then into that world intruded heavily armed, young North Americans, who succeeded only in making themselves targets of the Taliban and local fighters. Not only had the people of Korengal Valley never done anything to the U.S., when the Americans first got there the locals assumed they were Russian troops, still unaware the USSR had withdrawn and collapsed more than a decade before, much less that the U.S. had invaded more recently.[133] But the army was not there to fight these innocent villagers; they were there only to help them — to build a modern democratic nation for them. So, any killing, destroying and dying that had to be done to save the people there was deemed to be justified.

However, a statement by Specialist Kyle Steiner in *Korengal* helps to illustrate why America's nation-building project in Afghanistan can never work. The entire idea of young, heavily armed, foreign soldiers invading the valley to "bring good things" to win over the population, as another young soldier tried to explain, may be the clearest example of futility one could imagine. In any case, the concept cannot survive violent conflict. Steiner told Junger:

> You know, this whole 'go in there and act like their friend' thing doesn't work, especially when you've got, you know, the Afghani [*sic*] that we caught trying to put the roadside bomb, the IED [improvised explosive device], just spitting on us and calling us "infidel" and stuff, you know, "hearts and minds" is out the window then. "Hearts and minds" go out the window when you see the guy shooting at you and then he puts his wife and kids in front of him knowing full well that we won't shoot back. Or the guy who shakes our hand, takes the 10 bags of rice we give him for his family and school supplies and coats, and immediately walks up the mountain and shoots an RPG [shoulder-fired, rocket-propelled grenade] at us, walks back down and smiles at

2010), DVD; Sebastian Junger, *Korengal,* (New York: Virgil Films and Entertainment, 2014), DVD.
[132] Gopal, *No Good Men,* 141-143.
[133] Sebastian Junger, *War* (New York: Twelve, 2010), 47.

us the next morning when he's walking his goats. Fuck his heart. And fuck his mind.

When the military finally called it quits and left the Korengal Valley in 2010, it had accomplished exactly nothing in four years of fighting other than getting more than 40 American soldiers killed and hundreds wounded, along with uncounted civilian casualties among the Afghans.

Korengal veteran, U.S. Army Specialist Robert Soto could have been speaking about the entire Afghan war when he vented his frustration to the *New York Times* upon finally withdrawing from the valley, "It hurts on a level that — three units from the Army, we all did what we did up there. And we all lost men. We all sacrificed. I was 18 years old when I got there. I really would not have expected to go through what we went through at that age. It confuses me, why it took so long for them to realize that we were not making progress up there."[134]

The American government had left these soldiers stranded, killing and dying for nothing in a treacherous mountain valley in the middle of nowhere, on an unclear mission, frustrated at fighting ghosts sniping at them from afar and planting IEDs all around them, in a vain attempt to build a nation in a place that never had one and whose people had no intention of making one no matter how many of them the U.S. side killed. It was a crime and a mistake.

The Ghosts of Direct Action

U.S. Army Sgt. Anthony Walker, a psychological operations specialist and veteran of three tours in Afghanistan, who for a time was attached to the Joint Special Operations Command (JSOC) — top-tier special operations forces — later described how easy it was for completely innocent bystanders to get caught up in night raid missions. Walker explained, "out of over 100 raids, maybe one was based on human intelligence and the rest was based on signals [electronic] intelligence," and it seemed from his perspective to be "rather easy to get caught up in that dragnet that would place you on a list saying you're a bad guy." People would also get shot simply coming outside to investigate the late-night noise or for demanding that soldiers who were posting up on their roofs to provide cover for other raiding soldiers get off their property. Walker recalled that "we were raiding homes of people that were just distant family members to the target individual or were just in some way fulfilling their cultural duty [to protect those seeking shelter] and were not intending to

[134] Alissa J. Rubin, "US Forces Close Post in Afghan 'Valley of Death,'" *New York Times*, April 14, 2010, http://www.nytimes.com/2010/04/15/world/asia/15outpost.html.

facilitate an insurgency." Walker also described and provided photographic evidence of two war crimes committed, he said, by a young Army Ranger of the 75th Regiment on the outskirts of Khost City in eastern Afghanistan in 2008: two pictures, one of a woman's corpse with a large rectangular piece of her neck cut away, in what Walker says was the aftermath of a fellow soldier's cutting and taking this piece of her flesh as a trophy (which he then held up in the air in triumph), and another of a dead and bloody-faced teenage girl lying next to an AK-47 rifle, captioned by Walker as "the practice of placing weapons next to noncombatants for photo 'evidence.'"[135]

Walker says he tried but failed to stop the attack which led to the deaths of the woman and girl in the pictures. During a raid on a targeted individual in one house, the Rangers had stationed a sniper team on the roof of another nearby house to provide cover for the raid team. But there was one so-called "Military Aged Male" (MAM) in the house who grabbed an AK-47 and fired a warning shot into the thick stucco ceiling to scare away those on his roof. Walker says the "MAM" must have assumed they were criminals, as the Rangers' assault had not been announced by the noise of a Black Hawk helicopter or any other blatant signal. Instead, the team had driven into the area quietly, so there was no reason for the "MAM" to assume those on his roof were American soldiers. But when he fired off the round, "that's what got everything started," Walker says. "The atrocity." The only AK-47 rifle in the house was the one that had been fired through the ceiling. In response, Walker said, one Ranger killed the family — the woman and the young girl in the pictures, as well as the boy who had fired the warning shot into the ceiling.

As it turned out, the family was not just innocent, but the family of Awal Khan, a colonel in the U.S. created-and-funded Afghan National Army. His position in the ANA helped to generate some news coverage of the attack, which confirmed Walker's story and added more detail. The family had not assumed they were under attack by criminals, but since the father worked so closely with the U.S., they thought it was the Taliban who had come to get revenge. And the casualties, it turned out, were more than Walker recalled. Killed were the colonel's wife, a schoolteacher; their 17-year-old daughter; a 15-year-old son, presumably the one who had fired the warning shot; his brother, a seven-day-old baby; and the unborn baby of Khan's cousin who, despite being shot five times and losing her child, managed to survive. Another of Khan's daughters was also wounded but lived.[136]

---

[135] Due to the graphic nature of the photographs, the author has decided not to include them in the book itself. However, they may be viewed online at http://foolserrand.us/walker.

[136] Ali Daya, "Family of Afghan Army Colonel Killed in US Raid," *Taipei Times*, April 9, 2009, http://www.taipeitimes.com/News/world/archives/2009/04/12/2003440842; Douglas A. Wissing,

Walker said it was "standard practice" to plant a "drop gun" as evidence against innocent people, such as they did against this family. It was a "regular thing" to the Rangers of the 2nd Battalion. In fact, he said the "entire regiment did it all the time." Walker further claimed that a two-star general, and deputy to then-JSOC Commander Admiral McRaven, "investigated," then assembled the soldiers and instructed them on their story in case anyone asked. He told them to say that all four adults in the house — counting the teenage girl and her 15-year-old brother — went for the one AK-47 at the same time, giving the Ranger no choice but to waste them all.

Walker was witness to other unjustified killings during that Afghan deployment. On another mission near Khost City, the same battalion, possibly the same platoon, raided a house and killed a mother and father in a shooting justified by questionable claims that the woman had a gun. In another incident, an army dog bit a young boy during a raid near Forward Operating Base Salerno. Walker's memory seems to be confirmed by a report in RAWA News.[137]

Walker also describes another raid in Khost where a civilian poked his head around the side of his house as soldiers detonated explosives to breach the wall of a compound catty-corner from his. "I said 'It's a civilian,'" Walker later recalled. "I could see that he was unarmed." Walker, following the rules, asked for permission to use his hand-held megaphone to warn the man to go back inside. "I wasn't even going to wait for the translator." But it was already too late. Another soldier fired and killed the man.

Another instance took place out in the countryside in 2008 or 2009: Walker was assigned to do a "call out" at a local school, meaning make an announcement to those inside to, in effect, "come out with your hands up." Soon a group of preteen boys, Walker estimates they were approximately 11–13 years old, began to come out one by one. But the eighth boy to come out panicked. Completely terrified, the boy hesitated and acted confused when ordered about by the soldiers. One noticed a bulge in the boy's pocket and asked him what it was. And "just like you would do if someone asked you what was in your pocket," Walker explained, the boy reached into it. The Ranger shot him dead. The same Ranger, Walker says, who had killed the family in Khost.

In Writing: Uncovering the Unexpected Hoosier State (Bloomington, IN: Quarry, 2016), 131-132; Alie Daya, "Afghan Father Says His Baby Dies in Coalition Raid," Reuters, April 10, 2009, http://www.reuters.com/article/idUSSP477728._CH_.2400; Kalam Sadat, "US Military Concedes Afghan Civilian Casualties," Reuters, April 10, 2009, http://www.reuters.com/article/us-afghanistan-violence-idUSTRE5390FM20090410.
[137] Saboor Mangal, "Coalition Forces Kill Three of an Afghan Family in Khost," RAWA News, December 17, 2008, http://www.rawa.org/temp/runews/2008/12/17/coalition-forces-kill-three-of-an-afghan-family-in-khost.html.

Sgt. Walker says he joined the army because he really wanted to fight terrorism, but finally realized that this was not the way. "I interrogated children after we killed their parents — lied to them. How many, I don't know, but some must now be Taliban," he concluded.

One could argue these claims are too thinly sourced or are unrepresentative of the behavior of U.S. troops and special operations forces in Afghanistan. But even if they were embellished, it is not hard to imagine how infuriating just a few stories like these would be to Americans if this was happening to our population at the hands of a foreign occupying army. Even worse is the truth of what Sgt. Walker says: war crimes such as the killing and framing of innocent people are just a regular part of the war — "standard practice."

Americans must not be blind to the fact that, as Walker explained, no matter what their intentions are when joining the military or going to war, once men are put into these situations, awful things happen. Despite all the propaganda about our brave and glorious golden-idol soldiers, they are just men, often very young ones, and in the wrong circumstances, some of them will commit horrible atrocities. Even when soldiers stay within the rules, the nature of the war they are waging — against local militia men from, and hiding among, the local population — and all the "collateral damage" that comes with it, amounts to a campaign of terror waged against civilians by the U.S. and the Afghan National Army. The "ghosts of direct action," as Walker calls them — the consequence of new resistance fighters being created with each raid and each interrogation — are just as inevitable as the abuses that create them:[138]

> For years, Afghan villages targeted by the Rangers and Navy SEALs were subjected to numerous atrocities. These operations released shockwaves throughout entire communities as collateral damage became murderous aggression to Afghans. Afghans were killed, abused, humiliated in front of their families. And they haven't forgotten. …
>
> The ghosts of direct action make nation-building in Afghanistan very difficult. Rural Afghans see Afghan National Security Forces (ANSF) and American troops as one in the same. They don't trust the ANSF and in many cases they believe the Taliban is more likely to respect their cultural values. They harbor resentment and distrust as a result of

---

[138] Anthony Walker, interviewed by the author, *Scott Horton Show*, radio archive, July 27, 2016, http://scotthorton.org/interviews/2016/07/27/72716-anthony-walker/; Anthony Walker, email message to the author, July 25, 2016; Anthony Walker, interviewed by the author, August 6, 2016; Aaron Glantz and Anthony Swofford, eds., *Winter Soldier: Iraq and Afghanistan* (Chicago: Haymarket, 2008).

the many pre-dawn raids in their communities and they have no reason to believe they will end when America leaves Afghanistan for good.

Rural Pashtuns in the South and East of Afghanistan simply don't believe the Afghan government is even functional because it was utterly powerless for years when it came to controlling direct action missions. When a particularly appalling atrocity occurred when I was in Afghanistan, our task force would be shut down for two weeks. Then everything would resume as before until another atrocity. This has left Afghans with absolutely no faith in their government.[139]

In 2010 the muckraking, leaked-document-posting website WikiLeaks released the Afghan War Logs,[140] a collection of thousands of confidential- and secret-level military documents leaked to the site by a young army specialist named Bradley (now Chelsea) Manning. Though the press had a field day pushing the government's narrative that Manning and WikiLeaks' Julian Assange were traitors and spies with "blood on their hands" for releasing the documents, then-Secretary of Defense, Republican Robert Gates admitted in a letter to the chairman of the Senate Armed Services Committee that "the review to date has not revealed any sensitive intelligence sources and methods compromised by this disclosure," and that such allegations were "significantly overwrought."[141] Prosecutors at Manning's court martial and a secret Department of Defense report admitted the same.[142] So it was not true that the Manning leak was treasonous, unless you count letting the American people have access to facts which might give them reason to doubt the morality or utility of the war as betraying his country.[143]

For a brief moment in the news cycle, the brutality of the ongoing occupation was laid bare for all to see. As David Leigh wrote in the *Guardian*,

Behind the military jargon, the war logs are littered with accounts of civilian tragedies. The 144 entries in the logs recording some of these

---

[139] Anthony Walker, "The Ghosts of Direct Action," Antiwar.com, July 27, 2016, http://original.antiwar.com/anthony_walker/2016/07/26/ghosts-direct-action/.

[140] *The Afghan War Diary*, Wikileaks, July 25, 2010, https://wikileaks.org/afg/.

[141] Elisabeth Bumiller, "Gates on Leaks, Wiki and Otherwise," *New York Times*, November 30, 2010, https://thecaucus.blogs.nytimes.com/2010/11/30/gates-on-leaks-wiki-and-otherwise/.

[142] Ed Pilkington, "Bradley Manning Leak Did Not Result in Deaths by Enemy Forces, Court Hears," *Guardian*, July 31, 2013, https://www.theguardian.com/world/2013/jul/31/bradley-manning-sentencing-hearing-pentagon; Jason Leopold, "Secret Government Report: Chelsea Manning Leaks Caused No Real Harm," Buzzfeed News, June 20, 2017, https://buzzfeed.com/jasonleopold/secret-government-report-chelsea-manning-leaks-caused-no.

[143] C. J. Chivers et al., "View Is Bleaker Than Official Portrayal of War in Afghanistan," *New York Times*, July 25, 2010, http://www.nytimes.com/2010/07/26/world/asia/26warlogs.html.

so-called "blue on white" events, cover a wide spectrum of day-by-day assaults on Afghans, with hundreds of casualties.

They range from the shootings of individual innocents to the often massive loss of life from air strikes, which eventually led President Hamid Karzai to protest publicly that the U.S. was treating Afghan lives as "cheap." When civilian family members are actually killed in Afghanistan, their relatives do, in fairness, get greater solatia payments than cans of beans and Hershey bars. The logs refer to sums paid of 100,000 Afghani per corpse, equivalent to about £1,500 [approximately $1,900].

Spin artists in the U.S. mass media attempting to downplay the importance of the information in the leaked documents would often explain they were in fact "raw" and "unvetted," and that any claims within them would have to be independently verified. That was definitely true. When the War Logs were released, some journalists found insight by going back to compare the documents with established reporting on some previous incidents. In one example, another reporter for the *Guardian* went back to find a report by U.S. marines giving their version of a massacre of civilians they had perpetrated in March of 2007. After being caught in an IED blast that wounded a member of their patrol, four of the marines simply opened fire and shot every vehicle and person they saw on the way back to their base, including children, teenagers and the elderly. They ultimately killed 19 unarmed civilians and wounded 50 more. The marines claimed, contrary to contemporary media reports and the conclusions of an army investigation, to have been ambushed from three sides at the point of the bomb attack and neglected to mention firing on anyone during their retreat, stating simply that "the patrol returned to JAF [Jalalabad Air Field]."[144]

Innocent people trying to live a normal life apart from the war had no guarantee that they would not be swept up in the chaos. Most Americans would hardly believe it possible that their soldiers bombed young couples and families during their weddings, as has happened at least six times in America's Afghan war. Tom Engelhardt and Erika Eichelberger have kept track:

December 29, 2001, Paktia Province, Afghanistan (more than 100 revelers die in a village in Eastern Afghanistan after an attack by B-52 and B-1B bombers); May 17, 2002, Khost Province, Afghanistan (at least 10 Afghans in a wedding celebration die when U.S. helicopters

144 Declan Walsh, "Afghanistan War Logs: How US Marines Sanitized Record of Bloodbath," *Guardian*, July 26, 2010, https://www.theguardian.com/world/2010/jul/26/afghanistan-war-logs-us-marines; "(Explosive Hazard) IED Ambush RPT (SVBIED) CJTF-82: 1 CF WIA," *Afghan War Diary*, March 4, 2007, https://wikileaks.org/afg/event/2007/03/AFG20070304n586.html.

and planes attack a village); July 1, 2002, Oruzgan Province, Afghanistan (at least 30, and possibly 40, celebrants die when attacked by a B-52 bomber and an AC-130 gunship); ... July 6, 2008, Nangarhar Province, Afghanistan (at least 47 dead, 39 of them women and children, including the bride, among a party escorting that bride to the groom's house — from a missile attack by jet aircraft); August 2008, Laghman Province, Afghanistan (16 killed, including 12 members of the family hosting the wedding, in an attack by "American bombers"); June 8, 2012, Logar Province, Afghanistan (18 killed, half of them children, when Taliban fighters take shelter amid a wedding party.)[145]

In the July 6, 2008, attack listed above, the first strike killed most of the children who had run a little further up the road ahead of the main group. The second bomb landed in the middle of the group of adults who followed. The bride and another guest attempted to run down a hill to escape, but they were obliterated by the third strike. "Hajj Khan was one of four elderly men escorting the bride's party that day," the *Guardian* later reported. He told them, "We were walking, I was holding my grandson's hand, then there was a loud noise and everything went white. When I opened my eyes, everybody was screaming. I was lying meters from where I had been, I was still holding my grandson's hand but the rest of him was gone. I looked around and saw pieces of bodies everywhere. I couldn't make out which part was which."[146]

In June 2007, seven children were killed when U.S. forces bombed a building in which they believed insurgent fighters were hiding. The American ambassador at the time, William B. Wood, shrugged it off. These things "cannot be completely avoided," he told the *New York Times*.[147] More schoolchildren were killed in Ghazi Khan, in the eastern Kunar Province, in December 2009, when American CIA paramilitary forces and Navy SEALs slaughtered 10 innocent boys in a school — allegedly dragging them from their beds and executing them — in a night raid that had been launched on the basis of faulty intelligence. Initially, NATO falsely claimed their men had come under fire by Taliban forces upon entering the village, and that the boys must have been killed in the battle, before eventually conceding to the targeting mistake, if not the war crime.[148]

---

[145] Tom Engelhardt, "Washington's Wedding Album from Hell," TomDispatch, December 20, 2013, http://www.tomdispatch.com/blog/175787/tomgram%3A_engelhardt,_washington's _wedding_album_from_hell/.

[146] Clancy Chassay, "'I Was Still Holding My Grandson's Hand - the Rest Was Gone,'" *Guardian*, December 15, 2008, https://www.theguardian.com/world/2008/dec/16/afghanistan-taliban-us-foreign-policy.

[147] C. J. Chivers, "7 Children Killed in Airstrike in Afghanistan," *New York Times*, June 19, 2007, http://www.nytimes.com/2007/06/19/world/asia/19afghan.html.

[148] Jerome Starkey, "Western Troops Accused of Executing 10 Afghan Civilians, Including

In Farah Province, on May 4, 2009, U.S. airstrikes, apparently meant as air support for soldiers in a battle several miles away, killed as many as 120 innocent civilians. Though spokesmen tried to spin it as a Taliban attack, photographs showed no evidence of a ground battle, but plenty that the village had in fact been attacked from the air.[149]

The Taliban and related insurgent groups committed widespread atrocities of their own, oftentimes deliberately targeting and terrorizing civilians with suicide attacks.[150] But this tragedy had been a consequence of the war dragging on so long. What America needed, the Democrats and media experts said, was a real victory in Afghanistan. To put an end to the fighting that was causing so much unnecessary "collateral damage," America needed to escalate the war to finally win it. Toward the end of 2008, the Washington consensus began to form[151] around then-candidate Barack Obama's campaign spin that Bush had neglected the "good" and "necessary" war in Afghanistan and that the next year the new administration would need to launch a major escalation there.[152]

But the warnings were there, too. The previously-mentioned Robert A. Pape, professor of political science at the University of Chicago, has built his study of suicide terrorists into a major project backed by the Pentagon. Pape and his staff have created a database of every single suicide attack on earth since the year 1980.[153] From this data Pape has written two books about the suicide terrorist phenomenon, *Dying to Win: The Strategic Logic of Suicide Terrorism* and *Cutting the Fuse: The Explosion of Global Suicide Terrorism and How to Stop It*.[154] In the case of the Afghan escalation, he foresaw the inevitable:

> What we are talking about doing is adding some maybe 10,000 forces, maybe 20,000 forces, but nowhere near enough to actually suppress

---

Children," *London Times*, December 31, 2009, https://www.thetimes.co.uk/article/western-troops-accused-of-executing-10-afghan-civilians-including-children-p2tph3d7d76; Mark Mazzetti et al., "SEAL Team 6: A Secret History of Quiet Killings and Blurred Lines," *New York Times*, June 6, 2015, https://www.nytimes.com/2015/06/07/world/asia/the-secret-history-of-seal-team-6.htm; "NATO Admits That Deaths of 8 Boys Were a Mistake," *Nation* (Pakistan), February 25, 2010, http://nation.com.pk/international/25-Feb-2010/Nato-admits-that-deaths-of-8-boys-were-a-mistake-report.

[149] Cockburn, *Chaos and* Caliphate, 188-189.

[150] Gopal, *No Good Men,* 216.

[151] Michael Gordon, "Afghan Strategy Poses Stiff Challenge for Obama," *New York Times,* December 1, 2008, http://www.nytimes.com/2008/12/02/world/asia/02strategy.html.

[152] "Democratic Debate Transcript, Chicago, Speakers: Joseph R. Biden Jr., et al.," Council on Foreign Relations, August 7, 2007, http://bit.ly/2rJXuQK; Anne E. Kornblut, "Obama to Propose Funds for Afghanistan, Harder Line in Pakistan," *Washington Post*, July 31, 2007.

[153] Chicago Project on Security and Terrorism, "Suicide Attack Database."

[154] Robert A. Pape, *Dying to Win: The Strategic Logic of Suicide Terrorism*. New York: (Random House, 2005); Robert A. Pape and James K. Feldman, *Cutting the Fuse: The Explosion of Global Suicide Terrorism and How to Stop It*, (Chicago University Press, 2010).

and control large parts of the country. So right now in Afghanistan, I'm afraid that what our policy is heading towards is the worst of both worlds. We're basically putting enough ground forces in Afghanistan to foment a fairly large anti-American suicide terrorism campaign, but I'm afraid we are not putting in enough to actually get the benefit of actually suppressing enough of the violence in Afghanistan.

Pape also warned that any counterinsurgency campaign strong enough to "suppress violence" enough to theoretically allow for other types of political progress to be made would require adding hundreds of thousands of additional soldiers, which was obviously deemed prohibitively expensive and politically untenable. There was no real reason to think such a large-scale escalation would have solved America's problems in Afghanistan, but anything less was sure to only make matters worse.[155]

---

[155] Robert A. Pape, interviewed by the author, *Scott Horton Show*, radio archive, October 1, 2008, http://scotthorton.org/interviews/antiwar-radio-robert-a-pape-2/.

Chapter Four: The "Surge"

"We are in just so many deep holes that everybody had better grab a shovel and start digging out." — Secretary of State Hillary Clinton, June 7, 2009

"We're not leaving Afghanistan prematurely. In fact, we're not ever leaving at all." — Secretary of Defense Robert Gates, May 10, 2010

"Turns out I'm really good at killing people." — President Barack Obama, September 30, 2011

Jammed by the Blob

In the 2008 campaign season, Democratic presidential candidate Barack Obama, who ran on his opposition to the war in Iraq, made the strategic calculation to temper the perception that he was weak on terrorism by promoting escalation in Afghanistan and Pakistan instead and surrounded himself with foreign policy hawks as advisers and eventual cabinet members. Their maneuvering eventually forced Obama to commit to an escalation far beyond what even he believed was appropriate.

As a presidential candidate in August of 2007, Obama made his position clear in a speech delivered the Woodrow Wilson Center:

> Our troops have fought valiantly [in Afghanistan], but Iraq has deprived them of the support they need — and deserve. As a result, parts of Afghanistan are falling into the hands of the Taliban, and a mix of terrorism, drugs and corruption threatens to overwhelm the country. As president, I would deploy at least two additional brigades to Afghanistan to reinforce our counter-terrorism operations and support NATO's efforts against the Taliban. ... If we have actionable intelligence about high-value terrorist targets [in Pakistan] and President Musharraf won't act, we will.[1]

As the new president, Obama acted on his campaign promises by bombing Pakistan with a CIA drone strike on his third day in office, killing nine very real, innocent human beings and shattering the lives of their survivors.[2] Though the Bush administration had used drones in Yemen, Iraq and Afghanistan, Obama and his "cruise missile liberals" had inaugurated a whole new era of robotic warfare.[3] While an argument could be made that the Pakistan drone war at least made sense as an attempt to target and kill the last "core" members of al Qaeda hiding there, it has been a disaster for the civilians in the targeted areas,[4] and has increased

---

[1] Barack Obama, "Obama's Speech at Woodrow Wilson Center," delivered August 1, 2007, http://www.americanrhetoric.com/speeches/barackobamawilsoncenter.htm.

[2] Spencer Ackerman, "Victim of Obama's First Drone Strike: 'I Am the Living Example of What Drones Are,'" *Guardian*, January 23, 2016, https://www.theguardian.com/world/2016/jan/23/drone-strike-victim-barack-obama.

[3] The Other Scott Horton (no relation to the author), *Lords of Secrecy: The National Security Elite and America's Stealth Warfare* (New York: Nation, 2015) 109-128; Andrew Cockburn, *Kill Chain: The Rise of the High-Tech Assassins* (New York: Henry Holt, 2015); Chris Woods, *Sudden Justice: America's Secret Drone Wars* (Oxford: Oxford University Press, 2015); Jeremy Scahill et al., *The Assassination Complex: Inside the Government's Secret Drone Warfare Program* (New York: Simon & Schuster, 2016).

[4] Malik Jalal, "I'm On the Kill List. This is What it Feels Like to be Hunted by Drones," *Independent*, April 12, 2016, http://www.independent.co.uk/voices/i-am-on-the-us-kill-list-this-is-what-it-feels-like-to-be-hunted-by-drones-a6980141.html; Malik Jalal, interviewed by the author, *Scott Horton Show*, radio archive, April 13, 2016, https://scotthorton.org/interviews/41316-malik-jalal/; International Human Rights and Conflict Resolution Clinic (Stanford Law School) and Global Justice Clinic

"local anger and suspicion" of Americans among the Pakistani people.[5] Obama's Afghan policy, on the other hand, including the 2009–2012 "surge" — a massive increase of U.S. combat forces — seems to have been crafted for mostly political reasons. Together, they were one big "Af-Pak" war, the Democrats said,[6] and they meant to escalate it on both sides of the Durand Line.[7]

While Obama had been among those Bush administration critics who believed that diverting America's best forces from the mountains of Afghanistan to the deserts of Iraq was the fatal flaw in America's Afghan policy,[8] there is no real reason to believe that is the case. As has been shown, constant escalation by the U.S. in Afghanistan has only driven more and more people into the ranks of the insurgency. Obama's military escalation in that country would only have the same effect.

Al Qaeda was long gone from Afghanistan, and by 2009, only the most dishonest claimed, and most naïve believed, the NATO alliance could create a democratic, Westphalian nation-state in the heart of Central Asia — the project Bush had begun and called "unfinished business." They had already failed. But Obama, a young, liberal Democratic president with dark skin and a Muslim-sounding name, who was determined to pull virtually all U.S. forces from Iraq, concluded he would have to escalate in Afghanistan to avoid being seen as weak or soft on terrorism.[9] Just weeks after taking office, in February 2009, Obama began his escalation, ordering an increase of 17,000 soldiers and marines[10] on top of the 6,000 President Bush had sent in on his way out of office.[11] By March, 17,000 had grown

---

(NYU School of Law), "Living Under Drones: Death, Injury, and Trauma to Civilians from US Drone Practices in Pakistan," September 2012, http://chrgj.org/wp-content/uploads/2012/10/Living-Under-Drones.pdf.

[5] David Rhode, "The Obama Doctrine: How the President's Drone War is Backfiring," *Foreign Policy*, February 27, 2012, http://foreignpolicy.com/2012/02/27/the-obama-doctrine/; Doyle McManus, "US Drone Attacks in Pakistan 'Backfiring,'? Congress Told," *Los Angeles Times*, May 3, 2009, http://articles.latimes.com/2009/may/03/opinion/oe-mcmanus3.

[6] Peter Bergen, "The Ultimate AfPak Reading List," *Foreign Policy*, September 8, 2009, http://foreignpolicy.com/2009/09/08/the-ultimate-afpak-reading-list/.

[7] Gould and Fitzgerald, *Crossing Zero*.

[8] Rohde and Sanger, "How a 'Good War' in Afghanistan Went Bad."

[9] Steven Thomma et al., "More US Troops to Afghanistan? Obama's Caught in a Vise," McClatchy Newspapers, September 21, 2009, http://www.mcclatchydc.com/news/politics-government/article24556015.html; Paul D. Miller, "Setting the Record Straight on Obama's Afghanistan Promises," *Foreign Policy*, March 29, 2016, http://foreignpolicy.com/2016/03/29/setting-the-record-straight-on-obamas-afghanistan-promises/; Steve Holland, "Tough Talk on Pakistan from Obama," Reuters, August 2, 2007, http://www.reuters.com/article/us-usa-politics-obama-idUSN0132206420070802; "Obama Takes Campaign Trail Overseas," CNN, July 19, 2008, http://www.cnn.com/2008/POLITICS/07/18/obama.trip/index.html.

[10] Helene Cooper, "Putting Stamp on Afghan War, Obama Will Send 17,000 Troops," *New York Times*, February 17, 2009, http://www.nytimes.com/2009/02/18/washington/18web-troops.html.

[11] Karen DeYoung, "More Troops Headed to Afghanistan," *Washington Post*, February 18, 2009, http://www.washingtonpost.com/wp-dyn/content/article/2009/02/17/AR2009021702411.html.

to 21,000.[12] Then in October, he sent 13,000 more.[13]

Part of Obama's strategy for being perceived as tough enough to be president in wartime was keeping holdovers from the previous Republican government, including Robert Gates, Bush's second and final secretary of defense, and U.S. Army General "King" David H. Petraeus, the celebrated spinner of the myth of the successful "surge" in Iraq, who at that time was commander of U.S. Central Command. Obama also named his primary campaign rival, the consistently hawkish Hillary Clinton, to be his first secretary of state. Obama may have been wise to appoint Clinton to this role as a way to prevent her from joining with his general election opponent, Republican hawk John McCain, as a force against him in the U.S. Senate. But by keeping his enemy close, he had unfortunately brought her closer. Clinton, Gates and Petraeus together would prove to be a nearly irresistible force arguing in favor of an even bigger increase of at least another 40,000 troops and an expanded counterinsurgency mission in Afghanistan by the new year.

In 2008, at the end of the Bush administration, the president had asked his "war czar," Lt. Gen. Douglas Lute, to review the current state of the Afghan war. Lute had reported that it was fouled up beyond all recognition. There were, Lute told Bush, eight different wars being fought in Afghanistan: by the CIA, NATO, the Training and Equipping Force, Joint Special Operations Command (first-tier special operations forces), U.S. Special Operations Command (second-tier special operations forces), the Afghan National Army, the Afghan National Police (ANP) and the Afghan National Directorate for Security (their intelligence service). All of these wars were being fought completely uncoordinated with one another, with no underlying strategy and no one in charge.[14]

A few months later, in early 2009, as Obama was coming into office, Gen. Petraeus asked his friend Derek Harvey, a retired Defense Intelligence Agency officer, to do a review of his own. Harvey investigated and reported back to Petraeus that in the war "basic questions had gone unasked: *Who is the enemy? Where are they? What are their motivations?* We know too little about the enemy to craft a winning strategy." [emphasis added][15]

Perhaps these reports were being put forward simply to justify the coming escalation of the war, but it does not seem that these men had to stretch very far to paint a picture of approaching disaster. They merely had

---

[12] Michael Hastings, *The Operators: The Wild and Terrifying Inside Story of America's War in Afghanistan* (New York: Blue Rider, 2012), 22.

[13] Ewen MacAskill, "Obama Quietly Deploying 13,000 More US Troops to Afghanistan," *Guardian*, October 13, 2009, https://www.theguardian.com/world/2009/oct/13/obama-afghanistan-troop-deployment.

[14] Woodward, *Obama's Wars*, 41-43.

[15] Ibid., 77.

to ignore the previous, rose-colored spin and see reality for what it was to describe an insurgency rising in influence. Unfortunately, these men all leapt to the same conclusion that the Bush administration had simply failed to make the necessary commitment to getting the job done.

Next to write a policy review report was former CIA officer Bruce Riedel. He recommended what became the second increase of 4,000 troops that spring,[16] while admitting the war could not be won without accounting for Pakistan's ongoing support for the Afghan Taliban. There was not much that could be done there, Riedel conceded, since the U.S. could not try to bribe the Pakistanis to much effect, because it was already bribing them, and could not seriously threaten them since they have a nuclear weapons deterrent. He was certainly right about that. But Riedel's recommendations still made no sense: his report was based on the assumption that the U.S. had to win something for all its efforts in Afghanistan. All these different benchmarks and standards must be accounted for and achieved to show some level of success. But why was the U.S. in Afghanistan in the first place? What was the actual danger? Riedel was forced to stretch to conflate al Qaeda with the Pakistani Taliban, the Afghan Taliban and the Lashkar-e-Taiba, an anti-Indian force in the disputed Kashmir region between India and Pakistan, in order to portray a threat to the United States that would justify his recommended troop increase.[17]

While the president and vice president wanted to focus on killing the last of the leaders of old "core" al Qaeda in Pakistan with CIA drones, the military would not be denied their Afghan escalation. One story leaked to McClatchy news service emphasized the old, bogus "safe-haven" myth and accused the White House of "minimizing warnings" from the intelligence community that if the Afghan Taliban retook parts of Afghanistan, they would definitely invite al Qaeda back as well.[18] In fact, there was no new intelligence estimate on that point.[19] This was simply spin and conjecture by those who wanted to escalate, framing the issue in a way to make the president seem treasonous if he resisted them. Osama bin Laden was still alive and at large then, making the alleged threat of the return of al Qaeda to Afghanistan seem more urgent, though the danger was not any more real than it had been at any time since 2002.

---

[16] Woodward, *Obama's Wars*, 115.

[17] Ibid., 99-102.

[18] Jonathan S. Landay et al., "Are Obama Advisers Downplaying Afghan Dangers?," McClatchy Newspapers, October 11, 2009, http://www.mcclatchydc.com/news/nation-world/world/article24558898.html.

[19] Gareth Porter, "Gates Conceals Real Story of Gaming Obama on the Afghan War," Inter Press Service, January 10, 2014, http://www.ipsnews.net/2014/01/gates-conceals-real-story-gaming-obama-afghan-war/.

On the advice of the hawkish retired general and Petraeus ally, Jack Keane, General David McKiernan, who sincerely respected the president and looked forward to working with him, was unceremoniously fired in the middle of his command simply in order to "reset" the request for more troops.[20] McKiernan was a big supporter of Petraeus's counterinsurgency doctrine, but he had already pushed hard for the first 21,000 troops sent in the first half of 2009. The Pentagon wanted to send another 45,000 troops. With a new commander, they could get a fresh start on their demands for escalation under new leadership, so Secretary Gates persuaded Obama to fire McKiernan on the pretext that he was an ineffective commander. His replacement, General Stanley McChrystal, got to work on the push for the next troop increase right away, giving a statement to Congress that the most recent group of 22,000 that had just been sent was nowhere near enough, and a whole new escalation would be necessary to win the war. The military's "jamming" of the president, as Obama would later call it,[21] had already begun.[22]

McChrystal, who was close to CENTCOM Commander Petraeus, was put in charge of the war due to his alleged specialties in counterinsurgency warfare as former commander of the Joint Special Operations Command in Iraq where he was said to have overseen major progress against the Sunni and Shi'ite insurgencies during the "surge" of troops there in 2007. McChrystal had gained notoriety for playing a direct role in the cover-up in the case of the death of American football star and Army Ranger Pat Tillman in Afghanistan, falsely blaming his friendly fire death on the Taliban,[23] as well as for being the commander of a network of military prisons in Iraq, including the infamous Camp NAMA, short for "Nasty Ass Military Area," where men were tortured in interrogations on his watch.[24] However, to his loyal staff and the credulous Washington media, McChrystal was not just a comparatively efficient special operations commander. No, he was "Big Stan," "the Pope," a "rock star." Big Stan knew what to do. Unburdened by the restraint of the White House and

---

[20] Hastings, *The Operators*, 39.

[21] Jeffrey Goldberg, "The Obama Doctrine," *Atlantic*, April 2016, https://www.theatlantic.com/magazine/archive/2016/04/the-obama-doctrine/471525/.

[22] Woodward, *Obama's Wars*, 82-85, 123-125.

[23] Hastings, *The Operators*, 184.

[24] John H. Richardson, "Acts of Conscience," *Esquire*, September 21, 2009, http://www.esquire.com/news-politics/a879/esq0806terror-102/; Ian Cobain, "Camp Nama: British Personnel Reveal Horrors of Secret US Base in Baghdad," *Guardian*, April 1, 2013, https://www.theguardian.com/world/2013/apr/01/camp-nama-iraq-human-rights-abuses; Eric Schmitt and Carolyn Marshall, "In Secret Unit's 'Black Room,' a Grim Portrait of US Abuse," *New York Times*, March 19, 2006, http://www.nytimes.com/2006/03/19/world/middleeast/in-secret-units-black-room-a-grim-portrait-of-us-abuse.html; "'No Blood, No Foul'?: Soldiers' Accounts of Detainee Abuse in Iraq," Human Rights Watch, July 22, 2006, https://hrw.org/report/2006/07/22/no-blood-no-foul/soldiers-accounts-detainee-abuse-iraq/.

civilian leadership, which he held in near-total contempt, this ultimate American action hero was finally being allowed to move in and save the day. Retired U.S. Army colonel and foreign policy critic Andrew Bacevich has noted this adulation of both McChrystal and Petraeus as some sort of super-fit, super-sharp, even super-human machines of ultimate military brilliance and success, perpetuated throughout the media in 2009, certainly crossed the line of what should be proper in any kind of constitutional republic, and, in effect, amounted to a public campaign against the president by his own subordinates.[25]

McChrystal's report, which called for an increase of up to 85,000 more troops to stay for at least another ten years to attempt to implement Petraeus's counterinsurgency doctrine (COIN), was leaked to the *Washington Post*,[26] which, the *New York Times* reported, "some in the White House took as an attempt to box in the president," who was making it known he was skeptical about any further increases in troop levels beyond the tens of thousands he had already sent. The leak caused a minor uproar at the time, as it represented nearly unprecedented interference from those in the military chain of command into civilian decision making.[27]

Vice President Joe Biden led the argument in the administration for a more minimal plan focused on counter-terrorism, rather than escalating the war against the growing Taliban insurgency. This plan emphasized attacks on al Qaeda targets along with expanded training of the Afghan National Army, rather than a full-fledged counterinsurgency and nation-building campaign. But the Biden plan made no sense either since there were "less than 100" al Qaeda in Afghanistan, as National Security Advisor General Jim Jones pointed out in the White House debates. The war was not about al Qaeda, but fighting locals who are only fighting "because there are foreigners on their land."[28] In fact, as the late, great, doubting war reporter and muckraking journalist Michael Hastings wrote, "McChrystal's strategy has so little to do with al Qaeda that Senator Lindsey Graham has to remind McChrystal and Petraeus that they need to include more al Qaeda in their 'message' to sell the war." Al Qaeda then "became part of the regular message."[29] Not that anyone could show there were any al Qaeda members anywhere in Afghanistan. U.S. intelligence at

---

[25] Hastings, *The Operators*, 16; Bacevich, *America's War for the Greater Middle East*, 302-303.

[26] Bob Woodward, "McChrystal: More Forces or 'Mission Failure,'" *Washington Post*, September 21, 2009, http://www.washingtonpost.com/wp-dyn/content/article/2009/09/20/AR2009092002920.html; Stanley McChrystal, "COMISAF Initial Assessment (Unclassified)," *Washington Post*, September 21, 2009, http://www.washingtonpost.com/wp-dyn/content/article/2009/09/21/AR2009092100110.html.

[27] Peter Baker, "How Obama Came to Plan for 'Surge' in Afghanistan," *New York Times*, December 5, 2009, http://www.nytimes.com/2009/12/06/world/asia/06reconstruct.html.

[28] Woodward, *Obama's Wars*, 155-156, 162.

[29] Hastings, *The Operators,* 134-135.

the time said there were only between 20–100, and even they were largely mythological.[30]

In September 2009, Matthew Hoh, a former Marine Corps captain-turned State Department official, resigned his position, complaining to his superiors that the military and civilian missions in Afghanistan were an incoherent lost cause.[31] The enemy the U.S. was fighting, Hoh wrote in his resignation letter, which he released to the media, was an ethnic "Pashtun insurgency," one not necessarily tied to the Taliban movement, but simply tribesmen resisting

> what is perceived by the Pashtun people as a continued and sustained assault, going back centuries, on Pashtun land, culture, traditions and religion by internal and external enemies. The U.S. and NATO presence in Pashtun valleys and villages, as well as Afghan army and police units that are led and composed of non-Pashtun soldiers and police, provide an occupation force against which the insurgency is justified.

Citing the intractable differences between local Afghan factions across the country, the rigged re-election of President Karzai that August[32] and the government and contractors' legendary corruption — among other issues — Hoh concluded further escalation could not possibly succeed and that he needed to leave government to speak out publicly before President Obama decided on the final troop "surge." As Hoh told the *Washington Post*, "I want people in Iowa, people in Arkansas, people in Arizona, to call their congressman and say, 'Listen, I don't think this is right.'" Hoh's resignation letter concluded,

> The dead return only in bodily form to be received by families who must be reassured their dead have sacrificed for a purpose worthy of futures lost, love vanished and promised dreams unkept. I have lost confidence such assurances can anymore be made.[33]

Hoh explained a year later that counterinsurgency had actually been the policy in Afghanistan since 2004 or 2005 and that all the new escalations had ever accomplished was to drive more people into the resistance, growing its numbers and increasing its power. Hoh had no doubt Obama's new "surge" would be only more of the same but on a larger scale. By

---

[30] McKenzie, *Scott Horton Show*, September 9, 2009.

[31] Karen DeYoung, "US Official Resigns over Afghan War," *Washington Post*, October 27, 2009, http://www.washingtonpost.com/wp-dyn/content/article/2009/10/26/AR2009102603394.html.

[32] Sonia Verma, "Rival Accuses Karzai of 'Rigging' Vote," *Globe and Mail*, August 23, 2009, http://www.theglobeandmail.com/news/world/rival-accuses-karzai-of-rigging-vote/article1201677.

[33] Matthew Hoh, "Resignation Letter," *Washington Post*, September 10, 2009, http://washingtonpost.com/wp-srv/hp/ssi/wpc/ResignationLetter.pdf?sid=ST2009102603447.

then, he had already been proven correct.[34]

In fact, the military and intelligence services were so frustrated with President Karzai by this point that they considered moving him to a purely ceremonial position and making former American Ambassador Zalmay Khalilzad the "Chief Executive Officer" of the country in his place.[35]

In November, Lt. Gen. Karl W. Eikenberry, a former commander of NATO forces in the Afghan war, by then retired from the army and serving as ambassador to Afghanistan, came out in agreement with Hoh. Two of Eikenberry's recent memos that were leaked to the *New York Times* showed he had warned the White House that the Karzai government was hopelessly corrupt and that the recent rigged presidential election showed it would be a mistake to invest hundreds of billions of dollars toward another decade or more of war when failure was already a foregone conclusion. The ambassador had already explained his reasons before his colleagues in a Principals Committee meeting of the National Security Council. When his memo hit the news, the only importance it served inside the halls of power was that it publicly signaled a break between the now-ambassador and the military. It did not seem to matter that Eikenberry was correct in his assessment that the war was lost and that their plan could not work. The reaction to the memo was all outrage about broken processes and indignation on the part of these toughest of professional warriors over being contradicted in front of their peers. The same sort of childish conflict broke out leading to Director of National Intelligence James Clapper and CIA Chief Leon Panetta being temporarily excluded from the war cabinet after they were perceived to have crossed a line when one of them had commented on an issue under someone else's area of responsibility.[36]

Ambassador Eikenberry warned that the U.S. had already been trying to "Afghanize" the war, and the escalation would be a step backward in creating further central government dependency upon American military power to settle disputes. He said the Karzai regime did not seek to take over responsibility for security, development or anything else, based on their belief that the Americans would handle it. "They assume we covet their territory for a never-ending 'war on terror' and for military bases to use against surrounding powers," he explained. The ambassador also warned there existed in the country no national identity among the population or leaders beyond their local ethnicities, tribes and clans, nor any ability in the foreseeable future for the country to produce enough

[34] Matthew Hoh, interviewed by the author, *Scott Horton Show*, radio archive, September 25, 2010, http://scotthorton.org/interviews/2010/09/25/antiwar-radio-matthew-hoh/.

[35] Helene Cooper, "Ex-US Envoy May Take Key Role in Afghan Government," *New York Times*, May 18, 2009, http://www.nytimes.com/2009/05/19/world/asia/19diplo.html.

[36] Woodward, *Obama's Wars*, 261.

wealth to afford a central government without indefinite American support. Eikenberry expressed no confidence in the Afghan National Army or Afghan National Police's ability to take over for the American and allied forces, even after two more years of training. The U.S. had already been down this road — to a dead end.[37]

But the Republicans and the military were accusing Obama of "dithering" on the decision and would have certainly attacked him as soft on terrorism, or worse, if he had refused the escalation plan. So, at the end of November 2009, the president gave in to the generals, against his own better judgment, ordering another 30,000 soldiers and marines to Afghanistan.

The New York Times explained that through a "back-channel," Obama's Chief of Staff, Rahm Emanuel, was talking with Senator Lindsey Graham, key ally of Senate hawk and defeated 2008 Republican presidential candidate Senator John McCain, "who urged him to settle on a troop number 'that began with 3'" [i.e., 30-something thousand] to win the support of the GOP hawks. "I said as long as the generals are okay and there is a meaningful number, you will be okay," Graham told him. The hawks' agenda was perfectly clear: occupy Central Asia forever. As Sen. Graham put it, "nobody gives a shit" that the U.S. still occupies Europe and East Asia more than 70 years after the end of World War II, as long as there are no American casualties.[38]

"All hail Obama!" cried William Kristol, the noted neoconservative hawk and then-editor of the Weekly Standard magazine, signaling that the president had pleased and placated even the most belligerent pundits with the announced escalation.[39]

The counsel of Vice President Joe Biden, Gen. Douglas Lute and other opponents of the "surge" inside the administration, together with the Hoh and Eikenberry memos, gave Obama all the political cover he needed to reject the escalation and begin to draw down troop numbers instead. And it is "clear," as Obama would say, that he did agree with the more limited approach. As Secretary of Defense Robert Gates wrote in his memoir, the president did not "trust his commander [Petraeus], can't stand Karzai, doesn't believe in his own strategy, and doesn't consider the war to be his. For him, it's all about getting out." Gates wrongly thought the problem was that Obama just did not have enough faith, but his statement remains

---

[37] Greg Jaffe et al., "US Envoy Resists Troop Increase, Cites Karzai as Problem," Washington Post, November 12, 2009, http://www.washingtonpost.com/wp-dyn/content/article/2009/11/11/AR2009111118432.html; "Ambassador Eikenberry's Cables on US Strategy in Afghanistan," New York Times, accessed May 25, 2007, http://documents.nytimes.com/eikenberry-s-memos-on-the-strategy-in-afghanistan.

[38] Woodward, Obama's Wars, 206.

[39] Michael Goldfarb, "Kristol: All Hail Obama!" Weekly Standard, March 27, 2009, http://www.weeklystandard.com/kristol-all-hail-obama/article/28281.

evidence of the president's better judgment, and betrayal of it.[40] The political pressure on Obama to escalate the war, to attempt to replicate the so-called success of the Iraq "surge," and against withdrawing from both wars simultaneously, was too great. "Consensus" — in large part spurred on by Obama's earlier campaign rhetoric — had been achieved by the foreign policy establishment "Blob," as Obama and his advisers came to call it,[41] in the nation's capital. Escalation was the default, and those who were resistant had been put on the defensive. Would Obama snatch defeat from the jaws of victory when a sure win was just a short "surge" of troops away? No. He would escalate and lose anyway.

The choices of plans submitted to the president by the military were a "too cold" 10,000- to 11,000-man "training surge" to boost the strength of the Afghan National Army and Police, a "too hot" plan for an increase of another 85,000 troops for a "robust" counterinsurgency campaign, or 40,000 for the "just right" middle way with just enough men to implement the counterinsurgency doctrine (COIN), but with an emphasis on a quick handover of territory to the Afghan National Army.

Joint Chiefs Vice-Chairman, Marine Corps General James Cartwright, attempting to remain loyal to the president's wishes, had come up with a plan for a "hybrid" approach of adding only 20,000 more special operations forces, half of them for counter-terrorism missions and half for training, rather than the massive nation-building program that came with the Petraeus-McChrystal plan. Joint Chiefs Chairman Adm. Mike Mullen was reportedly outright insubordinate at this point, attempting to prevent Gen. Cartwright from presenting the plan the president and vice president had specifically requested.[42] Secretary of Defense Gates and Adm. Mullen "never forgave him" for persisting.[43]

At one point, frustrated beyond belief by the military's obstruction, Obama almost chose the most minimal option for the escalation: sending 10,000 more trainers only, to try to build up the Afghan National Army. Not that this plan would have succeeded either, but at least it was embracing the truth that the ANA could only do so much, and the gains it would be responsible for protecting in the future should only be those they could achieve on their own in the first place. But in the end, the president was too afraid Generals Petraeus and McChrystal,[44] as well as

---

[40] Robert M. Gates, *Duty: Memoirs of a Secretary at War*, (New York: Knopf, 2014), 557.

[41] David Samuels, "The Aspiring Novelist Who Became Obama's Foreign-Policy Guru," *New York Times Magazine*, May 5, 2016, https://www.nytimes.com/2016/05/08/magazine/the-aspiring-novelist-who-became-obamas-foreign-policy-guru.html.

[42] Woodward, *Obama's Wars*, 235-238.

[43] Josh Rogin, "General Cartwright is Paying the Price for Hillary Clinton's Sins," *Washington Post*, October 18, 2016, https://www.washingtonpost.com/news/josh-rogin/wp/2016/10/18/general-cartwright-is-paying-the-price-for-hillary-clintons-sins/?utm_term=.11c235f1b4ce.

[44] Hastings, *The Operators*, 135.

Secretary of Defense Gates,[45] would resign. It was Obama's fault for keeping Bush's men. It was his profound moral cowardice that prevented him from standing up to them when he knew giving in was wrong.

Even though Obama eventually settled on 30,000 troops and a slightly more limited mission, the generals took it as a victory for their 40,000 "just right" COIN plan and proclaimed it as such. The White House tried to emphasize Obama's insistence on limiting the number of troops to 30,000 instead of 40,000 and his moving the bell curve of force deployments to the left — the bulk of the troop increase was deployed in and out slightly faster than in the original plan. But in the end, once he conceded the principle, the president was signing up for the implementation of Petraeus and McChrystal's counterinsurgency strategy and to continue the war throughout the remainder of his two terms in office.[46]

President Obama made the call but was quick to attempt to deny responsibility for the failure of the escalation, complaining to the media he had been "jammed" by the U.S. foreign policy establishment into ordering it despite his better judgment.[47] There is no doubt this is true. Pressure from hawks in Congress, especially Senators McCain and Graham, was unrelenting. And the Pentagon, including Generals Petraeus and McChrystal, and Admiral Mike Mullen, the Chairman of the Joint Chiefs of Staff, were plainly insubordinate, leaking the "surge"-demanding assessment to the *Washington Post* and giving speeches,[48] interviews and quotes to major media sources such as *Newsweek*,[49] the *Washington Post*[50] and CBS News' *60 Minutes*,[51] to create a powerful echo-chamber effect in the media.[52] Nevertheless, the president's disavowal of responsibility is absurd. If Obama had had any real backbone, he would have refused to

[45] Woodward, *Obama's Wars*, 304.

[46] Woodward, *Obama's Wars*, 192, 278-279; Karl Eikenberry, "The Limits of Counterinsurgency Doctrine in Afghanistan," *Foreign Affairs*, September/October 2013, https://foreignaffairs.com/articles/afghanistan/2013-08-12/limits-counterinsurgency-doctrine-afghanistan.

[47] Jeffrey Goldberg, "The Obama Doctrine," *Atlantic*, April 2016, http://www.theatlantic.com/magazine/archive/2016/04/the-obama-doctrine/471525/.

[48] Alex Spillius, "White House Angry at General Stanley McChrystal Speech on Afghanistan," *Daily Telegraph*, October 5, 2009, http://www.telegraph.co.uk/news/worldnews/barackobama/6259582/White-House-angry-at-General-Stanley-McChrystal-speech-on-Afghanistan.html.

[49] Evan Thomas, "General McChrystal's Plan for Afghanistan," *Newsweek*, September 25, 2009, http://www.newsweek.com/general-mcchrystals-plan-afghanistan-79551.

[50] Ann Scott Tyson, "US Commander in Afghanistan Calls Situation 'Serious,'" *Washington Post*, September 1, 2009, http://www.washingtonpost.com/wp-dyn/content/article/2009/08/31/AR2009083101100.html; Michael Gerson, "US Has Reasons to Hope for Afghanistan," *Washington Post*, September 4, 2009, http://www.washingtonpost.com/wp-dyn/content/article/2009/09/03/AR2009090302862.html; Woodward, "McChrystal: More Forces or 'Mission Failure.'"

[51] David Martin, "McChrystal's Frank Talk on Afghanistan," *60 Minutes*, CBS News, September 24, 2009, http://www.cbsnews.com/news/mcchrystals-frank-talk-on-afghanistan/.

[52] Michael Hastings, "The Sins of General David Petraeus," Buzzfeed News, November 11, 2012, https://www.buzzfeed.com/mhastings/the-sins-of-general-david-petraeus.

order the escalation and instead given a speech saying that he had defeated John McCain fair and square in the election a year prior precisely because the American people had decided they wanted him, and not the George W. Bush-style hawks like Senator McCain, to decide these questions. That was why he won, and that was how he was going to lead, and the generals and appointees who did not like it could resign. That would have shown a lot more courage than sending other people's sons and daughters to die to prove their valor on his behalf.[53]

In truth, in purely domestic political terms, Obama may have been smart to go along with the Afghan escalation. Liberal and progressive Democratic voters had invested so much in the "hope" and "change" narrative that Obama's presidency supposedly represented, he could have been killing Afghan women and children personally and most would have just looked the other way. There were certainly plenty of notable and heroic exceptions to this, but overall the numbers do not lie. As Michael T. Heaney and Fabio Rojas show in their book, *Party in the Street: The Antiwar Movement and the Democratic Party after 9/11*, the mass of the antiwar movement from the Bush years vanished, not with the ongoing wars, but with the Bush administration itself.[54] Obama had successfully dodged an entire category of Republican political assault without jeopardizing the support of his Democratic base. Even some major feminist groups got on board to support Obama's great Afghan escalation.[55] Democrats in Congress, as well as European allies,[56] who had criticized the war in Iraq, had long treated Afghanistan as a useful scapegoat to demonstrate their commitment to national security issues by calling for escalation there instead.[57] Obama was just continuing this successful political strategy at the cost of tens of thousands of human lives.

The president gave in, escalated and extended a war he knew was destined to fail, at best betting on a slight chance of reaching some sort of settlement with the Taliban. Many Americans may be surprised to discover the purpose of the "surge" of troops to Afghanistan in 2009–2012 was never to defeat the Taliban or even to secure the country from their presence by forcing them back to their sanctuaries in Pakistan. Instead, the entire counterinsurgency doctrine promised nothing more than temporary

---

[53] Woodward, *Obama's Wars*, 194-197.

[54] Michael T. Heaney and Fabio Rojas, *Party in the Street: The Antiwar Movement and the Democratic Party after 9/11* (Cambridge, Cambridge University Press, 2015).

[55] Feminist Majority Foundation, Campaign for Afghan Women and Girls, http://feminist.org/afghan; Sonali Kolhatkar and Mariam Rawi, "Why Is a Leading Feminist Organization Lending Its Name to Support Escalation in Afghanistan?," Alternet, July 7, 2009, http://alternet.org/story/141165/why_is_a_leading_feminist_organization_lending_its_name_to_support_escalation.

[56] "CIA Report into Shoring Up Afghan War Support in Western Europe," WikiLeaks, March 26, 2010, https://file.wikileaks.org/file/cia-afghanistan.pdf.

[57] Suhrke, *When More is Less*, 49-50.

gains in certain parts of the country. As the *New York Times* described the administration's deliberations:

> Mr. Gates and others talked about the limits of the American ability to actually defeat the Taliban; they were an indigenous force in Afghan society, part of the political fabric. This was a view shared by others around the table, including Leon E. Panetta, the director of the CIA, who argued that the Taliban could not be defeated as such and so the goal should be to drive wedges between those who could be reconciled with the Afghan government and those who could not be. ...

> On Oct. 22, the National Security Council produced what one official called a 'consensus memo,' much of which originated out of the Defense Secretary's office, concluding that the United States should focus on diminishing the Taliban insurgency but not destroying it; building up certain critical ministries; and transferring authority to Afghan security forces.

Gates, Petraeus and the other military leaders promised Obama that with this plan they could have the Taliban sitting at the table, ready to concede to American terms within 18 months — by July 2011. By that time, the Afghan National Army would be trained up and ready to assume responsibility for the entire nation's security, which would allow the U.S. to begin withdrawing forces.[58]

This was the *official plan*: they were escalating an already eight-year-old war by a total of 60,000 U.S. soldiers and marines, along with tens of thousands of British, Canadian, Dutch, German, and other NATO forces, so that the Taliban would hopefully be somewhat "degraded" and "diminished" in a year and a half, while training an army they had already been training for years to virtually no effect. Gen. Petraeus, on the eve of launching his big "surge," seemed to already be climbing down from his promises, proclaiming that, "I don't think you win this war. I think you keep fighting." Comparing the Afghan occupation to the still-continuing violence in Iraq, Petraeus said, "This is the kind of fight we're in for the rest of our lives and probably our kids' lives."[59]

As Gen. McChrystal had explained at a Principals Committee meeting in the autumn of 2009, this phase of the project depended on building a 400,000-man Afghan National Army and a "reliable" partner in a strong, central Afghan government. Amb. Eikenberry reportedly interrupted and warned that a strong central government for Afghanistan did not exist, nor was it possible to create one. Corruption in Afghanistan, as partially

---

[58] Woodward, *Obama's Wars*, 113; Jonathan Alter, *The Promise: President Obama, Year One*, excerpted in *Newsweek*, May 14, 2010, http://www.newsweek.com/jonathan-alter-obama-year-one-promise-72479.

[59] Woodward, *Obama's Wars*, 332.

measured by the "Mansions of Kabul," was so far off the charts as to make a joke out of any proposal for reform, he insisted. Bob Woodward details how the Principals Committee of Obama's NSC would waste days on end arguing about how best to dump tens of billions more dollars into the Kabul government, while "fighting corruption," and bickering about what the definition of "defeat" was, while debating how to both defeat and negotiate with the Taliban at the same time, before quickly changing the subject to nothing and getting nowhere.

At the *eighth* strategy review meeting, in early November 2009, after months of this debate inside and outside of the administration and just three weeks before the big announcement, the White House was still asking the military, *"What is the mission? What are we trying to do? What are the objectives? For what purpose?"* [emphasis added] And they were still getting no good answers.[60]

It seems that at no point was it discussed or weighed in these deliberations that people would be killed — shot, bombed, blown apart — as a result of this "surge," other than in the context of public relations: how would the people's concern about casualties affect the military's timescales? Secretary of Defense Gates seemed to think virtue was to be found in steadfastly ignoring those concerns. He later wrote in his memoirs about how easily he believed the politicians could disregard the American people's will on such an important issue and his disdain for those in the cabinet who would take public opinion into account:

> Biden argued throughout the process, and would continue to argue, that the war was politically unsustainable at home. I thought he was wrong and that if the president remained steadfast and played his cards carefully, he could sustain even an unpopular war. Bush had done that with a far more unpopular war in Iraq and with both houses of Congress in the hands of the Democrats. The key was showing that we were being successful militarily, at some point announcing a drawdown of forces and being able to show that the end was in sight.[61]

Secretary of State Hillary Clinton's only obvious concern when it came to public opinion was that the national security establishment in Washington, D.C., perceive her as tough enough to be president herself one day — a calculation that evidently carried through to her failed 2016 presidential run.[62] It was obvious to the members the National Security Council at the time that the chief diplomat's choice to side with the military

[60] Woodward, *Obama's Wars*, 269.

[61] Robert M. Gates, *Duty*, 342.

[62] John Hudson, "Exclusive: Prominent GOP Neoconservative to Fundraise for Hillary Clinton," *Foreign Policy*, June 23, 2016, http://foreignpolicy.com/2016/06/23/exclusive-prominent-gop-neoconservative-to-fundraise-for-hillary-clinton/.

helped to "diminish" the president's political "running room" on the issue. She had "reduced his cover" for any "softer" approach, as they put it. Nobody in the cabinet was fooled. The rest of the team reportedly perceived this as political posturing for her own political future. The secretary's ultimately unsuccessful political ploy was not just at Obama's expense, but so many thousands of others as well.[63] Secretary Clinton's emails later revealed Gen. Wesley Clark and former National Security Advisor Sandy Berger, both of whom had served under her husband Bill Clinton during his presidency, told her the core issue was that the U.S. must convince the Pakistanis to abandon all alleged support for the members of al Qaeda hiding there, with Clark adding a word of caution about the dangers of "mission creep" in Afghanistan. However, Hillary's political adviser, Mark Penn, who had led her failed campaign for the Democratic nomination in 2008, told the secretary unequivocally that any failure to support escalation would be "politically, quite dangerous. ... Obama maintained throughout the campaign and the start of his presidency that [Afghanistan] is the one to fight and backing down here makes him and the administration vulnerable to losing moderate support and seeming weak and indecisive." Clinton seemingly took this political advice to heart, and consistently advocated for the generals' side in the administration's debates leading up to Obama's capitulation.[64] In fact, less than a week after Obama announced the "surge" escalation in a speech at West Point, Secretary of Defense Gates and Secretary of State Clinton both publicly suggested that the hard July 2011 deadline for the beginning of the drawdown was actually flexible, undermining the basis of the entire compromise with the military on the question.[65] Petraeus then followed their lead and began to publicly back down from his sworn promise to the president that he would never waver from the July 2011 date for the beginning of the withdrawal.[66]

The COINdinistas

With the incoming Obama presidency came a powerful new think tank, the Center for a New American Security (CNAS). CNAS was originally

---

[63] Woodward, *Obama's Wars*, 254.

[64] Jason Leopold and Alya Iftikhar, "Hillary Clinton Sought Advice on Afghanistan from Former Bill Clinton Advisers," Vice, July 1, 2015, https://news.vice.com/article/hillary-clinton-sought-advice-on-afghanistan-from-former-bill-clinton-advisors.

[65] Mary Katharine Ham, "Gates, Clinton Talk Afghanistan Deadlines That Aren't Really Deadlines on Sunday Shows," *Weekly Standard*, December 7, 2009, http://www.weeklystandard.com/gates-clinton-talk-afghanistan-deadlines-that-arent-really-deadlines-on-sunday-shows/article/272677; Baker, "How Obama Came to Plan for 'Surge' in Afghanistan."

[66] Woodward, *Obama's Wars*, 213-219, 224, 254.

created to groom national security officials in what was assumed would be the new Hillary Clinton administration and was dedicated to the "art" of counterinsurgency warfare. Funded by major defense contractors, investment banks, conservative foundations and foreign governments,[67] CNAS pushed hard for an escalation of the Afghan war and sought influence over and positions within the new Democratic administration. Together, the CNAS "COINdinistas" and fellow-travelers — such as former Army Ranger Andrew Exum; neoconservative intellectual Frederick Kagan and his wife Kimberly[68]; Australian COIN theorist and Petraeus adviser David Kilcullen; "Johnny Appleseed of COIN" and former military adviser to Paul Wolfowitz, John Nagl;[69] Stephen Biddle of the Council on Foreign Relations, who had previously championed the "Sunni turn" in Iraq;[70] "CNAS journalists," Thomas Ricks[71] of *Foreign Policy* and the "totally co-opted by the military" Robert Kaplan of the *Atlantic*;[72] and incoming Deputy Secretary of Defense for Policy, CNAS co-founder, Michèle Flournoy — pushed hard for an escalation of troop numbers and for the application of their counterinsurgency theories. The new Counterinsurgency Field Manual — written by Gen. Mattis along with Petraeus and his staff during the worst part of the second Iraq war — was said to contain the magic words which would help America achieve victory, or at least "success," in Afghanistan.[73]

The CNAS group may not have known the first thing about winning a war of any kind, but what a public relations coup. The cult of the military expert was in full swing. Never mind those dim-witted, Bush-era

[67] "CNAS Supporters," Center for a New American Security, accessed May 24, 2017, https://www.cnas.org/support-cnas/cnas-supporters.

[68] Frederick W. Kagan and Kimberly Kagan, "Afghan Surge Would Give US Leverage to Succeed," November 27, 2009, http://www.washingtonpost.com/wp-dyn/content/article/2009/11/25/AR2009112503537.html

[69] Tim Shorrock, "Making COIN," *Baffler*, Winter, 2016, https://thebaffler.com/salvos/making-coin-shorrock.

[70] Stephen Biddle, "Seeing Baghdad, Thinking Saigon," *Foreign Affairs*, March/April 2006, http://www.nytimes.com/cfr/international/20060301faessay_v85n2_biddle.html; Andrew Gray, "US Afghan Commander May Ask for More Troops," Reuters, July 30, 2009, http://in.reuters.com/article/idINIndia-41440620090730; Stephen Biddle, "Is There a Middle Way?," *New Republic*, October 19, 2009, https://newrepublic.com/article/70415/there-middle-way.

[71] Thomas E. Ricks, "The COINdinistas," *Foreign Policy*, November 30, 2009, http://foreignpolicy.com/2009/11/30/the-coindinistas/.

[72] Hastings, *The Operators*, 91.

[73] *Counterinsurgency FM 3-24*, Department of the Army, December 2006, http://usacac.army.mil/cac2/Repository/Materials/COIN-FM3-24.pdf; John A. Nagl, "A Better War in Afghanistan," *Joint Force Quarterly*, January 2010, https://www.questia.com/magazine/1G1-213855004/a-better-war-in-afghanistan; Andrew M. Exum, "Triage: The Next Twelve Months in Afghanistan and Pakistan," CNAS, June 10, 2009, https://www.cnas.org/publications/reports/triage-the-next-twelve-months-in-afghanistan-and-pakistan; David Galula, *Counterinsurgency Warfare: Theory and Practice* (Santa Barbara, CA: Praeger, 2006).

incompetents, the real war-scientists were in charge now, and they knew what to do.[74]

The new strategy would mean an end to stodgy old-think about the occupation and would focus instead on "clearing, holding and building" territory that had supposedly been "liberated" nearly a decade before. But this time the army was going to "*build and transfer*" — this was the all-important difference in the COINdinistas' brilliant new plan.[75]

CNAS war intellectuals promised — to credulous "expert" and media audiences everywhere — they could "*change entire societies*,"[76] even Afghanistan. All they had to do was install a little "government in a box" in each town, village or district across the country.[77] The wondrous, dedicated and experienced Afghan technocrats of these ready-made governments would then selflessly guide the country, finally, into our wonderful, Western, twenty-first century. America's COIN superheroes had "learned to eat soup with a knife."[78] Nothing could stop them now.

Persistent COIN critic Kelley Beaucar Vlahos was on the scene at a massive CNAS conference in Washington, D.C., in 2009. Vlahos described a "mix of Army brass, Navy officers in their starched whites, and soldiers in digital camo networking among the dark suits and smart skirts of the civilian elite. Defense contractors, lobbyists, analysts, journalists, administration reps, Hill staff — 1,400 of the 'best and brightest,' seeing and being seen." She could have stopped right there. Vlahos, it seems, had found the key to understanding the mystery of American foreign policy: a bunch of upper-middle class career civil servants doing their best to move up in the world. It did not matter that they were selling an obviously impossible war against an enemy hiding across the border of an allied state that would always support them. It did not matter that what they were selling was a "hearts and minds" nation-building campaign and military escalation in *Afghanistan*, or that the American people were decidedly against it.[79] All that mattered was that

---

[74] "Transcript: Gen. Petraeus, ABC News Exclusive Interview," interviewed by Martha Raddatz, ABC News, September 14, 2010, http://abcnews.go.com/WN/Afghanistan/transcript-abc-news-interview-gen-david-petraeus-afghanistan/story?id=11603013; Ricks, "The COINdinistas."

[75] Anthony H. Cordesman, "Obama's New Strategy in Afghanistan," Center for Strategic and International Studies, December 2, 2009, https://www.csis.org/analysis/obama%E2%80%99s-new-strategy-afghanistan.

[76] John Nagl, "Unprepared," review of *The Echo of Battle: The Army's Way of War*, by Brian Linn McAllister, *RUSI Journal* 153, no. 2 (2008): 82-83, http://smallwarsjournal.com/documents/naglunprepared.pdf.

[77] David Sanger, "A Test for the Meaning of Victory in Afghanistan," *New York Times*, February 13, 2010, http://www.nytimes.com/2010/02/14/weekinreview/14sanger.html.

[78] John A. Nagl, *Learning to Eat Soup with a Knife: Counterinsurgency Lessons from Malaya and Vietnam* (Chicago: University of Chicago Press, 2005).

[79] Paul Steinhauser, "Poll: Support for Afghan War at All-time Low," CNN Politics, September 15, 2009, http://www.cnn.com/2009/POLITICS/09/15/afghan.war.poll/index.html.

COIN and troop "surges" were the cool new fad in Washington, and, for those in a position to exploit it, this was the opportunity of a lifetime to get some attention and maybe a chance at that promotion they'd been hoping for. They all held panel discussions. They all said lots of important things. It was all very "heady" and exciting. And it was all junk. The COINdinista phenomenon might as well have been a study in social psychology at the local college. Dissenting military strategists like U.S. Army Colonels Gian Gentile[80] and Douglas Macgregor[81] were left to grumble under their breath on the sidelines.[82]

As Col. Gentile later wrote in *Wrong Turn: America's Deadly Embrace of Counterinsurgency*, faith in the brilliance and sure-fire success of the new counterinsurgency manual in the hands of men such as Generals McChrystal and Petraeus had grown into something like a religion. And yet the whole thing was obviously hogwash. COIN was already a proven failure. The historical examples cited of the successful use of similar doctrines were highly dubious victories, at best. The British had only won in Malaya because they were fighting against a marginal minority uprising that they simply defeated and removed in a massive conventional war and ethnic cleansing campaign. In Algeria and Vietnam, the French *lost* and were driven out in humiliation. When the Americans joined the French in defeat in Vietnam, the consequences were disastrous for all sides.[83]

Though common mythology has it that the U.S. could have finally won in Vietnam if only Congress had allowed time for the counterinsurgency doctrine to be implemented, in fact, the U.S. had been trying a "Clear, Hold, Build" strategy in Vietnam since 1962. America's attempted counterinsurgency war there showed that temporary security gains were meaningless if not combined with success in nation-building and establishing the legitimacy of the central state — something that has proved to be as impossible in Afghanistan as it was in Vietnam.[84]

Nor was the second Iraq war a model for progress in Afghanistan. The story of the success of Petraeus's Iraq troop "surge" in 2007, a major premise upon which the plan for the 2010 Afghan escalation was based, was never what the politicians and media portrayed it to be. The temporary, comparative reduction in violence in Iraq after the troop increase there was mostly due to the fact that the U.S. was fighting in a civil war on the side of the majority Shi'ite Arabs against a weak minority, the Sunni Arabs. The Sunni insurgency, after suffering major losses,

---

[80] Gian Gentile, *Wrong Turn: America's Deadly Embrace of Counterinsurgency* (New York: New, 2013).

[81] Hastings, "The Runaway General."

[82] Kelley Beaucar Vlahos, "One-Sided COIN," *American Conservative*, August 1, 2009, http://www.theamericanconservative.com/articles/one-sided-coin-2/.

[83] Gian, *Wrong Turn*, 35-58, 59-84.

[84] "The Strategic Hamlet Program, 1961-1963," *Pentagon Papers*.

including possession of the capital city of Baghdad, simply needed time to regroup before going back to war. The Sunni tribal fighters that dominated the Iraqi insurgency had already turned against and begun to marginalize the worst of their allies, al Qaeda in Iraq — which at that time was mostly led by foreigners from Saudi Arabia[85] and Egypt[86] — long before Petraeus ever took charge,[87] for overstepping their bounds of authority over local Sunnis. Additionally, al Qaeda in Iraq's terrorist tactics had helped to provoke a devastating "cleansing" campaign by Shi'ite militias in response. Insurgent leaders were therefore willing to accept American money and guns to stop fighting the U.S. occupation for a time and instead complete this ultimately temporary marginalization of al Qaeda in Iraq. This was the so-called Sunni Tribal "awakening" movement where former insurgent fighters became known as the "Concerned Local Citizens," or "Sons of Iraq," on the American payroll, and were, in essence, deputized to patrol their own neighborhoods and eliminate al Qaeda.[88] At the same time, the increase in numbers of U.S. forces in Iraq during the 2007 "surge" mostly served to abet the completion of Shi'ite forces' sectarian "cleansing" of Sunnis from Baghdad.[89] "Clearing, Holding and Building" and winning over the goodwill of the local population was never even really the plan. Nor did the relative peace of desolation in the capital city help to lead to any sort of political reconciliation and integration among the factions, which had been the stated goal of the entire project.[90] The winning majority Shi'ite side had been freed of their last incentive to compromise with their defeated rivals. They then promptly kicked the U.S. right out of the country without so much as a thanks or the rights to a single,

---

[85] Bill Roggio, "Profiles of Saudi Terrorists," FDD's Long War Journal, July 5, 2005, http://www.longwarjournal.org/archives/2005/07/profiles_of_sau.php.

[86] Kim Gamel, "A New Face at the Top of al-Qaeda in Iraq," *Washington Post*, June 16, 2006, http://washingtonpost.com/wp-dyn/content/article/2006/06/16/AR2006061600272_pf.html.

[87] Sabrina Tavernise and Dexter Filkins, "Local Insurgents Tell of Clashes with Al Qaeda's Forces in Iraq," *New York Times*, January 12, 2006, http://www.nytimes.com/2006/01/12/world/middleeast/local-insurgents-tell-of-clashes-with-al-qaedas-forces-in.html; John Ward Anderson, "Iraqi Tribes Strike Back at Insurgents," *Washington Post*, March 7, 2006, http://www.washingtonpost.com/wp-dyn/content/article/2006/03/06/AR2006030601596.html; Kathleen Ridolfo, "Iraq: Sunni Insurgents Turning Against Al-Zarqawi," Radio Free Europe/Radio Liberty, January 26, 2006, http://www.rferl.org/a/1065108.html.

[88] Hala Jaber, "American-backed Killer Militias Strut Across Iraq," *London Times*, November 25, 2007, http://timesonline.co.uk/tol/news/world/iraq/article2937104.ece or http://www.heal-online.org/iraq112507.pdf.

[89] Maggie Fox, "Satellite Images Show Ethnic Cleanout in Iraq," Reuters, September 19, 2008, http://www.reuters.com/article/us-iraq-lights-idUSN1953066020080919; "Baghdad's New Owners," *Newsweek*, September 9, 2007, http://www.newsweek.com/baghdads-new-owners-100331; Joel Wing, "Columbia University Charts Sectarian Cleansing of Baghdad," Musings on Iraq, November 19, 2009, http://musingsoniraq.blogspot.com/2009/11/blog-post.html.

[90] Lionel Beehner and Greg Bruno, "Backgrounder: What are Iraq's Benchmarks?," Council on Foreign Relations, March 11, 2008, http://www.cfr.org/iraq/iraqs-benchmarks/p13333.

permanent American base.[91] Within a few years, Iraq would completely fall apart, with the losing minority Sunni Arabs breaking away from Baghdad's rule and declaring bin Laden's once seemingly impossible dream, an Islamist caliphate, the so-called Islamic State, in the predominantly Sunni Arab areas of western and northwestern Iraq and eastern Syria — at least for a few years.[92] This was Obama's template for victory in Afghanistan.

As Col. Gentile pointed out, back in Malaya and Vietnam, the British and French had called this same doctrine "counter-revolutionary warfare." And so the American people, proud of their distant revolutionary past and deeply in denial about their position as the world's most powerful empire, had to be sold on the idea that rather than enforcing a British-style colonial repression of local populations, the Afghan occupation was good-old American liberation, just like when our grandfathers saved France from the Nazis in World War II. The Pentagon's public relations men thus changed the name of this military doctrine from "counter-revolutionary" to "counterinsurgency" to frame these wars not as invasions of conquest and domination, but heroic struggles to save nice civilians against those terrorists living among them who would try to thwart the benevolent forces of progress and freedom American troops were attempting to deliver.

This narrative successfully evades the real question COIN proponents have never truly been made to address: Does America not have to be an empire, dominating someone else's country, to even have an insurgency to pacify? When faced with this question, war proponents can always switch right back to the safe-haven myth: we still must never fully cut and run, or who knows what might happen? In the meantime, the U.S.A. has taken over the role of the region's oppressor from the hated English, with UK forces now acting as junior partners in almost all of America's wars.[93]

Gentile also notes that the U.S. had been practicing COIN-style nation building from the beginning of the Afghan occupation, with more than enough time and money spent on advancing governance here and democracy there, and working hard to build up local police so they can better protect the people. Just as in the Vietnam War, waging counterinsurgency in Afghanistan had been the doctrine from the very outset, it just never accomplished anything. "The idea that any of this ever made sense or has ever worked should be buried deep in the ground, yet

---

[91] "President Bush and Iraq Prime Minister Maliki Sign the Strategic Framework Agreement and Security Agreement," Office of the Press Secretary, December 14, 2008, https://georgewbush-whitehouse.archives.gov/news/releases/2008/12/20081214-2.html.

[92] Matt Bradley, "ISIS Declares New Islamist Caliphate," *Wall Street Journal*, June 29, 2014, https://www.wsj.com/articles/isis-declares-new-islamist-caliphate-1404065263; Gordon Lubold and Felicia Schwartz, "US Hails Reclamation of Mosul," July 10, 2017, *Wall Street Journal*, https://www.wsj.com/articles/u-s-hails-reclamation-of-mosul-1499735959.

[93] Gian, *Wrong Turn*, 6.

the belief that counterinsurgency works persists like a vampire among the living."[94] At one point the COINdinistas became so convinced of their coming success in the midst of the Afghan escalation, they began speaking of immediately stepping it up and embracing "GCOIN" — *Global* Counterinsurgency deployments "from Somalia to the Philippines,"[95] or anywhere an ally has some fighters who need keeping down. As Amb. Eikenberry later joked, "'COIN' [had] evolved from a noun to an adjective, and its overuse became almost a parody of faithful Red Guards chanting Maoist slogans during the Cultural Revolution."[96]

Writer Tom Engelhardt warned in late 2009 that the Afghan "surge" was to be a massive project, with the addition of tens of thousands of U.S. and coalition troops, including first- and second-tier special operations forces; huge numbers of new bases across the country — some of them literally the size of small towns, equipped with their own Burger Kings, Baskin-Robbins, Taco Bells, movie theaters and everything else an army with a bottomless budget could provide; a massive increase of civilian contractors, State Department officials and NGO do-gooders; mercenaries, CIA paramilitaries and spies; the creation of new extra-legal militias of different tribal groups; expanded training of the Afghan National Army and Afghan National Police forces; the escalation of the drone war in neighboring Pakistan; and expanded costs for all concerned, both financial and in terms of lost lives and limbs. Every bit of it played out just as Engelhardt predicted: the "surge" became a massive government program on the other side of the planet that could never "work" beyond giving these particular departments something to do and something to spend money on.[97]

Secretary of State Hillary Clinton had brought on her old friend Richard Holbrooke as Special Representative for Afghanistan and Pakistan to lead the diplomatic efforts that were meant to complement — or be complemented by — the increase in military force. Though Holbrooke never had the confidence of the president or his top staff,[98] even if Obama had given 100 percent support to the envoy's efforts, and Holbrooke had been as competent as he insisted he was, there is no reason to believe he could have succeeded. The insurgent tribes did not have enough incentive to deal, unless, as the hawks complained, Obama would have been willing to stay in overwhelming force and fight them forever,

---

[94] Ibid., 113-129, 135.

[95] Shorrock, "Making COIN."

[96] Karl Eikenberry, "The Limits of Counterinsurgency Doctrine in Afghanistan," *Foreign Affairs*, September/October 2013.

[97] Tom Engelhardt, "The Nine Surges of Obama's War," TomDispatch, December 10, 2009, http://www.tomdispatch.com/post/175176/tomgram%3A__state_of_surge%2C_afghanistan/.

[98] Woodward, *Obama's Wars*, 357.

and even then it is hard to see how that would have done anything but benefit the insurgency overall, just as the previous decade of occupation and escalation had. As it was, all the Taliban had to do was wait. On the other side, Holbrooke apparently envisioned a Grand Bargain agreed to by all the regional players to include Iran, Russia and China, and even a peaceful final resolution to the Indian-Pakistani dispute over control over the land of Kashmir. This was magical thinking for a set of intractable problems. Holbrooke died in December 2010, unable to see his impossible mission even get started enough to fail.[99]

The fact that the entire project was destined to fall apart was obvious to anyone who did not have a vested interest in believing the hype about the greatness of the CNAS and military COINdinistas. Patrick Cockburn described the problems the U.S. was facing just as President Obama was ordering his first wave of reinforcements in the spring of 2009. First was the Pakistan problem, "fighting the Taliban in one country [while] allied with its main supporters in another." The enormous common border between the two countries provided almost endless opportunities for insurgents to take shelter and strike when they saw fit. Indeed, the local tribesmen do not recognize the so-called Durand Line that supposedly separates ethnic Pashtuns in the two countries in the first place. The Afghan government was already warning that more fighting would not be enough to defeat the Taliban, especially if air power was used, as the resulting high level of civilian casualties would just drive more people into the insurgency. Cockburn also presciently warned that Obama's newly launched CIA drone war in Pakistan would have to have a large intelligence apparatus set up inside the country for it to work and that the U.S. would pay a big political price for operating there. He went on to cite a recent BBC report showing growing unpopularity of U.S. forces rising with their increased presence, as well as greater acceptance among locals of the Taliban insurgency against them, as reasons to be skeptical of all the claims about the good another big troop increase could accomplish.[100]

Gen. McChrystal's high-end request in his report to Obama was for 85,000 additional troops and a decades-long, open-ended commitment to counterinsurgency. Even then there was no reason to think such a commitment could have achieved victory. But escalating with fewer troops than that, COIN proponents conceded, was just politics, or "adding time to the Washington clock."[101] The plan was simply to let the military keep

[99] Nicholas Kristof, "What Holbrooke Knew," *New York Times,* May 14, 2011, http://www.nytimes.com/2011/05/15/opinion/15kristof.html.
[100] Patrick Cockburn, interviewed by the author, *Scott Horton Show,* radio archive, April 29, 2009, http://scotthorton.org/interviews/antiwar-radio-patrick-cockburn-8/.
[101] Julian E. Barnes, "Americans Won't Accept 'Long Slog' in Afghanistan War, Gates Says," *Los Angeles Times,* July 19, 2009, http://articles.latimes.com/2009/jul/19/nation/na-gates19.

fighting for a while longer. The Pentagon even created a new group, the Pakistan-Afghanistan Coordinating Cell (PACC) — a whole new chain of command — to allow McChrystal to evade all the other generals at the Pentagon who might want to stick their noses in. The general and his staff reportedly maintained virtually no relationships with the State Department officials they were supposed to be working with as partners on various "good government" projects around the country to guarantee the success of the pacification operation.[102]

As far as the failure of the State Department and associated civilian agencies and organizations to extend their reach to the majority of the people, in the end, it is just as well. As Astri Suhrke showed in *When More is Less: The International Project in Afghanistan*,[103] U.S. money spent on nation-building projects only makes every problem worse, not better. The best-case scenario is that the money is simply wasted, burned or dumped in a black hole before it falls directly into the hands of the insurgency. Without peace, "reconstruction" achieves no results other than worsening corruption. Authors of a late-2016 SIGAR report agreed that U.S. aid had not helped, but, in fact, had sabotaged the nation-building effort in Afghanistan by fueling the rise of one of the most corrupt and ineffective governments on the face of the earth.[104]

Karzai routinely complained that the Provincial Reconstruction Teams were building "parallel government institutions," which undermined the authority of the national government. Yet the more help the U.S. provided to Kabul, the more he appeared to be nothing but a puppet of NATO, undermining his authority even further. Eikenberry later wrote, "the more resources the Americans threw into the Afghan cauldron, the more Karzai felt compelled to burnish his own nativist credentials by lashing out at what he decried as pernicious U.S. influence. ... Ultimately ... a COIN approach is predicated on the general alignment of the foreign and host nations' overarching political and military strategies, and this was simply not the case in Afghanistan."[105]

---

[102] Gould and Fitzgerald, *Crossing Zero*, 130-131.

[103] Suhrke, *When More is Less*.

[104] Sune Engel Rasmussen, "US Funds Fed Corruption in Afghanistan, Eroding Security," *Guardian*, September 14, 2016, https://www.theguardian.com/world/2016/sep/14/afghanistan-corruption-us-military-taliban-security; SIGAR, "Corruption in Conflict."

[105] Karl Eikenberry, "The Limits of Counterinsurgency Doctrine in Afghanistan," *Foreign Affairs*, September/October 2013, https://www.foreignaffairs.com/articles/afghanistan/2013-08-12/limits-counterinsurgency-doctrine-afghanistan.

Escalation

In early 2009, Michael Hastings explained the mission in Afghanistan from the point of view of the troops fighting near the eastern border with Pakistan. In describing the role of U.S. soldiers under the command of U.S. Army Captain Terry Hilt, Hastings wrote,

> It's an accepted fact among Hilt and his men that the area they are responsible for is so large it's nearly impossible for them to have any lasting impact. So they do what they can, going out each day as long as the wrecker is around to pull the MRAPs (the million-dollar armored vehicles that can withstand a roadside bomb) out of the mud if they get stuck, teaching the Afghan police how not to be fuckups, trying to resolve the occasional complex tribal dispute, and running into the enemy and engaging in battle with increasing frequency.[106]

As Hastings described, the unit he was embedded with was "about 25 guys with about 350 square miles to cover, a good stretch of it along the Afghanistan-Pakistan border. They're not even going to be able to see most of the area they're responsible for. And essentially, a lot of it is the familiar story of riding around and waiting to get hit."

It was obvious to Hastings and the soldiers he was with then that the impending escalation of the war would likely fail to achieve anything of note. When it came to the new, celebrated counterinsurgency doctrine, the senior level officers and military planners involved were as skeptical as any grunt on the ground. Many officers would have preferred to focus on the last al Qaeda fighters in Pakistan than to expand the occupation even further. "There has been some push-back," Hastings said, "but unfortunately the guys who are pushing back are not the ones who are calling the shots." He went on to explain that because of the nature of the promotions system within the army bureaucracy, no matter how bad the war went, there was no incentive for anyone to recommend leaving. This, he said, coupled with a complete lack of urgency surrounding the entire mission, ultimately seemed a prescription for endless mission creep and war, even as military leaders admitted that "there is no military solution" to the problem of the Taliban. But who said anything about a solution? David Kilcullen, the Australian counterinsurgency adviser to Gen. Petraeus, had told Hastings he was calling for a full 25-year commitment to Afghanistan and Pakistan starting from the beginning of the escalation in 2009.[107]

---

[106] Michael Hastings, "Obama's War," *GQ*, March 31, 2009, http://www.gq.com/story/obama-afghanistan-iraq-war-troops.

[107] Michael Hastings, interviewed by the author, *Scott Horton Show*, radio archive, April 21, 2009, http://scotthorton.org/interviews/2009/04/21/antiwar-radio-michael-hastings/.

And yet, how much of the insurgency really was made up of the old Taliban anyway? As Bette Dam confirmed after spending time in the southern provinces interviewing the insurgents, Taliban control of the project was vastly overstated. Attacks of all kinds were just automatically blamed on the Taliban whether they had anything to do with them or not. According to Dam, even the existence of the Taliban itself was overstated, not just their role in the insurgency. For example, Mullah Akhtar Muhammad Mansour, Mullah Omar's successor as leader of the Taliban, was by all accounts a divisive figure who served only his tribe rather than the entire remnant of the old Taliban government that had existed before 2001. Not only was there no single and simple "Taliban insurgency" to focus the fight on, there was really no organized group to bring to the table even if all the renewed fighting was somehow successful.[108]

When the first wave of reinforcements was sent in early 2009, instead of going to the all-important southern Kandahar Province, the marines were sent to the much more sparsely populated Helmand Province next door. According to Rajiv Chandrasekaran, *Washington Post* reporter and author of *Little America: The War Within the War for Afghanistan*, this was primarily due to "a reliance on understaffed NATO partners for crucial intelligence, a misjudgment of Helmand's importance to Afghanistan's security, and tribal politics within the Pentagon." As current Afghan war commander, General John Nicholson explained then, the feelings of the Canadian troops who were allegedly already holding things down in Kandahar Province were considered very important, and the U.S. did not want to make them look bad. In Chandrasekaran's estimation, this decision was itself a fatal blow to the war effort as this force was completely wasted, with the "Marines … confining themselves to a far less important patch of desert." In fact, though Gen. McChrystal and everyone else in the U.S. command other than the Marine Corps agreed they were being wasted there,[109] he would later dispatch thousands more army soldiers to Helmand to reinforce the marines already out making new enemies in the middle of nowhere.[110]

Frank Ledwidge, author of *Investment in Blood: The True Cost of Britain's Afghan War*,[111] later explained why COIN had been such a failure for the British army in Helmand Province as well. The soldier-central planners did

---

[108] Dam, *Scott Horton Show*, August 24, 2016.

[109] Hastings, *The Operators*, 79-80.

[110] "'Little America' book excerpt: Obama's Troop Increase for Afghan War Was Misdirected," excerpted from *Little America: The War Within the War for Afghanistan,* by Rajiv Chandrasekaran, *Washington Post,* June 22, 2012, https://www.washingtonpost.com/world/war-zones/little-america-excerpt-obamas-troop-increase-for-afghan-war-was-misdirected/2012/06/22/gJQAYHrAvV_story.html.

[111] Frank Ledwidge, *Investment in Blood: The True Cost of Britain's Afghan War* (New Haven, CT: Yale University Press, 2013).

not understand who was who or what was happening on the ground in the country they were occupying. The troops instead "imposed their own reality" on the situation, one necessarily false and bound to backfire. Even though the British were supposedly the experts in counterinsurgency, there to show the Americans how it was done, journalist Jean MacKenzie had to clue them in to the fact that the locals absolutely hated them, even though they had just arrived. "The only place on the planet where the British army would be less welcome," she explained, "is the Bogside in Londonderry [in Northern Ireland]. You have a history here of four wars, this being the fourth, in each case you've been seen as rapacious invaders coming here for your own benefit. And furthermore, not 100 miles from here is where your worst defeat in Afghan eyes took place. You could not have come to a more hostile, anti-British environment than Helmand." This incredibly important history was news to Ledwidge, and would have been to the UK and U.S. armies as well.[112]

In fact, due to the legacy of historical British invasions and wars in Afghanistan, the presence of UK forces had been as much of a problem as a help for American goals since the very beginning of the U.S. war there. When they showed up at the Bagram air base in November 2001 without informing anyone in the Northern Alliance first, Abdullah Abdullah and others the U.S. was working to rally together in the face of the recent death of Shah Massoud were extremely angry, and it nearly had the effect of sabotaging initial U.S. efforts to put together the new government.[113]

It was impossible for the Pashtun population to see occupying U.S. and UK forces as anything but the primary threat to their lives and way of life.[114] In the places where the Afghan "surge" had temporarily reduced the numbers of Taliban attacks and the degree of their influence over the population, things were already returning to normal as the forces withdrew. It was never a question whether highly trained and well-equipped American and NATO troops could "clear and hold" territory wherever they went in Afghanistan, but the "build and transfer" part of the plan would predictably amount to nothing but discarded old slogan fragments.[115]

[112] Frank Ledwidge, interviewed by the author, *Scott Horton Show*, radio archive, January 2, 2015, https://scotthorton.org/interviews/10215-frank-ledwidge/.

[113] Berntsen and Pezzullo, *Jawbreaker*, 209-210.

[114] David Collins et al., "Rogue SAS Unit Accused of Executing Civilians in Afghanistan," *Sunday Times*, July 2, 2017, https://www.thetimes.co.uk/article/rogue-sas-unit-accused-of-executing-civilians-in-afghanistan-f2bqlc897; David Brown, "SAS Under Investigation Over 'Rogue Unit' Deaths in Afghanistan," July 3, 2017, *London Times*,https://www.thetimes.co.uk/article/sas-under-investigation-over-rogue-unit-deaths-in-afghanistan-2cbbt7ks3; "SAS 'Murderers' Ignored Warning of Wrong Targets in Afghanistan," *Sunday Times*, July 9, 2017, https://www.thetimes.co.uk/edition/news/sas-murderers-ignored-warning-of-wrong-targets-in-afghanistan-dqw9tgzst.

[115] Ledwidge, *Scott Horton Show*, January 2, 2015.

Operation Moshtarak, the invasion and occupation of an area called Marjah in the southern Helmand Valley beginning in February 2010, was said to be the first "test case"[116] for the implementation of Gen. Petraeus's rewritten counterinsurgency doctrine in Afghanistan. Hyped as a "city" of 80,000 people by the mainstream media, Marjah was, in fact, a small farming district[117] out in the vast, agricultural Helmand Province. The discrepancy in population size was part of the public relations effort by Marine Corps commanders to sell the escalation. If they could prove the success of COIN in Marjah while casting the village as a significant target, then they would look so much the better.[118] In terms of actual strategy, though, the invasion of the entirely rural and sparsely populated province made little sense. The war planners all agreed the marines would have been of much more use in the neighboring Kandahar Province, though there is little reason to believe they would have done more good than harm there either. Regardless, despite his well-justified reservations, McChrystal went ahead and embraced the mission entirely, and the marines stayed. This, he promised, would be the first successful test for COIN in Afghanistan before moving on to Kandahar City. The public was assured that the installation of handpicked administrators to run the town was certain to be a proven success in no time. "We've got a government in a box, ready to roll in," Gen. McChrystal told the *New York Times*.

> The gamble here is that once Afghans see the semblance of a state taking hold in Marjah, rank-and-file Taliban will begin to take more seriously the offers that Mr. Karzai and the West are dangling to buy them off. Enticed by the offer of some political role in Afghan society — and a regular paycheck — they will think twice about trying to recapture the town. "We think many of the foot soldiers are in it for the money, not the ideology," one British official said recently. "We need to test the proposition that it's cheaper to enrich them a little than to fight them every spring and summer."[119]

The "test case" was a complete failure. Again, no one doubted the power of U.S. marines to occupy the area, but as *Stars and Stripes* later noted in a post-mortem on the mission:

> Even the choice of the name for the operation carried foreboding for the pending governing and development portion of the

---

[116] Sue Pleming and Philip Barbara, eds., "Analysts Assess Marjah Offensive," Reuters, March 1, 2010, http://in.reuters.com/article/idININdia-46567720100301.
[117] "Marjah, Afghanistan," Google Maps, Earth View, https://www.google.com/maps/place/Marjeh,+Afghanistan.
[118] Gareth Porter, "Fiction of Marjah as City Was US Misinformation," Inter Press Service, March 9, 2010, http://original.antiwar.com/porter/2010/03/08/fiction-of-marjah-as-city.
[119] Sanger, "A Test for the Meaning of Victory in Afghanistan."

counterinsurgency effort, which pinned success on winning over the people. "Moshtarak" is a Dari word, and Dari is largely the language of the country's north; residents of the southern province of Helmand overwhelmingly speak Pashto and often feel little kinship with Dari speakers. ...

McChrystal's hand-picked Marjah district governor, Abdul Zahir Aryan, had spent the last 15 years in Germany, four of them in prison for stabbing his stepson, who intervened when Aryan was beating his wife. In Marjah, he lived on a U.S. military base, was out of touch with a country he had left so many years before and was despised by local residents. He lasted six months in the job before being quietly removed. He was later murdered under mysterious circumstances.

HBO's 2011 original documentary, *The Battle for Marjah*,[120] followed the Marines' Bravo Company during Operation Moshtarak. Innocent people were killed, including young girls. The marines patronized the victims' father with apologies and promises of a better future and distributed $2,500 "condolence payments" for each of the dead civilians, but no hearts or minds seem to be won. Since the Afghan National Army was almost entirely made up of Tajiks from Afghanistan's north,[121] and a local drive to recruit police failed, the marines are shown signing up a local militia to act as the "police." By this point, the complete make-work nature of this government job is too plain to be ignored. Pointing to the pathetic rag-tag militia before him, surely no match for the insurgency, a captain explains to a young marine with no small bit of irony that they are "our exit strategy. This [group], turn it into the police. Then go to the next village and turn them into the police, and then we go home." Though he did not say it, the captain's tone suggested he knew full-well the situation would never last, but that fact would just have to be someone else's problem in the future. These men were sent to accomplish an impossible task. Going through the motions and checking off boxes while trying not to get killed was the best anyone could expect. One young marine seems to begin to understand the locals' predicament when he explains the people they were "helping" kept telling them, "they just want to live their lives." The other marines explain the locals would always prefer the Taliban to the Americans for the simple reason that the Taliban are their husbands, sons and neighbors while the U.S. Army and Marine Corps are from ten million miles away. It was clear in the film that since the marines had been sent on a nonsensical mission to protect the people from themselves, they had decided instead simply to try to keep each other alive until the time came

---

[120] Ben Anderson, *The Battle for Marjah*, directed by Anthony Wonke, (New York: HBO Films, 2011), DVD, http://www.hbo.com/documentaries/the-battle-for-marjah/.

[121] Porter, "Tajik Grip on Afghan Army Signals New Ethnic War."

to rotate home.

McChrystal himself gave up on Marjah fairly quickly, admitting publicly it was a "bleeding ulcer," and that little progress was being made there. If only the COIN "surge" had lasted another 10–15 years, then we would have seen real progress, Kilcullen told *Stars and Stripes*, "We just didn't put the time in."[122]

On the contrary, even during the actual occupation of Marjah, the insurgents never went anywhere but inside their homes — and then only in the daytime. At night they still ruled, exacting vengeance on anyone who cooperated with the occupation and making sure U.S. and mostly Tajik Afghan National Army forces never made any progress. The marines never truly controlled the town the whole time they occupied it. If the military could not clear, hold or build an entire society while they were still there, then the final phase of the Obama administration's counterinsurgency doctrine — the "transfer" of authority from U.S. forces over to the central government in Kabul — was never going to happen. It never did. Today Marjah, and indeed virtually the entire Helmand Province, is controlled by the Taliban.[123]

This should have been no surprise. All the reasons for the failures of the Afghan "surge," in contrast to the supposedly successful one waged in Iraq, had been laid out by Petraeus himself: in Afghanistan, unlike Iraq, the insurgency was winning, not already badly losing to the majority population; they had sanctuary in a neighboring state; and they knew the U.S. had to leave sooner or later, while they would be around forever. In Petraeus-speak, they had "resolve" and faced no real pressure or reason to give up the fight; the political process in the country lacked even the legitimacy of the state in Baghdad, which was backed by the majority Shi'ite Arab population and their Kurdish allies there; they were unable to repeat the Iraqi Sunni Arab tribal "awakening" — these Afghan Taliban fighters were the "Concerned Local Citizens," but there were no foreign fighter, al Qaeda in Iraq-type terrorists for the U.S. to bribe the Taliban to split away from and to consider a common enemy; and, finally, according to Gen. Petraeus, the Taliban courts provided better security and fairer dispute resolution than the U.S. or the regime the U.S. had installed in power. The insurgents' shadow government was indigenous to the population and was not going anywhere, and the military knew it.[124]

---

[122] Heath Druzin, "A Look at How the US-Led Coalition Lost Afghanistan's Marjah District to the Taliban: Misunderstanding Afghan Ideology Key to Coalition's Failure to Maintain Control," *Stars and Stripes,* January 16, 2016, http://www.stripes.com/news/middle-east/a-look-at-how-the-us-led-coalition-lost-afghanistan-s-Marjah-district-to-the-taliban-1.389156.

[123] Taimoor Shah and Rod Nordland, "Taliban Take an Afghan District, Sangin, That Many Marines Died to Keep," *New York Times*, March 23, 2017, https://www.nytimes.com/2017/03/23/world/asia/afghanistan-taliban-helmand-sangin.html."

[124] Woodward, *Obama's Wars*, 243.

Drug Wars

Taxes on poppy farmers and opium producers provide hundreds of millions of dollars per year[125] in revenue for the Taliban. And yet, any attempt by the Kabul government or U.S. forces to eradicate it just enrages the population and increases support for their insurgency.[126]

As Reagan-era NSC official Oliver North wrote for Fox News, Marjah was also to be the test case for the American Drug Enforcement Agency's "surge"-era effort to eradicate poppy crops and bribe local farmers not to harvest the crops they had already sown. DEA "administrator" Michele Leonhart, who North claimed "may have made the most important contribution to bringing an end to the Taliban," told Fox:

> The DEA is completely committed to winning this battle. Our blood has been spilled here. Locking up corrupt officials involved with narcotics is not only good for the people of Afghanistan, it's good for these Marines and the American people too.[127]

The U.S. has spent at least $8.4 billion in Afghanistan trying to abolish poppy farming since 2001. As NBC News reported in 2015, over this same time frame Afghan opium had grown from 70 to 90 percent of the world black-market supply.[128] It is now a more than $3 billion per year industry.[129]

SIGAR explained, "Afghan farmers are growing more opium than ever. The Afghan insurgency receives significant funding from participating in and taxing the illicit narcotics trade, raising the question of whether the Afghan government can ever prevail without tackling the narcotics problem." Yet U.S. attempts to clamp down on poppy cultivation, and Afghan officials' increased ability to extort bribes from those seeking exceptions, have also helped drive Pashtun peasant farmers into the arms of the Taliban insurgency for protection.[130]

---

[125] Hashim Wahdatyar, "How Opium Fuels the Taliban's War Machine in Afghanistan," Diplomat, October 28, 2016, http://www.thediplomat.com/2016/10/how-opium-fuels-the-talibans-war-machine-in-afghanistan; Matthieu Aikins, "Afghanistan: The Making of a Narco State," Rolling Stone, December 4, 2014, http://www.rollingstone.com/politics/news/afghanistan-the-making-of-a-narco-state-20141204.

[126] Alissa J. Rubin, "In Marja, a Vice President Speaks with Warmth, but Reaps Cool," New York Times, March 1, 2010, http://www.nytimes.com/2010/03/02/world/asia/02marja.html.

[127] Oliver North, "Test Case: Marjah," Fox News, April 2, 2010, http://www.foxnews.com/story/2010/04/02/test-case-Marjah.html.

[128] Elizabeth Chuck, "As Heroin Use Grows in US, Poppy Crops Thrive in Afghanistan," NBC News, July 7, 2015, http://www.nbcnews.com/news/world/heroin-use-grows-u-s-poppy-crops-thrive-afghanistan-n388081.

[129] Taimoor Shah and Mujib Mashal, "Bountiful Afghan Opium Harvest Yields Profits for the Taliban," New York Times, May 4, 2016, https://www.nytimes.com/2016/05/04/world/asia/taliban-afghan-poppy-harvest-opium.html.

[130] "High-Risk List," SIGAR; Alissa J. Rubin, "In Afghanistan, Poppy Growing Proves Resilient,"

For this reason, among others, "tackling" the problem of opium farming in Afghanistan has proven virtually impossible. As SIGAR admitted, other important reconstruction projects have only helped to make the opium problem worse:

> Certain reconstruction projects such as improved irrigation, roads, and agricultural assistance can actually lead to increased opium cultivation. SIGAR found that affordable deep-well technology turned 200,000 hectares of desert in southwestern Afghanistan into arable land over the past decade. Due to relatively high opium prices and the rise of an inexpensive, skilled, and mobile labor force, much of this newly arable land is dedicated to opium cultivation. Poppy-growing provinces that were once declared "poppy free" have seen a resurgence in cultivation.[131]

It was U.S. and Pakistani support for Gulbuddin Hekmatyar and his mujahideen allies in the 1980s that had gotten the ball rolling on creating a new opium industry in Afghanistan and Pakistan to replace the traditional agriculture that the Soviet war was destroying.[132] The civil wars of the 1990s made matters even worse.

As historian Alfred McCoy explained:

> During this seemingly unending civil war, rival factions leaned heavily on opium to finance the fighting, more than doubling the harvest to 4,600 tons by 1999. Throughout these two decades of warfare and a twenty-fold jump in drug production, Afghanistan itself was slowly transformed from a diverse agricultural ecosystem — with herding, orchards, and over 60 food crops — into the world's first economy dependent on the production of a single illicit drug. In the process, a fragile human ecology was brought to ruin in an unprecedented way.
> …
>
> During these two decades of war, … modern firepower devastated the herds, damaged snowmelt irrigation systems, and destroyed many of the orchards. While the Soviets simply blasted the landscape with firepower, the Taliban, with an unerring instinct for their society's economic jugular, violated the unwritten rules of traditional Afghan warfare by cutting down the orchards on the vast Shomali plain north of Kabul.

New York Times, January 1, 2012, http://www.nytimes.com/2012/01/02/world/asia/in-afghanistan-a-troubling-resurgence-of-the-poppy-crop.html.

[131] "High Risk List," Special Inspector General for Afghanistan Reconstruction, December 2014, https://www.sigar.mil/pdf/spotlight/High-Risk_List.pdf.

[132] James Rupert and Steve Coll, "US Declines to Probe Afghan Drug Trade," *Washington Post*, May 13, 1990, https://www.washingtonpost.com/archive/politics/1990/05/13/us-declines-to-probe-afghan-drug-trade/f07eadd2-3d25-4dd5-9e8c-05beed819769/.

All these strands of destruction knit themselves into a veritable Gordian knot of human suffering to which opium became the sole solution. Like Alexander's legendary sword, it offered a straightforward way to cut through a complex conundrum. Without any aid to restock their herds, reseed their fields, or replant their orchards, Afghan farmers — including some 3 million returning refugees — found sustenance in opium, which had historically been but a small part of their agriculture.[133]

It seems like there may be no going back for Afghanistan. The laws of economics will always counteract attempts to eradicate opium in a country where poppies are not simply the largest cash crop,[134] but the largest domestic industry by far,[135] comprising as much as 50 percent of Afghanistan's entire economy.[136] But the DEA was also up against Ahmed Wali Karzai, the notoriously corrupt[137] CIA asset,[138] half-brother of the Afghan president, leader of the Kandahar City provincial council, and one of the biggest heroin kingpins in the whole country.[139] Like his president-brother, Wali Karzai's ties to the CIA predated September 11th and the subsequent invasion. And though McChrystal's then-assistant, Colonel Michael Flynn, compared him to Al Capone and said Wali Karzai's removal from power would be necessary for the installation of good governance in Kandahar City,[140] the generals quickly changed their minds. They were too dependent on his network for intelligence about alleged high-level Taliban targets and needed his help to operate one of the many paramilitary forces working for the CIA in and near Kandahar.[141]

Wali Karzai was eventually murdered in the summer of 2011, reportedly by a friend and trusted CIA asset who was turned and recruited by the Taliban.[142] Regardless, throughout the war, Afghanistan has been

[133] Alfred McCoy, "Afghanistan as a Drug War," TomDispatch, March 30, 2010, http://www.tomdispatch.com/blog/175225/tomgram:_alfred_mccoy,_afghanistan_as_a_drug_war.
[134] Reid Standish, "NATO Couldn't Crush Afghanistan's Opium Economy," Foreign Policy, November 13, 2014, http://foreignpolicy.com/2014/11/13/nato-couldnt-crush-afghanistans-opium-economy/.
[135] George Gavrilis, "The Good and Bad News about Afghan Opium," Council on Foreign Relations, February 10, 2010, http://www.cfr.org/afghanistan/good-bad-news-afghan-opium/p21372.
[136] Alfred McCoy, "Afghanistan as a Drug War."
[137] Tim McGirk, "A US Stumbling Block in Kandahar: Karzai's Brother," Time, March 19, 2010, http://content.time.com/time/world/article/0,8599,1973240,00.html.
[138] Woodward, Obama's Wars, 65.
[139] James Risen, "Reports Link Karzai's Brother to Afghanistan Heroin Trade," New York Times, October 4, 2008, http://www.nytimes.com/2008/10/05/world/asia/05afghan.html.
[140] Dexter Filkins et al., "Brother of Afghan Leader Said to Be Paid by CIA," New York Times, October 27, 2009, http://www.nytimes.com/2009/10/28/world/asia/28intel.html.
[141] Porter, "US, NATO Forces Rely on Warlords for Security."
[142] Julius Cavendish, "Bodyguard Who Killed Karzai's Brother Was Trusted CIA Contact,"

beating its own world records for domination of the global black market for narcotics. As mentioned, by 2015 Afghanistan supplied 90 percent of the world's heroin.[143] In many cases, U.S. soldiers and marines found they had "no choice" but to guard poppy fields for local warlords throughout the country.[144] These criminals were often the best people the U.S. could find to "serve" in desired roles. For all the rumors about top secret CIA missions to sell drugs to pay for their covert operations as they had done during previous wars in Southeast Asia[145] and Central America,[146] in Afghanistan there was no secret to the conspiracy. The drug dealers often were high-level government officials themselves.[147]

Reporter Michael Hastings once told a story of having a "heroin dealer" introduced to him at an Afghan wedding. "That's interesting," Hastings replied. "Do you have any trouble with the law?"

"Not at all," replied his new acquaintance, "I have one brother in the police and another brother in the Taliban. No problems."[148]

In 2016, even the *New York Times* described a "narco-state administered directly by government officials," from Helmand to Kabul:

More than ever, Afghan government officials have become directly involved in the opium trade, expanding their competition with the Taliban beyond politics and into a struggle for control of the drug traffic and revenue. At the local level, the fight itself can often look like a turf war between drug gangs, even as American troops are being pulled back into the battle on the government's behalf, particularly in Helmand, in southern Afghanistan.

"There are phases of government complicity, starting with accommodation of the farmers and then on to cooperation with

Independent, July 15, 2011, http://www.independent.co.uk/news/world/asia/bodyguard-who-killed-karzais-brother-was-trusted-cia-contact-2314580.html.

[143] "Afghanistan Opium Survey 2014," United Nations Office on Drugs and Crime, November 2004, https://www.unodc.org/documents/crop-monitoring/Afghanistan/Afghan-opium-survey-2014.pdf.

[144] David Axe, "US Kicks Drug-War Habit, Makes Peace with Afghan Poppies," *Wired*, May 9, 2015, https://www.wired.com/2013/05/afghan-poppies/.

[145] Alfred W. McCoy, *The Politics of Heroin: CIA Complicity in the Global Drug Trade*, revised ed. (Chicago: Lawrence Hill, 1991).

[146] Gary Webb, *Dark Alliance: The CIA, the Contras, and the Crack Cocaine Explosion* (Oakland: Seven Stories, 1998).

[147] Paul Harris, "Victorious Warlords Set to Open the Opium Floodgates," *Guardian*, November 24, 2001, https://www.theguardian.com/world/2001/nov/25/afghanistan.drugstrade; Azam Ahmed, "Tasked with Combating Opium, Afghan Officials Profit from It," *New York Times*, February 15, 2016, https://www.nytimes.com/2016/02/16/world/asia/afghanistan-opium-heroin-taliban-helmand.html; Alfred W. McCoy, "How a Pink Flower Defeated the World's Sole Superpower," TomDispatch, February 21, 2016, http://www.tomdispatch.com/post/176106/tomgram%3A_alfred_mccoy,_washington's_twenty-first-century_opium_wars; Jean McKenzie, *Scott Horton Show*, September 9, 2009.

[148] Hastings, *Scott Horton Show*, April 21, 2009.

them," said David Mansfield, a researcher who conducted more than 15 years of fieldwork on Afghan opium. "The last is predation, where the government essentially takes over the business entirely."[149]

Virtually every year since the very early years of the occupation has seen records set for poppy crops in Afghanistan.[150] This has led to a huge increase in opium supply worldwide, used mostly for black-market heroin instead of badly needed medicine. Heroin abuse and related overdose deaths are a growing problem in Afghanistan,[151] the U.S.[152] and globally.[153] Prohibition and efforts to subsidize the production of other crops have completely failed to rid Afghanistan of its poppy industry. As Voice of America admitted in the spring of 2017:

> Afghan authorities said poppies, which traditionally have been grown in southern provinces, have found fertile lands in several northern and northeastern provinces, including Balkh and Jawzjan.
>
> A large-scale increase also is expected in provinces with previously little opium crops, such as northwestern Badghis and Ghor.
>
> "Opium is cultivated in almost half of the province, including areas under the government influence," a resident in northeastern Baghlan province told VOA on condition of anonymity for safety concerns. "Poppy crops are seen everywhere in the northeastern region. Badakhshan — which borders Tajikistan and China — is the epicenter of narcotics in the north." ...
>
> The Afghan government says it, along with aid agencies, has been trying to help Afghans find a sustainable alternative crop source. But those efforts appear to be failing. ... Experts say worsening security and immediate economic benefits for farmers are major reasons for the rise in poppy cultivation. ...

---

[149] Azam Ahmed, "Tasked with Combating Opium, Afghan Officials Profit from It," *New York Times*, February 15, 2016, https://www.nytimes.com/2016/02/16/world/asia/afghanistan-opium-heroin-taliban-helmand.html.

[150] Andrea Germanos, "$7 Billion US Eradication Effort Delivers Record High Poppy Crop in Afghanistan," Common Dreams, October 21, 2014, http://www.commondreams.org/news/2014/10/21/7-billion-us-eradication-effort-delivers-record-high-poppy-crop-afghanistan.

[151] "UNODC Reports Major, and Growing, Drug Abuse in Afghanistan," United Nations Office on Drugs and Crime, June 21, 2010, https://www.unodc.org/unodc/en/press/releases/2010/June/unodc-reports-major-and-growing-drug-abuse-in-afghanistan.html.

[152] Maggie Fox, "Heroin Deaths Quadruple Across US," NBC News, July 7, 2015, http://www.nbcnews.com/health/health-news/heroin-deaths-quadruple-across-us-n388006.

[153] "Record 29 Million People Drug-Dependent Worldwide; Heroin Use Up Sharply – UN Report," United Nations Office on Drugs and Crime, June 23, 2016, http://www.un.org/apps/news/story.asp?NewsID=54302.

"[N]arco-entrepreneurs" control large portions of government lands in several provinces where they cultivate poppies.[154]

This raises the question of whether it would be better to legalize the production and trade in opiates and to invite the global pharmaceutical market to try to find a way for Afghan farmers to continue to survive, while diverting their product to productive medicinal uses.[155] This model has already been proven successful in India and Turkey.[156] But the U.S. government will never allow this, citing the "fight" against the opium trade, "for which there are no shortcuts."[157]

Tossing COIN

The decision to continue to tolerate Wali Karzai was the first major indication that while the increase of troops might come to Kandahar City, COIN and its nostrums would be discarded in favor of a renewed emphasis on targeted night raids against alleged insurgent leaders and mid-level coordinators, as opposed to making any real effort at "changing their entire society." But the "clear, hold, build and transfer a whole new world" counterinsurgency campaign was to have had its true showcase in Kandahar City, after the "proof-of-concept" test-run in Marjah. As Hastings wrote, Kandahar City "was supposed to be a decisive turning point in the war — the primary reason for the troop surge that McChrystal wrested from Obama." But now it was canceled in favor of escalated night raids and a "rising tide of security" provided by now better-funded Afghan soldiers and police. McChrystal gave a huge boost to the Afghan militia program in the north and in Kandahar, in conjunction with Wali Karzai.[158]

Hastings explained that during the "surge," American G.I.s were in way over their heads and they knew it. Morale was low because soldiers "didn't sign up to be cultural anthropologists" and street cops. In Afghanistan, we

---

[154] Noor Zahid and Akmal Dawi, "Afghanistan's Deadly Poppy Harvest on Rise Again," Voice of America News, May 16, 2017, https://www.voanews.com/a/afghanistan-deadly-poppy-harvest-on-rise-again/3853575.html.

[155] Abigail Hall, "Want to Hurt the Taliban? Legalize Opium in Afghanistan," Defense One, December 10, 2016, http://www.defenseone.com/ideas/2016/12/want-undermine-taliban-legalize-opium-afghanistan/133778/.

[156] Reza Aslan, "How Opium Can Save Afghanistan," Daily Beast, December 19, 2008, http://www.thedailybeast.com/articles/2008/12/19/how-opium-can-save-afghanistan.html.

[157] "US Opposes Efforts to Legalize Opium in Afghanistan," US Department of State Bureau of International Narcotics and Law Enforcement Affairs, February 20, 2007, http://2001-2009.state.gov/p/inl/rls/rpt/80734.htm.

[158] Gareth Porter, "McChrystal Strategy Shifts to Raids – and Wali Karzai," IPS News, May 25, 2010, https://original.antiwar.com/porter/2010/05/24/mcchrystal-strategy-shifts-to-raids---and-wali-karzai/; Hastings, *The Operators*, 338; Hastings, "The Runaway General."

"have the 'surge,' without the 'awakening,'" he said, in reference to the effort in Iraq to bribe Sunni tribal chiefs to turn against al Qaeda in Iraq in 2007. In this case, no matter how many local police forces the U.S. tried to create, they could never be the natural power in the region compared to the Taliban and related insurgent groups. This being the case, Hastings confirmed, U.S. forces were already abandoning the pretension of COIN and the establishment of "good government" in Kandahar City in favor of simply expanding night raids against alleged high- and medium-level targets instead. The discussion and indecision about what to do with Karzai's half-brother Wali, such as, for example, "whether or not we should try to kill him," just showed how much trouble the U.S. was having working with their allies. If that was true, Hastings asked, how would the Americans ever be able to successfully come to terms with the Taliban?[159]

Mainstream media coverage of the escalation of the war in 2010 was as ridiculous as it was predictable. Minor victories were cited as clear signs of long-term progress. "We have seized the initiative" and "sapped the momentum" from the Taliban, they reported. The U.S. is occupying space [the Taliban] have ruled for years, "at least for the moment."[160] The generals on the ground certainly took these temporary results as first steps in a great success story.[161] In fact, many of the retreating Taliban did not even flee to Pakistan, but had instead only temporarily gone to hide out in Kandahar City and other surrounding areas.[162] As Hastings explained, U.S. forces are from North America, on the far side of the planet, and will one day have to go home, and the Taliban knows this. All the insurgents have to do, as a guerrilla army, is "not lose," and they know that, too.[163]

Adding an increase of troops inevitably means putting them in more areas where they are not wanted, which leads to more casualties. The plan, however, was that the increase in casualties as a result of the escalation would reach an "inflection point" where, after making significant progress, casualties would start decreasing. Rather conveniently, this meant that any decrease *or increase* in the numbers of casualties would serve as an indication of substantial progress. But the "inflection point" never occurred. For all

[159] Michael Hastings, interviewed by the author, *Scott Horton Show,* radio archive, September 30, 2010, https://scotthorton.org/interviews/antiwar-radio-patrick-cockburn-michael-hastings-and-andy-worthington/.
[160] Carlotta Gall, "Coalition Forces Routing Taliban in Key Afghan Region," *New York Times,* October 20, 2010, http://www.nytimes.com/2010/10/21/world/asia/21kandahar.html.
[161] Ron Moreau, "David Rodriguez: The General Who Planned the Afghan Surge," *Newsweek,* June 26, 2011, http://www.newsweek.com/david-rodriguez-general-who-planned-afghan-surge-68011.
[162] Ben Farmer, "Taliban Quit Rural Areas for City After US Surge," *Irish Times,* June 20, 2011, http://www.irishtimes.com/news/taliban-quit-rural-areas-for-city-after-us-surge-1.601228; C.J. Chivers, "What Marja Tells Us of Battles Yet to Come," *New York Times,* June 10, 2010, http://www.nytimes.com/2010/06/11/world/middleeast/11marja.html.
[163] Michael Hastings, *Scott Horton Show,* September 30, 2010.

the talk of "protecting" the population to win them over and build their nation under the new counterinsurgency doctrine, casualties for civilians and fighters on both sides went up overall from the time McChrystal took over in 2009.[164]

This was despite the fact that McChrystal had greatly restricted the rules of engagement for U.S. troops during the escalation. "The Afghan people are the insurgency," he explained. If U.S. troops kill the people, then there is no one left to protect. American forces must go into battle so "heroically restrained" in their mission of "population protection" that the local civilians will choose them instead of choosing to fight against them. McChrystal even cited what he called "insurgent math" at a 1:10 ratio: if U.S. forces killed two insurgents, they were likely to end up having to face twenty more in the future. McChrystal taught his men, "Those two that were killed, their relatives don't understand that they're doing bad things. Okay [they think,] 'a foreigner killed my brother, I['ve] got to fight them.'"[165]

The U.S. Army and Marine Corps stationed infantry to stand around like targets on far-flung street corners, under these comparatively restrictive new rules of engagement, pretending to be Officer Friendly out "protecting civilians" during the day — doing "armed social work," as COIN "expert" and Petraeus adviser Kilcullen put it[166] — while special operations forces attacked supposed Taliban and other alleged "High-Value Targets" (HVTs) at night. Again, this was not meant to defeat the insurgency, just weaken it so much in the space of eighteen months that they would come to the negotiating table to accept American terms. The U.S. was supposed to convince the local population to turn against the Taliban and accept the Afghan army as their security force. Instead, as Hastings reported, these tactics led to growth in the ranks of the insurgent enemy and low morale — even near-mutiny — on the part of some U.S. soldiers, who had received new rules so restrictive after being passed down through the chain of command that they felt they were helpless to return fire even when fired upon and in imminent danger.[167]

McChrystal was relieved of command in June of 2010 after a *Rolling Stone* article by Hastings detailed McChrystal and his staff's total contempt for the U.S. government's civilian leaders and the soldiers in the field's total contempt for McChrystal and his restrictive and incoherent rules of engagement.[168] Even though McChrystal had already conceded that

---

[164] Gentile, *Wrong Turn*, 132.

[165] Hastings, *The Operators*, 141; Hastings, "The Runaway General."

[166] Shorrock, "Making COIN."

[167] Hastings, "The Runaway General."

[168] Ibid.

Marjah was a disaster and had abandoned his planned COIN operation in Kandahar City, his early dismissal might have meant that in the history of the era, the COINdinistas would not have to face judgment for their failure. But President Obama cleverly ambushed the Godfather of Counterinsurgency, the lionized Gen. David Petraeus himself, with the task of finishing the project McChrystal had started, demoting the general from commander of Central Command to lead the Afghan war, "boxing in" Petraeus for a change. Who better to finish the student's task than the master himself? In this way, Obama was attempting to ensure that their coming failure would forever be remembered as the generals' as well as the president's.[169]

But where his protégé McChrystal had attempted to actually apply the new counterinsurgency doctrine in Petraeus's Field Manual and restrict the rules of engagement on the ground, as well as the use of air power, in the hopes of winning over the loyalty of the local population, Petraeus ironically seemed to abandon his own COIN doctrine right away, loosening the rules of engagement, especially unleashing the use of night raids and air power against alleged Taliban and other insurgent targets, with the predictable effect of radicalizing even more fighters against the U.S. and the government it backed. Petraeus likewise abandoned any pretense of carrying out a counterinsurgency campaign in Kandahar City. McChrystal, the special operations expert in targeted killing, had tried to implement Petraeus's "people's war" counterinsurgency doctrine, while Petraeus himself, who had pushed so hard for the escalation in the name of counterinsurgency, abandoned it outright once he was put in charge of the war, instead focusing on simple, useless or even counter-productive "anti-insurgency," as Col. Flynn deridingly called it[170] — a heightened focus on increased targeted killings and airstrikes.[171]

For most of Afghanistan, the new COIN strategy was never implemented in any real sense. The "surge" mostly just meant vast increases in violence, signifying nothing. The military and CIA started a new program of training unaccountable local militias, the "Counterterrorism Pursuit Teams," and further empowered heroin

---

[169] "Afghan Shift: McChrystal Out, Petraeus In," NPR News, June 23, 2010, http://www.npr.org/templates/story/story.php?storyId=128029497.

[170] Michael T. Flynn et al., "Fixing Intel: A Blueprint for Making Intelligence Relevant in Afghanistan," CNAS, January 2010, https://s3.amazonaws.com/files.cnas.org/documents/AfghanIntel_Flynn_Jan2010_code507_voices.pdf.

[171] Carlotta Gall, "Night Raids Curbing Taliban, but Afghans Cite Civilian Toll," *New York Times*, July 8, 2011, http://www.nytimes.com/2011/07/09/world/asia/09nightraids.html; Noah Shactman, "Petraeus Launches Afghan Air Assault; Strikes Up 172 Percent," *Wired*, October 12, 2010, https://www.wired.com/2010/10/gloves-come-off-afghan-air-war-strikes-spike-172/; Jeremy Scahill, "America's Failed War of Attrition in Afghanistan," *Nation*, November 22, 2010, https://www.thenation.com/article/americas-failed-war-attrition-afghanistan/.

traffickers and warlords, such as Petraeus-favorite Abdul Razzik in southern Kandahar Province,[172] while U.S. special operations forces embarked on an expanded program of night raids on family homes of supposed high-value insurgent targets of the Taliban and Haqqani Network. The loosened rules of engagement led to increased mass-casualty attacks by ISAF forces, including apparent accidents such as airstrikes launched against local policemen.[173]

The new militia program, the Community Defense Initiative, was a failure. The same went for the Public Protection Force, the Local Defense Initiative and the Afghan Local Police. No matter the title, none of these amounted to much more than the military passing out cash and AK-47s to local militias and strongmen in the hopes they would fight the Taliban. Training, command and control were never truly established. But some money and time were spent, and as in much of the Afghanistan project, that seemed to be the most important thing.[174]

The most effective part of the 2009–2012 escalation was said to be the expanded focus on the use of night raids against suspected "High-Value Targets." Many Americans may only be able to imagine such missions from the point of view of U.S. special operations forces as they embark on such daring, far-away missions as shown through the green-tinted night vision footage of cable TV documentaries. This limited view may also be part of what has prevented U.S. military forces in Afghanistan from achieving their mission: they cannot imagine what it is like to be on the receiving end of one of these raids either. Frankly, it is probably true that Americans, by and large, do not care about how Afghans feel, particularly when their terror is at the hand of U.S. soldiers. But this was supposed to be the big COIN campaign: Clear, Hold, Build! Hearts and minds! Befriend the nice folks and protect the people from their real enemy, the Taliban, so we can build a new nation together! But how could their hearts and minds possibly be won when black helicopters full of special operations shock troops raid their homes and neighborhoods in the middle of the night, killing or capturing men in their bedrooms, in front of their wives and children, pointing weapons in their faces, shouting at them in a foreign language, scanning their irises with high-tech gadgets and

---

[172] Michael Hastings, "King David's War," *Rolling Stone*, February 2, 2011, http://rollingstone.com/politics/news/king-davids-war-20110202; Matthieu Aikins, "Our Man in Kandahar," *Atlantic*, November 2011, https://theatlantic.com/magazine/archive/2011/11/our-man-in-kandahar/308653/; Matthieu Aikins, "The Bidding War," *New Yorker*, March 7, 2016, http://newyorker.com/magazine/2016/03/07/the-man-who-made-millions-off-the-afghan-war.

[173] "Afghanistan: NATO Air Strike Kills Seven Policemen," *Daily Telegraph*, February 18, 2010, http://www.telegraph.co.uk/news/worldnews/asia/afghanistan/7265024/Afghanistan-Nato-air-strike-kills-seven-policemen.html.

[174] Dexter Filkins, "Afghan Militias Battle Taliban with Aid of US," *New York Times*, November 21, 2009, http://www.nytimes.com/2009/11/22/world/asia/22militias.html.

shooting any neighbors who might come outside to investigate the commotion or defend their town from attack, like some nightmare dystopia out of science fiction or the totalitarian regimes of the twentieth century? This night raid program amounted to what former Petraeus staffer, CNAS director, and lead COIN salesman John Nagl bragged was an "industrial strength counter-terrorism killing machine."[175] It was certainly an industrial strength killing machine, though the "counter-terrorism" boast was little more than that.

In 2012, the historian and investigative reporter Gareth Porter was awarded the Martha Gellhorn Prize for Journalism, in part for his assessment of the night raid program:

> Although the raids have undoubtedly killed a large number of Taliban commanders and fighters, it is now clear that they also killed and incarcerated thousands of innocent civilians. The failure to discriminate between combatants and civilians flows directly from a targeting methodology that is incapable of such discrimination.[176]

The military, desperate for some decent intelligence, would come to simply redefine the term. Since the Americans never really knew who was who on the ground, they would instead rely on "link analysis" to discover who *called* who and which phones had ever been co-located. The generals believed that combined with drone surveillance, "network science" was a close to certain way to identify and roll up the Taliban's leadership, dealing them a desperate blow.

As Porter explained, during the second Iraq war, McChrystal, Flynn and JSOC had used hovering drones and cellphone data to target insurgent leaders. The generals also used Woodward from the *Post*[177] to convince the American public that these efforts had led to decreased violence in that country. The plan was to replicate this alleged success in Afghanistan. The military would use supposedly advanced "social network analysis" to decode enemy identities and movements. And that was it. Rather than

[175] Dan Edge and Stephen Grey, "Kill/Capture," *Frontline*, PBS, May 10, 2011, http://pbs.org/wgbh/frontline/film/kill-capture/; Matthew Cole, "The Crimes of SEAL Team 6," Intercept, January 10, 2017, https://theintercept.com/2017/01/10/the-crimes-of-seal-team-6/.

[176] Gareth Porter, "How McChrystal and Petraeus Built an Indiscriminate 'Killing Machine,'" Truthout, September 26, 2011, http://www.truth-out.org/news/item/3588:how-mcchrystal-and-petraeus-built-an-indiscriminate-killing-machine.

[177] "Secret Killing Program is Key in Iraq, Woodward says," CNN, September 9, 2008, http://www.cnn.com/2008/WORLD/meast/09/09/iraq.secret/; Sharon Weinberger, "What Is Woodward's 'Secret Weapon' in Iraq?," *Wired*, September 9, 2008, https://www.wired.com/2008/09/whats-the-milit/; Tim Collie, "Bob Woodward: Secret US Weapon Can Find, Kill Terrorists in Iraq, Pakistan," Newsmax, September 16, 2008, http://www.newsmax.com/Newsfront/woodward-secret-weapon/2008/09/16/id/325368/; "What Is Woodward's 'Secret Weapon' in Iraq?," CBS News, September 10, 2008; http://www.cbsnews.com/news/what-is-woodwards-secret-weapon-in-iraq/.

attempting to verify their conclusions with new and human-based intelligence, the priority was simply on speed — true efficiency be damned. As Porter wrote:

> The key to JSOC's definition of a given insurgent "network" was the decision to maintain long-term aerial surveillance of a particular location. McChrystal's intelligence chief Col. Michael Flynn liked to call surveillance by drone aircraft "The Unblinking Eye" — an image suggesting a godlike power of observation. The implication of the new intelligence methodology developed by McChrystal and Flynn was that anyone who visited a location under surveillance or who communicated with a mobile phone associated with that location could be considered to be part of the insurgent network.

> In October 2009, when JSOC was carrying out roughly 90 raids per month, the target list for SOF night raids, called the Joint Prioritized Effects List (JPEL), included 2,058 names, according to one of the Afghan war logs documents released by WikiLeaks. A large proportion of the targets on the list were not identifiable individuals at all, but mobile phone numbers.[178]

By the summer of 2010, special operations forces were doing 20 raids per night. A year later it was as many as 40 raids per night, or more than 1,000 per month. In an interconnected world where even the lowliest Pashtun tribesman is hardly more than six degrees of separation from actor Kevin Bacon,[179] how could anyone expect military *computers* to guess which calls, locations and relationships are meaningful enough to justify capturing or killing people? As Dana Priest and William Arkin wrote in their "Top Secret America" series for the *Washington Post*, "JSOC's success in targeting the right homes, businesses and individuals was only ever about 50 percent, according to two senior commanders. They considered this rate a good one."[180] In practice, this meant, even by the military's own estimation, only 14 percent of those captured in the raids had any real links to the insurgency.[181]

For a period in the early part of 2011, it became an important talking point that U.S. forces under Petraeus had captured thousands of Taliban fighters in their night raids and, therefore, were proven to be getting

[178] Porter, "How McChrystal and Petraeus Built an Indiscriminate 'Killing Machine.'"

[179] Fiona MacDonald, "Are We Really All Connected by Just Six Degrees of Separation?," Science Alert, August 27, 2015, http://www.sciencealert.com/are-we-all-really-connected-by-just-six-degrees-of-separation.

[180] Dana Priest and William M. Arkin, "'Top Secret America': A Look at the Military's Joint Special Operations Command," *Washington Post*, September 2, 2011, https://www.washingtonpost.com/world/national-security/top-secret-america-a-look-at-the-militarys-joint-special-operations-command/2011/08/30/gIQAvYuAxJ_story.html.

[181] Porter, "How McChrystal and Petraeus Built an Indiscriminate 'Killing Machine.'"

something accomplished. However, their own numbers later showed that approximately 90 percent of those captured were released within an initial two-week limited time frame, demonstrating the fact that the officers in charge of their detainment could not show credible evidence of their ties to the insurgency.[182] There is no reason to believe those killed in the same night raids were any more guilty than the arrested had been.

One terrible example was a Delta Force raid on the house of a policeman which resulted in the killing of five people: the policeman, his brother, two pregnant women — one of them a mother of 11 children — and a teenage girl. The soldiers and commanders lied, claiming they had found the women bound and shot in an "honor killing," when in fact they had done it themselves. The Delta Force operators even tried to dig the bullets out of the women's wounds to complete the cover-up.[183] McChrystal's assistant, Flynn, had previously written a report famously criticizing the low quality of U.S. intelligence about Afghanistan,[184] but the new methods of Flynn's "intelligence revolution" proved no better at distinguishing fighters from civilians or diminishing the strength of the insurgency.[185]

Later, an anonymous whistleblower leaked top secret documents regarding much of the U.S. drone program to Jeremy Scahill, which he reported for the Intercept in "The Drone Papers," later published as *The Assassination Complex*. This reporting, by Scahill, Ryan Devereaux and others, covered the broader terror war across the Middle East. In the section about Afghanistan, they showed that from 2011–2013, JSOC, supported by the CIA, ran an operation known as Haymaker, a series of targeted killing operations against Taliban and Haqqani Network targets in the northeastern Afghanistan provinces of Kunar and Nuristan, near the Pakistan border. "The vast majority of those killed in airstrikes were not the direct targets." During one five-month period, nine out of ten people killed were simply innocent bystanders. According to leaked slides, this Task Force 3-10, otherwise known as Task Force Green, launched

---

[182] Gareth Porter, "Ninety Percent of Petraeus's Captured 'Taliban' Were Civilians," June 12, 2011, Inter Press Service, http://www.ipsnews.net/2011/06/ninety-percent-of-petraeuss-captured-taliban-were-civilians/.

[183] Jerome Starkey, "Nato 'Covered Up' Botched Night Raid in Afghanistan That Killed Five," *Times of London,* March 13, 2010,
http://www.thetimes.co.uk/tto/news/world/asia/afghanistan/article2464783.ece.

[184] Michael T. Flynn et al., "Fixing Intel: A Blueprint for Making Intelligence Relevant in Afghanistan," Center for a New American Security, January 4, 2010,
https://www.cnas.org/publications/reports/fixing-intel-a-blueprint-for-making-intelligence-relevant-in-afghanistan.

[185] Gareth Porter, "Trump's National Security Adviser Facilitated the Murder of Civilians in Afghanistan," Truthout, November 23, 2016, http://www.truth-out.org/news/item/38487-trump-s-national-security-adviser-facilitated-the-murder-of-civilians-in-afghanistan; Porter, "How McChrystal and Petraeus Built an Indiscriminate 'Killing Machine.'"

more than 2,000 missions over the course of a year, yet by "February 2013, Haymaker airstrikes had resulted in no more than 35 'jackpots,' a term used to signal the neutralization of a specific targeted individual, while more than 200 people were declared EKIA — 'enemy killed in action.'" But even then, as military sources told Devereaux, "If there is no evidence that proves a person killed in a strike was either not a MAM, or was a MAM but not an unlawful enemy combatant, then there is no question, they label them EKIA."[186]

The military's argument against Vice President Biden's much more limited plan had been that "CT+," Counter-terrorism Plus Training, could never work without a full-scale counterinsurgency campaign and immersion of U.S. forces with the population. Only then could accurate intelligence be developed for use in counter-terrorism operations. Yet even at the height of the "surge," the military never had good human intelligence, instead mostly relying on the paper-thin evidence of electronic tracking of cell phone SIM card data. This framing by the military amounted to an ironic admission that they were largely attacking innocents when the deployment of COIN in Kandahar City was later abandoned and Gen. Petraeus doubled down on night raids and drone strikes instead.[187]

The CIA had even warned in a report in July 2009, just as the escalation was being debated in the administration, that targeted killing of alleged "High-Value Targets" does not work any better than counterinsurgency doctrine.

> Potential negative effects of HVT operations include increasing insurgent support, causing a government to neglect other aspects of its counterinsurgency strategy, provoking insurgents to alter strategy or organization in ways that favor the insurgents, strengthening an armed group's popular support with the population, radicalizing an insurgent group's remaining leaders, and creating a vacuum into which more radical groups can enter.

> HVT operations may, by eroding the "rules of the game" between the government and insurgents, escalate the level of violence in a conflict, which may or may not be in a government's interest.

Specifically, the CIA warned against applying the doctrine in Afghanistan:

> The Coalition has led a sustained effort since 2001 to target Taliban leaders, but the government's limited influence outside of Kabul has impeded integration of high-value targeting (HVT) efforts with other

---

[186] Scahill, *The Assassination Complex*; Ryan Devereaux, "Manhunting in the Hindu Kush," Intercept, October 15, 2015, https://theintercept.com/drone-papers/manhunting-in-the-hindu-kush/.

[187] Woodward, *Obama's Wars*, 234.

military and nonmilitary counterinsurgency elements, such as reconciliation programs. Afghan Government corruption and lack of unity, insufficient strength of Afghan and NATO security forces, and the country's endemic lawlessness have constrained the effectiveness of these counterinsurgency elements. Senior Taliban leaders' use of sanctuary in Pakistan has also complicated the HVT effort. Moreover, the Taliban has a high overall ability to replace lost leaders, a centralized but flexible command and control overlaid with egalitarian Pashtun structures, and good succession planning and bench strength, especially at the middle levels, according to clandestine and U.S. military reporting.[188]

In 2010, Col. Flynn wrote in his famous paper calling for the further adoption of counterinsurgency doctrine and more sophisticated intelligence collection in the Afghan war,

> The … inescapable truth asserts that merely killing insurgents usually serves to multiply enemies rather than subtract them. This counterintuitive dynamic is common in many guerrilla conflicts and is especially relevant in the revenge-prone Pashtun communities whose cooperation military forces seek to earn and maintain. The Soviets experienced this reality in the 1980s, when despite killing hundreds of thousands of Afghans, they faced a larger insurgency near the end of the war than they did at the beginning.[189]

But the only two options Petraeus had allowed for was a full-on COIN deployment or a return to air attacks and night raids. In Washington, D.C.'s view, the latter was the more restrained approach. Afghans might be forgiven for not regarding being bombed from the sky and having their doors kicked open in the middle of the night in quite the same way.[190]

Importantly, the use of air power was not restricted to drone strikes and Black Hawk helicopters delivering SEALs to their target civilian homes at night. The bombers went back up in the air as well. In one case, U.S. Army Lt. Col. David Flynn, the commander of the Combined Joint Task Force 1-320th in Kandahar Province and no relation to Col. Flynn,[191] was happy to boast about ordering the complete obliteration of the towns of Tarok Kolache, Khosrow Sofla and Lower Babur in the nearby Arghandab River Valley in October 2010. According to Lt. Col. Flynn, there were too many improvised explosive devices and snipers there,

---

[188] "Best Practices in Counterinsurgency," CIA, posted by Wikileaks, July 7, 2009, https://wikileaks.org/cia-hvt-counterinsurgency/WikiLeaks_Secret_CIA_review_of_HVT_Operations.pdf.

[189] Flynn, "Fixing Intel."

[190] Anand Gopal, interviewed by the author, *Scott Horton Show,* radio archive, June 28, 2010, https://scotthorton.org/interviews/antiwar-radio-anand-gopal-2/.

[191] Email message from journalist Mark Perry, April 3, 2017.

leaving the army "little choice" but to completely destroy the three villages in order to save them, since they wanted to avoid "losing momentum" in their attempted pacification of the rest of the province. In an article in *Wired* magazine, Lt. Col. Flynn assured readers that all the civilians had long since fled and that the only casualties were Taliban fighters. Since they dropped nearly 50,000 pounds of bombs on the tiny village of Tarok Kolache alone, it is doubtful much would have been left of the people caught in the bombing that day if anyone wanted to verify Lt. Col. Flynn's claims.[192] Pictures published at the *Foreign Policy* website in a puff piece by public relations flack Paula Broadwell — who was later revealed to be Gen. Petraeus's mistress with whom he was convicted of sharing a large volume of documents classified at the highest levels of secrecy — showed the town to have been completely obliterated. Nothing but craters remained. Broadwell promised this was not a problem because a local "approved contractor" had been hired to rebuild the entire village — they had surveyed for culverts and everything — as she mocked a local man's "fit of theatrics" over the total annihilation of his family's property.[193] "Sure they are pissed about the loss of their mud huts ... but that is why the BUILD story is important here," she later added on her Facebook page by way of explanation.[194] One "surge" supporter nevertheless wrote:

> I still have a hard time believing that the Taliban would go to the expense and trouble of lining every vertical and horizontal surface with explosives in a town they had already spent a lot of money to occupy without violence. It's just so... wasteful, and while the Taliban are many kinds of evil they are not profligate. I don't understand where they would see the utility in doing this, at least to the extent [Broadwell] says. Furthermore, there is the appeal to sympathy — [Lt. Col.] Flynn, the U.S. commander, was gun-shy because he lost some men under him. Without minimizing that — and I know how this sounds — but war sucks. It sucks hard. Losing men in war sucks even worse, and I am not in any way ignoring or writing off the grief and pain that causes. But that does not give you an excuse to burn a village to the ground. Part of what makes war suck, especially for Americans, is that we do not scorch the earth when we suffer losses, however tempting it may be.[195]

---

[192] Spencer Ackerman, "25 Tons of Bombs Wipe Afghan Town Off Map," *Wired,* January 19, 2011, https://www.wired.com/2011/01/25-tons-of-bombs-wipes-afghan-town-off-the-map/.

[193] Thomas E. Ricks, "Travels with Paula (I): A Time to Build," *Foreign Policy,* January 13, 2011, http://foreignpolicy.com/2011/01/13/travels-with-paula-i-a-time-to-build/.

[194] Joshua Foust, "Revisiting the Village Razing Policies of ISAF in Kandahar," Registan, January 16, 2011, http://registan.net/2011/01/16/revisiting-the-village-razing-policies-of-isaf-in-kandahar/comment-page-1/.

[195] Ibid.

According to the *Washington Post*, three years later, Tarok Kolache was nothing but a "sandy ruin," with just a few unlivable concrete buildings where the people's homes — their home — used to be. While a few families had returned, the community has been obliterated. The population has mostly moved away in hopes of finding better luck somewhere else.[196]

In November of 2010, then-*Nation* reporter Jeremy Scahill reported from Taliban country on the state of the war from their point of view:

> Contrary to the rhetoric emanating from NATO and Washington, the Taliban are not on the ropes and, from their perspective, would gain nothing from negotiating with the United States or NATO. As far as they are concerned, time is on their side. "The bottom line for [NATO and the U.S.] is to immediately implement what they would ultimately have to implement ... after colossal casualties," stated the Taliban declaration after the recent NATO summit. "They should not postpone withdrawal of their forces."

It was clear to Scahill then that

> along with Afghan government corruption, including a cabal of war lords, drug dealers and war criminals in key positions, the so-called Petraeus strategy of ratcheting up airstrikes and expanding night raids is itself delivering substantial blows to the stated U.S. counterinsurgency strategy and the much-discussed battle for hearts and minds. The raids and airstrikes are premiere recruiting points for the Taliban and, unlike Senator Graham and the Obama administration, Karzai seems to get that. In the bigger picture, the United States appears to be trying to kill its way to a passable definition of a success or even victory. This strategy puts a premium on the number of kills and captures of anyone who can loosely be defined as an insurgent and completely sidelines the blowback these operations cause.[197]

By the summer of 2011, Michael Hastings reported, soldiers on the ground in Afghanistan were convinced their efforts and lives were going to waste. It was the lowest level of morale he had ever seen, and he said everyone agreed COIN was failing. Hastings reiterated that the alleged success of the "surge" was a mirage. When U.S. forces are concentrated, they can certainly run the enemy off and stabilize things for a short period of time, but the Americans were spending so much money and time that

---

[196] Kevin Sieff, "Years Later, a Flattened Afghan Village Reflects on US Bombardment," *Washington Post*, August 25, 2013, https://www.washingtonpost.com/world/years-later-a-flattened-afghan-village-reflects-on-us-bombardment/2013/08/25/d8df9e62-05cf-11e3-bfc5-406b928603b2_story.html.

[197] Scahill, "America's Failed War of Attrition in Afghanistan."

it was apparent to all that the strategy was not sustainable. Insurgents would simply move to another part of the country to wait them out in an endless game. Importantly, Hastings also said that by this time — July 2011, right when the success of the "surge" was supposed to have brought the Taliban crawling to the table to negotiate with the U.S. and Afghan national government on Washington's terms — the U.S. had given up on the idea of creating a strong central government in Kabul. They would just pretend the various criminals, heroin kingpins and warlords ruling their provinces were part of some real central government, and accept them — as long as they were not Taliban. As horrible as it was, this at least made more sense than the previous policy, but was only accepted in the face of reality's total victory over previous American goals.[198]

Robert Pape's predictions that President Obama's troop increase and counterinsurgency campaign would succeed only at inaugurating a massive increase in the number of suicide attacks across Afghanistan soon proved to be correct. According to a UN report released during the height of the "surge" in the summer of 2010, there had been a massive increase in the insurgency's use of suicide strikes. The *New York Times* summarized:

> With an average of an assassination a day and a suicide bombing every second or third day, insurgents have greatly increased the level of violence in Afghanistan, and have become by far the biggest killers of civilians here, the United Nations said. ...

> The most striking change has been in suicide bombings, whose numbers have tripled this year compared with 2009. Such attacks now take place an average of three times a week compared with once a week before. In addition, two of three of those suicide attacks are considered "complex," in which attackers use a suicide bomb as well as other weapons.[199]

The claims by the U.S. Army and Marine Corps about "progress" achieved in this or that district in Helmand and Kandahar Provinces, based on statistics showing a relative increase or decrease in violent attacks by the insurgency, started to become something of a sick joke, even in mainstream media.[200] But if the Taliban had not been defeated, and they had not been brought to the negotiating table to sign on to American terms, then they had won the war.

---

[198] Michael Hastings, interviewed by the author, *Scott Horton Show,* radio archive, July 14, 2011, http://scotthorton.org/interviews/2011/07/14/antiwar-radio-michael-hastings-9/; Hastings, *The Operators,* 334.

[199] Rod Nordland, "Violence Up Sharply in Afghanistan," *New York Times,* June 19, 2010, http://www.nytimes.com/2010/06/20/world/asia/20afghan.html.

[200] Spencer Ackerman, "What Surge? Afghanistan's Most Violent Places Stay Bad, Despite Extra Troops," *Wired,* October 23, 2012, https://wired.com/2012/08/afghanistan-violence-helmand/.

"Surge"-Era War Crimes

In 2009, 33 civilians were killed in two separate massacres in the village of Garloch. The first was an airstrike that targeted the wrong house in a case of mistaken identity. In the second, U.S. forces attempting to raid a home shot a dog and then a concerned neighbor who had come out to investigate the noise or intervene to help, and then another, and another, ultimately killing 17 civilians. After the government backed down from their initial claims that "most" of the dead were "militants," they offered "condolence payments" of $2,000 to the survivors of the second attack. "That's what our lives are worth to you Americans — two thousand dollars? You want to kill us and then pay to keep us quiet?" Malek Hazrat railed to journalist Anand Gopal. "My daughter is buried in the ground!" a nearby old man added. "You can give me every dollar on earth, but I won't touch it. It won't bring her back." The rest of the village gave up and fled their homes en masse to a makeshift refugee camp "of tarps and plastic" on the side of the road to Pakistan, where they have been left to scavenge and beg to survive.[201]

In February 2010, drone operators launched an attack on some families on the side of a road in Uruzgan Province, which killed 23 men, women and children and wounded more than a dozen more.[202] This one was unique in that the transcript of the drone pilots and their decision making was published in Andrew Cockburn's book, Kill Chain,[203] and later dramatized in the documentary National Bird,[204] revealing how dehumanizing military jargon and technology help to contribute to bad decision making and the slaughter of innocents.[205] Filmmaker Sonia Kennebeck's interviews with the survivors convey just a small sense of the pain and grief Afghan civilians have suffered at the hands of their supposed liberators and protectors.

In February 2011, when a U.S. offensive killed 64 innocent people in Kunar Province, Gen. Petraeus infamously claimed in a meeting with Karzai and other Afghan dignitaries that the survivors had really killed and burned their own children just to make the U.S. look bad. Later, backpedaling slightly, a Pentagon spokesman denied the general had said anything beyond something about how everyone knows Afghans like to burn their kids sometimes, an assertion which the military continued to

---

[201] Gopal, No Good Men, 215-222.

[202] David S. Cloud, "Anatomy of an Afghan War Tragedy," Los Angeles Times, April 10, 2011, http://www.latimes.com/world/la-fg-afghanistan-drone-20110410-story.html.

[203] Andrew Cockburn, Kill Chain: The Rise of the High-Tech Assassins, 1-16, (Henry Holt, 2015).

[204] National Bird, by Sonia Kennebeck, (New York: FilmRise, 2016), http://nationalbirdfilm.com/.

[205] David Swanson, "How Drone Pilots Talk," November 4, 2016, http://davidswanson.org/node/5336.

insist upon.[206]

A few days later, nine young boys between the ages of 9 and 15, mistaken for insurgents, were massacred by U.S. attack helicopters while out gathering firewood. One boy, Hemad, lived to describe the experience:

> We were almost done collecting the wood when suddenly we saw the helicopters come. There were two of them. The helicopters hovered over us, scanned us and we saw a green flash from the helicopters. Then they flew back high up, and in a second round they hovered over us and started shooting. They fired a rocket which landed on a tree. The tree branches fell over me and shrapnel hit my right hand and my side.

Hidden by the fallen tree branches, Hemad watched as the helicopters "shot the boys one after another."

"News of the attack enraged Afghans and led to an anti-American demonstration … in the village of Nangalam, where the boys were from," reported the *New York Times*. "We are deeply sorry," Gen. Petraeus assured the boys' families.[207]

The Afghan war has also seen outright deliberate atrocities by rogue American soldiers such as the "Kill Team,"[208] a group of U.S. Army infantry from Bravo Company who went on an atrocity-spree, beginning with the cold-blooded murder of a 15-year-old farm boy, and then the mocking, desecration and mutilation of his corpse. The same group went on to murder and mutilate at least three more innocent civilians in the coming months. Eleven men were eventually convicted.[209] According to journalist Mark Boal,

> [A] review of internal Army records and investigative files obtained by *Rolling Stone*, including dozens of interviews with members of Bravo Company compiled by military investigators, indicates that the dozen infantrymen being portrayed as members of a secretive "kill team"

---

[206] "Afghan Governor: Women and Children Killed in Military Operation," CNN, February 20, 2011, http://cnn.com/2011/WORLD/asiapcf/02/20/afghanistan.civilians.killed/; Joshua Partlow, "Petraeus's Comments on Coalition Attack Reportedly Offend Karzai Government," *Washington Post*, February 21, 2011, http://washingtonpost.com/wp-dyn/content/article/2011/02/21/AR2011022103256.html; Hastings, *The Operators*, 355; Larry Shaughnessy, "Tension Between Petraeus, Afghans over Airstrike, Children," CNN, February 22, 2011, http://www.cnn.com/2011/WORLD/asiapcf/02/22/us.afghan.strikes/.

[207] Alissa J. Rubin and Sangar Rahimi, "Nine Afghan Boys Collecting Firewood Killed by NATO Helicopters," *New York Times*, March 2, 2011, http://www.nytimes.com/2011/03/03/world/asia/03afghan.html.

[208] Paul Harris, "US Soldier Admits Killing Unarmed Afghans for Sport," *Guardian*, March 23, 2011, https://www.theguardian.com/world/2011/mar/23/us-soldier-admits-killing-afghans.

[209] Chris McGreal, "'Kill Team' US Platoon Commander Guilty of Afghan Murders," *Guardian*, November 10, 2011, https://www.theguardian.com/world/2011/nov/11/kill-team-calvin-gibbs-convicted.

were operating out in the open, in plain view of the rest of the company. Far from being clandestine, as the Pentagon has implied, the murders of civilians were common knowledge among the unit and understood to be illegal by "pretty much the whole platoon," according to one soldier who complained about them. Staged killings were an open topic of conversation, and at least one soldier from another battalion in the 3,800-man Stryker Brigade participated in attacks on unarmed civilians. "The platoon has a reputation," a whistle-blower named Pfc. Justin Stoner told the Army Criminal Investigation Command. "They have had a lot of practice staging killings and getting away with it."[210]

On March 11, 2012, a steroid-raging, drunken, revenge-obsessed U.S. Army staff sergeant, Robert Bales, infuriated the local population when he murdered 17 innocent Afghan villagers — nine of them children, including a two- and a three-year-old — and desecrated many of the corpses by burning them.[211]

As recently as 2015, Bales was still insisting the people of Afghanistan had no right to resist his and the U.S. Army's righteous domination of their neighborhoods, even if (since he has been sentenced to life in prison) he now says he regrets slaughtering their toddlers.[212]

That autumn, a group of Special Forces stationed in Wardak Province, Operational Detachment Alpha 3124, known as the "A-Team," along with their translator, murdered at least 18 civilians in cold blood, first kidnapping and torturing 10 of them, and then buried most of their bodies in different spots just outside their base's fence. Other villagers were also tortured, but later released.

While the military insisted the translator had acted alone and that the locals must all be lying, journalist Matthieu Aikins found many civilian witnesses to Special Forces' complicity "scattered across Nerkh District" telling the same story and found it "difficult to believe … dozens of illiterate Afghan villagers … could have maintained an elaborate and consistent set of lies over a period of months." In fact, Aikins showed the villagers photos of the soldiers and interpreters from ODA 3124 mixed

---

[210] Mark Boal, "The Kill Team: How US Soldiers in Afghanistan Murdered Innocent Civilians," *Rolling Stone*, March 27, 2011, http://www.rollingstone.com/politics/news/the-kill-team-20110327.

[211] "Officials: Bales Sneaked Off Base Twice During Rampage," CNN, March 26, 2012, http://www.cnn.com/2012/03/26/world/asia/afghanistan-killings/; Eric M. Johnson, "US Soldier Pleads Guilty to Murdering 16 Afghan Civilians," *Bangor Daily News*, June 5, 2013, http://bangordailynews.com/2013/06/05/news/nation/us-soldier-pleads-guilty-to-murdering-16-afghan-civilians/; Gene Johnson, "Army: Bales, Wife Laughed About Killing Charges," *USA Today*, August 19, 2013, http://www.usatoday.com/story/news/world/2013/08/19/army-soldier-wife-laughed-about-killing-charges/2674853/.

[212] Brendan Vaughan, "Robert Bales Speaks: Confessions of America's Most Notorious War Criminal," *GQ*, October 21, 2015, http://www.gq.com/story/robert-bales-interview-afghanistan-massacre.

with pictures of random Green Berets and Afghans from the internet, as in a police photo array, and they consistently recognized the soldiers involved, as well as their interpreter. An Afghan government investigation, led by an official who initially disbelieved the claims, later found them to be credible. Separate investigations by the International Committee of the Red Cross and United Nations agreed. Three different U.S. military investigations have exonerated the soldiers completely. A fourth remains unresolved. As Aikins later said, it "stretches the limits of credulity to think that someone above these guys didn't understand that crimes had been committed and that it took the Red Cross to open a criminal investigation. How could there not be some official complicity in what amounted to an official cover-up?"[213]

"There is compelling evidence that [these] U.S. soldiers were involved in war crimes," Joanne Mariner of Amnesty International told the *Guardian* newspaper. One former Green Beret explained to Aikins, "Too many deployments with too many friends lost. And the locals get it every time, especially in Afghanistan." As Hazrat Mohammad Janan, the former deputy head of Wardak's provincial council, told the *Guardian*, when protests broke out after the discovery of the bodies of the disappeared, "We tried to get them to hand over the bodies to resolve the protests peacefully," but were unsuccessful. "As a result, people's hatred of the government grew. ... It strengthened the Taliban."[214]

SEAL Team 6, or the Naval Special Warfare Development Group (DEVGRU), considered to be among the top tier of U.S. special operations forces — the men who eventually killed Osama bin Laden in Pakistan in 2011 — have committed war crimes against the people of Afghanistan since the very beginning of the war. Journalist Matthew Cole has reported their use of supposedly ceremonial hatchets to kill and dismember their victims, as well as the practice of "canoeing" dead men with a shot to the very top of their head which splits it open, spilling brains out, as a special kind of trademark of the team. And they commit these atrocities with near-total impunity. The SEALs invoke plainly bogus excuses about the efficacy of such brutality and depravity as "psychological warfare" that will convince the enemy to give up their resistance, when, of

[213] Matthieu Aikins, interviewed by the author, *Scott Horton Show,* radio archive, November 25, 2013, http://scotthorton.org/interviews/2013/11/25/112513-matthieu-aikins/.

[214] Matthieu Aikins, "The A-Team Killings," *Rolling Stone,* November 6, 2013, http://www.rollingstone.com/feature/a-team-killings-afghanistan-special-forces; Matthieu Aikins, "US Special Forces May Have Gone on a Murder Spree in Afghanistan — Did the Army Cover It Up?" *Nation,* September 2, 2015, https://www.thenation.com/article/us-special-forces-may-have-gone-on-a-murder-spree-in-afghanistan-did-the-army-cover-it-up/; Sune Engel Rasmussen, "Afghan Families Skeptical as US Reopens Investigation of Bodies Found Near Base," *Guardian,* November 5, 2015, https://www.theguardian.com/world/2015/nov/05/afghanistan-bodies-us-military-base-a-team-investigation.

course, it only hardens their determination, the same way American soldiers react when the Taliban does it to them. A former SEAL told Cole,

> When you see your friend killed, recover his body, and find that the enemy mutilated him? It's a schoolyard mentality. "You guys want to play with those rules?" "Okay." You ask me to go living with the pigs, but I can't go live with pigs and then not get dirty.

"Most SEALs did not commit atrocities," Cole reported, "but the problem was persistent and recurrent, like a stubborn virus," because there was no accountability:

> [A]fter 9/11, [a] code emerged that made lying — especially to protect a teammate or the command from accountability — the more honorable course of action.

> "You can't win an investigation on us," one former SEAL Team 6 leader told me. "You don't whistleblow on the teams … and when you win on the battlefield, you don't lose investigations."[215]

In 2011, the UN put out a report documenting systemic torture of prisoners at Afghan detention facilities at the hands of Afghan police and intelligence officers,[216] causing a small hypocritical controversy over the transfer of detainees by the U.S. to the forces it was installing in charge of the country. Soon the media's interest faded and the captured were sent on to their fate. The infamous Bagram prison was finally transferred to Afghan control in 2013. CIA-backed militias have also continued fighting and committing war crimes at least through 2015, and likely to this day.[217]

So-called "collateral damage" to Afghan civilians during the counterinsurgency "surge" escalated as the numbers of soldiers and marines in the country grew. Gen. McChrystal himself conceded that at various checkpoints on Afghan roads, "We've shot an amazing number of people and killed a number and, to my knowledge, none has proven to have been a real threat to the force." Sgt. Maj. Michael Hall instructed soldiers, "There are stories after stories about how these people are turned into insurgents. Every time there is an escalation of force we are finding that innocents are being killed."[218]

---

[215] Matthew Cole, "The Crimes of SEAL Team 6," Intercept, January 10, 2017, https://theintercept.com/2017/01/10/the-crimes-of-seal-team-6/.

[216] "Systematic Torture in Afghan Detention Facilities – UN Report," UN News Centre, October 10, 2001, http://www.un.org/apps/news/story.asp?NewsID=39985.

[217] Sudarsan Raghavan, "Inside the CIA's Shadow War in Afghanistan: Agency Oversees Militias Implicated in Torture, Civilian Killings," *Washington Post*, December 3, 2015, https://www.washingtonpost.com/world/cia-backed-afghan-militias-fight-a-shadow-war/2015/12/02/fe5a0526-913f-11e5-befa-99ceebcbb272_story.html.

[218] Richard Oppel Jr., "Tighter Rules Fail to Stem Deaths of Innocent Afghans at Checkpoints,"

Losing Anyway

Throughout his reign in Afghanistan, Petraeus continued to insist the escalation was working. Despite the fact that the overall numbers of attacks by insurgents[219] and civilian casualties[220] had only increased, these seeming setbacks were actually indications of real "progress," he said, though always "fragile and reversible" at best.[221] For a general who emphasized the importance of "information operations" — setting the narrative within which the escalation would be fought — this framing simply highlighted the fact that, as Michael Hastings reported, the U.S. Congress and the American people were considered targets of his information war as much as the Taliban-led insurgency was.[222] "Fragile and reversible progress" is the perfect public relations cop-out phrase. Real progress, by definition, would not be fragile or reversible.

In February 2012, U.S. Army Lt. Col. Daniel Davis wrote a classified whistleblower report to Congress and then released an unclassified version to the public[223] along with an accompanying article in the *Armed Forces Journal*.[224] Davis had a unique job in, and view of, the Afghan war. A veteran of the first two Iraq wars, and a previous tour in Afghanistan, Davis spent his final tour as an acquisitions officer in the army's Rapid Equipping Force, making sure the soldiers in the field had all the equipment they needed without getting caught up in departmental snafus and delays. In this capacity, he traveled the entire country and talked with hundreds of troops and commanders from all different branches, brigades, platoons and battalions, including both regular infantry and special operations forces. They virtually all told him the same thing: this is not working now, and it is not going to work eventually either. At least a few of these soldiers were tragically killed in battle shortly after expressing their

New York Times, March 26, 2010, http://www.nytimes.com/2010/03/27/world/asia/27afghan.html.

[219] Thomas Joscelyn and Bill Roggio, "Analysis: The Taliban's 'Momentum' Has Not Been Broken," Long War Journal, September 6, 2012, http://longwarjournal.org/archives/2012/09/analysis_the _taliban.php.

[220] Laura King, "UN: 2010 Deadliest Year for Afghan Civilians," *Los Angeles Times*, March 10, 2011, http://articles.latimes.com/2011/mar/10/world/la-fg-afghan-civilian-deaths-20110310.

[221] Luis Martinez and Huma Khan, "Gen. Petraeus: Progress in Afghanistan 'Fragile and Reversible,'" ABC News, March 15, 2011, http://abcnews.go.com/Politics/afghanistan-gen-david-petraeus-calls-progress-fragile-reversible/story?id=13140052.

[222] Michael Hastings, "Another Runaway General: Army Deploys Psy-Ops on US Senators," *Rolling Stone*, February 23, 2011, http://www.rollingstone.com/politics/news/another-runaway-general-army-deploys-psy-ops-on-u-s-senators-20110223.

[223] Daniel L. Davis, "Dereliction of Duty II: Senior Military Leaders' Loss of Integrity Wounds Afghan War Effort," United States Army, February 6, 2012, https://info.publicintelligence.net/USArmy-Dereliction-of-Duty-II.pdf.

[224] Daniel L. Davis, "Truth, Lies and Afghanistan," *Armed Forces Journal*, February 1, 2012, http://armedforcesjournal.com/truth-lies-and-afghanistan/.

reservations about the war to Davis. When Davis came home and heard Gen. Petraeus proclaim his supposed success to the public and Congress, he decided enough was enough. As Davis put it, the general was not just spinning or putting on a brave face in a tough situation, he was lying — engaging in "information operations" against U.S. lawmakers and the American people to convince them there was progress being made or a light at the end of the tunnel. It was simply false that the Afghan National Army could ever be built up to hold its own or that the Taliban or other insurgent groups could be defeated or weakened to the point of marginalization in the society, or at least to compliance with American wishes. The truth, Davis wrote, had become "unrecognizable."

In fact, the number of shootings and IED attacks had increased across the country from 2010 to 2011. While Gen. Petraeus pretended he was halting the insurgency's momentum, he was actually just swelling their ranks in opposition to the expanded occupation with devastating effect. Even small successes could only ever be temporary, Davis warned in his report.

> There are three key factors which must go our way in order to succeed in this war: 1. We must militarily degrade the insurgency to a sufficiently low level of capability that will enable the Afghan security forces to handle them alone; 2. The ANSF must concurrently be trained to a sufficiently high level that they are able to handle the weakened insurgency; and 3. The GoIRA [Government of the Islamic Republic of Afghanistan] must be minimally corrupt and sufficiently able to govern, providing a viable economy, secure environment, and a fair judiciary. It is reasonable to assume that if the American public came to believe that even after 10 years of effort we were no closer to success in attaining those three requirements than in 2007 or 2008 — even after two full years of a 30,000-person troop surge — support would almost certainly come into question.

The Davis report went on to demonstrate the impossibility of the mission on those terms. The Afghan National Army was a complete joke that constantly reached ceasefires and non-aggression deals with the insurgency and would abandon their positions at the mere rumor of impending Taliban attacks. In one example cited by Davis, dozens of Americans were killed in two separate battles to take control of the Marawara Valley in Kunar Province. Yet when the U.S. passed authority over to the ANA to hold the territory, they immediately turned and ran. By 2012 the valley was permanently back in the hands of the insurgency.

The Afghan National Army was plagued with rampant drug use, and a large percentage of soldiers on the rolls were just "ghost soldiers," no-shows who either appeared a couple of times for the free rifle and boots and then went home or never even existed except as a name on a padded roll-call sheet for the purpose of raising the take-home pay of the commanding officers.

As Davis warned in 2012, American forces had nothing but contempt for the incompetent and unmotivated ANA and never believed government forces would be able to accept and sustain whatever supposed security gains the U.S. had made.

> In August [2011], I went on a dismounted patrol with troops in the Panjwai district of Kandahar province. Several troops from the unit had recently been killed in action, one of whom was a very popular and experienced soldier. One of the unit's senior officers rhetorically asked me, "How do I look these men in the eye and ask them to go out day after day on these missions? What's harder: How do I look [my soldier's] wife in the eye when I get back and tell her that her husband died for something meaningful? How do I do that?"

Davis was so concerned that decisions were being made based on bad information, he felt compelled to break the chain of command and go straight to Congress and the American people.

Davis later elaborated that in the late-"surge" era, when he served his second Afghan tour, violence was increasing, not diminishing, and he clarified that this was certainly not incidental, but directly due to the movement of troops into areas where they had never previously been stationed, creating situations "where people who would [normally] never join the Taliban" did. Davis told the story of one Taliban regional commander who got angry under questioning and told his interrogators, "Hey, I didn't want to join the Taliban, but you guys came in and as part of your operations, more violence was brought into my area, some of my family members were killed [by U.S. or allied Afghan National Army forces or police],[225] and I have an obligation to try to protect them. So you drove me into the Taliban."[226]

Davis was adamant that the "surge" was a "fool's errand" from the very beginning, which could never have worked, even with different generals making better decisions and having more infantry to deploy.[227] Even Petraeus's limited goal of hitting the Taliban so hard they would come to the negotiating table after a year and a half, like in the deal he had promised Obama and the American people, was an impossibility. The simple arithmetic of the situation precluded it: fight the insurgency and it grows; fight them harder and it grows even faster. At some point, we have to recognize that the Taliban is not the invading army: we are. The reason

---

[225] Daniel Davis, email message to author, August 6, 2016.

[226] Daniel Davis, interviewed by the author, *Scott Horton Show*, radio archive, February 3, 2016, http://scotthorton.org/interviews/2016/02/03/2316-daniel-davis/.

[227] Ibid.

the enemy does not run out of soldiers is that they are not soldiers. They are the people of the land America has failed to conquer.

The U.S. has been sending the most highly trained, elite military forces on the planet after mid-level nobodies in a rag-tag insurgency, and look at the results: the U.S. still cannot even beat *them*. America's military and intelligence services have shown that there is nothing they can do to decide the future of Afghanistan.

The entire "surge" was a disaster for everyone but the undertaker and the Taliban.[228] In *Little America*, Rajiv Chandrasekaran reported that President Obama refused to read a CIA assessment of Afghanistan explaining the situation there was already "trending to stalemate" in mid-2011, right around the time Petraeus had promised Obama the Taliban would have been brought to heel. The White House claimed they were concerned the report would be used to thwart the president's proposed timeline for withdrawal. This seems like an unnecessary dodge since it could have been just as easily interpreted to indicate that the whole thing should never have been tried and that it was already time to call it off.[229]

But America must keep fighting this impossible, self-defeating mission because if we quit, al Qaeda will come back, the media insists, forever invoking the safe-haven myth. What if they attack us again? In reality, there was no reason to think al Qaeda would come back to Afghanistan were the Taliban to return to power, especially considering the trouble they had brought the last time around. When the authors Alex Strick van Linschoten and Felix Kuehn contacted representatives of the Taliban's Quetta Shura after bin Laden was killed in May 2011, they did not seem to care in the slightest that he was dead or how he had died. "We are fighting for Mullah Muhammad Omar. He is our emir. We have never fought for Osama bin Laden. His death does not matter to us. We will continue with our struggle." In fact, al Qaeda did not have a single representative on the Quetta Shura council.[230] Vice President Joe Biden, Special Representative Holbrooke and then-head of counter-terrorism, later CIA director, John Brennan also conceded that there was no reason to believe that even if the Taliban did come back to power, that they would allow al Qaeda back into Afghanistan as well.[231]

Just six months into the official beginning of the 2010 troop "surge," CIA director Leon Panetta finally admitted to ABC News that when it came to numbers of al Qaeda fighters in Afghanistan, "I think at most,

---

[228] Spencer Ackerman, "Military's Own Report Card Gives Afghan Surge an F," *Wired*, September 27, 2012, https://www.wired.com/2012/09/surge-report-card/.

[229] "Biden, In Leaked Memo, Told Obama War Plan Flawed," Daily Caller, June 25, 2012, http://dailycaller.com/2012/06/25/biden-in-leaked-memo-told-obama-war-plan-flawed.

[230] Van Linschoten and Kuehn, *An Enemy We Created*, 3-4, 301.

[231] Woodward, *Obama's Wars*, 170, 227.

we're looking at maybe 50 to 100, maybe less. There's no question that the main location of al Qaeda is in tribal areas of Pakistan." It is too bad the reporter did not press a little more to get Panetta to confess that he could not prove there had been a single Saudi or Egyptian mujahideen fighter left in the whole country for years, much less any real associates of Osama bin Laden. But his concession should have been enough to cause a scandal: If "maybe less than 50" illusory al Qaeda fighters can keep us in the country for now, is there any possible future context in which the government could actually declare victory over al Qaeda there, much less the Taliban? And if their presence was the reason for the war, why was eliminating them not the focus of the escalation instead of the broader, obviously impossible, Pashtun-pacification effort?[232]

Later, Panetta, by then the secretary of defense, in announcing the end of the post-"surge" drawdown, claimed that at least the escalation had given the U.S. the chance to really train up the Afghan National Army to take over for U.S. and allied forces there. It is possible that he meant, but forgot to say, "at least for long enough to let me retire and get the heck out of town."[233] In addition to the problem of "ghost soldiers," continuing problems with retention, training, morale, drug abuse, and insider — or, "green on blue" — attacks by trainees against U.S. troops and each other remained.[234] The ANA's ability to secure the government's rule in the country was never in anything but doubt. This was as obvious then as it is today. Richard Holbrooke had previously complained that low retention rates meant training and equipping new soldiers was "like pouring water into a bucket with a hole in it."[235]

Like Robert Gates and Leon Panetta, David Petraeus also escaped any accountability for his failed "surge" and the loss of the Afghan war by bailing out after just one year in charge to head the CIA in the summer of 2011 — just as the Taliban were supposed to be meekly submitting to U.S. demands at the point of his bayonet. While at the CIA, Petraeus, who had already tried to manipulate the National Intelligence Estimate process and conclusions while still deployed to Afghanistan,[236] ordered analysts to

---

[232] Felicia Sonmez, "Panetta: 'Maybe 50 to 100' al Qaeda left in Afghanistan," *Washington Post*, June 27, 2010, http://voices.washingtonpost.com/44/2010/06/cia-chief-maybe-50-to-100-al-q.html.

[233] Karen Parrish, "Panetta Announces Completion of Afghanistan Surge Drawdown," American Forces Press Service, September 21, 2012, http://archive.defense.gov/news/newsarticle.aspx?id=117955.

[234] Richard Sisk, "Wave of Insider Attacks Hits Afghan Army," Military, October 31, 2016, http://www.military.com/daily-news/2016/10/31/wave-of-afghan-on-afghan-insider-attacks-hits-afghan-army.html.

[235] Woodward, *Obama's Wars*, 226; Leo Shane III, "Pentagon Scrambles to Account for Afghan 'Ghost' Troops," *Military Times*, February 16, 2016, http://www.militarytimes.com/story/military/pentagon/2016/02/16/dod-scrambling-afghan-ghost-troops/80446110/.

[236] Hastings, *The Operators*, 356.

"consult more closely with commanders on the ground as they put together future war zone intelligence estimates," to put a "separate agency approval" gloss on his failed policies in the war. "The directive," reported the *Washington Post*, "was seen by some as an affront to the agency's mandate to provide policymakers with independent, fact-based analysis."[237] This gambit by Petraeus to "grade his own homework"[238] on the war may have played a role in the other scandal which served to obscure Petraeus's disastrous legacy in Afghanistan, the previously mentioned revelations he was guilty of exposing sensitive information classified at the very highest degrees to his mistress and biographer, including "above top secret" level papers describing discussions of war policy with the president.[239] Some former CIA officers believe it was "the agency" itself that fed evidence of his indecencies and illegalities to the FBI, leading to the scandals which brought Petraeus down in mild-compared-to-what-he-deserved disgrace.[240]

Michèle Flournoy, co-founder of CNAS, had been a key COIN promoter and the deputy secretary of defense for policy in charge of implementing it during Obama's Afghan "surge." Flournoy left the Department of Defense in humiliation after her failure, claiming the old "spend more time with my family" excuse, usually only invoked by disgraced politicians. But once former Republican senator Chuck Hagel, Obama's third secretary of defense, was forced out in an apparent bureaucratic struggle over Syria policy,[241] Flournoy's name was floated as a possible successor. Apparently seeing how quickly her name had been rehabilitated — who cares about Afghanistan? — she let it be known in

---

[237] Ernesto Londoño et al., "Afghanistan Gains Will Be Lost Quickly After Drawdown, US Intelligence Estimate Warns," *Washington Post*, December 28, 2013, https://www.washingtonpost.com/world/national-security/afghanistan-gains-will-be-lost-quickly-after-drawdown-us-intelligence-estimate-warns/2013/12/28/ac609f90-6f32-11e3-aecc-85cb037b7236_story.html.

[238] Associated Press, "Petraeus Tells CIA to Consult Troops on War in Afghanistan," Fox News, October 14, 2011, http://www.foxnews.com/world/2011/10/14/petraeus-tells-cia-to-consult-troops-on-war-in-afghanistan.html; Kimberly Dozier, "CIA to Fuse Troops' Opinions in Afghan War Analysis," Newspapers, October 14, 2011, https://www.newspapers.com/newspage/132352431/; Pam Benson, "CIA Director Petraeus Defends Change in War Analysis," CNN, October 14, 2011, http://security.blogs.cnn.com/2011/10/14/cia-director-petraeus-defends-change-in-war-analysis/.

[239] Justin Miller and Nancy Youssef, "Petraeus Mistress Got Black Books Full of Code Words, Spy Names, and Obama Briefings," Daily Beast, March 3, 2015, http://www.thedailybeast.com/articles/2015/03/03/petraeus-mistress-got-secret-black-books-full-of-code-words-spy-names-and-briefings-with-obama.html.

[240] Philip Giraldi, "The Fall of Petraeus: A CIA Coup?," *American Conservative*, November 11, 2012, http://www.theamericanconservative.com/2012/11/11/a-cia-coup/.

[241] "US Defense Secretary Chuck Hagel Resigns," BBC News, November 24, 2014, http://www.bbc.com/news/world-us-canada-30182410; Eric Bradner, "Hagel: Focus on ISIS, Not Assad," CNN, November 22, 2015, http://www.cnn.com/2015/11/22/politics/chuck-hagel-syria-isis-assad/.

the papers that she did not seek and would not accept the nomination of her president to replace Hagel. Flournoy, who her friends called the "Defense Secretary in Waiting," was holding out for the position in the assumed-to-be-upcoming Hillary Clinton administration instead.[242]

In December 2013, a post-Petraeus National Intelligence Estimate, representing the consensus of all seventeen U.S. intelligence agencies, assessed that the Afghan "surge" had been useless after all. Every bit of their supposed success there would be lost by the time Obama left office, even if he decided to leave a few thousand troops behind, they predicted. "Some have interpreted the intelligence assessment as an implicit indictment of the 2009 troop surge," according to those who leaked it to the press. For all the media hype about the escalation's necessity back in 2009, this official pronunciation of the policy's failure a few years later went almost completely unnoticed.[243]

[242] Rowan Scarborough, "Flournoy May Be Holding Out for a Clinton Presidency to Become Defense Chief," *Washington Times*, November 26, 2014, http://www.washingtontimes.com/news/2014/nov/26/passing-muster-in-presidents-obamas-protective-inn/; Mike Emanuel and Justin Fishel, "Ex-Defense Official Michele Flournoy Takes Self Out of Running to Succeed Hagel at Pentagon," Fox News, November 25, 2014, http://www.foxnews.com/politics/2014/11/25/ex-defense-official-michele-flournoy-takes-self-out-running-to-succeed-hagel-at.html; Bradley Clapper, "Hagel's Departure Could Pave Way for 1st Woman Leader at Pentagon as Flournoy Heads Shortlist," *U.S. News and World Report,* November 24, 2014, https://usnews.com/news/politics/articles/2014/11/24/glass-shattering-flournoy-tops-pentagon-shortlist; Jeremy Herb, "Hillary Clinton's Defense Secretary in Waiting," Politico, November 2, 2016, http://politico.com/tipsheets/morning-defense/2016/11/hillary-clintons-defense-secretary-in-waiting-217183.
[243] Londoño et al., "Afghanistan Gains Will Be Lost Quickly After Drawdown."

Chapter Five: Falling Action

"Can you believe that the Afghan war is our 'longest war' ever — bring our troops home, rebuild the U.S., make America great again." — Donald Trump, January 14, 2013

"We've spent $2 trillion in Iraq, probably a trillion in Afghanistan. We're destroying our country. We owe $19 trillion. We're bogged down. Russia was bogged down in Afghanistan, meaning the Soviet Union. It broke up the Soviet Union." — Donald Trump, October 4, 2015

"I think you have to stay in Afghanistan for a while." — Donald Trump, March 4, 2016

Criminal Cops

In 2013, media company Vice produced the documentary *This Is What Winning Looks Like*, revealing U.S. Army efforts to persuade powerless peasant villagers to resist the Taliban themselves in the post-"surge" era since local police forces would not. The film showed that the national police force that the U.S. has built up in the predominantly Pashtun areas of the country is, in fact, made up of the worst criminals of all.[1] As just one example, Pashtun and larger Afghan culture has long had a terrible problem of systemic sexual abuse of children, particularly by those with petty amounts of power like tribal chiefs, soldiers and cops.[2] The U.S. troops shown in the video were clearly furious about the role they were being made to play: installing the lowest kind of criminal to be police chief over the people they were supposedly there to help. When America and its allies create these new police forces, they become complicit in the crimes these men commit. The worse it gets, the greater the pressure on Western forces to engage in cover-ups on their behalf. NATO even suppressed Canadian soldiers' reports of child rape committed by members of the Afghan National Army, rather than having to own up to their involvement in creating the situation.[3]

A U.S. Army Special Forces sergeant and his commanding officer were both punished after the sergeant punched an Afghan militia commander for raping a young boy. He was nearly kicked out of the army until a public outcry and congressional intervention prevented it. However, his captain was still relieved of command.[4] This problem remains "endemic" to Afghan National Security Forces,[5] and American and NATO politicians and generals continue to act as accomplices to it as they, once more, artificially build up the power of those who could not maintain it otherwise. In the mid-1990s, the Taliban had actually come to power by arresting kidnappers and rapists of women and young boys, and when they

---

[1] Ben Anderson, "This Is What Winning Looks Like: My Afghanistan War Diary," Vice, December 23, 2013, https://www.vice.com/en_us/article/this-is-what-winning-looks-like-full-length.

[2] Joel Brinkley, "Afghanistan's Dirty Little Secret," *San Francisco Chronicle*, August 29, 2010, http://www.sfgate.com/opinion/brinkley/article/Afghanistan-s-dirty-little-secret-3176762.php; Chris Mondloch, "An Afghan Tragedy: The Pashtun Practice of Having Sex with Young Boys," *Independent*, October 29, 2013, http://www.independent.co.uk/voices/comment/an-afghan-tragedy-the-pashtun-practice-of-having-sex-with-young-boys-8911529.html.

[3] Ann Jones, "Meet the Afghan Army," in *The Case for Withdrawal from Afghanistan*, ed. Nick Turse, 75.

[4] Christine Houser, "Green Beret Who Beat Up Afghan Officer for Raping Boy Can Stay in Army," *New York Times*, April 29, 2016, https://www.nytimes.com/2016/04/30/us/green-beret-who-beat-up-afghan-officer-for-raping-boy-can-stay-in-army.html.

[5] Hastings, *The Operators*, 270.

ruled the country, they had enforced the laws against it.[6] It is easy to see why people would welcome any armed group capable of putting a halt to such depravity. It is unquestionably a reason why many areas of the country are tolerating the return of the Taliban now.

By 2016, America had done so much to empower serial child rapists that the Taliban decided to start using "honey traps" of children to lure, ambush and kill Afghan police. Three American marines have also been murdered by one of their Afghan National Police ally's young sex slaves, though it is unclear if he was recruited to do so by the Taliban or other insurgent groups, or had just taken the opportunity to do so on his own.[7] The "bacha bazi," or dancing boys, are the police chiefs' "biggest weakness," a former official told French media in June 2016, explaining how the Taliban would recruit these young boys, who would then drug, poison and even shoot their U.S.-backed slave-masters.[8] If these policemen cannot find a steady supply of boys to rape who will not suddenly turn around and kill them in their sleep, then they could be alienated from their U.S. partners, undermining the military's entire strategy there.[9]

This is what military strategist William S. Lind identified as the "operational art" of the Taliban insurgency against U.S. and allied rule in Kabul: the use of scores of deadly insider attacks against American and Afghan National Army targets.[10] When the U.S. Army's strategy became reduced to a doubled focus on the continued training up of the Afghan army, the Taliban went straight for the gut, sending recruits to join up, begin training, and then ambush their trainers or fellow recruits on base. This rapidly led to further isolation between American trainers and their wards and increased demoralization on the part of both the trainers and

---

[6] Margolis, *American Raj,* 197; Ahmed, *Taliban,* 25; Van Linschoten and Kuehn, *An Enemy We Created,* 114-115.

[7] Kevin Sieff, "Deadly Insider Attack That Left 3 US Marines Dead Was Work of an Afghan Teenager," *Washington Post*, August 17, 2012, https://www.washingtonpost.com/world/asia_pacific/deadly-insider-attack-that-left-3-us-marines-dead-was-work-of-an-afghan-teenager/2012/08/17/20916eca-e7b8-11e1-936a-b801f1abab19_story.html; Dan Lamothe, "Navy Analysis Found That Marine's Case Would Draw Attention to Afghan 'Sex Slaves,'" *Washington Post*, September 1, 2016, https://www.washingtonpost.com/news/checkpoint/wp/2016/09/01/navy-analysis-found-that-a-marines-case-would-draw-attention-to-afghan-sex-slaves/.

[8] Agence France-Presse, "Taliban Use 'Honey Trap' Boys to Kill Afghan Police," *Inquirer* (Philippines), June 16, 2016, http://newsinfo.inquirer.net/790975/taliban-use-honey-trap-boys-to-kill-afghan-police.

[9] Lamothe, "Navy Analysis Found That Marine's Case Would Draw Attention to Afghan 'Sex Slaves.'"

[10] William S. Lind, "Unfriendly Fire," *American Conservative*, June 27, 2012, http://www.theamericanconservative.com/articles/unfriendly-fire/; William S. Lind, interviewed by the author, *Scott Horton Show,* radio archive, July 3, 2012, https://scotthorton.org/interviews/william-s-lind/.

trainees as well. These insider attacks continue to undermine U.S. training efforts and threaten the long term stability of Afghan security forces.[11]

Despite all the claims on the TV news, progress on the advancement of women's rights in Afghanistan under the Karzai regime was largely "illusory," according to journalist Ann Jones. For instance, the "Shi'ite personal status law" regarding the Hazaras, which was passed in 2009, legalized marital rape, denied women rights to divorce or inherit property, and treated the rape of women and children only as property crimes against the victims' husbands or fathers.[12] In fact, U.S.-trained Afghan National Police spend more time chasing runaway women and girls than criminals.[13] Afghanistan is a real rape culture, north and south. The U.S. cannot change this, but it can at least cease being part of it. Even if the Taliban does return to power, with their long record of oppressing women, at least on this issue it might be an improvement over the situation as it stands now.[14]

Attempts to Negotiate

The Afghan insurgency was never going to negotiate with the United States. As a Taliban commander explained to reporter Jeremy Scahill in 2010, "We don't want to fight after the withdrawal of foreigners, but as long as there are foreigners, we won't talk to Karzai."

"While Taliban leaders acknowledge that commanders are regularly killed," Scahill wrote, "they say the targeted killings are producing more radical leaders who are far less likely to negotiate than the older-school Taliban leaders who served in the government of Mullah Mohammed Omar. 'If today Mullah Omar was captured or killed, the fighting will go on,' says [Abdul Salam] Zaeef, [a former senior member of the former Taliban government], adding: 'It will be worse for everyone if the [current] Taliban leadership disappears.'"[15]

---

[11] Shawn Snow and Andrew deGrandpre, "Another Insider Attack in Afghanistan Leaves 7 Americans Wounded," *Military Times*, June 17, 2017, http://www.militarytimes.com/articles/us-wounded-afghanistan-base; IANS, "Six Afghanistan Policemen Killed, Nine Injured in 'Insider Attack,'" First Post, June 4, 2017, http://www.firstpost.com/world/afghanistan-two-policemen-kill-six-colleagues-injured-five-others-in-two-insider-attacks-3515999.html.

[12] Jaclyn Belczyk, "Amended Afghanistan Personal Status Law Still Restricts Women's Rights: HRW," Jurist, August 14, 2009, http://www.jurist.org/paperchase/2009/08/amended-afghanistan-personal-status-law.php.

[13] Ann Jones, "Remember the Women?," in *The Case for Withdrawal from Afghanistan*, ed. Nick Turse, 97, 104-106.

[14] Rashid, *Taliban*, 95-116.

[15] Gareth Porter, "Long-Term Afghan Presence Likely to Derail Peace Talks," Antiwar.com, March 29, 2011, http://original.antiwar.com/porter/2011/03/28/long-term-afghan-presence-likely-to-derail-peace-talks/; Scahill, "America's Failed War of Attrition in Afghanistan."

The closest the U.S. ever came to a settlement with the Taliban was after blowing nine full months negotiating with — and handsomely paying — a complete impostor who presented himself as high-level Taliban leader Mullah Akhtar Muhammad Mansour. The man, it turned out, was not Mansour and had no ties to the Taliban or insurgency, much less authority to negotiate on their behalf.[16]

In early 2010, the Pakistani government arrested a handful of Afghan Taliban leaders in Quetta. On the surface, this was a blow to Taliban power, but rather than the kind of help the U.S. had long been requesting from the Pakistanis, this move was seen as an attempt by the Pakistani intelligence agency, ISI, to prevent the Taliban from cutting a deal with the U.S. or Kabul that did not also include them.[17] As a result, in 2011 there was a brief series of meetings held in Qatar that went nowhere. The Americans and the British apparently had the idea that if they made specific offers to the Taliban, while cutting out their primary, Pakistani patrons, they could accentuate the distrust between the two and angle for a better deal later. And yet the Americans refused to allow the Taliban to have a permanent office in Turkey or Qatar where they could have had a base from which their negotiators could operate free from Pakistani influence. Regardless, the Taliban, and the Pakistanis along with them, continued to behave as though time was on their side, refusing to change their position that they would not agree to further talks until the U.S. and its allies agreed to withdraw all forces — an obviously poison-pill ultimatum to which the U.S. and its allies would never concede.[18] As the deputy secretary of defense for policy, CNAS's Michèle Flournoy testified to Congress on March 15, 2011, the U.S. military would be staying past 2014, no matter what, for counter-terrorism operations from "joint bases," a certain deal-killer for any negotiations with the insurgency.

In 2013, 2015 and 2016, the same false start to negotiations began and stalled. In 2013, this was over petty objections by the Kabul government over protocol. In the latter two, it was due to the continued Taliban insistence that they would not even begin formal discussions with the Kabul government until all foreign forces left Afghan soil — a promise it

---

[16] Dexter Filkins and Carlotta Gall, "Taliban Leader in Secret Talks Was an Impostor," *New York Times,* November 22, 2010, http://www.nytimes.com/2010/11/23/world/asia/23kabul.html.

[17] Anand Gopal, "Half of Afghanistan Taliban leadership arrested in Pakistan," *Christian Science Monitor,* February 24, 2010, http://www.csmonitor.com/World/Asia-South-Central/2010/0224/Half-of-Afghanistan-Taliban-leadership-arrested-in-Pakistan; Joshua Partlow and Karen DeYoung, "Afghan Officials Say Pakistan's Arrest of Taliban Leader Threatens Peace Talks," *Washington Post,* April 10, 2010, http://www.washingtonpost.com/wp-dyn/content/article/2010/04/09/AR2010040904807.html.

[18] Jonathon Burch, "Taliban Says No Peace Talks with Leader Mullah Omar," Reuters, March 16, 2009, http://in.reuters.com/article/idINIndia-38528220090316; Gareth Porter, "US Uses Peace Talks to Divide Taliban from Pakistan," Inter Press Service, May 31, 2011, http://www.ipsnews.net/2011/05/us-uses-peace-talks-to-divide-taliban-from-pakistan/.

could never make or enforce against the will of the U.S. administration, which itself would never give in to such demands. The Taliban's bet remained, as always, on winning the longer game.[19]

In 2014, Hamid Karzai finally stepped down from power after another disastrous election. Huge portions of the population were excluded. Voting had not even really taken place out in the countryside.[20] The process was so crooked both opponents succeeded in stealing it from each other, one on the first ballot, the other on the second.[21] The contest came down to Ashraf Ghani, an ally of Gen. Dostum, against his nemesis, Abdullah Abdullah, who himself is aligned with Gulbuddin Hekmatyar's Taliban-allied Hizb-e-Islami movement. After initial fights over ballot counts, recounts, runoffs and assassination attempts,[22] Obama's secretary of state, John Kerry, flew in and forced the opponents to compromise and agree to a completely ad-hoc and unconstitutional co-presidency. Ghani, who had previously been the Obama administration's first choice in the crooked election of 2009,[23] would be president while Abdullah Abdullah would become the new "Chief Executive."

The Voice of America conceded in April 2017,

> The September 2014 deal led to the creation of a Chief Executive Officer position, which was given to Abdullah, while Ghani became president. The CEO post was supposed to be turned into the role of prime minister within two years by a constitutional Loya Jirga or Grand Assembly.
>
> That never happened and differences in the way supporters of Abdullah and Ghani interpreted the agreement led to infighting.
>
> Abdullah believed the agreement gave him an equal share in government, while Ghani thought the ultimate authority rested with him. Many Afghans complained the "genuine and meaningful

---

[19] Jessica Donati and Margherita Stancati, "Taliban Detail Conditions for Afghan Peace Talks," *Wall Street Journal,* January 24, 2016, http://www.wsj.com/articles/taliban-detail-conditions-for-afghan-peace-talks-1453673527.

[20] Aikins and Gopal, "The Ghost Polls of Afghanistan."

[21] Associated Press, "Afghanistan Election Goes to 2nd Round; Runoff Between Abdullah Abdullah, Ashraf Ghani Ahmadzai," CBS News, May 15, 2014, http://cbsnews.com/news/afghanistan-election-2nd-round-abdullah-abdullah-ashraf-ghani-ahmadzai/; Matthew Rosenberg and Azam Ahmed, "Tentative Results in Afghan Presidential Runoff Spark Protests," *New York Times,* July 7, 2014, https://www.nytimes.com/2014/07/08/world/asia/afghan-preliminary-results-put-ashraf-ghani-ahead-of-abdullah-abdullah.html.

[22] Yaroslav Trofimov and Ehsanullah Amiri, "Afghan Presidential Front-Runner Escapes Assassination Attempt," *Wall Street Journal,* June 6, 2014, https://www.wsj.com/articles/afghan-presidential-front-runner-escapes-assassination-attempt-1402043894.

[23] Hastings, *The Operators,* 94-95.

partnership" the agreement was supposed to generate between the two was missing from the start.[24]

The major question seems to be when, not if, the "National Unity Government" will unravel, which leaves them in a very weak position from which to negotiate, if they ever get the chance. If the "co-presidents" cannot figure out how to get along, how can they be expected to negotiate peace with a broad-based insurgency?[25]

Taliban Back in Force

American hawks argue that since the Taliban-led insurgency will not negotiate, and especially considering they currently control more of the countryside than at any time since the turn of the century, the only option is to escalate militarily again, and forever.[26] There is another choice: just forget the whole thing. If the United States withdraws the last fifteen thousand[27] troops, airmen, spies and mercenaries, there is little doubt the insurgency could seize control of at least the predominantly Pashtun areas in the south and east of the country along the border with Pakistan in relatively short order. It is even possible, perhaps likely, that the capital city of Kabul could be lost soon thereafter. The Taliban's shadow government — the "Islamic Emirate of Afghanistan"[28] — already has the run of much of the Pashtun tribal lands as it is.[29] The National Unity Government can meet in their parliament all day long, but without the U.S. there to fund their entire operation, it would cease to exist in no time. Yes, the next phase of the Afghan civil war will probably be a bloody disaster, but that is in great measure due to the distortions of power the

---

[24] Ayesha Tanzeem, "International Crisis Group Calls Afghan Government 'Shaky,'" Voice of America News, April 10, 2017, http://www.voanews.com/a/inernational-crisis-group-calls-afghan-government-shaky/3803905.html.

[25] Pamela Constable, "Afghan Political Crisis Intensifies as Two-year Anniversary Nears," *Washington Post*, August 12, 2016, https://www.washingtonpost.com/world/asia_pacific/afghan-political-crisis-intensifies-as-two-year-anniversary-nears/2016/08/12/3575a5aa-6085-11e6-9fd0-0b47b4fac0a4_story.html.

[26] Bill Roggio, "US Officials Give Up on Prospects for Peace Deal with Taliban," Long War Journal, October 2, 2012, http://longwarjournal.org/archives/2012/10/us_officials_give_up_on_prospe.php; Thomas Joscelyn and Bill Roggio, "Are We Losing Afghanistan Again?" Long War Journal, October 21, 2015, http://longwarjournal.org/archives/2015/10/are-we-losing-afghanistan-again.php.

[27] Courtney Kube, "US Has Thousands More Troops in Afghanistan Than the Pentagon Admits," NBC News, August 23, 2017, https://www.nbcnews.com/news/military/u-s-has-thousands-more-troops-afghanistan-pentagon-admits-n795141.

[28] C. J. Chivers, "In Eastern Afghanistan, at War with the Taliban's Shadowy Rule," *New York Times*, February 6, 2011, http://www.nytimes.com/2011/02/07/world/asia/07taliban.html.

[29] Van Linschoten and Kuehn, *An Enemy We Created*, 272.

U.S. has created. Whether the U.S. government throws in the towel now or years from now, the result will be the same: the Pashtun population will throw off whatever degree of rule the national government attempts to maintain over them, and then, in all probability, they will be right back where they were in the 1990s, with a bloody civil war, possibly leading to Taliban dominance in all but the far north of the country.

The Taliban may refrain from pushing their luck and trying to assert dominance in non-Pashtun areas, possibly having learned the lesson of the difficulty of doing so from their previous rule over those areas, as well as witnessing the trouble the other major ethnic groups' coalition government has had in extending its rule over the Pashtun areas over the past 16 years. There is little doubt, though, that the Pashtun regions will remain independent of Kabul, at the very least. This is especially true considering America's renewed efforts to bring in India to support the Afghan National Army's fight against the Taliban is certain to provoke a further reaction from the Pakistanis.[30]

In the end, the country may just split apart. Afghanistan was never a truly unified state to begin with. After 40 years of war, divisions are as deep as they have ever been. There may not be much to hold together. Trust requires peace and vice versa.

It is clear President Ghani's regime desperately needs Western troops and air power to survive.[31] This is why he has constantly invoked the presence of the Taliban and local alleged ISIS affiliates for virtually any significant attack that takes place, in order to get more reinforcements for the thousands of U.S. troops stationed there.[32] In 2014, a small insurgent faction claimed the name of ISIS, "the Islamic State Khorasan Province," or "ISKP,"[33] and declared their loyalty to its "caliph," Omar Bakr al-Baghdadi.[34] This new ISIS affiliate is really just comprised of former

---

[30] Anand Gopal, interviewed by the author, *Scott Horton Show,* radio archive, January 14, 2011, https://scotthorton.org/interviews/antiwar-radio-anand-gopal-5/.

[31] Matthew Rosenberg and Michael D. Shear, "In Reversal, Obama Says US Soldiers Will Stay in Afghanistan to 2017," *New York Times,* October 15, 2015, https://www.nytimes.com/2015/10/16/world/asia/obama-troop-withdrawal-afghanistan.html; Mark Landler, "Obama Says He Will Keep More Troops in Afghanistan Than Planned," *New York Times,* July 6, 2016, https://www.nytimes.com/2016/07/07/world/asia/obama-afghanistan-troops.html; Jamie Tarabay, "US Commander: We Still Need Thousands of Troops in Afghanistan," Vocative, February 2, 2016, http://www.vocativ.com/277458/us-commander-we-still-need-thousands-of-troops-in-afghanistan/; Ahmed Rashid, "Air Cover is What Afghanistan Needs from the West," *Financial Times,* October 16, 2015, http://blogs.ft.com/the-exchange/2015/10/16/west-needs-to-provide-air-cover-to-afghans/.

[32] David Martin, "Pentagon Plans to Send Thousands More US Troops to Afghanistan," CBS News, June 16, 2017, http://www.cbsnews.com/news/pentagon-to-send-nearly-4000-more-u-s-troops-to-afghanistan/.

[33] Khorasan is a province in northeastern Iran, but the term is sometimes used to denote a much larger territory, including parts of Central Asia and northern Afghanistan.

[34] Priyanka Boghani, "ISIS is in Afghanistan, but Who Are They Really?," *Frontline,* PBS, November

members of the Pakistani Taliban — local Pashtun tribesmen, not international Arab terrorists[35] — who had fled from a Pakistani army offensive back in 2010. They had even been supported by the Afghan government for a time, reportedly in the hopes that they could be used against the Pakistani government in revenge for Pakistani support for the Afghan Taliban, and against the Afghan Taliban as well.[36] As Dutch reporter Bette Dam lamented, we are seeing the rest of the exact same dynamic play out with them as with the entire insurgency over all these years as well: seeing this new threat, the army and air force have launched a massive response against them. Since January 2015, the U.S. has been bombing the eastern Nangarhar Province in an attempt to fight this small insurgent faction now claiming ISIS's name. As a result, "they are creating unrest, hopelessness and new enemies" for the future. The anti-occupation violence Dam predicted has continued to escalate.[37]

In the meantime, it was revealed that Taliban leader Mullah Omar had died back in 2013,[38] though the rank and file Taliban fighters had been told he was alive and still their leader. Interestingly, it turned out that Omar had been in Afghanistan, not hiding in Pakistan as had been assumed. As Dam explained, Omar had not been in control of the Taliban part of the insurgency for quite some time, but had instead been sitting quietly at home, studying, for the last decade or so before his death.[39]

Omar's successor as leader of the Taliban, the previously discussed Mullah Mansour, was assassinated by a JSOC drone strike in Pakistan in

17, 2015, http://www.pbs.org/wgbh/frontline/article/isis-is-in-afghanistan-but-who-are-they-really/; Euan McKirdy and Ehsan Popalzai, "ISIS Kidnaps, Kills 30 in Afghanistan," CNN, October 26, 2016, http://www.cnn.com/2016/10/26/asia/isis-abduction-killings-afghanistan/.

35 Tim Craig and Haq Nawaz Khan, "Pakistani Taliban Leaders Pledge Allegiance to Islamic State," *Washington Post*, October 14, 2014, https://www.washingtonpost.com/world/pakistan-taliban-leaders-pledge-allegiance-to-islamic-state/2014/10/14/34837e7e-53df-11e4-809b-8cc0a295c773_story.html; "Top ISIS Commander Killed in US Airstrike in Afghanistan," BNO News, August 12, 2016, http://bnonews.com/news/index.php/news/id5030.

36 Borhan Osman, "The Islamic State in 'Khorasan': How It Began and Where It Stands Now in Nangarhar," Afghan Analysts Network, July 27, 2016, https://www.afghanistan-analysts.org/the-islamic-state-in-khorasan-how-it-began-and-where-it-stands-now-in-nangarhar/; Tahir Khan "Senior TTP Commander Daud Khan 'Switches Loyalty' to Daesh," *Daily Times*, July 31, 2017, http://dailytimes.com.pk/pakistan/31-Jul-17/senior-ttp-commander-daud-khan-switches-loyalty-to-daesh.

37 Dam, *Scott Horton Show*, August 24, 2016; Mujib Mashal, "Afghan Police Chief Is Killed as He Tries to Turn Tide Against Taliban," *New York Times*, September 11, 2016, http://www.nytimes.com/2016/09/12/world/middleeast/afghan-police-chief-is-killed-as-he-tries-to-turn-tide-against-taliban.html; "Man, 2 Sons Allegedly Killed in Encounter with US Troops," CBS News, June 12, 2017, http://www.cbsnews.com/news/afghanistan-civilians-killed-us-troops-nangarhar-afghan-official-says/.

38 Jibran Ahmad, "Taliban's Mullah Omar Died of Natural Causes in Afghanistan, Son Says," Reuters, September 14, 2015, http://www.reuters.com/article/us-pakistan-taliban-idUSKCN0RE0RC20150914.

39 Dam, *Scott Horton Show*, August 24, 2016; Bette Dam, email message to the author, August 29, 2016.

May 2016. Revealingly, the strike took place in the southwestern Pakistani Baluchistan region. This again raises questions about why the U.S. had spent so much time and effort on the drone war in that country helping the Pakistanis hunt and kill members of the Pakistani Taliban, a separate group up in the Northwestern Federally Administered Tribal Areas, North and South Waziristan, and the Swat Valley, all hundreds of miles away from where the Afghan Taliban had been hiding, which was in the land adjacent to Afghanistan's southern Kandahar and Helmand Provinces, the latter of which is now almost entirely controlled by the Taliban.[40]

If killing Mansour was intended to throw the Taliban off balance, it seems to have backfired. It turns out that the controversial Mansour's successor, Mullah Haibatullah Akhundzada, had previously been a mentor to Taliban founder Mullah Omar and commanded far more respect among the rank and file than his immediate predecessor. His appointment apparently helped unite the group. Shortly after Mansour's assassination, a suicide attack on a bus outside of Kabul, which killed 11 and was attributed to the Taliban,[41] seemed to show that they remain nowhere near ready to negotiate with the Ghani government.[42]

As foreign policy analyst Micah Zenko wrote, one year after the killing of Mansour, the stated objectives of the strike had not been achieved. The State Department's Office of the Inspector General had reported, the Taliban were still refusing to negotiate,[43] and would continue to refuse as long as U.S. forces remained in the country.[44] And insurgent violence had only grown worse:

> According to Department of Defense bi-annual Afghanistan progress reports released in June and December 2016, the number of "effective enemy-initiated attacks — that is, attacks that resulted in casualties" totaled 4,480 in the six months before Mansour's death. In the six months after (from June 1 to November 20, 2016), there were a total

---

[40] Kathy Gannon and Amir Shah, "Taliban Take Key Afghan District in Helmand Province," Military, March 23, 2017, http://www.military.com/daily-news/2017/03/23/taliban-take-key-afghan-district-helmand-province.html.

[41] Rahim Faiez, "Taliban Bomber Hits Court Minibus in Kabul, Killing 11," Associated Press, May 25, 2016, http://bigstory.ap.org/article/cd924d45f6774f2a8096f2d2817417b6/afghan-official-suicide-bombing-kabul-kills-10-people.

[42] Hamzah Rifaat Hussain, "Haibatullah Akhundzada and the Resurgence of the Taliban," Diplomat, June 4, 2016, http://thediplomat.com/2016/06/haibatullah-akhunzada-and-the-resurgence-of-the-taliban/.

[43] Lead Inspector General for Overseas Contingency Operations, "Operation Freedom's Sentinel," Report to the US Congress, October 1, 2016 - December 31, 2016, https://oig.state.gov/system/files/ofs1_dec2016_gold_11_-_a.pdf.

[44] Ayaz Gul, "Taliban: Peace Talks Not Possible Until Foreign 'Occupation' of Afghanistan Ends," Voice of America News, December 23, 2016, http://www.voanews.com/a/taliban-says-peace-talks-not-possible-until-foreign-occupation-of-afghanistan-ends/3648205.html.

of 5,271 effective enemy-initiated attacks. Those 791 additional attacks represent an increase following the killing of the terrorist leader.[45]

The Taliban's strength in the north of the country was demonstrated in September 2015, when they took over the provincial capital of Kunduz in northern Afghanistan for more than two weeks before finally being driven out by the Afghan National Army and American special operations forces. Though far from traditional "Pashtunistan," Kunduz has had a strong minority Pashtun population since the early twentieth century.[46] During one of the battles, U.S. special operations forces flying an AC-130 Gunship blasted a Doctors Without Borders hospital. Approximately 42 people were killed with more than 30 injured. Patients burned in their hospital beds, their surgeons alongside them.[47]

The building was of a unique and highly recognizable shape and clearly marked as a hospital. Among the first half dozen excuses offered by officials was the claim U.S. forces had believed there to be Taliban forces in positions around the hospital, or alternatively, that a Pakistani spy had been helping the Taliban from inside the hospital. Since these excuses amounted to admissions that this had been a deliberate assault against an international volunteer hospital full of non-combatants, they were quickly abandoned in favor of blaming local Afghan National Army units for giving bad information and the hasty actions of the air crew instead.[48]

A year later, the Taliban returned and nearly seized the city once more. Only the late arrival of U.S. Army special operations forces could again beat them back.[49]

Even when the Taliban do not control the city outright, ANA forces in Kunduz remain under constant attack, with the Taliban making four major attempts to take the city in the year between their two semi-successful attempts. The German daily Der Spiegel complained, "In

---

[45] Micah Zenko and Jennifer Wilson, "Did Killing Mullah Mansour Work?," Council on Foreign Relations, May 25, 2017, https://www.cfr.org/blog-post/did-killing-mullah-mansour-work.

[46] Christian Bleuer, "State-building, Migration and Economic Development on the Frontiers of Northern Afghanistan and Southern Tajikistan," Science Direct, October 8, 2011, http://www.sciencedirect.com/science/article/pii/S1879366511000297.

[47] Hannah Parry, "Doctor from MSF Hospital Bombed by US Forces Says Staff Died 'Screaming Out for Help That Never Came,'" Daily Mail, April 7, 2016, http://www.dailymail.co.uk/news/article-3528574/Our-colleagues-didn-t-die-peacefully-like-movies-Doctor-MSF-hospital-bombed-forces-says-staff-died-screaming-help-never-came.html.

[48] Glenn Greenwald, "The Radically Changing Story of the US Airstrike on Afghan Hospital: From Mistake to Justification," Intercept, October 5, 2015, https://theintercept.com/2015/10/05/the-radically-changing-story-of-the-u-s-airstrike-on-afghan-hospital-from-mistake-to-justification/; Robert Burns, "16 Blamed for Mistakes in Deadly US Attack on Afghan Clinic," Associated Press, April, 29, 2016, http://bigstory.ap.org/article/99f076ae2568408e90020b29bb5b514e/punishments-no-criminal-charges-us-attack-hospital.

[49] Najim Rahim and Fahim Abed, "Afghan Troops Hold Off the Taliban in Kunduz," New York Times, August 20, 2016, http://www.nytimes.com/2016/08/21/world/asia/kunduz-in-afghanistan-teeters-toward-taliban-control.html.

September and October of last year, the Islamists were able to occupy Kunduz for 15 days — enough for them to plunder and burn down almost everything the Germans had built up over the course of a decade." They explain also that the anti-Pashtun violence of Vice President Dostum's lawless militias had been driving more and more people into the arms of the rising insurgency for protection.[50] By May 2017, they had the town completely surrounded, and only last-minute reinforcements of ANA Special Forces troops kept the city from falling to the insurgents once again.[51]

Just a month before, Taliban suicide bombers and gunmen, in Afghan National Army uniforms, kicked off the 2017 fighting season by infiltrating a base in Balkh Province in Afghanistan's far north near the city of Mazar-e-Sharif, where they killed over 135 soldiers.[52] While the U.S. may have never lost a battle in the Afghan war — though they have come close[53] — they certainly have not won it.

Finally, in May of 2017, Gen. Dostum left Afghanistan for Turkey. The previous December he had ordered his bodyguards to hold down a former governor of the northern Jowzjan Province and rape him with the barrel of an AK-47. According to the *Guardian*, though President Ghani had claimed that the prosecution of Dostum for his crimes was essential to the establishment of the rule of law, he, in fact, had urged Dostum to temporarily leave the country instead.[54] Dostum remains Vice President and has made it clear that he is far from retirement.[55]

In early August 2016, the U.S. announced it was suspending $300 million in military aid to Pakistan, which was to be reimbursement for their costs in allowing the U.S. to use their ports, roads and other infrastructure to transport goods through Pakistan to U.S. and ISAF forces in Afghanistan, as a punishment for their long-standing support for the Afghan Taliban and Haqqani Network. Secretary of Defense Ashton Carter refused to certify their cooperation to Congress and suspended the

[50] Susanne Koelbl, "The Taliban Erases Western Gains in Afghanistan," *Der Spiegel*, October 12, 2016, http://www.spiegel.de/international/world/taliban-in-kunduz-is-erasing-gains-of-afghanistan-deployment-a-1116101.html.

[51] Mirwais Harooni, "Afghan Forces Try to Push Back Taliban from Kunduz City," Reuters, May 9, 2017, http://www.reuters.com/article/us-afghanistan-taliban-idUSKBN1851WN.

[52] Aref Musawi, "Survivors Say Insurgents Had Help from Inside Base," Tolo News, April 22, 2017, http://www.tolonews.com/afghanistan/survivors-claim-insurgents-had-help-inside-base.

[53] Candace Rondeaux, "Nine US Soldiers Killed in Firefight," *Washington Post*, July 14, 2008, http://www.washingtonpost.com/wpdyn/content/article/2008/07/13/AR2008071300292.html.

[54] Sune Engel Rasmussen, "Vice-President Leaves Afghanistan Amid Torture and Rape Claims," *Guardian*, May 19, 2017, https://www.theguardian.com/world/2017/may/19/vice-president-leaves-afghanistan-amid-torture-and-claims.

[55] Karim Amini, "Three Afghan Political Parties Form New Coalition in Ankara," Tolo News, June 29, 2017, http://tolonews.com/afghanistan/three-afghan-political-parties-form-new-coalition-ankara.

aid around the same time the U.S. was also announcing it was stepping up cooperation with India and requesting the Indians help the U.S. work around its own sanctions against Russia by purchasing even more MI-25 attack helicopters from them for the ANA.[56] India's continued willingness to train and equip Afghan National Army forces in their fight against the Afghan Taliban and the Haqqani Network amounted to nothing less than a "proxy war" between India and Pakistan in Afghanistan, in the words of reporter Charles Tiefer, a proxy war in which the U.S. remains on both sides.[57] All this virtually guarantees the Pakistani state will increase aid to their favored insurgent forces in response. The Americans could not be employing a more self-defeating strategy at this point if sabotage was their actual goal.[58]

A Trojan Horse?

In the autumn of 2016, the "Butcher of Kabul," Gulbuddin Hekmatyar, the infamous, formerly CIA-backed Pashtun warlord, former Afghan Prime Minister and insurgent leader, signed a peace deal with the new government in Kabul without the precondition of full foreign withdrawal. Betting the occupation was as good as over at that point, Hekmatyar had apparently decided that he and his Hizb-e-Islami group were better off consolidating their position in the capital before his sometimes-allies, the Taliban, beat him to it. As the *New York Times* reported, he made a pretty good bet. According to the deal, Hekmatyar and his entire group received protection, money, homes and offices as well as his group's removal from U.S. and UN terrorist lists. His captured soldiers were released from Afghan prisons, and Hekmatyar himself will get a high-level advisory position under President Ashraf Ghani.

While on its face this deal takes one of the smaller insurgent groups off

---

[56] Idrees Ali, "Pentagon Not to Pay Pakistan $300 Million in Military Reimbursements," Reuters, August 4, 2016, http://www.reuters.com/article/us-usa-pakistan-military-idUSKCN10F07O; Vivek Raghuvanshi, "US General Asks India for Military Assistance in Afghanistan," Defense News, August 11, 2016, http://www.defensenews.com/story/defense/land/weapons/2016/08/11/india-afghanistan-nicholson-russia-us-sanctions/88556746/.

[57] Charles Tiefer, "A Proxy War Between India and Pakistan is Under Way in Afghanistan," *Forbes*, August 13, 2016, http://www.forbes.com/sites/charlestiefer/2016/08/13/war-between-india-with-the-us-and-pakistan-started-this-week-in-afghanistan-proxy-war-that-is/; "India Pledges Full Support in Strengthening Afghanistan's Defense Capabilities," Khaama Press, June 22, 2016, https://www.khaama.com/india-pledges-full-support-in-strengthening-afghanistans-defense-capabilities-01328.

[58] "Pakistan 'Harboring Terrorists' in Afghanistan to Counter Indian Influence, Says Top US Official," *India Times*, May 24, 2017, http://www.indiatimes.com/news/world/pakistan-harbouring-terrorists-in-afghanistan-to-counter-indian-influence-says-top-us-official-322310.html; "Pentagon Praises India in Afghanistan," *American Interest*, June 22, 2017, https://www.the-american-interest.com/2017/06/22/pentagon-praises-india-afghanistan/.

the battlefield, and could set a precedent for negotiations with the Taliban, having Hekmatyar and 20,000 of his followers suddenly return to Kabul means he will either need to adjust to the new reality in the capital, or the new reality in the capital will need to adjust to him. For example, either Hizb-e-Islami is going to have to learn to accept the increased role of women in public life, or the women are going to have to get used to trying to dodge acid attacks again.[59] The whole thing could also be a Trojan horse, a clever ploy by Hekmatyar to position his men inside the capital city for the day he attempts to seize power for himself.[60] One day after returning to Kabul, Hekmatyar held a rally in front of thousands of supporters denouncing the National Unity Government and "co-presidents" Ghani and Abdullah.[61]

Politicians in Kabul have already begun to express second thoughts on the matter since, they say, Hekmatyar refuses to disarm thousands of militia men loyal to him and has already begun agitating against the Shi'ite Hazaras, complaining that they are being granted unfair privileges. "We welcomed the peace deal, but instead of surrendering to the government, Mr. Hekmatyar is acting as if the government has surrendered to him," a rival told the *Washington Post*.[62]

Shortly after his return, a group of Afghans petitioned the United Nations to ignore the immunity deal and prosecute Hekmatyar for war crimes. There is no doubt his victims deserve justice. As many as 50,000 people were killed by his forces during the 1990s civil war.[63] However, this is another example of the intractability of so many of Afghanistan's

---

[59] Fariba Nawa, "Kabul's Women Seek Refuge Indoors After a Series of Acid Attacks," *New York Times*, August 10, 2016, http://nytlive.nytimes.com/womenintheworld/2016/08/10/kabuls-women-seek-safety-indoors-after-a-series-of-acid-attacks/.

[60] Mujib Mashal and Jawad Sukhanyarmay, "Gulbuddin Hekmatyar, Exiled Afghan Insurgent, Nears a Comeback," *New York Times*, May 11, 2016,
http://www.nytimes.com/2016/05/12/world/asia/afghanistan-gulbuddin-hekmatyar.html; Mir Aq, "Hezb-e-Islami Takes Preconditions off the Peace Talks Table," Tolo News, April 6, 2016, http://www.tolonews.com/en/afghanistan/24626-hezb-e-islami-takes-preconditions-off-the-peace-talks-table; Ali Reza Sarwar, "How Will Kabul Welcome Gulbuddin Hekmatyar?," Diplomat, June 13, 2016, http://thediplomat.com/2016/06/how-will-kabul-welcome-gulbuddin-hekmatyar/; "Ghani Formalizes Peace Deal with 'Butcher of Kabul,'" *Hindu*, September 30, 2016, http://www.thehindu.com/news/ghani-formalises-peace-deal-with-butcher-of-kabul/article9163912.ece; "Afghan Warlord Hekmatyar Sanctions Dropped by UN," BBC News, February 4, 2017, http://www.bbc.com/news/world-asia-38867280.

[61] Hamid Shalizi, "Afghan Former Warlord Hekmatyar Rallies Supporters in Kabul," Yahoo! News, May 5, 2017, https://www.yahoo.com/news/afghan-former-warlord-hekmatyar-rallies-supporters-kabul-101311305.html.

[62] Pamela Constable, "Return of Warlord Hekmatyar Adds to Afghan Political Tensions," *Washington Post*, May 21, 2017, https://www.washingtonpost.com/world/asia_pacific/return-of-warlord-hekmatyar-adds-to-afghan-political-tensions/2017/05/18/1fa9fb20-398a-11e7-a59b-26e0451a96fd_story.html.

[63] Dexter Filkins, "Afghans Round Up Hundreds in Plot Against Leaders," *New York Times*, April 4, 2002, http://www.nytimes.com/2002/04/04/world/a-nation-challenged-kabul-afghans-round-up-hundreds-in-plot-against-leaders.html.

problems. If the deal is not respected, and Hekmatyar is jailed, it could make it that much harder for any other armed groups to come in and negotiate with the government the next time the opportunity might arise. Yet failing to hold him accountable now could just as easily lead to a disaster of a different kind.[64]

Even as Hekmatyar and his part of the Hizb-e-Islami group comes in from the cold, the Afghan government's enemies keep multiplying. There are now the various groups of Pashtun tribal fighters, the Taliban, the Haqqani network, the Islamic Movement of Uzbekistan and the groups now declaring allegiance to ISIS.[65] In August 2016, Taliban and Islamic State forces announced a temporary alliance in the fight against the Afghan National Army and allied militias in eastern Afghanistan,[66] though their infighting soon resumed.[67]

Staying Forever

On March 12, 2014, General Joseph Dunford, then commander of U.S. efforts in Afghanistan, conceded to the Senate Armed Services Committee that despite the tens of billions of dollars spent to build up the Afghan National Army, it could not hold territory where the U.S. had made temporary gains and had attempted to "transfer" that ground to them. Dunford warned against the president's planned drawdown, "If we leave at the end of 2014, the Afghan security forces will begin to deteriorate. The security environment will begin to deteriorate, and I think the only debate is the pace of that deterioration."[68]

True believers in American interventionism, like Dunford and former National Security Council staffer Paul D. Miller, cannot admit they were wrong to support escalating the Afghan war. No, Miller insists, it was just that more money should have been spent and longer commitments should have been made. The "surge" really did work, he says, citing, like Petraeus,

---

[64] "UN Mission to Afghanistan Receives Petition Against Hekmatyar," Radio Free Europe/Radio Liberty, May 26, 2017, https://www.rferl.org/a/afghanistan-un-petition-hekmatyar/28510387.html.

[65] Muhammad Shafiq, "Threats from All Sides," July 9, 2017, The News on Sunday, http://tns.thenews.com.pk/threats-sides-parachinar/#.WYYNxIqQwy4

[66] Jessica Donati and Habib Khan Totakhil, "Taliban, Islamic State Forge Alliance of Convenience in Eastern Afghanistan," Wall Street Journal, August 7, 2016, http://www.wsj.com/articles/taliban-islamic-state-forge-informal-alliance-in-eastern-afghanistan-1470611849.

[67] "Tora Bora Falls to Daesh After Heavy Clashes With Taliban," Tolo News, June 5, 2017, http://tolonews.com/afghanistan/tora-bora-falls-daesh-after-heavy-clashes-taliban.

[68] Ernesto Londoño, "US Commander in Afghanistan Warns That Full Withdrawal Will Allow Al-Qaeda to Regroup," Washington Post, March 12, 2014, https://www.washingtonpost.com/world/national-security/us-commander-in-afghanistan-warns-that-full-withdrawal-will-allow-al-qaeda-to-regroup/2014/03/12/4f7f6288-aa20-11e3-8599-ce7295b6851c_story.html.

statistics that actually only show Afghan guerrilla fighters learned to melt away to fight another day when faced with the full force of the U.S. military. The "surge" was doing great and would have worked even better, Miller is certain, if only Obama had given in to McChrystal's full request for 80,000 to 85,000 more troops, instead of just the 30,000. If only they had stayed longer and "invested" more aid in the national government, then, at some point, everything would have been fine. The central failure of the Obama administration, Miller says, was their inability to understand that political violence in Afghanistan will continue until "the creation of an alternate, just political order." What he and other hawks seem unable to understand is that the United States government, which has been fighting for a minority coalition against the country's plurality population for more than a decade and a half now, does not have the slightest idea how to achieve such results. The best and the brightest had their chance to try to give the Afghans a "government in a box," and it was a complete failure. Petraeus and McChrystal swore they could force the Taliban to submit to U.S. demands and have the Afghan army ready to take over for the Americans to maintain whatever supposed gains they made against the insurgency. They were wrong. But we've just got to give them another chance now! Have you not heard? ISIS![69] How could any president withdraw in such a situation?[70]

In May 2017, the Council on Foreign Relations' journal, *Foreign Affairs*, ran an article describing America's "four options" for Afghanistan: (1) spend another 25 years building a state in Kabul, (2) increase "kinetic efforts to secure a negotiated peace settlement," (3) continue containment and counter-terrorism strikes, and (4) focus on establishing permanent bases. As the article itself acknowledges, these approaches have already been tried and have failed, and there is little reason to believe that present circumstances would lend themselves to better outcomes. The author is also quite candid about America's imperial interest in southern Central Asia:

> The basing strategy with an open-ended American military presence would ensure sufficient forces to defend important population centers, retain bases critical for counterterrorism, and maintain a U.S. foothold in Central Asia. Although little has been explicitly written, a range of arguments imply that some strategists are thinking seriously about a semi-permanent Central Asian foothold from which to counter terrorism, monitor developments ranging from increased influence of

---

[69] Ahmed Mengli, "Kabul Hospital Attack: ISIS Claims Responsibility After 30 Killed by Gunmen Disguised as Doctors," NBC News, March 8, 2017, http://www.nbcnews.com/news/world/kabul-military-hospital-attack-taliban-denies-responsibility-n730516.

[70] Paul D. Miller, "Obama's Failed Legacy in Afghanistan," *National Interest*, February 15, 2016, http://www.the-american-interest.com/2016/02/15/obamas-failed-legacy-in-afghanistan/.

the Shanghai Cooperation Organization to China's Belt and Road Initiative, and potentially pressure the more vulnerable flanks in any future contingency with China, Iran, or Russia.

But the author then concedes the inherent futility of that mission as well:

> The downside, of course, is that the United States would necessarily accept a state of long-term instability in Afghanistan because a permanent U.S. presence in Afghanistan will incentivize regional actors to competitively back proxies. For example, they could support new militant groups and inject new capabilities into the conflict, similar to what the United States did in the 1980s against the Soviet Union. Moreover, the Afghan government's acquiescence to a permanent foreign occupier could very well weaken its own legitimacy in the eyes of the Afghan public. Finally, without alternative lines of communication, a sustained American presence in Afghanistan would only deepen its dependence upon Pakistan, frustrating U.S. cooperation with India as a balance against China.[71]

Never can proponents of government action entertain the possibility that intervention was the wrong thing to do in the first place. The conclusion of interested parties is always that the government should do more. And when more does not work, it only proves to them that more should have been done sooner and more must be done now and in the future. It is acceptable to adjust strategies or excuses, sure, but never to give up.[72]

But as Col. Bacevich observed about the war in Afghanistan, and the broader War on Terrorism, "We've done counterinsurgency, we've done counter-terrorism, we've done advise-and-assist, we've done targeted assassination, we've done nation-building… We have run the gamut of approaches in terms of tactics and methods, and none of them have yielded the success that proponents have argued that we would achieve. So you come back to that basic question, maybe the entire enterprise is misguided."[73]

Who really believes that if only the U.S. Marine Corps stays a few years longer they'll turn Lashkar Gah, Helmand Province into Cleveland,

---

[71] Sameer Lalwani, "Four Ways Forward in Afghanistan," *Foreign Affairs*, May 25, 2017, https://www.foreignaffairs.com/articles/afghanistan/2017-05-25/four-ways-forward-afghanistan.

[72] Ludwig von Mises, *Two Essays by Ludwig von Mises: Liberty and Property; Middle-of-the-Road Policy Leads to Socialism* (Auburn, AL: Ludwig Von Mises, 1991); Ludwig von Mises, *Planned Chaos* (Atlanta: Foundation for Economic Education, 1947); Murray N. Rothbard, "The Myth of Efficient Government Service," in *Man, Economy, and State, with Power and Market* (Auburn, AL: Ludwig von Mises, 2009), 1260–1272.

[73] Andrew Bacevich, interviewed by the author, *Scott Horton Show*, radio archive, April 2, 2017, https://scotthorton.org/interviews/4317-andrew-bacevich/.

Ohio?[74] Gen. McChrystal's original high-end plan, which he did not even bother submitting to Obama, called for an increase of another 100,000 troops and an indefinite commitment to counterinsurgency.[75] The fact that McChrystal was willing to go forward with less than a third of the increase he believed he needed just serves to emphasize the political, rather than strategic, nature of the "surge" decision in the first place. According to Col. Gian Gentile, going by the standard ratios, a true counterinsurgency project with successful results that lasted would require at least 300,000 U.S. soldiers and marines and decades longer to accomplish.[76] Some estimates said the U.S. would need more than 500,000 troops[77] — more than the U.S. Army's entire active force[78] — to achieve victory. Even then there is no reason to think the Afghans, especially the Pashtuns, would be somehow "won over" by American power in their country. As Elizabeth Gould and Paul Fitzgerald point out in *Crossing Zero: The AfPak War at the Turning Point of American Empire*, judging by the results in Marjah, where the occupation ratio was one U.S. marine *per two civilians* and the results were disastrous, even if the U.S. sent its entire million-man military to Afghanistan to stay, it could still never "work."[79] There would continue to be terrible violence and civilian deaths — and even more war crimes. There is every reason to conclude that any war against the Afghans short of genocidal annihilation will only ultimately fuel further reaction and insurgency against U.S. rule, even if America stayed for another 100 years.

In June 2016, many of those responsible for waging, escalating and losing the Afghan war signed an open letter to President Obama urging him to freeze troop levels. The letter was signed by former ambassadors to Afghanistan like Ryan Crocker and Zalmay Khalilzad, as well as military commanders, such as Generals John Allen, Stanley McChrystal and David Petraeus. Without admitting the slightest bit of failure, much less taking responsibility for those who had been killed on their watch for no good reason, the hawks instead continued to invoke the terrorist safe-haven myth and, much more realistically, the threat of increased Afghan civil war if the U.S. were to withdraw. The 5,000 Afghan soldiers and police killed

---

[74] Mohammad Stanekzai, "Dozens Killed in Afghanistan Car Bombing," *Herald Sun,* June 22, 2017, http://www.heraldsun.com.au/news/breaking-news/dozens-killed-in-afghanistan-car-bombing/news-story/9ff6fc5476639394ddf491e7845b5eb4.

[75] Spencer Ackerman, "Michael Hastings: McChrystal Was 'Complex,' Obama Was Naive, Afghanistan Is Hopeless," *Wired,* January 5, 2012, https://www.wired.com/2012/01/michael-hastings/.

[76] Gentile, *Wrong Turn,* 133-134.

[77] Fred Kaplan, "Obama's Middle Course," Slate, October 13, 2009, http://slate.com/articles/news_and_politics/war_stories/2009/10/obamas_middle_course.html.

[78] "2016 Index of Military Strength," Heritage Foundation, http://index.heritage.org/military/2016/assessments/us-military-power/us-army/.

[79] Gould and Fitzgerald, *Crossing Zero,* 166.

each year over the "past several years," are invoked as martyrs to the cause of progress instead of cited as proof of failure in one big, bloody, decade and a half-long, sunk-cost fallacy in action. "Afghanistan is a place where we should wish to consolidate and lock down our provisional progress into something of a more lasting asset," Petraeus and friends insisted.[80]

The hawks did not have to worry. Just four days later, on June 7, 2016, Obama announced that he had decided it would be necessary to leave 8,400 troops in Afghanistan through the end of his presidency in early 2017.[81] He had previously climbed down from his promise to have all troops out of the country by the end of his second term, even though the war had supposedly ended in December 2014.[82] Back in May 2012, Obama had signed a deal with Afghan President Karzai to leave U.S. forces in Afghanistan "until the end of 2024 and beyond," for the purpose of continuing to train the Afghan army and police forces and protect them with counter-terrorism units and air power stationed permanently in the country.[83] Therefore, when the promised "end" of the war, or "formal combat operations" came and went at the end of 2014 without the final withdrawal of U.S. combat forces, it came as no surprise to those watching closely — nor did President Obama's effort to prostrate himself before the great American fraud, Gen. David Petraeus, one last time before leaving office. The U.S. presence in Afghanistan will continue to prevent the negotiated settlement with the Taliban that the U.S. itself says must be the ultimate goal of any administration in Kabul.

These remaining forces are still accompanied by thousands of CIA officers and agents, mercenaries and other contractors, not to mention the presence of JSOC operators and U.S. Air Force bombers and drones. The Washington, D.C., consensus remains that the U.S. can never leave Afghanistan because all of its gains have been, in the immortal words of Gen. Petraeus, "fragile and reversible." The military and State Department have built nothing that can stand on its own after all this time. And so, they stay. Though the numbers of troops remaining are small enough to raise the question of whether they have enough firepower for much more than their own force protection.[84]

[80] Ryan Crocker et al., "Keep Troop Levels Steady in Afghanistan: An Open Letter," *National Interest,* June 3, 2016, http://nationalinterest.org/feature/keep-troop-levels-steady-afghanistan-16450.

[81] Landler, "Obama Says He Will Keep More Troops in Afghanistan Than Planned."

[82] Rosenberg and Shear, "In Reversal, Obama Says US Soldiers Will Stay in Afghanistan to 2017."

[83] "Security and Defense Cooperation Agreement Between the Islamic Republic of Afghanistan and the United States of America," Ministry of Foreign Affairs for the Islamic Republic of Afghanistan, May 2, 2012, http://mfa.gov.af/Content/files/BSA%20ENGLISH%20AFG.pdf; Ben Farmer, "US Troops May Stay in Afghanistan until 2024," *Telegraph,* August 19, 2011, http://www.telegraph.co.uk/news/worldnews/asia/afghanistan/8712701/US-troops-may-stay-in-Afghanistan-until-2024.html.

[84] Greg Jaffe and Missy Ryan, "The US Was Supposed to Leave Afghanistan, 2017. Now It Might

If 2015 had been considered the worst year of the war so far,[85] 2016 would prove to be worse. In January, one full year after the "end" of the war, President Obama authorized U.S. Air Force strikes against ISIS targets "under any circumstance," according to the *Air Force Times*.[86] In May, at a press conference held after a briefing with new Afghan war commander, Gen. John Nicholson, the Supreme Allied Commander of NATO, U.S. Army General Curtis Scaporrotti, invoked the old safe-haven myth, declaring that NATO troops would be staying until they "realize [their] objective of a stable and secure Afghanistan that is not a haven for terrorists any longer."[87] In July 2016, Obama ordered the air force to loosen rules of engagement against all targets and vastly increase air support for the Afghan National Army just as he was announcing that the final drawdown of troops on his watch would stop at 8,400, rather than the previously planned 5,500.[88] B-52 Stratofortress heavy bombers were brought back into the country for the once-again expanded mission as the Taliban continued to make major gains.[89] This led to mass casualty attacks such as one in Nangarhar Province in September that killed 15 civilians.[90] By April, the Taliban already controlled nearly half of the country.[91]

In June 2016, Obama lifted restrictions on U.S. ground troops fighting insurgents. "Under the new rules, airstrikes will no longer have to be justified as necessary to defend American troops," reported the *New York Times*. "United States commanders will now be allowed to use air power against the Taliban when they see fit, Pentagon and administration officials said. American forces will also be permitted to accompany regular Afghan troops into combat against the Taliban."

Take Decades," *Washington Post*, January 26, 2016, https://washingtonpost.com/news/checkpoint/wp/2016/01/26/the-u-s-was-supposed-to-leave-afghanistan-by-2017-now-it-might-take-decades/.

[85] Dawood Azami, "The Taliban's Resurgence in Afghanistan," Al Jazeera, December 27, 2015, http://www.aljazeera.com/news/2015/12/analysis-taliban-resurgence-afghanistan-isil-151227065817409.html.

[86] Oriana Pawlyk, "US Air Force Reports Sharp Climb in Air Strikes Against Militants in Afghanistan," *Air Force Times,* July 29, 2016, http://www.airforcetimes.com/story/military/2016/07/29/us-air-force-reports-sharp-climb-air-strikes-against-militants-afghanistan/87737638/.

[87] Dan Lamothe, "Top NATO Commanders Signal Support for Keeping Troops in Afghanistan," *Washington Post,* May 18, 2016, https://washingtonpost.com/news/checkpoint/wp/2016/05/18/top-nato-commanders-signal-support-for-keeping-troops-in-afghanistan/.

[88] Landler, "Obama Says He Will Keep More Troops in Afghanistan Than Planned."

[89] Tom Vanden Brook, "Pentagon Acknowledges New Airstrikes in Afghanistan," *USA Today,* June 24, 2016, http://www.usatoday.com/story/news/politics/2016/06/24/pentagon-acknowledges-new-airstrikes-afghanistan/86345966/.

[90] Pamela Constable, "UN Officials Criticize Fatal US Airstrike in Afghanistan," *Washington Post*, September 29, 2016, https://www.washingtonpost.com/world/un-officials-criticize-fatal-us-airstrike-in-afghanistan/2016/09/29/9d06d122-8672-11e6-a3ef-f35afb41797f_story.html.

[91] Sarah Almuktar and Karen Yourish, "More Than 14 Years After US Invasion, the Taliban Control Large Parts of Afghanistan," *New York Times*, April 19, 2016, http://www.nytimes.com/interactive/2015/09/29/world/asia/afghanistan-taliban-maps.html.

The justification for this shift in policy was explained:

> The Afghan Army and police, riddled by corruption and hampered by poor leadership, have proved outmatched by the Taliban. The Afghan government remains weak and unstable, despite tens of billions of dollars in American aid. ...

> The fight against the Taliban was intended to be left to Afghan forces, not Americans, who were supposed to strike the insurgents only if under direct threat. But in the 18 months since, the administration has allowed the self-defense rationale to be stretched to its limits. ...

> American officials insisted that the new rules would not pull United States troops back into the kind of daily fighting that they saw before the end of the combat mission in 2014.[92]

By returning U.S. troops to the front lines in the battle against the insurgency, the government was again exposing them to murderous "green on blue," insider attacks at the hands of their supposed allies in the Afghan National Army.[93]

And things keep getting worse. After a massive suicide attack at a hotel in Kabul on August 1, 2016, CNN reported, "The rash of kidnappings and Taliban bombings have heightened security fears in Kabul. U.S. and other diplomats have been barred from traveling by road the short distance from the city's international airport to their diplomatic missions. Instead, they've been ferried by helicopter."[94] Never mind the countryside, Americans and their collaborators are not even safe driving around in the capital city. Security in Kabul is as precarious now as it has been at any time since 2001.[95]

The insurgency is reported to now have as many as 25,000 fighters in Pakistan and southern Afghanistan. Though there is really no need for them to hurry, with a committed effort, some clever planning and a little bit of luck, they could even threaten Kabul.[96]

---

[92] Matthew Rosenberg, "Obama Loosens Restrictions on US Forces Fighting Taliban in Afghanistan," *New York Times,* June 10, 2016,
http://www.nytimes.com/2016/06/11/world/asia/obama-us-forces-taliban.html.

[93] Aleem Agha and Luis Martinez, "3 US Service Members Killed in Attack by Afghan Soldier; Taliban Claims Responsibility," ABC News, June 10, 2017,
http://abcnews.go.com/International/us-soldiers-killed-wounded-attack-afghan-soldier/story?id=47956850; Jay Croft, "7 US Troops Wounded in Insider Attack in Afghanistan," CNN, June 17, 2017, http://www.cnn.com/2017/06/17/politics/us-casualties-afghanistan-attack/index.html.

[94] Steve Visser and Masoud Popalzai, "Kabul's Northgate Hotel Bombed, Attacked," CNN, August 1, 2016, http://www.cnn.com/2016/07/31/asia/kabul-blast/.

[95] Laura Cesaretti, "Afghanistan's Militias: The Enemy Within?," Diplomat, January 4, 2017, http://thediplomat.com/2017/01/afghanistans-militias-the-enemy-within/.

[96] Ioannis Koskinas, "Afghanistan on the Brink, Part 1," *Foreign Policy*, February 18, 2016,

In the summer of 2016, the chief of police in Helmand Province himself complained that half of his policemen were "ghosts."[97] In October, near the capital city of Lashkar Gah, the last part of the massive province not under the full control of the Taliban, approximately 100 ANA and ANP troops were double-crossed and massacred by Taliban forces who had pretended to accept their surrender and offered them a safe retreat from the battlefield before gunning them down.[98] Just in the second quarter of 2016, 4,500 ANA soldiers were killed and another 8,000 were wounded. The entire army was falling apart, desertions were rampant, recruitment rates down through the floor.[99] As SIGAR warned in early 2017, "the ANDSF [Afghan National Defense and Security Forces] has not yet been capable of securing all of Afghanistan and has lost territory to the insurgency. As of August 28, 2016, USFOR-A [U.S. Forces-Afghanistan] reported that only 63.4% of the country's districts were under Afghan government control *or influence*."[100] [emphasis added]

In May of 2017, the *Wall Street Journal* reported:

> The Taliban wielded significant control over 8.4 million Afghans — almost a third of the population — at the end of 2016, up from 5 million a year earlier, according to a confidential United Nations report reviewed by *The Wall Street Journal*. The report showed that the territory over which the insurgents have significant influence or control increased from 30% to 40% of the country over the same period.[101]

In July of 2017, SIGAR reported that more than 12,000 ANA soldiers were AWOL or non-existent. The ones fighting were being killed at a rate of 5,000 per year.[102] Though the government still claims at least nominal control over the country's provincial capitals, chaos reigns over the capital of Kabul itself. On May 31, 2017, a massive car bomb was detonated in what was believed to be a secure area of Kabul near the Presidential Palace, killing more than 150 people.[103] Two days later, security forces opened fire

---

http://foreignpolicy.com/2016/02/18/afghanistan-on-the-brink-part-1/.

[97] "High-Risk List," SIGAR.

[98] Stanekzai Zainullah, "Fighters Ambush, Kill Dozens of Retreating Afghan Troops," Reuters, October 13, 2016, http://www.reuters.com/article/us-afghanistan-helmand-idUSKCN12D16M.

[99] Mujib Mashal and Fahim Abed, "Afghan Forces, Their Numbers Dwindling Sharply, Face a Resurgent Taliban," *New York Times*, October 12, 2016, http://www.nytimes.com/2016/10/13/world/asia/afghanistan-kabul-taliban-massacre.html.

[100] "High-Risk List," SIGAR.

[101] Jessica Donati and Habib Khan Totakhil, "Taliban Broaden Their Reach in Villages Across Afghanistan," *Wall Street Journal*, May 8, 2017, https://www.wsj.com/articles/taliban-broaden-their-reach-in-villages-across-afghanistan-1494235804.

[102] Quarterly Report, Special Inspector General for Afghanistan Reconstruction, July 30, 2017, https://www.sigar.mil/pdf/quarterlyreports/2017-07-30qr.pdf.

[103] Josh Smith, "Kabul Truck-bomb Toll Rises to More Than 150 Killed: Afghan President," Reuters, June 6, 2017, http://www.reuters.com/article/us-afghanistan-blast-idUSKBN18X0FU.

on a crowd protesting the lack of security, killing seven more.[104] And the bomb attacks continue.[105] SIGAR complained in July 2017 that "U.S. officials, whether at State, USAID, Justice, Treasury, Commerce or elsewhere, cannot oversee the billions of dollars the United States is dedicating to Afghan reconstruction if, for the most part, they cannot leave the U.S. embassy compound."[106]

U.S. forces under Donald Trump have stepped up the level of air strikes, dropping bombs at a higher rate in the first half of 2017 than at any time since the Obama "surge" ended in 2012.[107] Partly due to this bombing, a record number of civilians have been killed in violent attacks in this same timeframe, according to the UN.[108]

As previously mentioned, though the Taliban-led insurgency — and planeloads of American dollars — have helped to solidify the National Unity Government alliance between the Tajiks, Uzbeks, Hazaras and other tribal and ethnic factions in Kabul and the north, this is still Afghanistan; loyalties are so divided, hatreds are so bitter and power allocations so distorted that at any time alliances could change and multi-sided civil war could break out again. Without that money, it is virtually guaranteed.[109]

Nizamuddin Nashir, the district chief of Khanabad, told journalist Dexter Filkins in 2012, "Mark my words, the moment the Americans leave, the civil war will begin. This country will be divided into twenty-five or thirty fiefdoms, each with its own government. Mir Alam will take Kunduz. Atta will take Mazar-e-Sharif. Dostum will take Sheberghan. The Karzais will take Kandahar. The Haqqanis will take Paktika. If these things don't happen, you can burn my bones when I die."[110]

104 "Afghanistan: 7 Demonstrators Killed as Clashes Erupt at Kabul Anti-government Protest," Almasdar News, June 2, 2017, https://www.almasdarnews.com/article/afghanistan-7-demonstrators-killed-clashes-erupt-kabul-anti-government-protest/.

105 Hamid Shalizi and James Mackenzie, "Taliban Suicide Car Bomber Kills Dozens in Afghan Capital," Reuters, July 23, 2017, http://www.reuters.com/article/us-afghanistan-blast-idUSKBN1A9067.

106 SIGAR, Quarterly Report, July 30, 2017.

107 Thomas Gibbons-Neff, "US Airstrikes in Afghanistan Are at Levels Not Seen Since Obama Troop Surge," Washington Post, July 17, 2017, https://www.washingtonpost.com/news/checkpoint/wp/2017/07/17/u-s-airstrikes-in-afghanistan-are-at-levels-not-seen-since-obama-troop-surge/.

108 Mujib Mashal and Taimoor Shah, "Afghanistan More Deadly for Women and Children, U.N. Says," New York Times, July 17, 2017, https://nytimes.com/2017/07/17/world/asia/afghanistan-civilian-deaths-united-nations-report.html.

109 Brahma Chellaney, "Afghanistan's Partition Might Be Unpreventable," Japan Times, February 27, 2013, http://www.japantimes.co.jp/opinion/2013/02/27/commentary/world-commentary/afghanistans-partition-might-be-unpreventable/.

110 Dexter Filkins, "After America," New Yorker, July 9, 2012, http://www.newyorker.com/magazine/2012/07/09/after-america-2.

Costs and Consequences

The occupation of Afghanistan and fight against the insurgency has become, by far, the longest foreign war in American history. Osama bin Laden must have died content, knowing that his plan to bog the U.S. down in such a long, bloody and expensive war that cannot possibly be won was at the very pinnacle of its success at the time he was finally put down by the Navy SEALs in Pakistan in the spring of 2011.[111] The financial cost has been *over a trillion dollars*, with unimaginable and incalculable sacrifices made in terms of opportunity costs. Again, as the special inspector general and others have pointed out, the "reconstruction" of Afghanistan has cost more than the entire Marshall Plan for aid to Western Europe after World War II.[112]

Twenty-four hundred American soldiers and marines have been killed in the Afghan war — the vast majority of them during Obama and Petraeus's useless "surge" — along with more than 1,000 from the UK and other NATO-allied countries.[113] More than 17,000 U.S. troops have been wounded.[114] Tens, possibly hundreds, of thousands of Afghans, a large proportion of them civilians, have also been killed in the violence of the war, though no one really knows.[115] The wounded certainly number in the hundreds of thousands. Unlike in Iraq War II, no one has been able to do a reliable survey of the overall "excess death" rate in Afghanistan since the U.S. invasion in 2001.[116] Of course the country was in the middle of a generation-long civil war by that time, and had suffered a very harsh famine in the late 1990s, so such a survey, were it ever to take place, may not show very much change — but that itself would show a total failure of American policy for the last 15 years and counting. Laura Bush and

---

[111] Jeff Huber, "Osama bin Laden, Dead and Lovin' It," Pen and Sword, May 24, 2011, http://zenhuber.blogspot.com/2011/05/preview-bin-laden-dead-and-loving-it.html.

[112] "High-Risk List," SIGAR; Geoff Dyer and Chloe Sorvino, "$1 Trillion Cost of Longest US War Hastens Retreat from Military Intervention," *Financial Times*, December 14, 2014, https://www.ft.com/content/14be0e0c-8255-11e4-ace7-00144feabdc0.

[113] "Operation Enduring Freedom, Coalition Military Fatalities By Year," iCasualties, accessed July 31, 2017, http://icasualties.org/OEF/index.aspx.

[114] "Operation Enduring Freedom: U.S. Wounded Totals," iCasualties, accessed July 31, 2017, http://icasualties.org/OEF/USCasualtiesByState.aspx.

[115] International Physicians for the Prevention of Nuclear War, Physicians for Social Responsibility and Physicians for Global Survival, "Casualty Figures After 10 Years of the 'War on Terror,' Iraq, Afghanistan, Pakistan," Physicians for Social Responsibility, March 2015, http://www.psr.org/assets/pdfs/body-count.pdf; Neta C. Crawford, "Death Toll from War in Afghanistan and Pakistan Climbs to 173,000," News from Brown, August 9, 2016, https://news.brown.edu/articles/2016/08/costs-war.

[116] Neta C. Crawford, "Civilian Death and Injury in Afghanistan, 2001-2011," Boston University, September 2011, http://watson.brown.edu/costsofwar/files/cow/imce/papers/2011/Civilian%20Death%20and%20Injury%20in%20Afghanistan,%202001-2011.pdf.

John Nagl promised they were going to change Afghan society into the kind of place where young women in miniskirts would be able to fly their kites on the way to vote in their local party primaries at their new government schools in peace and security. Instead, the country is still in chaos, and when the U.S. eventually does leave Afghanistan — whether in 2024, 2034 or 2044 — the civil war there will likely continue without us.

The signature weapon of the Afghan war has been the improvised explosive device, makeshift landmines, usually made from old artillery shells or household chemical explosives.[117] The corresponding signature wounds of the war for U.S. soldiers and marines, therefore, has been lost legs and genitals.[118] Modern medical technology has made it possible to save lives that would surely have been lost in any previous era, but this also means that many thousands of Americans have been horribly and permanently maimed, including in ways that make quality of life very poor and guarantee dependence on public welfare and military medicine for the rest of their lives.[119]

Suicide is a phenomenon so wrapped up in individual pain and shame that it remains largely taboo and undiscussed in our society. With some great exceptions, this is all the more true in military culture where the crisis is even more widespread than in the general population. From traumatic brain injuries, to "shell shock," or Post Traumatic Stress Disorder (PTSD), to "survivors' guilt" and "moral injury," many American men and women have been unable to cope with the consequences of the war on their lives. Their suicides multiply their grief, transferring it to all those who knew and cared about them.[120]

---

[117] Mujib Mashal, "Afghanistan's IED Complex," *Time*, January 2, 2013, http://world.time.com/2013/01/02/afghanistans-ied-complex-inside-the-taliban-bomb-making-industry/.

[118] Mary Kekatos, "'Unprecedented' Rate of Genital Injuries Among US Soldiers: Devastating Study Reveals More Than 1,300 Iraq and Afghanistan Vets Left with Life-Changing Wounds to Sexual Organs," *Daily Mail,* January 16, 2017, http://www.dailymail.co.uk/health/article-4125068/More-1-300-vets-left-wounds-sexual-organs.html.

[119] Ann Jones, *They Were Soldiers: How the Wounded Return from America's Wars: The Untold Story* (Chicago: Haymarket, 2014).

[120] Asked about mental health support for U.S. vets, Matthew Hoh writes: "First is Veterans Crisis Line, 1-800-273-8255, https://www.veteranscrisisline.net. The crisis line is not reserved only for individuals who are about to kill themselves, it is for anyone in a crisis, for anyone looking for help, who needs to reach out and talk. It is a really good place for anyone to start, a safe place for someone to speak anonymously with someone who is compassionate, who will care and who can give qualified answers. The crisis line can also make referrals and consultations to the VA on behalf of people who are calling into the crisis line. Here is the site for the VA PTSD program: https://www.ptsd.va.gov. I recommend everyone go to the VA. The VA PTSD program is the best thing we have. There are a lot of other programs out there, but, honestly, a lot of them are niche, tailored, advanced, or quirky. The results from the VA suicide treatment have been good, not great, but good. And it's free. Most of the guys who have problems, who need the most help, by the time they are willing to get help, may not have the money or the health insurance to get the help. Which is why this is also a good program: https://www.giveanhour.org. This program matches up veterans in need with health professionals who are willing to donate their time. I also recommend this program as a program for veterans and their families to go to for general forms of assistance:

Many others face broken families and marriages.[121] Children grow up in broken homes. Mothers and fathers lose their sons and daughters. Young men and women, who had been promised that military service would give them an edge and a head start on adulthood and a career, often come home physically and mentally wounded, unemployed,[122] deep in debt,[123] disillusioned and changed for the worse.

Another of the major dangers facing U.S. troops, Afghans and Iraqis alike has been the military's obscene "burn pits" where all manner of toxic material is "disposed of" in ways that ultimately douse the soldiers and population in carcinogenic smoke. There is strong reason to believe that former Vice President Joe Biden's son, Beau, died due to his exposure to the smoke from burn pits on the bases where he was deployed in Iraq. His death is only the most prominent of many, though no one really knows for sure just how many. War is hell, as they say. What is the Pentagon supposed to do, bring Greenpeace and the EPA into battle with them? (We should not give them any bright ideas.) Perhaps inevitable environmental devastation should get more attention as a reason to oppose these wars in the first place. However badly the Americans have felt the terrible effects of these poisons, the people of Afghanistan and Iraq have gotten it that much worse. As with the Gulf War Illnesses in the 1990s, the Pentagon would prefer to deny the problem even exists.[124]

According to the UN, the year 2015 set a record for most civilians killed in a year for the entire war, at more than 3,500, "a quarter of them children — and nearly 7,500 [were] wounded." Nearly a fifth of these casualties were from attacks by Afghan security forces.[125] In 2015, U.S. airstrikes in Afghanistan were killing civilians at the highest rate in seven

---

https://semperfifund.org. They are not as well-known as some of the larger veteran's charities, but Semper Fi Fund has been around for a while now, is administratively sound and they do solid, good work that is actually needed by veterans and their families."

[121] James Hosek, "Lengthy Military Deployments Increase Divorce Risk for U.S. Enlisted Service Members," RAND Corporation, September 3, 2013,
https://www.rand.org/news/press/2013/09/03.html.

[122] Dianna Cahn, "Survey: Demands on Troops, Families 'Unsustainable,'" *Stars and Stripes*, December 7, 2016, https://www.stripes.com/survey-demands-on-troops-families-unsustainable-1.443167.

[123] Herb Weisbaum, "Survey: Military Families Carry More Debt, Have Fewer Assets Than Civilians," NBC News, July 13, 2015, http://www.nbcnews.com/business/personal-finance/survey-military-families-carry-more-debt-have-fewer-assets-civilians-n390046.

[124] Kelley B. Vlahos, "The New Agent Orange?," *American Conservative*, October 16, 2012, http://www.theamericanconservative.com/articles/the-new-agent-orange/; Joseph Hickman, *The Burn Pits: The Poisoning of America's Soldiers* (New York: Hot, 2016), 27-33; Jennifer Percy, "The Things They Burned," *New Republic*, November 22, 2016, https://newrepublic.com/article/138058/things-burned.

[125] "Afghan Casualties Hit Record High 11,000 in 2015 – UN Report," UN News Centre, February 2016, http://www.un.org/apps/news/story.asp?NewsID=53229.

years, according to the Bureau of Investigative Journalism.[126] The numbers for 2016 were even worse.[127] The population of this desperately poor country remains mired in violent conflict, with no end in sight. More than half a million Afghans were forced to flee the violence, becoming "internally displaced" refugees, in 2016 alone.[128] According to the United Nations, the violence is only getting worse. There were 5,243 civilian casualties in the first half of 2017, which they blamed primarily on insurgent bombings as well as Afghan and U.S. airstrikes.[129] Another 2,531 Afghan troops and police were killed in action, with 4,238 wounded.[130]

So many people have died in this pointless war, Operation Enduring Freedom, now Operation Freedom's Sentinel. It was a waste. All in vain. All along. A "useless sacrifice," as one of America's more thoughtful founders might have put it.

Backdraft

As far as the American people know, the whole thing must have worked out fairly well. They certainly have not heard much news out of Afghanistan lately. Nor did they have a chance to hear the future of the war debated in the 2016 presidential electoral campaign. In fact, if the American people have heard anything about Afghanistan at all lately it was probably from the 2016 popcorn flick, *Whisky, Tango, Foxtrot*, where we learn that Afghanistan is a place where older, single women can go to at least find themselves if they cannot find a husband. And they can get drunk and party and have a great time, too. The Afghanistan war is a fun little rite of passage for a North American white person to go through, like hiking up Machu Picchu or going on the scariest roller coaster at Six Flags. The war is not brutal and pointless, but very exciting. "Oorah! Get some, Tina Fey!" cries Marine Corps Capt. Billy Bob Thornton. Hey, why not?

---

[126] Jack Serle et al., "US Airstrikes in Afghanistan Killing Civilians at Greatest Rate for Seven Years, New Figures Show," Bureau of Investigative Journalism, February 18, 2016, https://www.thebureauinvestigates.com/2016/02/18/us-airstrikes-afghanistan-killing-civilians-greatest-rate-seven-years-new-figures-show/.

[127] Sayed Salahuddin and Pamela Constable, "UN Says Civilian Toll in Afghanistan is Highest in Years," *Washington Post*, February 6, 2017, https://washingtonpost.com/world/un-says-civilian-toll-in-afghanistan-higher-than-ever/2017/02/06/4866259e-ec59-11e6-b4ff-ac2cf509efe5_story.html.

[128] Jelena Bjelica, "Over Half a Million Afghans Flee Conflict in 2016," Afghan Analysts, December 28, 2016, https://www.afghanistan-analysts.org/over-half-a-million-afghans-flee-conflict-in-2016-a-look-at-the-idp-statistics/.

[129] "2017 Mid-Year Report on the Protection of Civilians in Armed Conflict in Afghanistan," the Human Rights Unit of the United Nations Assistance Mission in Afghanistan (UNAMA), July 30, 2017, https://unama.unmissions.org/sites/default/files/protection_of_civilians_in_armed_conflict_midyear_report_2017_30-july_2017.pdf.

[130] Quarterly Report, Special Inspector General for Afghanistan Reconstruction, July 30, 2017.

But reality is catching up to the U.S. and its allies. Gone are the days when Western countries could invade and dominate the poorer parts of the globe with impunity. That could have been the lesson of the September 11th attacks if anyone had wanted to admit the truth behind the attackers' motives. But now we can see the direct consequences right before our eyes.

In December of 2009, just after Obama had announced the launch of the "surge," journalist Patrick Cockburn explained that the continued occupation of Afghanistan, rather than preventing terrorist attacks by denying our antagonists safe-haven, actually increased the likelihood of attacks in Western countries.[131] Granted, this was obvious enough, especially since just a month before, a U.S. Army major named Nidal Hasan, due to deploy to Afghanistan and upset both about the reports of war crimes being committed against civilians there and the prospect of being made to kill fellow Muslims himself,[132] instead killed 13 soldiers and wounded 30 others in a massacre on base at Ft. Hood in central Texas.[133] It was later revealed that Hasan had been in contact with prominent American al Qaeda preacher Anwar al-Awlaki.[134] Insistent on pretending they had won the terror war, and to deny that blowback from U.S. policies was to blame for this "lone wolf" attack, the Obama administration tried to spin the entire thing as "workplace violence," as though Hassan had simply "gone postal" under the work-a-day pressures of his job.[135]

But this was not truly "blowback," properly defined as long-term consequences of secret foreign policies returning to haunt the United States, surprising the population and leaving them vulnerable to misinformation about the context of the conflict.[136] A more accurate way to identify this phenomenon would be to call it "backdraft," when the direct consequences of the government's openly declared foreign policies blow up right in all of our faces, undeniable to anyone but the most

[131] Patrick Cockburn, interviewed by the author, *Scott Horton Show*, radio archive, December 8, 2009, http://scotthorton.org/interviews/antiwar-radio-patrick-cockburn-11/.

[132] "Emails from Nidal Malik Hasan," *New York Times*, written in 2009, published August 20, 2013, http://www.nytimes.com/interactive/2013/08/21/us/21hasan-emails-document.html.

[133] Robert D. McFadden, "Army Doctor Held in Ft. Hood Rampage," *New York Times*, November 5, 2009, http://www.nytimes.com/2009/11/06/us/06forthood.html.

[134] David Johnston and Scott Shane, "US Knew of Suspect's Tie to Radical Cleric," *New York Times*, November 9, 2009, http://www.nytimes.com/2009/11/10/us/10inquire.html; Mariah Blake, "Internal Documents Reveal How the FBI Blew Fort Hood," *Mother Jones*, August 27, 2013, http://www.motherjones.com/politics/2013/08/nidal-hasan-anwar-awlaki-emails-fbi-fort-hood.

[135] Michael Daly, "Nidal Hasan's Murders Termed 'Workplace Violence' by US," Daily Beast, August 6, 2013, http://www.thedailybeast.com/articles/2013/08/06/nidal-hasan-s-murders-termed-workplace-violence-by-u-s.html.

[136] Chalmers Johnson, *Blowback: The Costs and Consequences of American Empire* (New York: Holt, 2004), 8; Chalmers Johnson, interviewed by the author, *Scott Horton Show*, radio archive, January 3, 2008, https://scotthorton.org/interviews/antiwar-radio-chalmers-johnson-2/; Risen, "Oh, What a Fine Plot We Hatched"; Wilber, "CIA Clandestine Service History."

committed war hawks. This is borrowed from the term used by firefighters for when their ax-wielding or door-kicking intervention inadvertently provides oxygen to a heated and fuel-filled room, causing a massive explosion.

Approximately a month before Hassan's attack, Najibullah Zazi, an Afghan-American who traveled to Pakistan in 2008 and received training in making bombs, supposedly from al Qaeda members, was arrested along with two others, thwarting their plot to attack the New York subway system. One of the small number of "al Qaeda" or "ISIS" terrorism plots in the U.S. that was not[137] originally cooked-up by undercover FBI informants,[138] Zazi later told the court the motive for his "martyrdom operation" was not some abstract religious duty to attack innocents. "I would sacrifice myself to bring attention to what the United States military was doing to civilian [sic] in Afghanistan by sacrificing my soul for the sake of saving other souls," Zazi explained during his confession in court. Of course, Zazi is a horrible hypocrite, who himself was targeting innocent civilians, but the conclusion remains the same. He was radicalized against the U.S. in political terms, not religious ones, because of the conduct of our government in the ongoing occupation of his former country. It was fortunate that in this case no one on this side was killed.[139]

Just a few months later, a young Pakistani-American named Faisal Shahzad attempted to detonate a truck bomb in crowded Times Square in New York City — an attack that, luckily, failed. Shahzad, never known to be a religious fundamentalist, was living the American dream. He had an advanced degree, a professional career and a family. But then he took a trip back to his home country of Pakistan where he reportedly saw the results of a CIA drone strike first hand. Shahzad then offered his services to the Pakistani Taliban — who had never attacked America before — to take revenge inside the United States on their behalf.[140] At his sentencing in federal court, Shahzad said he was avenging the innocents killed by the U.S. drone war in Pakistan, part of the Obama administration's combined "Af-Pak" war. When the judge excoriated Shahzad for risking the lives of innocent children, he replied,

---

[137] Kerry Burke et al., "How the Feds Caught Najibullah Zazi," *New York Daily News*, September 27, 2009, http://www.nydailynews.com/news/crime/feds-caught-najibullah-zazi-pieced-9-11-terror-plot-article-1.380680.

[138] Trevor Aaronson, *The Terror Factory: Inside the FBI's Manufactured War on Terrorism* (Singapore: Ig Publishing, 2013).

[139] "Najibullah Zazi Reveals Chilling Details on Al Qaeda Training and Terrorist Plot to Blow Up Subways," *New York Daily News*, February 23, 2010, http://www.nydailynews.com/news/crime/najibullah-zazi-reveals-chilling-details-al-qaeda-training-terrorist-plot-blow-subways-article-1.169311.

[140] Howard Chua-Eoan, "Faisal Shahzad: The Broadway Bomber," *Time*, May 8, 2010, http://content.time.com/time/magazine/article/0,9171,1987579-1,00.html.

Well, the drone hits in Afghanistan and Iraq, they don't see children, they don't see anybody. They kill women, children, they kill everybody. It's a war, and in war, they kill people. They're killing all Muslims.

The judge and the terrorist continued to go back and forth:

Judge: Now we're not talking about them; we're talking about you.

Shahzad: Well, I am part of that. I am part of the answer to the U.S. terrorizing the Muslim nations and the Muslim people. And, on behalf of that, I'm avenging the attack. Living in the United States, Americans only care about their own people, but they don't care about the people elsewhere in the world when they die.

Similarly, in Gaza Strip, somebody has to go and live with the family whose house is bulldozed by the Israeli bulldozer. There's a lot of aggression…

Judge: In Afghanistan?

Shahzad: In Gaza Strip.

Judge: I see.

Shahzad: We Muslims are one community. We're not divided.

Judge: Well, I don't want to get drawn into a discussion of the Qur'an.

Who said anything about the Qur'an? Just how obtuse can a federal judge be? We may have found the limit.[141]

Dzhokhar Tsarnaev, co-conspirator in the deadly Boston Marathon attacks with his brother Tamerlan,[142] told investigators they were motivated by the U.S. wars in Iraq and Afghanistan.[143]

Omar Mateen, the American-born perpetrator of the horrific Orlando Pulse nightclub massacre of June 2016, explicitly told witnesses he was taking revenge for the continuing U.S. war in Afghanistan, the country of his family's origin. "When I saw his picture on the news, I thought, of

---

[141] Lorraine Adams and Ayesha Nasir, "Inside the Mind of the Times Square Bomber," *Guardian*, September 18, 2010, https://www.theguardian.com/world/2010/sep/19/times-square-bomber.

[142] Michele McPhee, "Tamerlan Tsarnaev: Terrorist. Murderer. Federal Informant?," *Boston Magazine*, April 2017, http://www.bostonmagazine.com/news/article/2017/04/09/tamerlan-tsarnaev-fbi-informant/.

[143] Thomas Gibbons-Neff, "I Could Justify Fighting in Afghanistan — Until the Boston Bombing," *Washington Post*, April 26, 2013, https://www.washingtonpost.com/opinions/i-could-justify-fighting-in-afghanistan--until-the-boston-bombing/2013/04/26/e483321c-ad26-11e2-b6fd-ba6f5f26d70e_story.html; Scott Wilson et al., "Boston Bombing Suspect Cites US Wars as Motivation, Officials Say," *Washington Post*, April 23, 2013, https://www.washingtonpost.com/national/boston-bombing-suspect-cites-us-wars-as-motivation-officials-say/2013/04/23/324b9cea-ac29-11e2-b6fd-ba6f5f26d70e_story.html.

course, he did that," a co-worker of Mateen told *New York Newsday*. "He had bad things to say about everybody — blacks, Jews, gays, a lot of politicians, our soldiers. He had a lot of hate in him. He told me America destroyed Afghanistan."[144]

A young woman named Patience Carter, who was shot in the leg by Mateen and held hostage in the bathroom of the club for three hours with the gunman, said, "The motive was very clear to us who are laying in our own blood and other people's blood, who are injured, who were shot. Everybody who was in that bathroom who survived could hear him talking to 911, saying the reason why he's doing this is because he wanted America to stop bombing his country."[145]

In the middle of committing his atrocity — Mateen slaughtered 49 people and wounded 53 — he stopped to post on his Facebook page: "You kill innocent women and children by doing us airstrikes... now taste the Islamic state vengeance." [errors in original][146] The transcript of his call to 911, released much later after all the attention died down, is more explicit. As Mateen declared his loyalty to the leaders of ISIS, he explained his demands:

> [Y]ou have to tell America to stop bombing Syria and Iraq. They are killing a lot of innocent people. What am I to do here when my people are getting killed over there. You get what I'm saying? ... You need to stop the U.S. airstrikes. They need to stop the U.S. airstrikes, okay? ... You have to tell the U.S. government to stop bombing. They are killing too many children, they are killing too many women, okay? ... I feel the pain of the people getting killed in Syria and Iraq and all over the Muslim [world]. A lot of innocent women and children are getting killed in Syria and Iraq and Afghanistan, okay?[147]

The government's narrative was that Omar Mateen was a wife-beating psychopath and bully who had issues with his sexuality and that particular

---

[144] Kevin Deutsch, "Orlando Shooting Suspect Showed Signs of Violence, Reports Say," *New York Newsday*, June 13, 2016, http://www.newsday.com/news/nation/orlando-shooting-suspect-showed-signs-of-violence-reports-say-1.11906792.

[145] Katie Zezima et al., "Orlando Gunman Said He Carried Out Attack to Get 'Americans to Stop Bombing His Country,' Witness Says," *Washington Post*, June 14, 2016, https://www.washingtonpost.com/news/post-nation/wp/2016/06/14/fbi-director-orlando-shooting-probe-also-looks-backward-into-agency-files-on-shooter/; "Orlando Shooting: Omar Mateen 'Wanted US to Stop Bombing Afghanistan,' Survivor Says," ABC News (Australia), June 14, 2016, http://www.abc.net.au/news/2016-06-15/orlando-gunman-wanted-to-stop-us-bombing-afghanistan/7511586.

[146] Brian Bennett and Del Quentin Wilber, "Orlando Gunman, During Pause in His Rampage, Searched Social Media for News of It," *Los Angeles Times*, June 16, 2016, http://www.latimes.com/nation/la-na-orlando-cellphone-20160615-snap-story.html.

[147] Omar Mateen, "Transcript of 911 Calls," Public Intelligence, June 12, 2016, https://info.publicintelligence.net/FL-OmarMateenTranscripts.pdf.

nightclub,[148] but all evidence is that the attack was political. Mateen could have gotten in drunken fistfights his whole short life long, but instead, he chose to sign on with the agendas of Syrian al Qaeda and the Islamic State and attack a crowded nightclub as a strike against the United States. Mateen specifically cited the perpetual occupation and bombing of Afghanistan as he slaughtered dozens of innocent Americans, showing the strong possibility that these kinds of plots and attacks will keep happening. The government said U.S. forces were "fighting them over there so we don't have to fight them here." Instead, the war over there is causing more and more of this deadly backdraft against us here.[149]

Long-time Afghan-war partner Germany was hit a month after the Orlando attack when a young Pakistani refugee, Riaz Khan Ahmadzai, a.k.a. Mohammed Riyadh, who by all accounts had been adjusting quite well to his new life in Germany over the previous year, took out a hatchet and started attacking people on a train in northern Bavaria. He then attacked one more innocent woman during his attempted escape, wounding a total of six people, several of them severely. It was, police said, revenge over a friend who had recently been killed in an airstrike in Afghanistan. In a video released by the Islamic State group soon after the attack, Ahmadzai says, "I am one of the soldiers of the Islamic Caliphate, and I am going to conduct an attack in Germany. It is about time to stop you from coming to our homes, killing our families and getting away with it. Our apostate politicians have never tried to stop you, and Muslims have never been able to fight you back or even speak against what you do. But these times are gone now."[150]

Back in 2010, WikiLeaks released a CIA document describing the propaganda techniques and pressure they would bring to bear against the governments and populations of NATO allies France and Germany out of fear that rising casualties in the "surge" could cause their withdrawal from the war. The document identified appeals from Obama, threats to women's rights and the risk of civilian casualties as the best issues to highlight while appealing to the liberal French to ensure their support of the occupation, while Germans would be more susceptible to threats of

---

[148] James Rothwell and Harriet Alexander, "Orlando Shooter Omar Mateen Was 'Mentally Unstable Wife-Beating Homophobe,'" *Daily Telegraph*, June 13, 2016, http://www.telegraph.co.uk/news/2016/06/13/orlando-shooter-omar-mateen-was-mentally-unstable-wife-beating-h/.

[149] James Bradley, interviewed by the author, *Scott Horton Show*, radio archive, June 27, 2016, https://scotthorton.org/interviews/62716-james-bradley/.

[150] Melissa Eddy, "Afghan Teenager Spoke of Friend's Death Before Ax Attack in Germany," *New York Times*, July 19, 2016, http://www.nytimes.com/2016/07/20/world/europe/germany-train-ax-attack.html; Jennifer Newton and Alan Hall, "ISIS Train Axe Attacker is a Pakistani Who Lied About Being Afghan," *Daily Mail*, July 20, 2016, http://www.dailymail.co.uk/news/article-3698818/Did-ISIS-axe-attacker-LIE-Afghanistan-Claims-train-jihadi-hid-Pakistani-background-higher-immigration-status-Germany.html.

an influx of terrorists, heroin and refugees from Afghanistan.[151] They stayed, the war was still lost and the CIA's threats all came true anyway.

In September 2016, an Afghan-born U.S. citizen named Ahmad Khan Rahami set off two bombs on public streets, one in New York and one in New Jersey — thankfully, again, killing no one. Just like Zazi and Shahzad before him, Rahami seemed to be happy and well-assimilated into American culture. His family owned a small restaurant in New York, and he spent most of his free time souping up Honda Civics and racing them.[152] Then he traveled to Afghanistan and Pakistan. It is unknown whether he had any actual contact with members of al Qaeda or any Taliban faction while there, but he reportedly came back a changed, much more "serious" man, and soon went to war on their behalf.[153]

On June 21, 2017, a Canadian Muslim named Amor M. Ftouhi attacked and wounded a police officer at a Michigan airport with a knife, but was thankfully subdued by other police and a maintenance man before he could get the cop's gun and do any more damage. According to police, during the actual stabbing, the attacker yelled, "You have killed people in Syria, Iraq and Afghanistan and you are going to die." He also yelled "Allahu Akbar," while he was being taken down.[154] The latter statement received far more attention.[155]

Every time this happens, foreign policy hawks and social media commentators announce that their biased expert opinions have been confirmed again: Islam makes people into insane killers! The deeper their religious devotion, the more dangerous they are! But people can only persist in this belief as long as they presume, even after 16 years of war, that it is impossible that anyone on America's side could do anything to provoke such hatred, a premise that cannot withstand an honest scrutiny

151 "CIA Report into Shoring Up Afghan War Support in Western Europe, 'CIA Red Cell: A Red Cell Special Memorandum, Afghanistan: Sustaining West European Support for the NATO-led Mission — Why Counting on Apathy Might Not Be Enough,'" March 11, 2010, WikiLeaks release: March 26, 2010, https://file.wikileaks.org/file/cia-afghanistan.pdf; "Report Says Afghan Women Can Help Sell War to Europeans," Deutsche Welle, March 27, 2010, http://www.dw.com/en/report-says-afghan-women-can-help-sell-war-to-europeans/a-5404617.
152 "Ahmad Khan Rahami: US Blasts Suspect a 'Very Friendly Guy,'" BBC News, September 20, 2016, http://www.bbc.com/news/world-us-canada-37410115.
153 Barney Henderson et al., "New York Bombing: Suspect Ahmad Rahami 'May Have Been Radicalized After Visiting Afghanistan,'" Daily Telegraph, September 20, 2016, http://www.telegraph.co.uk/news/2016/09/19/new-york-bombing-fbi-names-28-year-old-suspect-as-authorities-pr/.
154 David Komer, "Terror Suspect Who Stabbed Flint Airport Officer ID'd as Canadian Amor Ftouhi," Fox 2 WJBK News, http://www.fox2detroit.com/news/local-news/262988142-story.
155 Google News search result, "'Allahu Akbar' Michigan knife Airport June 2017," 313,000 results, June 23, 2017, https://www.google.com/search?q=%22allahu+akbar%22+michigan+knife+airport+june+2017&tbm=nws; Google News search result, "'Syria, Iraq and Afghanistan' Michigan knife airport June 2017," 1,050 results, June 23, 2017, https://www.google.com/search?q=%22Syria%2C+Iraq+and+Afghanistan%22+Michigan+knife+airport+June+2017&ie=UTF-8&tbm=nws.

of the history of U.S. intervention and the words of our enemies: killing them makes their survivors want to kill us.

The U.S. government is perfectly content to blame foreign policy blowback, rather than religious extremists' hatred of freedom, even for ISIS attacks, when the victims are from countries that are designated American adversaries, going so far as to imply that the innocent victims deserved it. In one example, after the killing of 224 people in the October 2015 bombing of Russian Metrojet flight 9268 out of Sharm El Sheikh, Egypt, U.S. officials "delighted" in its destruction.[156] After the June 2017 attacks on Parliament and the Ayatollah Khomeini's tomb in Tehran, Iran, the Trump administration's official statement read, "We underscore that states that sponsor terrorism risk falling victim to the evil they promote."[157]

A 2011 report written by the Los Angeles office of the FBI determined that an increase in attacks against U.S. targets was due to "a broadening U.S. military presence overseas and outreach by Islamist ideologues." The outreach they refer to was the propaganda of those like American al Qaeda preacher and propagandist, Anwar Awlaki, who consistently framed terrorism as a defense against the U.S. military waging war in the Middle East.[158]

To be sure, when the FBI launches an entrapment sting on a target here in America, they virtually always prey on their victim's sympathy for people dying in the wars overseas — and desperate need for money.[159] Never in the history of all 800-plus terrorism cases the U.S. government has successfully prosecuted since September 11th has anyone claimed to have been motivated by a hatred of the freedom and innocence of the American people. They only ever cite the U.S. government's tyranny and violence.[160]

Additionally, all these domestic attacks are driving the massive expansion of the American government's police powers in the name of security to protect us from terrorism. With the rise of the Department of

---

[156] Nancy Youssef and Shane Harris, "US Spies Root for an ISIS-Russia War," Daily Beast, November 9, 2015, http://www.thedailybeast.com/us-spies-root-for-an-isis-russia-war.

[157] "Statement by the President on the Terrorist Attacks in Iran," June 7, 2017, https://www.whitehouse.gov/the-press-office/2017/06/07/statement-president-terrorist-attacks-iran; Claire Shaffer, "Trump White House Blames ISIS Attack on Tehran and the 'Evil They Promote,'" Newsweek, June 7, 2017, http://www.newsweek.com/donald-trump-islamic-state-terrorist-iran-evil-622727.

[158] "Anwar Nasser Aulaqi CT-Sunni Extremist – Middle East," Federal Bureau of Investigation, November 26, 2010, http://nsarchive.gwu.edu/NSAEBB/NSAEBB529-Anwar-al-Awlaki-File/documents/18)%20FBI%20notes%20Awlaki%20video%20calling%20for%20killing%20Ameri can%20Nov%202010.pdf.

[159] Aaronson, The Terror Factory.

[160] Waqas Mirza, "2011 FBI Report Finds 'Broadening US Military Presence' Responsible for Rise in Terror Attacks," Muckrock, September 14, 2016, https://www.muckrock.com/news/archives/2016/sep/14/CVE-military-presence/.

Homeland Security, the war is coming back home.[161] Police are becoming more militarized and are turning the arms and equipment procured in the name of fighting terrorism against the American people. From military-style, rifle-toting sheriff's deputies in combat fatigues, to the endless groping of men, women and children at the airports, to new restrictions against free speech and assembly, the public is becoming well accustomed to the rituals and practices of arbitrary and unaccountable tyranny.

The unleashing of the surveillance powers of the CIA[162] and National Security Agency (NSA)[163] against Americans and the decreased legal restraints on the sharing of information with other agencies[164] has given the federal government a much greater ability to intrude on ordinary Americans' lives. While the PATRIOT Act has helped to erode our Fourth Amendment protections against unreasonable searches and seizures,[165] the less well-known National Defense Authorization Act of 2012 has language which permits formerly Bill of Rights-protected "U.S. persons" — *including American citizens* — to be detained by the military indefinitely, without charges. Really.[166]

Barack Obama even assassinated an American citizen, Anwar Awlaki, with a drone attack in Yemen, with barely the slightest pretension that the law authorized him to do so.[167]

---

[161] Christopher J. Coyne and Abigail Hall, "Perfecting Tyranny: Foreign Intervention as Experimentation in State Control," *Independent Review* 19, no. 2 (Fall 2014): 165–189.

[162] Andrew Griffin, "Wikileaks Publishes Massive Trove of CIA Spying Files in 'Vault 7' Release," *Independent*, March 7, 2017, http://www.independent.co.uk/life-style/gadgets-and-tech/news/wikileaks-cia-vault-7-julian-assange-year-zero-documents-download-spying-secrets-a7616031.html.

[163] "NSA Primary Sources Catalog of Edward Snowden Documents and Articles," Electronic Frontier Foundation, accessed May 23, 2017, https://www.eff.org/nsa-spying/nsadocs.

[164] Charlie Savage, "NSA Gets More Latitude to Share Intercepted Communications," *New York Times,* January 12, 2017, https://www.nytimes.com/2017/01/12/us/politics/nsa-gets-more-latitude-to-share-intercepted-communications.html.

[165] Robert A. Levy, "The USA Patriot Act: We Deserve Better," *Liberty*, November 1, 2001, https://www.cato.org/publications/commentary/usa-patriot-act-we-deserve-better.

[166] Yunji De Nies, "With Reservations, Obama Signs Act to Allow Detention of Citizens," ABC News, December 31, 2011, http://abcnews.go.com/blogs/politics/2011/12/with-reservations-obama-signs-act-to-allow-detention-of-citizens/; "President Obama Signs Indefinite Detention Bill into Law," American Civil Liberties Union, December 31, 2011, https://www.aclu.org/news/president-obama-signs-indefinite-detention-bill-law; Zuri Davis, "Detained Without a Trial: Sen. Rand Paul's New Legislation Will Combat Unconstitutional Indefinite Detention," Rare, June 8, 2017, http://rare.us/rare-politics/rare-liberty/liberty-rising/detained-without-a-trial-sen-rand-pauls-new-legislation-will-combat-unconstitutional-indefinite-detention/.

[167] "Attorney General Eric Holder Speaks at Northwestern University School of Law," United States Department of Justice, March 5, 2012, https://www.justice.gov/opa/speech/attorney-general-eric-holder-speaks-northwestern-university-school-law; "Memorandum for the Attorney General Re: Applicability of Federal Criminal Laws and the Constitution to Contemplated Lethal Operations Against Shaykh Anwar al-Aulaqi," Office of the Assistant Attorney General, July 16, 2010, https://www.washingtonpost.com/r/2010-2019/WashingtonPost/2014/06/23/National-Security/Graphics/memodrones.pdf.

There are fewer separations of police power than ever in the United States as the different levels of government join together in multi-jurisdictional task forces, fusion centers, information sharing and military training programs, while courts uphold this dismemberment of constitutional federalism and the Bill of Rights in the name of the emergency. This is what Osama bin Laden called "the choking life,"[168] which he wished to see the U.S. government inflict on the American people, primarily to cause a reaction.

Do we really want to give up our freedom when all we have to do to guarantee our safety is call off the unnecessary interventions in the Middle East? The U.S. should not capitulate to the demands of terrorists. But that is, ironically, exactly what the government has done in waging this war, provoking so many new enemies and destroying so much of our privacy and freedom that they claim to be fighting to protect.

It is the right thing to stop doing the wrong thing, and ceasing intervention is the best first step in deterring the terrorist attacks that have cost so many lives and driven so much of the expansion of government's powers in recent years.

Another World

A couple of weeks or so after the September 11th attacks, the author saw the strangest thing on TV. A reporter asked two young American brothers about what they thought the new war meant for their future, and whether they were now looking forward to a life of military service fighting America's enemies. The older of the two boys may have been around 16, but his younger brother was no more than 12 years old — a child. It should have been an absurd proposition to ask these boys if they planned, as adults, to fight in a war just getting underway against a few hundred outlaws hiding in Afghanistan. But, it turns out that this reporter was right to assume it would still be going on years later. Indeed, everything had changed. It was the start of a war with no end: a conflict set, in the words of the Bush, Obama and now Trump administrations, to last for "generations" — a "long war" to be fought for decades into the future against rag-tag militiamen in their mountain hideouts, fighting for their own territory, on the far side of the planet from here.

There was such a feeling of unreality back then. Remember it? "Everything changed on September 11th!" "United We Stand!" From coast to coast, reason was disregarded in favor of feelings, symbols and

---

[168] "Bin Laden's Sole Post-September 11 TV Interview Aired," CNN, February 5, 2002, http://edition.cnn.com/2002/US/01/31/gen.binladen.interview/; Osama bin Laden, *Quotations from Osama Bin Laden*, ed. Brad K. Berner (Oracle, AZ: Peacock, 2006), 77.

slogans. Even after the single greatest failure of the national government in U.S. history, the September 11th attacks, the Bush administration, through its compliant media, demanded the presumption of total legitimacy, total knowledge and total capability from everyone. "You are either with us, or you are with the terrorists!"[169] We will "fight for freedom"[170] and "rid the world of evil,"[171] the government vowed. The media, led by the major papers and TV networks, were all happy to toe the line. "U.S.A.! We're Number One!" they chanted. "Countdown to the Next Conflict!" blared the fancy, twenty-first century cable-TV news graphics. There is nothing our government can't accomplish, in Afghanistan or anywhere else, they promised. To challenge the consensus was blasphemy against the state religion and its priests.

But now, after more than a decade and a half of failure, reality is impossible to ignore any longer. There is no reason to think the current mess would be any better if the occupation was 30 years old instead of 15. Before he died, even establishment oracle Zbigniew Brzezinski had finally become convinced that America had overreached in the Bush and Obama years and desperately needed to retrench, cooperate more with Russia and China and deputize more of the imperial law-enforcing to smaller allied nations before the entire thing fell apart.[172]

The real lesson of America's war in Afghanistan is that we should never have had one. Even if all negotiations truly had broken down, leaving the U.S. no choice but to send in troops after Osama bin Laden and Ayman al Zawahiri and their few hundred followers, they could have been caught or killed by the end of 2001 had the government kept the target narrowly defined to those guilty of orchestrating the attacks on our country. As it was, U.S. forces had great success against al Qaeda in Afghanistan in December 2001, bin Laden's escape notwithstanding. As one intelligence officer involved in the initial war against al Qaeda in the winter of 2001 told journalist Robert Dreyfuss, "We came in with B-52s and F-16s, and at Tora Bora, we dropped a 15,000-pound device on them. We blew them to bits. If you wanted to do a body count, you would have needed to pick up the pieces with Q-Tips." Even after 180 or so al Qaeda escaped into Pakistan, the group was virtually defeated. Brian Jenkins, a veteran intelligence expert at the RAND Corporation, estimated that by 2006, the top leadership of al Qaeda, "that is, bin Laden and the boys," was "a core

[169] "Bush: 'You Are Either with Us, or with the Terrorists,'" Voice of America News, October 27, 2009, http://www.voanews.com/a/a-13-a-2001-09-21-14-bush-66411197/549664.html.

[170] George W. Bush, "Address to a Joint Session of Congress and the American People."

[171] Manuel Perez-Rivas, "Bush Vows to Rid the World of 'Evil-Doers,'" CNN, September 16, 2001, http://edition.cnn.com/2001/US/09/16/gen.bush.terrorism/.

[172] Zbigniew Brzezinski, "Toward a Global Realignment," *American Interest,* April 17, 2016, http://www.the-american-interest.com/2016/04/17/toward-a-global-realignment/.

of only tens to scores of individuals involved in managing this thing." Old "core" al Qaeda — not including Abu Musab al Zarqawi's then-new "al Qaeda in Iraq" — had been "virtually eliminated as a threat," thanks to good police work based on intelligence gathered early in the war:

> In Afghanistan, the CIA reaped an intelligence bonanza, seizing al Qaeda's computers, files and organizational records. "Once we got Al Qaeda's hard drives, our knowledge expanded exponentially," says a retired CIA station chief. That intelligence has enabled counter-terrorism officers to target al Qaeda operatives around the world, all but eviscerating the group's foreign presence. "We've killed or captured at least one or two terrorists a day for five years, all over the world," says an experienced CIA hand. "More than 4,000 in all."[173]

The ranks had been blasted, bin Laden was "marginalized," as Bush had put it, and Khalid Sheikh Mohammad, chief planner of the September 11th attack, and his associate Ramzi bin al Shibh, who had helped run the operation, had been captured in Pakistan.[174] That was pretty much it. The Terror War had been won. The Bush administration instead portrayed the terrorist threat as a huge ongoing menace that threatened to establish a totalitarian terrorist caliphate in all the territory "from Spain to Indonesia."[175] In fact, al Qaeda had no true state sponsors in the world aside from some Saudi and other Persian Gulf princes who financed them under the table. The Iranian Shi'ite regime was their enemy,[176] as was the Ba'athist secular-socialist government in Iraq[177] and every corrupt king,

---

[173] Dreyfuss, "The Phony War."

[174] Terry McDermott and Josh Meyer, "Inside the Mission to Catch Khalid Sheikh Mohammed," *Atlantic*, April 2, 2012, http://www.theatlantic.com/international/archive/2012/04/inside-the-mission-to-catch-khalid-sheikh-mohammed/255319/; Maria Ressa et al., "Top Al Qaeda Operative Caught in Pakistan," CNN, March 1, 2003, http://www.cnn.com/2003/WORLD/asiapcf/south/03/01/pakistan.arrests/; James Vicini, "Key al Qaeda 911 Figure Captured In Pakistan," *Dawn* (Pakistan), September 14, 2002, https://www.dawn.com/news/57343/suspect-is-osama-s-top-aide-moin-extradition-possible-if-asked-for; Jackie Lyden and Steve Inskeep, "Ramzi Binalshibh Captured," *All Things Considered*, NPR News, September 13, 2002, http://www.npr.org/templates/story/story.php?storyId=1149966.

[175] George W. Bush, "Remarks to the Woodrow Wilson International Center for Scholars," 41 Weekly Comp. Pres. Doc. 1855 (December 14, 2005).

[176] Philip Giraldi, "Shaping the Story on Iran," Antiwar.com, May 20, 2010, http://original.antiwar.com/giraldi/2010/05/19/shaping-the-story-on-iran/; Gareth Porter, "Burnt Offering," *American Prospect*, May 21, 2006, http://prospect.org/article/burnt-offering; Robert Windrem, "US, Iran Secretly Discussed Swap of al Qaeda Detainees for Iranian Dissidents," NBC News, March 15, 2003, http://investigations.nbcnews.com/_news/2013/03/15/17315494-us-iran-secretly-discussed-swap-of-al-qaeda-detainees-for-iranian-dissidents; Gareth Porter, "US Treasury Claim of Iran-Al-Qaeda 'Secret Deal' Is Discredited," Inter Press Service, May 10, 2012, http://www.ipsnews.net/2012/05/us-treasury-claim-of-iran-al-qaeda-secret-deal-is-discredited/.

[177] Matt Barganier, "Scheuer Corrects *National Review*, *Weekly Standard*," Antiwar.com, April 18, 2007, https://www.antiwar.com/blog/2007/04/18/scheuer-corrects-national-review-weekly-standard/; Walter Pincus, "CIA Learned in '02 That Bin Laden Had No Iraq Ties, Report Says," *Washington Post*, September 15, 2006, http://www.washingtonpost.com/wp-

emir, sultan and "president" in the region. That was what al Qaeda was so angry about in the first place. But on TV in the United States in 2002, there were constant "Orange Alerts" warning us there could be an attack here, there or any place CIA captives could be tortured into pretending was threatened, at any time.[178] The terrorists were dead or gone, but they were also *everywhere* — and the war was just getting started.

President Bush, who liked to talk about al Qaeda as though it had already conquered large areas of the earth, at one point conceded the truth, that the group was really just a "loose network with many branches,"[179] suitable to be rolled up by a little bit of simple police and intelligence work, such as we had seen with the early arrests of so many al Qaeda figures in Pakistan.

But he would fix that.

By turning one small manhunt into the Global War on Terrorism, complete with regime change campaigns against al Qaeda's enemies such as Saddam Hussein in Iraq, Muammar Ghaddafi in Libya and Bashar al-Assad in Syria, the George W. Bush and Barack Obama administrations have served the interests of these only true enemies of the American people. Bin Laden's goals were to bog us down and bleed us dry, radicalize the people of the region, swell his ranks, destabilize America's Arab satellite dictatorships and ultimately create a new caliphate in Arabia, Mesopotamia and the Levant. The U.S. has spent trillions, which has helped to break our economy and that of the entire world. Local groups of fighters claiming loyalty to al Qaeda and its leader Zawahiri continue to expand, with factions now in Iraq, Yemen, Libya, Syria and even Mali, in the western Sahara Desert, where consequences of the 2011 Libya war have spread.[180] Governments have been destabilized or have been

---

dyn/content/article/2006/09/14/AR2006091401545.html; Robert H. Reid, "Man Thought to Be Bin Laden Urges Iraqi Suicide Attacks," *Southeast Missourian*, February 12, 2003, http://www.semissourian.com/story/101414.html.

[178] Tom Vanden Brook, "Waterboarding Didn't Work, Committee Report Finds," *USA Today*, December 9, 2014, http://www.usatoday.com/story/news/nation/2014/12/09/waterboarding-ksm/20151103/; Marcy Wheeler, "KSM Had the CIA Believing in Black Muslim Convert Jihadists Arsonists in Montana for 3 Months," Emptywheel, December 15, 2014, https://www.emptywheel.net/2014/12/15/ksm-had-the-cia-believing-in-black-muslim-jihadist-converts-in-montana-for-3-months/; Dexter Filkins, "Khalid Sheikh Mohammed and the CIA," *New Yorker*, December 31, 2014, http://www.newyorker.com/news/news-desk/khalid-sheikh-mohammed-cia; "FBI Warns of Terrorist Attacks on US Banks," *Irish Times*, April 20, 2002, http://www.irishtimes.com/news/fbi-warns-of-terrorist-attacks-on-us-banks-1.420710; Toni Locy, "Some Question Motives Behind Series of Alerts," *USA Today*, May 24, 2002, http://usatoday30.usatoday.com/news/attack/2002/05/24/alerts-motives.htm; David Rose, "Tortured Reasoning," *Vanity Fair*, December 2008, http://www.vanityfair.com/magazine/2008/12/torture200812.

[179] George W. Bush, "Remarks to the National Endowment for Democracy," 41 Weekly Comp. Pres. Doc. 1502 (October 6, 2005).

[180] Jeremy Keenan, "How Washington Helped Foster the Islamist Uprising in Mali," *New Internationalist*, December 2012, https://newint.org/features/2012/12/01/us-terrorism-sahara/.

overthrown in Yemen, Egypt, Tunisia, Bahrain, Syria and, of course, Iraq. The Kingdom of Saudi Arabia still stands, but, in 2014–2017, the predominantly Sunni Arab parts of western Iraq and eastern Syria actually did fall to the forces of the so-called Islamic State,[181] the Iraqi-dominated faction of "al Qaeda in Iraq," a spin-off of bin Laden's original al Qaeda, which had only come into being in late 2004, a full year and a half into America's invasion and occupation of that country. The regional sectarian war touched off by America's overthrow of minority Sunni Arab power in Iraq in 2003 will continue to rage for decades to come, even long after the current versions of al Qaeda and the Islamic State have been sidelined and replaced.

In the aftermath of the monetary and political destabilization set off by the U.S. war in Iraq, the loyal dictatorship of Hosni Mubarak in Egypt was overthrown in a popular revolution in 2011, which ended when the conservative Islamist Muslim Brotherhood won the presidency and a bare majority in Parliament. America and Saudi Arabia's allies in the Egyptian military overthrew the new government in a violent coup and bloody massacre a little more than a year later.[182] This proved, al Qaeda leader Ayman al Zawahiri then claimed, that he was right all along that the United States would never allow democratic election results in Arab countries to supersede their declared "interests," that the conservative old Muslim Brotherhood were damned fools for even trying to participate in Western-style processes and that the "far enemy" would have to continue to be targeted.[183] Since then, terrorist attacks in Egypt have increased and an insurgency has broken out in the Sinai Peninsula in resistance to the revived military regime.[184]

In short, America "fell for it." U.S. political and military leaders exploited the September 11th attacks to get away with pursuing unrelated agendas, ultimately to the point of imperial over-extension and the detriment of American power, just as Osama bin Laden and Ayman al-Zawahiri were hoping and betting they would. By granting these leaders

---

[181] Patrick Cockburn, *The Rise of Islamic State: ISIS and the New Sunni Revolution*, rev. ed. (New York: Verso, 2015).

[182] Cheryl K. Chumley, "John Kerry: Egypt's Army Was Only 'Restoring Democracy,'" *Washington Times*, August 2, 2013, http://www.washingtontimes.com/news/2013/aug/2/john-kerry-egypt-army-was-only-restoring-democracy/.

[183] "Ayman al-Zawahiri Says US Behind Coup Against Mohamed Morsi," *Guardian*, August 3, 2013, https://theguardian.com/world/2013/aug/03/ayman-zawahiri-coup-mohamed-morsi; "Al-Qaeda Head Ayman al-Zawahiri Accuses US of Plotting Removal of Mohammed Morsi in Egypt," *Telegraph*, August 3, 2013, http://telegraph.co.uk/news/worldnews/al-qaeda/10220281/Al-Qaeda-head-Ayman-al-Zawahiri-accuses-US-of-plotting-removal-of-Mohammed-Morsi-in-Egypt.html.

[184] Yusri Mohamed et al., "Islamic State Kills 12 Military Personnel in Egypt's Sinai," Reuters, October 14, 2016, http://www.reuters.com/article/us-egypt-insurgency-idUSKBN12E14Q; Omar Fahmy, "Egypt Says Air Strikes Kill Islamic State Leaders in Sinai," Reuters, April 20, 2017, http://www.reuters.com/article/us-egypt-security-idUSKBN17M1AS.

the writ to "keep us safe" at any cost in this new, fearful age, the people of this country have instead placed themselves in much greater danger. Our government helped create this international terrorist movement that they then provoked into turning against the American people. Then they exploited the blowback terrorist attacks, using them as an excuse to spread the war to countries that had nothing to do with al Qaeda or their war against America. In playing the role of the rampaging empire, America's leaders have not only created the space for the spread of bin Ladenite fighters across the Middle East, but have allowed some of these most savage and formerly marginal groups of criminals and terrorists on earth to portray themselves as brave heroes who saw the danger first and would dare to stand up to such overwhelming military power. In doing so, America's leaders have helped to add tens of thousands of combatants to the enemy's ranks and guarantee blowback and backdraft against the U.S. and its allies into the indefinite future, all the while using terrorism as an excuse for further erosions of our freedoms. And they did it all in the name of keeping us safe.

Instead of reacting the way our enemy wanted us to, America should have played it smart and cool. President Bush could have focused diplomatic or military efforts very narrowly on the few hundred true associates of bin Laden hiding in Afghanistan and then pulled right back out again. He could have announced that, on second thought, the U.S. was sorry for its military presence in the Middle East and interference in Arab domestic politics — that we had only been trying to protect them from the dark forces of international Soviet Communism after all, we swear, but that, yes, the USSR is long gone now, and it is past time to close up the foreign bases and come home. Americans could have insisted that he do so.

The United States could have made its best intentions clear to the world right then and there. Those few who were guilty of attacking us would pay, but otherwise America would prove that we were exactly who we claimed to be. We could have refrained from unleashing America's virtually limitless military power and taking advantage of our newfound victimhood to accomplish other, unrelated goals. We could have closed our bases and withdrawn our troops from the Middle East, where they had overstayed their welcome and were only causing problems.

Instead, America has given itself another Vietnam in Afghanistan and beyond. The impossible pipe-dream of Osama bin Laden and his few hundred associates at the turn of the twenty-first century has been brought to life by the Bush and Obama administrations. Further battlegrounds have been seeded across the Middle East and northern Africa. The Ba'athist regime in Syria and the revolutionary Shi'ite government in Iran — both of which Osama bin Laden would have loved to see America overthrow[185] — remain under threat of regime change.[186]

And the U.S. has proven the terrorists right about us. They attacked, saying Americans were hypocrites and barbarians who lie and murder and support dictators, while claiming to be champions of human rights and democratic values. In reaction, our government bombed and shot and tortured and made refugees out of *millions* of people[187] who had nothing to do with attacking us whatsoever. America has invaded nations, overthrown regimes and fomented chaos, national and regional civil wars and mass deprivation for a thousand miles in every direction.

Bin Laden's ultimate desire[188] is now in danger of being fulfilled. The War on Terrorism is becoming an escalating conflict between Western and Islamic civilizations, which could continue to destroy the Middle East while driving more people to adopt al Qaeda and ISIS's point of view and further divide humanity from itself.[189] There are plenty of factions in American politics that have an interest in pushing a similar narrative as the terrorists — that the bin Ladenites are the true representatives of Islam, just as they claim, and that their existence proves this world is not big enough for their civilization and ours.[190] In fact, while most Muslims in the world oppose American foreign policy, they consistently answer that they admire the American people and our society and do not support

[185] Paul Richter, "US Designates Anti-government Iran Militant Group as Terrorist," *Los Angeles Times*, November 4, 2010, http://articles.latimes.com/2010/nov/04/world/la-fg-iran-terror-list-20101104; Brian Murphy and Kareem Fahim, "Islamic State Claims New Reach into Iran with Twin Attacks in Tehran," *Washington Post*, June 7, 2017, https://www.washingtonpost.com/world/rare-double-attacks-hits-irans-capital/2017/06/07/d9f101c2-4b50-11e7-9669-250d0b15f83b_story.html; "Al-Qaeda's Zawahiri Calls for 'Guerrilla War' in Syria," al-Jazeera, April 24, 2017, http://www.aljazeera.com/news/2017/04/al-qaeda-zawahiri-calls-guerrilla-war-syria-170424115728643.html.

[186] Max Greenwood, "Tillerson: 'No role' for Assad in Governing Syria," *Hill*, April 6, 2017, http://thehill.com/policy/international/327660-tillerson-no-role-for-assad-in-syria; "Secretary of State Rex Tillerson testimony, House Foreign Affairs Committee hearing on State Department's Fiscal Year 2018 Budget Request," C-Span 3, June 14, 2017, https://www.c-span.org/video/?429946-1/secretary-tillerson-testifies-fy-2018-state-department-budget.

[187] International Physicians for the Prevention of Nuclear War et al., "Casualty Figures After 10 Years of the 'War on Terror,' Iraq, Afghanistan, Pakistan."

[188] Syed Saleem Shahzad, *Inside al Qaeda and the Taliban: Beyond bin Laden and 911* (Chicago: Pluto, 2011); 137-139.

[189] "The Extinction of the Gray Zone," *Dabiq*, Issue 7, https://media.clarionproject.org/files/islamic-state/islamic-state-dabiq-magazine-issue-7-from-hypocrisy-to-apostasy.pdf.

[190] Stephen M. Walt, "Don't Give ISIS What It Wants," *Foreign Policy*, November 16, 2015, http://foreignpolicy.com/2015/11/16/dont-give-isis-what-it-wants-united-states-reaction/; Max Blumenthal, "How Western Militarists Are Playing into the Hands of ISIS," AlterNet, November 16, 2015, http://www.alternet.org/world/how-western-militarists-are-playing-hands-isis; Emma Ashford, "What We Get Wrong About the Clash of Civilizations," Cato Institute, February 6, 2017, https://www.cato-unbound.org/2017/02/06/emma-ashford/what-we-get-wrong-about-clash-civilizations; Caner K. Dagli, "The Phony Islam of ISIS," *Atlantic*, February 27, 2015, https://www.theatlantic.com/international/archive/2015/02/what-muslims-really-want-isis-atlantic/386156/; Amir Tibon, "AIPAC Gave $60K to Group That Inspired Trump's Muslim Ban," *Ha'aretz*, March 16, 2017, http://www.haaretz.com/us-news/.premium-1.777541.

terrorism.[191] U.S. Muslims remain well-assimilated, loyal Americans.[192] But if the terrorists and hawks' common version of recent history continues to gain influence, we could be in for a very long war, indeed.

Mattis and McMaster's War

Donald Trump consistently denounced the Afghan war for at least five years before becoming president[193] and was clearly hesitant to continue to sacrifice lives and dollars on an obviously impossible mission, before he gave in to the generals and ordered a new escalation in August of 2017. The president seems to understand that by sending more soldiers and marines back to Afghanistan to reinforce those attempting to hold the line there, he is only prolonging this deadly exercise in wishful thinking and government make-work.

Trump won the election partly on a platform of stated reluctance to get involved in new conflicts and regret over the last decade and more of war. He was correct when he said the U.S. would have been better off if we had never gone over there in 2001:

> We've spent trillions of dollars overseas, while allowing our own infrastructure to fall into total disrepair and decay. In the Middle East, we've spent as of four weeks ago, $6 trillion. Think of it. And by the way, the Middle East is in … much worse shape than it was 15 years ago. If our presidents would have gone to the beach for 15 years, we would be in much better shape than we are right now, that I can tell you. Be a hell of a lot better. We could have rebuilt our country three times with that money.[194]

But Trump also warned,

> I would stay in Afghanistan. It's probably the one place we should have gone in the Middle East because it's adjacent and right next to Pakistan which has nuclear weapons. So I think you have to stay and do the best you can, not that it's ever going to be great but I don't think we have much of a choice. That's one place, frankly, instead of going to

[191] Esposito and Mogahed, *Who Speaks for Islam?*

[192] Michael Hirsh, "Inside the FBI's Secret Muslim Network," Politico, March 24, 2016, http://www.politico.com/magazine/story/2016/03/fbi-muslim-outreach-terrorism-213765; "US Muslims Concerned About Their Place in Society, but Continue to Believe in the American Dream," Pew Research Center, July 26, 2017, http://www.pewforum.org/2017/07/26/findings-from-pew-research-centers-2017-survey-of-us-muslims/.

[193] Twitter search results, "Afghanistan from:realdonaldtrump," https://twitter.com/search?f=tweets&vertical=default&q=Afghanistan%20from%3Arealdonaldtrump&src=typd

[194] Donald Trump, "Remarks at the Conservative Political Action Conference in National Harbor, Maryland," DCPD-201700137 (February 24, 2017).

Iraq we probably should have gone there first. I would stay in Afghanistan and only, again, because of its location next to Pakistan. … I hate doing it. I hate doing it so much. But again, you have nuclear weapons in Pakistan, so I would do it.[195]

By this, the president apparently means the U.S. must maintain a military presence within striking distance to protect Pakistan's nuclear weapons from falling into the hands of extremists. However, hypothetically accepting the necessity of such a policy and all other things being equal, he ignores the fact that U.S. special operations forces, marines, and navy aviators can remain stationed on aircraft carriers off Pakistan's coast in the Indian Ocean on a permanent basis for use in such an emergency. Ten or fifteen thousand troops busy hunting insurgent fighters in Afghanistan next door would seem to make little difference.

But the military leadership apparently decided they did not want to take any chances with the unpredictable new president. Just before the inauguration, in January 2017, the Marine Corps announced a new deployment back to Helmand Province to "advise and assist" Afghan forces desperately trying to hang on to control of Lashkar Gah.[196] In February, before Trump had seen the results of any formal review or received any official recommendation, Afghan war commander, Gen. John Nicholson publicly told Sen. John McCain's Armed Services Committee that "thousands" more troops needed to be sent back to Helmand Province immediately to "break the stalemate" between the insurgents and the Afghan National Army there.[197] General Joseph Votel, the current commander of Central Command, publicly agreed just a few weeks later.[198] This seems to have been the beginning of the military's attempt to "jam" Donald Trump the way they did Barack Obama in 2009.

[195] "Donald Trump On His Foreign Policy Strategy," interview with Bill O'Reilly, Fox News, April 29, 2016, http://www.foxnews.com/transcript/2016/04/29/donald-trump-on-his-foreign-policy-strategy/; Greg Jaffe and Missy Ryan, "In Afghanistan, Trump Will Inherit a Costly Stalemate and Few Solutions," *Washington Post*, January 18, 2017, https://www.washingtonpost.com/world/national-security/in-afghanistan-trump-will-inherit-a-costly-stalemate-and-few-solutions/2017/01/18/aacdf742-dc06-11e6-ad42-f3375f271c9c_story.html.

[196] Hope Hodge Seck, "300 Marines Will Deploy to Helmand This Spring, Corps Confirms," Military, January 6, 2017, http://www.military.com/daily-news/2017/01/06/300-marines-will-deploy-to-helmand-this-spring-corps-confirms.html; Hope Seck, interviewed by the author, *Scott Horton Show,* radio archive, January 11, 2017, https://scotthorton.org/interviews/11117-hope-hodge-seck-on-the-deployment-of-300-marines-to-afghanistan/.

[197] Kevin Baron, "Afghanistan Needs 'Thousands' More Troops, US General Says," Defense One, February 9, 2017, http://www.defenseone.com/threats/2017/02/afghanistan-needs-thousands-more-troops-us-general-says-stunning-assessment/135280/?oref=defense_one_breaking_nl; Joshua Fatzick, "Top US General: Afghanistan War Still a 'Stalemate,'" Voice of America News, February 9, 2017, http://www.voanews.com/a/top-us-general-says-afghanistan-war-still-a-stalemate/3716256.html.

[198] Shawn Snow, "CENTCOM Commander Supports Troop Increase in Afghanistan," *Military Times*, March 9, 2017, http://www.militarytimes.com/articles/syria-votel-afghanistan-troops.

This was probably unnecessary, and may have even backfired somewhat on the military leadership. Trump ran for office opposing nation-building and regime change operations against secular Middle Eastern governments, but promised to completely destroy "radical Islamic terrorism" in short order. Upon taking office, Trump quickly authorized expanded special operations[199] and CIA[200] strikes against al Qaeda and ISIS targets across the Middle East: he has launched major strikes against al Qaeda,[201] as well as their enemies, the Houthi movement in Yemen;[202] sent the army to fight the al Qaeda-linked militia al Shabaab in Somalia;[203] sent the marines to fight the Islamic State in western Iraq and eastern Syria;[204] launched airstrikes against al Qaeda[205] and against government targets in western Syria;[206] bombed ISIS in what used to be Libya;[207] and presumably sent troops to many more places we do not know about.[208] Trump's reluctance to escalate the war in Afghanistan seemed to be the exception to his overall point of view about the War on Terrorism.

Possibly in part as a reaction to his military advisers' presumptuousness, in the first months of his presidency, Trump repeatedly delayed the decision to escalate troop strength and ordered his

---

[199] James Gordon Meek, "US Special Ops Step Up Strikes on Al-Qaeda and ISIS, Insiders Say," ABC News, March 3, 2017, http://abcnews.go.com/International/us-special-ops-step-strikes-al-qaeda-isis/story?id=45889665.

[200] Gordon Lubold and Shane Harris, "Trump Broadens CIA Powers, Allows Deadly Drone Strikes," *Wall Street Journal*, March 13, 2017, https://www.wsj.com/articles/trump-gave-cia-power-to-launch-drone-strikes-1489444374.

[201] Eric Schmitt, "United States Ramps Up Airstrikes Against Al Qaeda in Yemen," *New York Times*, March 3, 2017, https://www.nytimes.com/2017/03/03/world/middleeast/yemen-us-airstrikes-al-qaeda.html.

[202] Gordon Lubold and Jay Solomon, "US Boosts Military Backing for Saudi-Led Coalition in Yemen," *Wall Street Journal*, March 27, 2017, https://www.wsj.com/articles/u-s-boosts-military-backing-for-saudi-led-coalition-in-yemen-1490651993.

[203] Tom O'Conner, "Trump Expands US Military Campaign in Africa with Somalia Offensive," *Newsweek*, March 31, 2017, http://www.newsweek.com/trump-expand-military-campaign-africa-somalia-offensive-577347; Abdi Guled, "First US Military Member Killed in Somalia Since 1993," *Chicago Tribune*, May 5, 2017, http://www.chicagotribune.com/news/nationworld/ct-us-military-somalia-al-shabab-20170505-story.html.

[204] Dan Lamothe and Thomas Gibbons-Neff, "Marines Have Arrived in Syria to Fire Artillery in the Fight for Raqqa," *Washington Post*, March 8, 2017, https://www.washingtonpost.com/news/checkpoint/wp/2017/03/08/marines-have-arrived-in-syria-to-fire-artillery-in-the-fight-for-raqqa/.

[205] "US Forces Killed 11 al-Qaeda Operatives in Two Air Strikes in Syria Says Pentagon," *Telegraph*, February 9, 2017, http://www.telegraph.co.uk/news/2017/02/09/us-forces-killed-11-al-qaeda-operatives-two-air-strikes-syria/; "Al-Qaeda's Deputy Leader Reportedly Killed by US Drone Strike in Syria," *Telegraph*, February 27, 2017, http://www.telegraph.co.uk/news/2017/02/27/al-qaedas-deputy-leader-reportedly-killed-us-drone-strike-syria/.

[206] "US-led Coalition Strikes Pro-government Forces in Syria," ABC News, June 6, 2017, http://www.cbsnews.com/news/us-led-coalition-strikes-pro-government-forces-in-syria/.

[207] Eric Schmitt, "Warnings of a 'Powder Keg' in Libya as ISIS Regroups," *New York Times*, March 21, 2017, https://www.nytimes.com/2017/03/21/world/africa/libya-isis.html.

[208] Nick Turse, "America's War-Fighting Footprint in Africa," TomDispatch, April 27, 2017, http://www.tomdispatch.com/blog/176272/.

National Security Council to continually return to the drawing board to come up with a new strategy to justify doing so.[209]

Virtually the entire Principals Committee of President Trump's National Security Council is heavily implicated or invested in America's failed war in Afghanistan: Secretary of Defense Mattis was a Marine Corps general in the initial invasion,[210] helped Petraeus write the new counterinsurgency manual[211] and was later commander of Central Command in charge of the war overall;[212] National Security Advisor, Army Lt. Gen. H. R. McMaster helped advise Petraeus's staff during the rewrite of the army's counterinsurgency doctrine[213] and was formerly in charge of anti-corruption efforts in Kabul during the Obama "surge";[214] Chairman of the Joint Chiefs of Staff, Marine Corps Gen. Joseph Dunford was commander of ISAF and U.S. forces in Afghanistan from February 2013 to August 2014;[215] Chief of Staff and retired Marine Corps Gen. John Kelly's son, Robert, also a marine, was killed by an IED on patrol in Helmand Province in 2010.[216] Former Representative, now CIA director, Mike Pompeo,[217] and former Senator, now director of national intelligence, Dan Coats,[218] have also both been big war supporters in

---

[209] Idrees Ali and Phil Stewart, "In Afghan Review, Trump's Frustration Carries Echoes of Obama Years," Reuters, August 6, 2017, http://www.reuters.com/article/us-usa-afghanistan-trump-idUSKBN1AM0F5.

[210] Travis J. Tritten, "Retired Green Beret Says Mattis Left 'My Men to Die' in Afghanistan," *Stars and Stripes*, December 2, 2016, https://www.stripes.com/news/retired-green-beret-says-mattis-left-my-men-to-die-in-afghanistan-1.442367.

[211] Dan Lamothe, "Mattis: The Man, the Myths and the Influential General's Deep Bond with His Marines," *Military Times*, April 5, 2013, http://www.militarytimes.com/story/military/archives/2013/04/05/the-man-the-myths-mattis-as-chaos-retires-marines-recall/78538642/.

[212] Jim Garamone, "Mattis Discusses Afghan Transition at Marine Symposium," American Forces Press Service, August 31, 2001, http://www.centcom.mil/MEDIA/NEWS-ARTICLES/News-Article-View/Article/884380/mattis-discusses-afghan-transition-at-marine-symposium/.

[213] Mackubin Thomas Owens, "Counterinsurgency from the Bottom Up: Colonel H.R. McMaster and the 3rd Armored Cavalry Regiment in Tel Afar, Spring-Fall 2005," Foreign Policy Research Institute, March 17, 2017, http://www.fpri.org/article/2017/03/counterinsurgency-bottom-colonel-h-r-mcmaster-3rd-armored-cavalry-regiment-tel-afar-spring-fall-2005/.

[214] David Feith, "H.R. McMaster: The Warrior's-Eye View of Afghanistan," *Wall Street Journal*, May 12, 2012, https://www.wsj.com/articles/SB10001424052702304451104577392281146871796.

[215] "Dunford Takes Command of Foreign Forces in Afghanistan," Radio Free Europe/Radio Liberty, February 10, 2013, http://www.rferl.org/a/dunford-afghanistan-command/24897927.html; "Biography of General Joseph F. Dunford, Jr., Chairman, Joint Chiefs of Staff," Department of Defense, accessed May 23, 2017, https://www.defense.gov/About/Biographies/Biography-View/Article/621329/general-joseph-f-dunford-jr.

[216] Rowan Scarborough, "Border Security Hawk Gen. John Kelly Attracts Trump Cabinet Interest," *Washington Times*, November 27, 2016, http://www.washingtontimes.com/news/2016/nov/27/john-kelly-trump-cabinet-mention-a-border-security/; Kevin Baron, "What You Don't Know About Gen. John Kelly," Defense One, December 7, 2016, http://www.defenseone.com/politics/2016/12/what-you-dont-know-about-gen-john-kelly/133703/.

[217] "Mike Pompeo on War & Peace," On the Issues, last modified February 26, 2016, http://www.ontheissues.org/House/Mike_Pompeo_War_+_Peace.htm.

[218] "A Conversation with Senator Dan Coats," interviewed by Charles Lane, Council on Foreign

Congress. For these men, to concede that America's longest foreign war has failed, to cut and run in a fight where staying forever means never quite losing, to suffer disgrace by admitting defeat and allowing the Taliban to openly rule the predominantly Pashtun parts of the country in the U.S. military's absence is unthinkable.

As Kelly put it,

> If you think this war against our way of life is over because some of the self-appointed opinion-makers and chattering class grow "war weary," because they want to be out of Iraq or Afghanistan, you are mistaken. This enemy is dedicated to our destruction. He will fight us for generations, and the conflict will move through various phases as it has since 9/11.[219]

With the principle of perpetual conflict established, coming up with an actual plan that made sense would have to come second. In the meantime, the fighting continued. After a Green Beret was killed fighting ISIS in Nangarhar Province in April 2017,[220] U.S. Special Operations Command took revenge by dropping a 21,000-pound MOAB, "Massive Ordnance Air Blast" or "Mother of All Bombs," on an enemy position. Since B-52s still regularly bomb ISIS and Taliban targets — U.S. forces dropped more bombs in April 2017 than any other single month since 2012[221] — the use of the MOAB in this instance seemed to be more about sending a message than anything else, though the military said the use of a fuel-air bomb was necessary to reach fighters hiding in tunnels deep underground.[222] The military also claimed there were still hundreds of ISIS fighters left to be dealt with in eastern Afghanistan, giving the safe-haven myth a whole new lease on life. We can forget the threat of long-dead al Qaeda leaders one day returning from Pakistan, now local Afghan and Pakistani Pashtun tribal fighters resisting the occupation and Kabul-based government, while declaring themselves part of ISIS, provide another enemy to fight into the indefinite future.[223]

Relations, January 24, 2013, http://www.cfr.org/budget-debt-and-deficits/conversation-senator-dan-coats/p35379.

[219] Scarborough, "General: Millennial Marines Shun Self-absorbed Culture."

[220] Meghann Myers, "DoD Identifies Green Beret Killed While Fighting ISIS in Afghanistan," *Army Times*, April 10, 2017, https://www.armytimes.com/articles/dod-identifies-green-beret-killed-while-fighting-isis-in-afghanistan.

[221] Stephen Losey, "US, Coalition Strikes in Afghanistan Spike, Hit Highest Number in Five Years," *Air Force Times*, May 26, 2017, https://airforcetimes.com/articles/us-coalition-strikes-in-afghanistan-spike-hit-highest-number-in-five-years; Gabriel Dominguez, "USAF Increases Use of Air Power in Afghanistan," *IHS Jane's Defence Weekly*, May 25, 2017, http://janes.com/article/70795/usaf-increases-use-of-air-power-in-afghanistan.

[222] Emily Dreyfuss, "That 'Mother of All Bombs' Was Just Waiting for the Right Target," *Wired,* April 13, 2017, https://www.wired.com/2017/04/mother-bombs-just-waiting-right-target/.

[223] Lucas Tomlinson, "US Drops Largest Non-Nuclear Bomb in Afghanistan After Green Beret

As expert Borhan Osman wrote shortly afterward,

> Having been eclipsed by the Taliban, the Islamic State seems to be focused on marketing itself to potential and active jihadists. For that, it needs publicity. President Trump's big bomb provided exactly that. The destruction of a network of caves is the perfect advertisement to lure radicals undecided about joining a jihadist group and attract members from other groups.

> After the bombing and the subsequent military operations, the Islamic State in Khorasan's radio station in Nangarhar has been roaring. One preacher called the bomb a blessing from God that affirmed the group's jihadist status. This is a message skillfully tailored for young radicals, since for them American hostility is a stamp of a group's credibility. The more a group is targeted by the United States, the greater its jihadi legitimacy.

> The United States military's increased engagement will attract more foreign militants to Afghanistan to wage a jihad against the Americans. A less prominent role for the United States on the battlefield and a less passionate rhetoric of confrontation would perhaps improve the chances that Afghan forces will vanquish the group.[224]

But the illogic of further escalation remains irresistible to the foreign policy establishment, despite the fact that U.S. troops have never, in 16 years, achieved anything but "fragile and reversible" gains in rolling back the insurgency in certain areas, while driving up long-term enemy recruitment in response. Stephen Biddle of the Council on Foreign Relations — one of McChrystal's advisers from his review during the summer of 2009 — told the media in April 2017 that the failure of the last Afghan counterinsurgency "surge" was that it ended too soon. He called for the addition of 90,000 soldiers and marines, which would bring troop levels back to their 2010–2011 high of 100,000 — indefinitely.[225]

Former Deputy Secretary of Defense for Policy Michèle Flournoy, while taking no personal responsibility whatsoever for her role in the failure of the last escalation, continues to claim that her and Obama's "surge" was working great, but that the former president had sabotaged

---

Killed," Fox News, April 13, 2017, http://www.foxnews.com/world/2017/04/13/us-drops-largest-non-nuclear-bomb-in-afghanistan-after-green-beret-killed.html; Jawad Sukhanyar and Rod Nordland, "ISIS, Aided by Ex-Taliban Groups, Makes Inroads in Northern Afghanistan," *New York Times*, June 28, 2017, https://nytimes.com/2017/06/28/world/asia/isis-northern-afghanistan.html.

[224] Borhan Osman, "The Wrong Enemy in Afghanistan," *New York Times*, May 9, 2017, https://www.nytimes.com/2017/05/09/opinion/the-wrong-enemy-in-afghanistan.html.

[225] Alex Pfeiffer, "After More Than a Decade and a Half in Afghanistan the US Needs to Deploy More Troops to Win, Experts Say," Daily Caller, April 17, 2017, http://dailycaller.com/2017/04/17/after-more-than-a-decade-and-a-half-in-afghanistan-the-u-s-needs-to-deploy-more-troops-to-win-experts-say/.

his own victory by announcing withdrawal dates and encouraging the enemy to bide their time. *That* is the only reason the Taliban decided to keep fighting. The only way to get it right, Flournoy also insists, is for the U.S. to escalate and make an "indefinite" commitment to Afghanistan.[226] Much of the rest of the "expert" foreign policy commentator community was quick to agree. It's not that the policy they had supported was wrong, the military just hadn't implemented their ideas quite hard enough. The "surge" had been temporary. That was the problem before. No wonder it didn't work. But once the U.S. announces — after 16 years — that it is staying forever, no matter what, then the Taliban will finally stop resisting.[227]

The plan the generals had in mind was more modest than sending another 90,000 men, though perhaps Biddle's recommendation was more of an example of the "art of the deal." By proposing to rehash the entire "surge," he was helping to make the increase they later requested sound more reasonable by contrast.[228] Though Nicholson and Mattis made it known that they meant to ask for between 3,000 and 5,000 more troops in the spring of 2017 — seemingly a fairly small and last-ditch response to shore up a failing status quo — by summer, the high-end plan being talked about at the Pentagon was for as many as 20,000 additional soldiers to be sent to attempt to slow and then reverse the Taliban's gains.[229] Whether this represented real panic on the part of some of those reviewing the war or simply another attempt to play the game of providing the president with multiple options with an emphasis on the middle choice is unknown. One official complained that the Obama administration had left the Afghan government "losing slowly" and that "the Taliban will overrun the government eventually" if the escalation was not approved.[230] But this increase in troop numbers would only be required for the time it takes to again train an Afghan National Army powerful enough to "sustain [the fight] and bring the stability that is needed to bring the Taliban to negotiation," Gen. Curtis Scaparrotti, the NATO supreme allied commander Europe, insisted. He did not make the mistake of saying how long that might take.[231]

---

[226] Michèle Flournoy and Richard Fontaine, "The Afghan War Is Not Lost," *National Interest*, July 11, 2017, http://nationalinterest.org/feature/the-afghan-war-not-lost-21499.

[227] Peter Bergen, "Trump's Emerging Plan for Afghanistan Breaks with Obama Approach," CNN, June 21, 2017, http://www.cnn.com/2017/06/21/opinions/trump-plan-for-afghanistan-breaks-with-obama-approach-bergen/index.html.

[228] Alex Pfeiffer, "After More Than a Decade and a Half in Afghanistan."

[229] Mark Perry, interviewed by the author, *Scott Horton Show*, radio archive, June 28, 2017, https://scotthorton.org/062817-mark-perry/.

[230] Eli Lake, "Trump Has to Decide," Bloomberg News, May 17, 2017, https://bloomberg.com/view/articles/2017-05-17/trump-has-to-decide-50-000-troops-to-afghanistan.

[231] Marcus Weinberger, "NATO Laying Groundwork to Send More Troops to Iraq, Afghanistan,"

National Security Advisor McMaster has reportedly made a "do-over" against the Taliban insurgency and long-term war in Afghanistan his "personal mission." His war strategy is said to be built around a "four-year plan to push back the Taliban" — a plan that is not even meant to "yield significant results," in terms of forcing the Taliban to the negotiating table, "until its later stages."[232] No more promises of results in 18 months as before. The plan is just keep fighting, and maybe, someday years from now, negotiate with an insurgency that has no intention of doing so, from a position of strength that cannot be achieved.

The military got a head start on the new escalation before it was even decided. In May, the U.S. announced they were giving 159 sophisticated Black Hawk helicopters to the ANA to assist in their fight against the Taliban. This was either a subtle indication of the coming escalation or total ineptitude. As one expert told the *Military Times*, "Given that it takes substantial U.S. support to maintain the airframes that the Afghan Air Force has already, it doesn't seem feasible that they would be able to support that many Black Hawks without a significant contribution from NATO."[233] Reuters reported that this was part of a "four-year, $7 billion expansion plan … aimed at training more flight and maintenance crews and increasing the number of aircraft in the Afghan Air Force (AAF)."[234]

The military also expanded their mission criteria so that U.S. infantry could once again join special operations forces in returning to the front lines to fight the insurgency.[235] Though the initial increase of four or five thousand troops did not sound like much of a "surge" at first, it turned out the generals' plan included delegating the setting of troop levels from the White House to the Pentagon in the future as well.[236] They made it

Defense One, May 18, 2017, http://defenseone.com/threats/2017/05/nato-laying-groundwork-send-more-troops-iraq-afghanistan/137997/.

[232] Greg Jaffe, "Trump Suggests That More US Troops Might Not Be Needed in Afghanistan," *Washington Post*, July 20, 2017 https://www.washingtonpost.com/world/national-security/trump-has-rare-meeting-of-full-national-security-team-to-discuss-afghanistan/2017/07/19/05c25cc6-6cc4-11e7-9c15-177740635e83_story.html.

[233] Shawn Snow and Mackenzie Wolf, "US to Provide Afghanistan with 159 Black Hawks to Help Break 'Stalemate,'" *Military Times*, May 17, 2017, http://militarytimes.com/articles/blackhawks-airforce-afghanistan-stalemate; "Trump Administration Outlines Emerging Strategy On Afghanistan," NPR News, June 30, 2017, http://www.npr.org/2017/06/30/535059255/trump-administration-outlines-emerging-strategy-on-afghanistan.

[234] James Mackenzie, "As US Weighs Afghan Strategy, Hopes Set on Fledgling Air Force," July 23, 2017, Reuters, http://www.reuters.com/article/us-afghanistan-airforce-idUSKBN1A80MX.

[235] "Pentagon Seeks to Ramp Up US Role in Afghan War," CBS News, May 8, 2017, http://www.cbsnews.com/news/us-afghanistan-troop-levels-role/.

[236] Missy Ryan and Greg Jaffe, "US Poised to Expand Military Effort Against Taliban in Afghanistan," *Washington Post*, May 8, 2017, https://www.washingtonpost.com/world/national-security/us-poised-to-expand-military-effort-against-taliban-in-afghanistan/2017/05/08/356c4930-33fa-11e7-b412-62beef8121f7_story.html.

clear that further eventual increases were intended from the beginning.[237]

The center-left Brookings Institute scholar, Michael O'Hanlon, argued in his May 2017 case for renewed escalation that, though there is no end to the Afghan war in sight, "*maybe that's okay*, given how relatively modest in scale and risk the mission has become, and how modest it will remain even if President Trump adds several thousand more troops to the mix." [emphasis added] Though O'Hanlon concedes parenthetically that "Afghan forces have been taking 5,000 or more fatalities a year in recent years, akin to U.S. losses in Vietnam ... [and] are not as far advanced as we would like. We have remedial work to do."[238]

Laurel Miller, the State Department's Special Representative for Afghanistan and Pakistan (SRAP) until the Trump administration closed her office down, later seemed sympathetic with the non-interventionist view, conceding to the press that, "I don't think there is any serious analyst of the situation in Afghanistan who believes that the war is winnable. It's possible to prevent the defeat of the Afghan government and prevent military victory by the Taliban, but this is not a war that's going to be won, certainly not in any time horizon that's relevant to political decision-making in Washington."[239]

Though this view seems to be near-universal, and even when the administration was all but admitting failure was inevitable, they continued to plan to escalate the war anyway. A senior administration official told the media that their "victory problem" could not seem to be resolved. "Not everyone agrees on how to define it, and definitely not everyone agrees on how to pursue it. We don't completely agree on ends, and we definitely don't completely agree on means. And we won't, even after a strategy rolls out."[240]

Director of National Intelligence Dan Coats testified before the U.S. Senate Intelligence Committee on May 12. Arguing for the troop increase, he admitted that "Afghan security forces' performance will probably worsen due to a combination of Taliban operations, combat casualties, desertions, poor logistics support and weak leadership. ... [Security will] almost certainly deteriorate through 2018, even with a modest increase in

---

[237] Carlo Muñoz, "Pentagon Set to Send More US Troops to Afghanistan," *Washington Times*, July 19, 2017, http://washingtontimes.com/news/2017/jul/19/afghanistan-campaign-to-get-more-us-troops-pentago/.

[238] Michael E. O'Hanlon, "Time for a (Mini) Surge in Afghanistan," *USA Today*, May 17, 2017, https://www.usatoday.com/story/opinion/2017/05/16/afghanistan-taliban-troops-surge-michael-ohanlon-column/101690634/.

[239] Susan B. Glasser, "The Trump White House's War Within," Politico magazine, July 24, 2017, http://www.politico.com/magazine/story/2017/07/24/donald-trump-afghanistan-215412.

[240] Olivier Knox, "Trump Faces a 'Victory Problem' in Afghanistan," Yahoo News, July 14, 2017, https://www.yahoo.com/news/trumps-faces-victory-problem-afghanistan-090031034.html

the military assistance by the U.S. and its partners."[241]

Forced to concede that defeating the Taliban was out of the question,[242] the generals insisted that if only the U.S. would escalate again, they could at least force the Taliban to the table to negotiate.[243] Chairman of the Joint Chiefs of Staff Dunford was optimistic. "The goal is not to defeat the Taliban, but to convince them they cannot win and are better off seeking a negotiated end to the war. ... It comes down to which side cracks first. We can be tired, but war is a clash of wills, right? So who wins? And who loses? Who loses is whose will is lost first."[244] Dunford said that if the Taliban think the U.S. is leaving in one year, then they will hang on, "but if there is an extended commitment by the international community that says we are prepared to do what has to be done as long as it takes to get the Afghans where they need to be ... that's a different story."[245]

But the story was not different. As though in answer to Dunford, the Taliban simultaneously announced the beginning of their spring offensive[246] like it was just another day at the office.[247]

While McMaster was showing slides of women walking in skirts in 1970s Kabul as though the former communist era represented the true status-quo ante in Afghanistan and that this would somehow soon translate to modern Western capitalism and democracy if only he had a little more time to defeat the insurgency, Trump was reportedly in "no mood" to give in to his national security advisor's plan, putting off the decision for months. Trump had reportedly been complaining to his staff "about how great powers throughout history — from Alexander's Macedonians to the British Empire — have failed to pacify the country."[248]

With these statements Trump has shown that, like Obama before him, he *could* differentiate between international anti-American terrorists and

---

[241] "US Intelligence: Afghanistan Will 'Almost Certainly' Deteriorate," Deutsche Welle, May 12, 2017, http://www.dw.com/en/us-intelligence-afghanistan-will-almost-certainly-deteriorate/a-38808558.

[242] CBS News, "Pentagon Seeks to Ramp Up US Role in Afghan War."

[243] Michael R. Gordon, "Trump Advisers Call for More Troops to Break Afghan Deadlock," *New York Times*, May 8, 2017, https://www.nytimes.com/2017/05/08/us/politics/donald-trump-afghanistan-troops-taliban-stalemate.html; Missy Ryan and Greg Jaffe, "US Poised to Expand Military Effort Against Taliban in Afghanistan," *Washington Post*, May 8, 2017, https://www.washingtonpost.com/world/national-security/us-poised-to-expand-military-effort-against-taliban-in-afghanistan/2017/05/08/356c4930-33fa-11e7-b412-62beef8121f7_story.html.

[244] CBS News, "Pentagon Seeks to Ramp Up US Role in Afghan War."

[245] Jim Garamone, "US Officials Studying Force Size in Afghanistan, Dunford Says," Department of Defense News, May 9, 2017, https://www.defense.gov/News/Article/Article/1177743/us-officials-studying-force-size-in-afghanistan-dunford-says/.

[246] "Taliban Announce Launch of Spring Offensive," Panarmenian, April 28, 2017, http://www.panarmenian.net/eng/news/238640/.

[247] "Taliban Announce Start of Spring Offensive," *New York Post*, April 27, 2013, http://nypost.com/2013/04/27/taliban-announce-start-of-spring-offensive/.

[248] Eli Lake, "Trump Has to Decide."

local resistance fighters battling for their own territory on their own territory, and that he knew better than to believe the mission to subdue them could ever succeed.

Part of the delay in announcing the escalation was reportedly due to major disagreements within the White House "over whether sending more troops would make a decisive difference, how much NATO allies should contribute and whether the United States should pressure Pakistan to rein in Taliban insurgents believed to be operating from safe havens there."[249] Some of the president's political advisers had been pushing back against the generals and recommending a much more limited strategy.

> On the [political advisers'] side are those who want to maintain the current level of troops but limit U.S. involvement in the war. That option would leave it up to the Afghan government and the Taliban to resolve the conflict, but assist the Afghan government with a minimal train-and-advise mission, also known as "foreign internal defense," and assist local partners in fighting extremist ideology. It would also include a counterterrorism presence to target high-value targets. It would take notably longer than the kinetic plan but would be significantly cheaper.

> "We don't fight other people's wars," the official said. "We help our friends fight their own wars for themselves."[250]

Just as when President Obama could have resorted to Vice President Biden's much more limited and realistic "Counter-terrorism Plus Training" option instead of ordering the troop increase of 2010–2012, this project would also fail. It remains impossible that the U.S. could ever build a national army that would be able to dominate Afghanistan's plurality Pashtun population. The ANA could not even fend off the Taliban insurgency without indefinite U.S. assistance. But at the very least, the civilian advisers staking out this minimalist position are arguing from an acknowledged reality that the Afghan National Army can never be expected to hold ground they cannot take for themselves in the first place.

Trump's political advisers, his son-in-law and senior advisor, Jared Kushner, and former chief strategist, Stephen Bannon, even went so far as to advocate a new strategy where the U.S. would withdraw all forces only to replace them with mercenaries under the command of firms such

---

[249] Pamela Constable and Sayed Salahuddin, "Afghan War Faces Flurry of Setbacks as New US Military Policy Nears," *Washington Post*, June 18, 2017, https://www.washingtonpost.com/world/asia_pacific/afghan-war-faces-flurry-of-setbacks-as-new-us-military-policy-nears/2017/06/18/e24acaf2-5383-11e7-b064-828ba60fbb98_story.html.

[250] Kristina Wong, "Exclusive: Trump Has 'Less Kinetic' Option in Afghanistan," Breitbart, May 11, 2017, http://www.breitbart.com/national-security/2017/05/11/exclusive-trump-has-less-kinetic-option-in-afghanistan/.

as DynCorp International, run by Steve Feinberg,[251] and Frontier Services Group (FSG), the latest project of notorious Blackwater founder Erik Prince. This was referred to as the "Laos option," after the CIA's practice of supporting mercenaries there during the Vietnam war.[252] Prince had proposed in a piece for the *Wall Street Journal* that the U.S. should appoint a "viceroy" to rule Afghanistan on the model of the old British East India Company.[253] Mattis and McMaster both reportedly opposed this idea due to their previous history of dealing with Blackwater forces in Iraq War II, where they remained outside of the military chain of command and operated with such lawlessness that they caused extra problems for U.S. forces.[254] According to journalist Mark Perry, the DynCorp plan would have put the company under the control of the CIA instead of the military.[255]

Bringing in Steve Feinberg may have been the trick that turned Trump around and bridged the gap between the president's military and civilian advisers. Appealing to Trump's "to the victor go the spoils" mentality, revealed by his many statements that the U.S. should have somehow "taken" Iraq's oil after invading in 2003, as well as his competitiveness toward China, Trump's aides have once again brought up Afghanistan's supposed trillion dollars-worth of rare earth minerals as a reason to continue the occupation. A company has already been lined up to develop the mines, and Feinberg has reportedly indicated that his DynCorp contractors would like to take the contract to guard them. This was reportedly music to the ears of a president who the *New York Times* said was "searching for a reason" to keep U.S. forces there. One catch: many of these minerals were said to be in the Taliban stronghold of the southern Helmand Province where the marines and their charges in the Afghan National Army, facing insurgents armed to the teeth with American weapons bought or confiscated from the Afghan military,[256] are

[251] Tim Shorrock, "Kushner and Bannon Team Up to Privatize the War in Afghanistan," *Nation*, July 14, 2017, https://www.thenation.com/article/kushner-and-bannon-team-up-to-privatize-the-war-in-afghanistan/.

[252] Mark Landler, "Trump Aides Recruited Businessmen to Devise Options for Afghanistan," *New York Times*, July 10, 2017, https://www.nytimes.com/2017/07/10/world/asia/trump-afghanistan-policy-erik-prince-stephen-feinberg.html.

[253] Erik Prince, "The MacArthur Model for Afghanistan," *Wall Street Journal*, May 31, 2017, https://www.wsj.com/articles/the-macarthur-model-for-afghanistan-1496269058.

[254] Mark Perry, "Bannon & Kushner Want to Outsource Afghanistan to Mercenaries," *American Conservative*, July 18, 2017, http://theamericanconservative.com/articles/exclusive-bannon-kushner-want-to-outsource-afghanistan-to-mercenaries/; Mark Perry, interviewed by the author, *Scott Horton Show*, radio archive, July 19, 2017, https://scotthorton.org/71917-mark-perry/.

[255] Mark Perry, "Bannon & Kushner Want to Outsource Afghanistan to Mercenaries."

[256] Mujib Mashal, "Back in Afghan Hot Spot, US Marines Chase Diminished Goals," *New York Times*, July 14, 2017, https://www.nytimes.com/2017/07/14/world/asia/back-in-afghan-hot-spot-us-marines-chase-diminished-goals.html; Shawn Snow, "US Weapons Complicate Afghan war," *Army Times*, July 25, 2017, https://www.armytimes.com/flashpoints/2017/07/25/us-weapons-

desperately trying to simply hang on to the capital city. Even though the plan to extract any resources located there is unrealistic, the argument may satisfy both sides of the dispute in the administration, those who wish to increase the numbers of contractors there, and those hoping to give the U.S. Army and Marine Corps something to do for a while longer.[257]

It turns out that Trump was more willing to resist the generals' advice than anyone might have guessed, holding out for months against their pressure to escalate. The fact that his political advisers had gone so far as to come up with a plan to hire mercenaries to replace the troops left in Afghanistan represented the president's hesitance to adopt the recommendations of Lt. Gen. McMaster when they were originally proposed in May.[258] But the generals kept the heat on Trump through the media to send more soldiers and marines, just as they had done eight years before. Retired Army Gen. Jack Keane, Gen. Petraeus's mentor and a powerful force in arguing for the 2007 "surge" in Iraq as well as the 2010–2012 "surge" in Afghanistan, told Fox News that Trump would have to send at least 10,000–20,000 more soldiers to reinforce and expand the mission there, and implied that perhaps a full escalation back to 2010-levels would be necessary. Arguing from the presumption that the only problem with the war was that Obama had ever reduced troop strength, Keane maintained that, "when we took the 100,000 plus troops out of Afghanistan — just left 8,000 — we took all the support that the Afghan Army had," including "attack helicopters and anti-IED intelligence, communications and logistics. We have to put that back if they're going to be effective."[259]

As another part of the military's drumbeat for Trump's new escalation, the Pentagon and the Ghani government in Kabul began making vague accusations that the Russians had "perhaps" recently begun arming the Taliban.[260] In March, Gen. Joseph Votel, commander of Central Command, testified before the House Armed Services Committee. "I think it is fair to assume [the Russians] may be providing some sort of support to [the Taliban], in terms of weapons or other things that may be there," he claimed, though his statement was loaded with disclaimer and

complicate-afghan-war/.

[257] Mark Landler and James Risen, "Trump Finds Reason for the US to Remain in Afghanistan: Minerals," *New York Times*, July 25, 2017, https://www.nytimes.com/2017/07/25/world/asia/afghanistan-trump-mineral-deposits.html.

[258] Susan B. Glasser, "The Trump White House's War Within," Politico magazine, July 24, 2017, http://www.politico.com/magazine/story/2017/07/24/donald-trump-afghanistan-215412.

[259] Cristina Corbin, "Gen. Keane: 10,000 to 20,000 Additional Troops Needed in Afghanistan," Fox News, June 16, 2017, http://www.foxnews.com/us/2017/06/16/gen-keane-10000-to-20000-additional-troops-needed-in-afghanistan.html

[260] "US General: Russia May Be Supplying Taliban Fighters," al Jazeera, March 24, 2017, http://www.aljazeera.com/news/2017/03/general-russia-supplying-taliban-fighters-170323161613169.html.

deniability. This was an interesting take since the U.S. had been backing the Russians' friends among the northern tribes in Afghanistan against the Taliban since 2001, and the Russians had been helping the U.S. do it by allowing access to their territory for a supply route for U.S. and NATO forces.[261] In fact, those making this claim provided no evidence that the Russians had turned around and begun to support their enemies in the Taliban. Accusations in the press seemed to be almost completely speculative or based solely on the claims of local government officials.[262] The Russians[263] and Taliban[264] both immediately denied it, though the Taliban readily admitted to being in contact with the Russians, saying simply that communication with regional powers was important for protecting their interests. After the initial media hype had died down, Marine Corps Lt. Gen. Vincent Stewart admitted to the U.S. Senate that, "I have not seen real physical evidence of weapons or money being transferred."[265]

One thing Russia actually had done, perhaps under the mistaken impression that the American mission in Afghanistan really was winding down, was hold a series of peace talks in Moscow with various groups from inside Afghanistan and interested nearby governments. The Americans and the Taliban both boycotted the talks, with the U.S. saying that it was merely an attempt by Russia to gain influence in the region.[266] The reality seems to be that the Russians have decided that focusing on support for the military of Tajikistan and the buffer states of Central Asia makes more sense than continuing to rely on the U.S.-installed government in Afghanistan to keep a lid on the rising Taliban or the new

---

[261] "Northern Distribution Network [NDN]," GlobalSecurity.org, http://www.globalsecurity.org/military/facility/ndn.htm.

[262] Arif Rafiq, "Russia Returns to Afghanistan," *National Interest*, January 12, 2017, http://nationalinterest.org/feature/russia-returns-afghanistan-19040; Usman Sharifi and Sajjad Tarakzai, "Russia and Iran Ties with Taliban Stoking Afghanistan Anxiety," Yahoo! News, December 30, 2016, https://www.yahoo.com/news/russia-iran-ties-taliban-stoke-afghan-anxiety-040857785.html; Nick Paton Walsh and Masoud Popalzai, "Videos Suggest Russian Government May be Arming Taliban," CNN, July 25, 2017, http://cnn.com/2017/07/25/asia/taliban-weapons-afghanistan/index.html; Jared Keller "CNN Crashes And Burns With 'Exclusive' Report On Russia Arming The Taliban," Task and Purpose, July 27, 2017, http://taskandpurpose.com/cnn-russia-taliban-weapons/.

[263] "Russia Denies Supplying Taliban After NATO Claim," *News International*, March 24, 2017, https://www.thenews.com.pk/latest/194269-Russia-denies-supplying-Taliban-after-NATO-claim.

[264] "Claims of Russian Assistance Towards the Mujahideen are Baseless," Taliban statement, posted on al Emarah English, April 14, 2017, https://alemarah-english.com/?p=13164.

[265] Idrees Ali and Phil Stewart, "US Official: No Physical Evidence Russia Gave Weapons to Taliban," Reuters, May 23, 2017, https://www.reuters.com/article/us-usa-afghanistan-russia-idUSKBN18J25R.

[266] "US Skips Out on Afghanistan-Taliban Conference in Moscow," Deutsche Welle, April 14, 2017, http://www.dw.com/en/us-skips-out-on-afghanistan-taliban-conference-in-moscow/a-38426486.

groups declaring loyalty to ISIS.[267] In any case, the Afghan, Pakistani and Indian governments actually agreed that U.S. participation in the talks was essential. The Taliban echoed the Trump administration, telling the Voice of America that "this meeting stems from political agendas of the countries who are organizing it. This has really nothing to do with us, nor do we support it." The report continued, "The spokesman reiterated insurgents' traditional stance that U.S.-led foreign troops would have to leave Afghanistan before any conflict resolution talks could be initiated."[268]

They certainly seemed to make little progress without the participation of the most powerful players in the game. Though one account of the talks on the Indian website the Wire seemed to reveal a completely intractable situation where, even if all sides within Afghanistan and all their foreign backers truly wanted peace and a fair deal for all, they could never agree to a common vision in a hundred years.[269]

For one example, China and Pakistan are extremely worried about India's gains and designs on Afghanistan and vice-versa.[270] Just as China has supported the Afghan mujahideen against India's allies in Afghanistan in the 1980s, in the 1990s and very early 2000s, India and the U.S. have both trained and supported Muslim Uighur fighters in Afghanistan for use against the government in the Western Chinese Xinjiang Province — possibly some of the same men who were later detained in Guantánamo Bay prison.[271] These facts can perhaps serve as reminders that the problems of Afghanistan cannot be solved by American intervention. All of America's friends and adversaries on all sides of this war have their own interests, issues and history that will be worked out much faster when the 800-pound American gorilla is no longer tilting the scales and determining unsustainable outcomes.

But that's not what the administration believes. Lisa Curtis, a former CIA analyst and scholar at the conservative Heritage Foundation, and her co-author, former Pakistani ambassador to the U.S., Husain Haqqani, wrote a paper just after the Trump presidency began making the case that

---

[267] Dan Simpson, "Vietnam Redux?," *Pittsburgh Post-Gazette*, February 23, 2016, http://www.post-gazette.com/opinion/columnists/2016/02/24/Dan-Simpson-Vietnam-redux/stories/201602230025.

[268] Ayuz Gul, "Afghan Taliban Declines to Support Moscow-Backed Peace Talks," Voice of America News, April 13, 2017, http://www.voanews.com/a/afghan-taliban-declines-to-support-moscow-backed-peace-talks/3808505.html.

[269] Devirupa Mitra, "At Russia-Led Regional Talks, Afghanistan Says Talks with Taliban Can Only Be Held on Its Soil," Wire (India), April 15, 2017, https://thewire.in/124530/afghanistan-taliban-talks-russia/.

[270] "Pakistan Fears Indian Influence in Afghanistan, May Rope in China to Balance New Delhi's Sway: US Intel," First Post, May 29, 2017, http://www.firstpost.com/world/pakistan-fears-indian-influence-in-afghanistan-may-rope-in-china-to-balance-new-delhis-sway-us-intel-3492929.html.

[271] Eric Margolis, interviewed by the author, *Scott Horton Show*, radio archive, March 25, 2008, https://scotthorton.org/interviews/antiwar-radio-eric-margolis-3/.

the Obama government's attempts to encourage the Pakistanis to cease their support for the Afghan Taliban, Haqqani Network and other insurgent groups with increased aid and high-level talks had failed. Instead, they recommended, it was time to get tough.[272] As a result, Curtis was hired by Lt. Gen. McMaster to be senior director for South and Central Asia on the National Security Council at the White House where she could help to shape the new strategy.[273]

But none of the relatively mild measures the authors propose in their paper would seem to be enough to convince the Pakistanis to abandon their primary national interest in keeping friendly forces in play in Afghanistan. Curtis and Haqqani write that if the Pakistanis refuse to cease support for the Afghan Taliban, Haqqani Network and other Afghan insurgent groups or intervene in any possible talks between the U.S. and the Taliban in an attempt to secure their interests, the U.S. should threaten to cut off military aid and revoke Pakistan's status as a "Major Non-NATO Ally" (MNNA). They further suggest that certain individual Pakistani military officers could be banned from traveling to the United States. Additionally, the administration could threaten to begin a new drone war against Afghan Taliban targets inside Pakistan, withhold aid money and, eventually, even designate them a state sponsor of terrorism. If all that does not work, Curtis and Haqqani suggest asking China to pressure them on our behalf.

The fact that Pakistan has a core national security interest in continuing to support these groups is barely raised, and then only to be dismissed without proper context or argument. American interests, they write, are not "fully compatible" with Pakistani "desires to … counter India's role" in Afghanistan. But why would China pressure Pakistan for the U.S. when the reason the U.S. supports India is to balance against China in the first place? The authors write that if, as a result of these actions, the U.S. predictably pushes Pakistan into a deeper alliance with China, it would still have been worth a try: "In any case, Washington's policy should not be constrained by fear that other countries will displace the U.S. role in Pakistan."

It seems as though Mattis began implementing Curtis's plan before Trump announced the new strategy in August. In late July, Mattis said the U.S. would be withholding $50 million in military aid to Pakistan as punishment for their continued support for the Afghan insurgency.[274]

---

[272] Husain Haqqani and Lisa Curtis, "A New US Approach to Pakistan: Enforcing Aid Conditions without Cutting Ties," Hudson Institute, February 6, 2017, https://hudson.org/research/13305-a-new-u-s-approach-to-pakistan-enforcing-aid-conditions-without-cutting-ties.

[273] Mark Perry, interviewed by the author, *Scott Horton Show*, radio archive, July 19, 2017, https://scotthorton.org/71917-mark-perry/.

[274] Carla Babb, "Pentagon Withholds $50 Million in Pakistan Military Aid," Voice of America, July

When the Obama administration did the same in 2016, it apparently did not achieve the desired result. The administration has also said they are considering increasing support for an Indian role in "providing stability" in Afghanistan as part of their broader strategy.[275] As part of Trump's speech announcing that he was finally adopting Mattis and McMaster's strategy, the president invoked America's trade relationship with India, seemingly demanding further intervention on their part, while at the same time insisting that Pakistan cease all support for the Afghan insurgency.[276] Rather than solve any problems, these types of actions are more likely to only push the government of Pakistan back toward the military hard-liners' position and increased support for the Afghan Taliban and Haqqanis.[277]

Despite the administration and Pentagon's repeated statements that only a political, diplomatic solution could solve the Afghan crisis, in June 2017, Secretary Mattis quite clearly dismissed the idea of a deal with the Taliban. He based this not on the reality that the insurgents are winning and feel no pressure to give in to American demands, but on the completely false claim that the insurgents have no legitimacy among the local population — like the U.S. apparently has — and so America's war must continue on behalf of the Afghan people:

> We're up against an enemy that knows that they cannot win at the ballot box, and you think — we have to sometimes remind ourselves of that reality. That's why they use bombs, because ballots would ensure they never had a role to play, and based upon that foundation, that they cannot win the support, the affection, the respect of the Afghan people. We will stand by them. They've had a long, hard fight … and the fight goes on. But the bottom line is we're not going to surrender civilization to people who cannot win at the ballot box.[278]

With this statement, Mattis is apparently ruling out the very "negotiated settlement" his colleagues all say is the only solution to the violent conflict. At least he's honest. Can anyone imagine the U.S. or, for that matter, the other major political and ethnic factions that control the government in

---

21, 2017, https://www.voanews.com/a/pentagon-withholds-50-million-in-pakistan-military-aid/3954665.html.

[275] "US Looking into Potential Role of India in Afghanistan, says Daniel Coats," Financial Express, July 25, 2017, http://www.financialexpress.com/india-news/us-looking-into-potential-role-of-india-in-afghanistan-says-daniel-coats/777685/.

[276] "Full Transcript: Donald Trump Announces His Afghanistan Policy," Defense One, August 22, 2017, http://www.defenseone.com/politics/2017/08/full-transcript-donald-trump-announces-his-afghanistan-policy/140414/.

[277] Adam Weinstein, "Washington's Big Mistake in Isolating Pakistan," Daily Times, July 16, 2017, http://dailytimes.com.pk/opinion/16-Jul-17/washingtons-big-mistake-in-isolating-pakistan.

[278] "Press Availability with Secretary of Defense James Mattis, Australian Foreign Minister Julie Bishop, and Australian Defense Minister Marise Payne," delivered in Sydney, Australia, June 5, 2017, https://www.state.gov/secretary/remarks/2017/06/271571.htm.

the capital making a deal to bring the Taliban, or any of the other major insurgent groups, into a power-sharing arrangement with Kabul at this point? Could the current form of the government survive such a deal? When American politicians and policymakers do invoke a future "diplomatic solution" to Afghanistan's problems, they almost never elaborate about what they imagine that would look like and often seem to imply a belief in the same old policy that by building up the civilian government and police of the country, they will somehow win over the people and make the insurgency obsolete, driving it out of existence.[279] Some, like former Special Representative Miller, push for an honest compromise, but this is wishful thinking. As she concedes, "the tools for implementing these kinds of policies do not change. No one has any new, quick fixes that people before failed to consider."[280]

In mid-July, months after the review was supposed to have been complete, Secretary Mattis announced that the administration was kicking the can down the road on the troop decision yet again. It later became clear that Trump was still not convinced to go ahead. The July 19 Principals Committee meeting had turned into a "shit show," where "words were exchanged," and President Trump refused to sign off on the plan the rest of the National Security Council had approved[281] and repeatedly suggested that Mattis fire Gen. Nicholson.[282] The president publicly expressed more doubts in McMaster's strategy when he explained that he had brought some Afghan war vets to the White House to "find out why we've been there for 17 years," and refused to commit beyond "we'll see," in response to a reporter's question about the pending escalation.[283] In fact, at the very end of July, the *Wall Street Journal* reported that Trump was considering his political advisers' minimal strategy of withdrawal of all but special operations forces and drones for a "limited counter-terrorism strategy." A senior administration official told the *Journal* that full-scale nation-building "doesn't work unless we are there for a long time, and if we don't have the appetite to be there a long time, we should just leave."[284]

---

[279] Victoria McGrane, "After Afghan Trip, Elizabeth Warren Calls for Broader Strategy," *Boston Globe*, July 4, 2017, https://www.bostonglobe.com/news/nation/2017/07/04/after-afghan-trip-elizabeth-warren-calls-for-broader-strategy/N4WwOV2GUDJPkK6dzoaBYO/story.html.

[280] Sean Illing, "America's Former Envoy to Afghanistan Says the War Can't be Won," Vox, August 1, 2017, https://www.vox.com/world/2017/8/1/16049272/afghanistan-donald-trump-mineral-deposits-imperialism.

[281] Susan B. Glasser, "The Trump White House's War Within."

[282] Carol E. Lee and Courtney Kube, "Trump Says US 'Losing' Afghan War in Tense Meeting with Generals," NBC News, August 2, 2017, http://www.nbcnews.com/news/us-news/trump-says-u-s-losing-afghan-war-tense-meeting-generals-n789006.

[283] Susan B. Glasser, "The Trump White House's War Within."

[284] Dion Nissenbaum, "White House Looks at Scaling Back US Military Presence in Afghanistan,"

Though Trump tried to pass the buck by authorizing the secretary of defense to raise troop levels by up to 5,000,[285] Mattis decided to wait to deploy them until after the new strategy was approved.[286] In the end, the pressure on the president to escalate was intense enough, and his instincts already hawkish enough, that Trump finally, despite his obvious misgivings, gave in and signed off on an initial increase of about 4,000 additional troops and the larger regional strategy proposed by the military.[287] It is remarkable that Trump put up as much resistance as he did. In the end though, he rolled over for the military just as Obama had done before him. Trump announced the new plan on August 21, in a speech invoking no good reason to fight, just safe-haven myths and sunk cost fallacies.[288] Seeming to entirely adopt McMaster's narrative of the reasons for the failure of Obama's "surge," Trump said that the U.S. would no longer have timetables of any kind since that would be equivalent to announcing to the insurgency in advance what our plans are so they can wait us out. Instead the U.S.'s help for the Afghan government would be "conditions-based," meaning, on the face of it, that the U.S. can never withdraw, since the conditions under which they have deemed it proper to do so have already been proven unattainable. Meanwhile, the Taliban-based insurgency has nothing but time. This change in semantics means nothing to them, as they made clear in their response to Trump's speech.[289]

The president also seemed to accept McMaster's line on negotiations with the insurgency, saying, "nobody knows if or when that will ever happen." Instead, Trump promised a "clear definition" of "victory," and then went on not to describe an end-state of any kind, but instead simply gave a list of ever-present tense "-i n g words," amounting to not much more than slogans: "attacking our enemies, obliterating ISIS, crushing al Qaeda, preventing the Taliban from taking over the country, and stopping mass terror attacks against Americans before they emerge" — in other words, the new strategy is the same strategy in place since the end of the

---

Wall Street Journal, July 30, 2017, https://www.wsj.com/articles/white-house-looks-at-scaling-back-u-s-military-presence-in-afghanistan-1501426803.

[285] Joe Gould, "Mattis: Trump Authorized Military to Set Troop Levels in Afghanistan," Defense News, June 14, 2017, https://defensenews.com/congress/2017/06/14/mattis-trump-authorized-military-to-set-troop-levels-in-afghanistan/.

[286] Michael Callahan et al., "Mattis on Afghanistan Troops Decision: 'We are Working to Get It Right,'" CNN, July 21, 2017, http://www.cnn.com/2017/07/21/politics/mattis-trump-afghanistan-strategy/index.html.

[287] "Trump Approves Sending 4,000 More Troops to Afghanistan, Senior Official Says," Fox News, August 21, 2017, http://www.foxnews.com/politics/2017/08/21/trump-approves-sending-4000-more-troops-to-afghanistan-senior-official-says.html.

[288] "Full Transcript: Donald Trump Announces His Afghanistan Policy," Defense One.

[289] Mushtaq Yusufzai et al., "Afghan Taliban 'Happy to Continue' War After Trump Vows Victory," NBC News, August 22, 2017, https://www.nbcnews.com/news/world/afghan-taliban-happy-continue-war-after-trump-vows-victory-n794776.

"surge" in 2012: just hold the line a while longer.

The endlessly threatened return of al Qaeda has not taken place, though as far as the local Pashtun insurgency is concerned, Gen. McChrystal's old "insurgent math" still applies. The more people the U.S. kills, the more fighters join the ranks of their enemies. So increasing American troop strength is far more likely to make matters worse by driving a whole new generation of young men into the insurgency to oppose it. This is especially true considering that Trump has also ordered the loosening of the military's rules of engagement in the conflict.[290] This may protect him from criticism that during his term he did not allow the army to do its best job fighting, but in the end will probably make their task even more difficult. The Afghan National Army continues to be a dysfunctional, corrupt and ineffective force, who provoke more resistance wherever they go as well.

Trump had been right to resist the military's insistence on escalation. But short of ending the war, it would seem to make little difference either way. After all, even if the president gave the generals full authority to escalate troop levels back up to 100,000, what difference could they make in terms of accomplishing U.S. objectives? At the height of Obama's troop "surge," there were more than 100,000 soldiers, marines and special operators in the country, along with another 40,000 troops from NATO coalition countries. Their goal of "clearing, holding, building and transferring" the predominantly Pashtun south to the rule of the central government in Kabul was not achieved. Democracy has not taken root, as shown by the disastrous elections of 2009 and 2014. Nor was the U.S. able to force the Taliban to negotiate, even at the height of the last escalation, as Gen. Petraeus assured us he would. Is holding Bagram Air Base, bombing Nangarhar and Helmand and sending checks to Kabul the Pentagon's long-term plan?

Better would be to just call the whole thing off.

Come Home

The occupation of Afghanistan is not just America's longest foreign war. It may also have the distinction of being both the least supported[291] and least opposed[292] war in our history.

---

[290] "Full Transcript: Donald Trump Announces His Afghanistan Policy," Defense One.

[291] Steven Shepard, "Trump's Challenge: A Wall of Public Skepticism on Afghanistan War," Politico, August 21, 2017, http://www.politico.com/story/2017/08/21/trump-afghanistan-war-troops-241871.

[292] "Most Important Problem," Gallup Poll, May 2017, http://www.gallup.com/poll/1675/most-important-problem.aspx.

Regardless, the permanent war system in Washington, D.C., is like a big snowball rolling downhill. The incentives are all set up for the war to continue forever. A major part of this is policymakers' fear of being accused of being soft on terrorism or weak on protecting the security of the American people. Doing something must always be preferable to doing nothing, even when doing something is not working. Barack Obama and Hillary Clinton's political careers certainly have demonstrated the way this dynamic is particularly strong when it comes to Democratic leaders in power, since they are thought to be the less-hawkish of the two parties. The pressure on Hillary Clinton in Washington to prove how tough she was ended up costing her support among the general public in the election of 2016,[293] where seemingly counter-intuitively, the Republican candidate took a somewhat softer line on at least some foreign policy issues. More importantly, Trump turned Clinton's hawkishness against her, characterizing her as reckless "Trigger-happy Hillary" and threatened more chaos and a worsening refugee crisis were she to win.

The fact that the American people are tired enough of war that it caused Hillary's hawkishness to undermine, rather than bolster, her support also highlights the opportunity that Trump could still have to make peace. As they used to say, "Only Nixon could go to China." If a Democratic president had gone to China to end that part of the Cold War, as Nixon did in 1972, Nixon himself would have red-baited them, or at least implied they were soft on defense against communism. But when Nixon, a Republican and well-known anti-Communist, made the trip, it went without saying: the president is doing this because he's smart; because he decided that the time had come to make peace. His move was not interpreted as weakness or a blunder somehow benefiting the Communist bloc, but instead was an ingenious plan to break it for the patriotic good of America's security interests. This decision by Nixon, like his détente with the Soviet Union at around the same time, has gone down in history as a brave and brilliant move by an otherwise infamous president to make a major step forward for peace. The same dynamic was at play when the governments of Ronald Reagan and George Bush Sr. negotiated a final end of the Cold War with the USSR 17 years later, and for that matter, when George W. Bush ran for president promising to back down from the dangerous interventions of the Bill Clinton years and adopt a "more humble foreign policy" in 2000.

---

[293] Douglas L. Kriner and Francis X. Shen, "Battlefield Casualties and BallotBox Defeat: Did the Bush-Obama Wars Cost Clinton the White House?" Social Science Research Network, June 19, 2017, https://papers.ssrn.com/sol3/papers.cfm?abstract_id=2989040; Asma Khalid and Joel Rose, "Millennials Just Didn't Love Hillary Clinton the Way They Loved Barack Obama," National Public Radio, November 14, 2016, http://www.npr.org/2016/11/14/501727488/millennials-just-didnt-love-hillary-clinton-the-way-they-loved-barack-obama.

This is why Trump was able to characterize Clinton's "toughness" as highly risky and reckless, turning her hawkishness into a national security liability instead of an asset, and his presumed reluctance to be not weakness, but characteristic of his superior understanding of the limits and proper uses of U.S. power. In other words, like other Republican politicians, Trump can afford to be peaceful. Where a Democrat like Obama must spend all of his political capital to temporarily withdraw from Iraq or make a nuclear inspection agreement with Iran, a Republican — particularly one seen as very nationalistic, as President Trump is — should be able to cut deals and make peace wherever he wishes and only gain politically from doing so. There is no real faction of prominence to the right of President Trump in a position to try to attack him and his national security cabinet as being anything less than patriotic Americans or as wimps and pushovers who would turn and run from an enemy, as Republicans might do to a Democratic president in the same position.

What the Trump administration could do, rather than concede defeat, is simply announce a change in priorities to a real America First foreign policy in regard to Afghanistan: declare that the Pashtun militiamen of that poor country are no longer our enemy and the Bush-Obama government in Kabul is no longer our responsibility — loose ends be damned. They cannot be tied up at a reasonable price, if any. It would be wrong to ask more young people to kill and die, and more mothers and fathers to lose them, for a mission that was ill-conceived from the start. Remaking Afghanistan is impossible. Fighting there does not prevent terrorism, but provokes it. America's true national interests lie far from Central Asia. Invasion, regime change, occupation and disruption across the so-called Muslim World is no way to fight terrorism. Not anymore. The best way to prevent terrorism is to cease intervention. It is time to return to peace, to return to normalcy. It is time to just come home.

If the Taliban took all of Afghanistan, the U.S. still only has nothing to lose but face. But why should Donald Trump worry about that? This president is known for changing his positions regularly. In fact, it was reported that his military advisers were afraid that Trump would change his mind between the time he approved the new strategy at their meeting at Camp David and time he announced the plan two days later.[294] Though he has missed his first opportunity to separate his Afghan policy from his predecessors', Trump could still turn around and correctly place the blame for their failures on the previous administrations and make a clean break with the past. Just as when President Obama was in the same situation in 2009, we know that Trump knows better than to continue waging this

---

[294] Kimberly Dozier and Spencer Ackerman, "Team Trump Worried He'll Change His Mind Again on Afghanistan War Plan," August 21, 2017, Daily Beast, http://www.thedailybeast.com/team-trump-worried-hell-change-his-mind-again-on-afghanistan-war-plan.

disastrous war. But the American people will ultimately have to force the issue and create an overwhelming demand for complete withdrawal from Afghanistan, ideally before the new escalation makes things there much worse.

In 2009 when Obama was deciding on Petraeus and McChrystal's "surge," virtually all of the political pressure was coming from the Pentagon, Republicans in Congress and the media. The American people remained opposed, by and large, and yet the rank and file of the Republican Party were pro-military enough that they did not object too strongly to the mission, while members of the Democratic Party were too infatuated with the new president to oppose it. So, politically speaking, it seemed there was no real downside to the escalation since "the people" had mostly fallen silent on the issue.

But in the summer of 2013, when the Obama government was threatening airstrikes against the Bashar al-Assad government in Damascus, Syria, in response to its alleged use of chemical weapons, virtually the entire American public rose up to demand that Congress stop him. The massive audiences of American conservative talk radio found common cause with liberal, left and libertarian groups of every description. Republican and Democratic representatives and senators were deluged with negative calls and letters, and people turned out in large numbers to various town halls and meetings across the country. The people made their voices heard — and they won. The escalation of American intervention in Syria at that point was stopped in its tracks. It truly was a remarkable victory for the antiwar movement and average citizens of all parties over Washington, D.C.'s consensus for more war.[295]

So it is possible for the American people to have their way, even on issues of foreign policy, which are usually left to the so-called experts to decide.

If the Trump administration could be certain that the American people were overwhelmingly opposed to the war[296] and that we would stand by his decision if and when he ordered the generals to pack it up and come home, it would, at least theoretically, give him a context in which it would make political sense to do so.

[295] John Harwood, "House Republicans Say Voters Oppose Intervention," New York Times, September 6, 2013, http://www.nytimes.com/2013/09/07/us/politics/house-republicans-say-constituents-are-strongly-opposed-to-a-syria-strike.html; Kevin Liptak, "McCain Gets an Earful from Voters on Syria," CNN, September 5, 2013, http://politicalticker.blogs.cnn.com/2013/09/05/mccain-gets-an-earful-from-voters-on-syria/; "The Hill's Syria Whip List: Obama Seeks to Turn Tide with House, Public," Hill, September 9, 2013, http://thehill.com/homenews/administration/319933-the-hills-syria-whip-list.
[296] Contact the White House, U.S. House of Representatives and U.S. Senate here https://www.whitehouse.gov/contact/write-or-call; http://www.house.gov/representatives/; https://www.senate.gov/.

There are many important issues that face and divide the American people. But so many of these problems — economic cronyism, disruption and hardship, deepening enmity between those of left and right cultural and political distinctions, and the growth of government police power at the expense of so many of our natural and civil rights and liberties — have, at their root, America's permanent war system and the demands it makes on society to perpetuate itself at the expense of the people and our way of life.

It does not have to be this way.

Americans must prioritize opposition to the destructive war in Afghanistan and work together to end it now.

Acknowledgments

Thanks to Eric Garris, Gareth Porter, Grant F. Smith, Anand Gopal, Eric Margolis, Jeffrey Kaye, Anthony Gregory, Ramzy Baroud, Anne Frost, Damon Hatheway, Phil Brown, Jonathan Koop, Adam McDonald, Nico Palomino, Mike Dworski, James Reilly, Harley Abbott, Noah Pugsley, Matthew Hampton, "Mr. Ivan Johnson," Robert Blumen, Mike Swanson, Tim Frey, Rick McGinnis and all my great guests, listeners, advertisers, volunteers and supporters over the years.

About the Author

Scott Horton is managing director of The Libertarian Institute at LibertarianInstitute.org, host of *Antiwar Radio* for Pacifica, 90.7 FM KPFK in Los Angeles and 88.3 FM KUCR in Riverside, California, host of the *Scott Horton Show* podcast from ScottHorton.org and the opinion editor of Antiwar.com. Horton has conducted more than 4,500 interviews since 2003. He lives in Austin, Texas with his wife, investigative reporter Larisa Alexandrovna Horton.

To listen to *Antiwar Radio*, tune in to KPFK 90.7 FM, Pacifica, in the Los Angeles area at 8:30 am Pacific Time Sundays, http://kpfk.org. You may also subscribe to the podcast feed of the radio shows on Scott's website, on iTunes at http://apple.co/2u66y3E or listen on Stitcher at https://www.stitcher.com/podcast/the-scott-horton-show.

Appendices

Appendix I: Frequently Used Abbreviations

ANA: Afghan National Army
ANSF: Afghan National Security Forces
ANP: Afghan National Police
CENTCOM: Central Command
CIA: Central Intelligence Agency
COIN: Counterinsurgency doctrine
COINdinistas: People who make coin selling COIN
DOD: Department of Defense
EKIA: Enemy Killed in Action
HVT: High-Value Target
IS, ISIS: The Islamic State in Iraq and Syria
ISKP (ISIS-K): Islamic State Khorasan Province
ISAF: International Security Assistance Force
ISI: Pakistani Inter-Service Intelligence
JSOC: Joint Special Operations Command
MAM: Military Aged Male
NATO: North Atlantic Treaty Organization
NGO: Non-Governmental Organization
SIGAR: Special Inspector General for Afghanistan Reconstruction
UBL: Osama (Usama) bin Laden
USAID: United States Agency for International Development
USFOR-A: U.S. Forces-Afghanistan

Appendix II: Cast of Characters

Al Qaeda (alphabetical by last name)
Mohammed Atta: lead hijacker, leader of September 11th plot in the U.S.
Anwar al Awlaki: American al Qaeda propagandist, killed in drone strike in Yemen in 2011.
Abdullah Yusuf Azzam: founder "Afghanistan Services Bureau."
Omar bin Laden: Osama's non-terrorist son.
Osama bin Laden: former leader of al Qaeda (1990s-2011).
Khalid Sheikh Mohammed (KSM): Ramzi Yousef's uncle; ringleader, September 11th plot.
Abdul Hakim Murad: Yousef's associate.
Mohammad al-Qahtani: would-be 20th hijacker, denied entry to U.S., tortured at Guantánamo.
Omar Abdel Rahman, "The Blind Sheik": leader Egyptian Islamic Jihad.
Ahmad Salem: FBI informant.
Wali Khan Amin Shah: Yousef's associate.
Ramzi bin al Shibh: Atta's friend, helped plan September 11th attacks.
Ramzi Yousef: bomb maker, WTC 1993, ringleader "Bojinka" plots.
Abu Musab al Zarqawi: former leader of al Qaeda in Iraq.
Ayman al Zawahiri: current leader of al Qaeda (2011–).
Abu Zubaydah: accused, tortured, but actually not a member of al Qaeda.

ISIS
Abu Bakr al-Baghdadi, a.k.a. Caliph Ibrahim: ruler of Islamic State/leader of ISIS (2014–).

Afghan Taliban (alphabetical by last name)
Mullah Haibatullah Akhundzada: current Taliban Leader.
Mullah Mohamed al Mansour: former Taliban Leader.
Wakil Ahmed Muttawakil: former Foreign Minister.
Mullah Omar: former Taliban Leader.

Afghan Mujahideen/Warlords (alphabetical by last name)
Rashid Dostum
Mohammed Fahim
Abdul Haq
Mawlawi Jalaluddin Haqqani
Sirajuddin Haqqani

Gulbuddin Hekmatyar
Ahmed Wali Karzai (AWK)
Jan Muhammad Khan (JMK)
Ahmad Shah Massoud
Abdul Razzik
Pacha Khan Zadran (PKZ)
Hajji Zaman

Regional Politicians (alphabetical by last name)
Abdullah Abdullah: Chief Executive Officer of Afghanistan (2015–).
Ashraf Ghani: president of Afghanistan (2015–).
Saddam Hussein: former dictator of Iraq (1979–2003).
Hamid Karzai: former president of Afghanistan (2001–2015).
Ruhollah Khomeini: former supreme leader of Iran (1979–1989).
Pervez Musharraf: former dictator of Pakistan (2001–2008).
Jaber Al-Ahmad Al-Sabah: former king of Kuwait (1977–2006).
Fahd bin Abdulaziz Al Saud: former king of Saudi Arabia (1982–2005).

U.S. Politicians, Generals, Intelligence Officers, Journalists

Presidents (in chronological order)
Jimmy Carter
Ronald Reagan
George H. W. Bush
Bill Clinton
George W. Bush
Barack Obama
Donald Trump

Secretaries of Defense (in chronological order)
Dick Cheney (H. W. Bush)
Donald Rumsfeld (W. Bush)
Robert Gates (W. Bush, Obama)
Leon Panetta (Obama)
Ashton Carter (Obama)
James Mattis (Trump)

Secretaries of State (in chronological order)
Madeleine Albright (Clinton)
Colin Powell (W. Bush)
Condoleezza Rice (W. Bush)
Hillary Clinton (Obama)
John Kerry (Obama)

National Security Advisors (in chronological order)
Zbigniew Brzezinski (Carter)
Gen. Jim Jones (Obama)
H. R. McMaster (Trump)

U.S. House of Representatives
Rep. Ron Paul (R-Texas)

U.S. Senate
Sen. Lindsey Graham (R-South Carolina)
Sen. John McCain (R-Arizona)

Selected Military Leaders (alphabetical by last name)
James Cartwright: presented minimal escalation plan to Obama.
Karl Eikenberry: after leading Afghan war became Ambassador to Afghanistan, COIN dissenter.
Michael Flynn: McChrystal's deputy in Iraq and Afghan wars, Trump's first National Security Advisor.
Tommy Franks: botched the initial war.
Jack Keane: major force behind Iraq, Afghan "surges."
James Mattis: Marine Corps general in initial war, current Secretary of Defense, decided 2017 escalation.
Stanley McChrystal: Obama's first "surge" general, dropped COIN after Marjah failure.
David McKiernan: fired by Gates so he could re-start troop request.
H. R. McMaster: Petraeus protégé, part of Obama "surge," current National Security Advisor, pushed for current "surge."
Mike Mullen: as Chairman of the Joint Chiefs of Staff, tried to prevent Vice-Chairman Cartwright from presenting minimalist plan to Obama.
John Nicholson: current general in charge of Afghan war, requested 2017 escalation.
David Petraeus: escalated, lost Afghan war, hailed as genius.
Joseph Votel: current commander of CENTCOM.

State, Defense Department Whistleblowers, Dissenters (alphabetical by last name)
Daniel L. Davis: whistleblower during the "surge," in 2012.
Gian Gentile: author of articles, book dissenting from COIN doctrine.
Matthew Hoh: whistleblower before the "surge," in 2009.
Anthony Walker: witnessed war crimes in 2008 and 2009.

CIA (alphabetical by last name)
Gary Berntsen: second commander in charge in Afghanistan, began Tora Bora fight.
Henry Crumpton: commander of initial invasion based in U.S.
Robert Grenier: Islamabad Station Chief during initial war.
Leon Panetta: Obama's first CIA director.
David Petraeus: as CIA director, reviewed his own performance as general.
Bruce Riedel: retired officer, did Afghan policy review for Obama government.

Neoconservatives (alphabetical by last name)
Zalmay Khalilzad: helped pick Hamid Karzai for interim president, later Ambassador to Afghanistan.
Laurie Mylroie: promoter of "Saddam Hussein backs bin Laden" theory.
Richard Perle: promoter of Mylroie's "Saddam Hussein backs bin Laden" theory.
Paul Wolfowitz: Deputy Secretary of Defense under W. Bush.

Highly Cited Journalists (alphabetical by last name)
Matthieu Aikins
Abdel Bari Atwan
Andrew Cockburn
Patrick Cockburn
Alan Cullison
Bette Dam
Anand Gopal
Michael Hastings
Ann Jones
Sebastian Junger
Felix Kuehn
Frank Ledwidge
Alex Strick van Linschoten
Jean MacKenzie
Eric Margolis
Gareth Porter
Ahmed Rashid
Jeremy Scahill
Astri Suhrke

Appendix III: Selected Readings on U.S. Torture

Akinyode, Funmi, Jason Leopold and Ky Henderson. "Unmasked: CIA Officially Identifies Architects of Its Post-9/11 Torture Program." Vice. November 7, 2016. https://news.vice.com/story/james-mitchell-bruce-jessen-cia-torture-program.

Apuzzo, Matt, and Sheri Fink. "Secret Documents Show a Tortured Prisoner's Descent." *New York Times.* November 12, 2016. https://www.nytimes.com/interactive/2016/10/17/world/cia-torture-guantanamo-bay.html.

Apuzzo, Matt, Sheri Fink and James Risen. "How US Torture Left a Legacy of Damaged Minds." *New York Times.* October 9, 2016. https://www.nytimes.com/2016/10/09/world/cia-torture-guantanamo-bay.html.

Boumediene, Lakhdar and Mustafa Ait Idir. *Witnesses of the Unseen: Seven Years in Guantanamo.* Stanford: Redwood, 2017

Carle, Glenn L. *The Interrogator: An Education.* New York: Nation, 2011.

Clark, Kate. "Kafka in Cuba: The Afghan Experience in Guantánamo." Afghanistan Analysts Network. November 2016. https://www.afghanistan-analysts.org/wp-content/uploads/2016/11/20161101-Kafka-final-ES-SV.pdf.

Camerino, Tony [Matthew Alexander], and John R. Bruning. *How to Break a Terrorist: The U.S. Interrogators Who Used Brains, Not Brutality, to Take Down the Deadliest Man in Iraq.* New York: Free, 2008.

Eviatar, Daphne. "Detained and Denied in Afghanistan." Human Rights First. May 2011. https://www.humanrightsfirst.org/wp-content/uploads/pdf/Detained-Denied-in-Afghanistan.pdf.

Fink, Sheri. "Where Even Nightmares Are Classified: Psychiatric Care at Guantánamo." *New York Times.* November 12, 2016. https://www.nytimes.com/2016/11/13/world/guantanamo-bay-doctors-abuse.html.

Fink, Sheri and James Risen. "Psychologists Open a Window on Brutal CIA Interrogations." *New York Times.* June 21, 2017. https://www.nytimes.com/interactive/2017/06/20/us/cia-torture.html.

Gordon, Rebecca. *American Nuremberg: The U.S. Officials Who Should Stand Trial for Post-9/11 War Crimes.* New York: Hot, 2016.

Grey, Stephen. *Ghost Plane: The True Story of the CIA Rendition and Torture Program*. New York: St. Martin's, 2006.

Hersh, Seymour M. *Chain of Command: The Road from 9/11 to Abu Ghraib*. New York: Harper Perennial, 2005.

————. "The Gray Zone." *New Yorker*. May 24, 2004. http://www.newyorker.com/magazine/2004/05/24/the-gray-zone.

————. "Torture at Abu Ghraib." *New Yorker*. May 10, 2004. http://www.newyorker.com/magazine/2004/05/10/torture-at-abu-ghraib.

Hickman, Joseph. *Murder at Camp Delta: A Staff Sergeant's Pursuit of the Truth About Guantánamo Bay*. New York: Simon & Schuster, 2015.

Hicks, David. *Guantánamo: My Journey*. New York: Random House, 2012.

Human Rights Watch. "CIA Activities." Landing page for articles related to the CIA. https://www.hrw.org/topic/terrorism/counterterrorism/cia-activities.

Impey, Joanna, and Deutsche Welle. "Guantánamo Inmate Claims He Underwent Medical Experiments." *Deutsche Welle*. March 3, 2011. http://www.dw.com/en/guantanamo-inmate-claims-he-underwent-medical-experiments/a-14887255.

International Committee of the Red Cross. "ICRC Report on the Treatment of Fourteen 'High Value Detainees' in CIA Custody." February 2007. http://www.nybooks.com/media/doc/2010/04/22/icrc-report.pdf.

Kaye, Jeffrey S. *Cover-up at Guantánamo: The NCIS Investigation into the "Suicides" of Mohammed Al Hanashi and Abdul Rahman Al Amri*. Independently published, 2017.

————. "New Revelations Suggest DoD Cover-Up Over Detainee Drugging Charges." Truthout. September 21, 2012. http://www.truth-out.org/news/item/11640-new-revelations-suggest-dod-cover-up-over-detainee-drugging-charges.

Kaye, Jeffrey S., and Jason Leopold. "DoD Report Reveals Some Detainees Interrogated While Drugged, Others 'Chemically Restrained.'" Truthout. July 11, 2012. http://www.truth-out.org/news/item/10248-exclusive-department-of-defense-declassifies-report-on-alleged-drugging-of-detainees.

Klippenstein, Ken, and Joseph Hickman. "CIA Documents Expose the Failed Torture Methods Used on Guantánamo's Most Famous Detainee." AlterNet. May 15, 2017. http://www.alternet.org/grayzone-project/failed-torture-guantanamo.

Kurnaz, Murat. *Five Years of My Life: An Innocent Man in Guantánamo*. New York: St. Martin's, 2008.

Leopold, Jason. "Revealed: Senate Report Contains New Details on CIA Black Sites." Al Jazeera. April 9, 2014. http://america.aljazeera.com/articles/2014/4/9/senate-cia-torture.html.

Leopold, Jason, and Jeffrey Kaye. "CIA Psychologist's Notes Reveal True Purpose Behind Bush's Torture Program." Truthout. March 22, 2011. http://www.truth-out.org/news/item/205-exclusive-cia-psychologists-notes-reveal-true-purpose-behind-bushs-torture-program.

Mayer, Jane. *The Dark Side: The Inside Story of How the War on Terror Turned into a War on American Ideals*. Norwell, MA: Anchor, 2009.

McCoy, Alfred. *A Question of Torture: CIA Interrogation, from the Cold War to the War on Terror*. New York: Metropolitan, 2006.

———. *Torture and Impunity: The U.S. Doctrine of Coercive Interrogation*. Madison, WI: University of Wisconsin Press, 2014.

Otterman, Michael. *American Torture: From the Cold War to Abu Ghraib and Beyond*. London: Pluto, 2008.

Phillips, Joshua E.S. *None of Us Were Like This Before: American Soldiers and Torture*. New York: Verso, 2012.

Pitter, Laura. "US: Ex-Detainees Describe Unreported CIA Torture." Human Rights Watch. October 3, 2016. https://www.hrw.org/news/2016/10/03/us-ex-detainees-describe-unreported-cia-torture.

Richardson, John H. "Acts of Conscience." *Esquire*. September 21, 2009. http://www.esquire.com/news-politics/a879/esq0806terror-102/.

Risen, James, and Bryan Denton. "After Torture, Ex-Detainee Is Still Captive of 'The Darkness.'" *New York Times*. October 12, 2016. https://www.nytimes.com/2016/10/12/world/cia-torture-abuses-detainee.html.

Sands, Philippe. *Torture Team: Rumsfeld's Memo and the Betrayal of American Values*. New York: St. Martin's, 2008.

Savage, Charlie. "CIA Torture Left Scars on Guantánamo Prisoner's Psyche for Years." *New York Times*. March 17, 2017. https://www.nytimes.com/2017/03/17/us/politics/guantanamo-bay-abd-al-rahim-al-nashiri.html.

———. *Takeover: The Return of the Imperial Presidency and the Subversion of American Democracy*. Reprint. New York: Back Bay, 2008.

Somini Sengupta and Marlise Simons. "US Forces May Have Committed War Crimes in Afghanistan, Prosecutor Says." *New York Times*. November 14, 2016. https://www.nytimes.com/2016/11/15/world/asia/united-states-torture-afghanistan-international-criminal-court.html.

Slahi, Mohamedou Ould. *Guantánamo Diary*. Boston: Little, Brown, 2005.

United States Senate Select Committee on Intelligence. "Committee Study of the Central Intelligence Agency's Detention and Interrogation Program." December 3, 2014. https://www.amnestyusa.org/pdfs/sscistudy1.pdf.

Wikileaks. Gitmo Files. https://wikileaks.org/gitmo/.

Worthington, Andy. *The Guantánamo Files: The Stories of the 774 Detainees in America's Illegal Prison*. London: Pluto, 2007.

Yachot, Noa. "Video: CIA Officials Forced to Testify About Torture Program." ACLU. June 21, 2017. https://www.aclu.org/blog/speak-freely/video-cia-officials-forced-testify-about-torture-program.

Appendix IV: Selected Readings on Afghanistan

Atwan, Abdul Bari. *The Secret History of al Qaeda.* Updated ed. Oakland: University of California Press, 2008.

Bacevich, Andrew J. *America's War for the Greater Middle East: A Military History.* New York: Random House, 2016.

Bamford, James. *A Pretext for War: 9/11, Iraq, and the Abuse of America's Intelligence Agencies.* New York: Doubleday, 2004.

Berntsen, Gary, and Ralph Pezzullo. *Jawbreaker: The Attack on Bin Laden and Al-Qaeda; A Personal Account by the CIA's Key Field Commander.* Portland: Broadway, 2006.

Bin Laden, Osama. *Messages to the World: The Statements of Osama Bin Laden.* Edited by Bruce Lawrence. Translated by James Howarth. Annotated, New York: Verso, 2005.

———. *Quotations from Osama Bin Laden.* Edited by Brad K. Berner. Oracle, AZ: Peacock, 2006.

Blum, William. *Freeing the World to Death: Essays on the American Empire.* Monroe, MN: Common Courage, 2004.

Bovard, James. *Attention Deficit Democracy.* New York: Palgrave MacMillan, 2005.

Brzezinski, Zbigniew. *The Grand Chessboard: American Primacy and Its Geostrategic Imperatives.* Lebanon, IN: Basic, 1997.

Clarke, Richard. *Against All Enemies: Inside America's War on Terror.* New York: Free, 2004.

Cockburn, Andrew. *Kill Chain: The Rise of the High-Tech Assassins.* New York: Henry Holt, 2015.

Cockburn, Patrick. *The Age of Jihad: Islamic State and the Great War for the Middle East.* New York: Verso, 2016.

———. *Chaos and Caliphate: Jihadis and the West in the Struggle for the Middle East.* New York: OR Books, 2016.

———. *The Rise of Islamic State: ISIS and the New Sunni Revolution.* Revised ed. New York: Verso, 2015.

Coll, Steve. *The Bin Ladens: An Arabian Family in the American Century.* London: Penguin, 2008.

———. *Ghost Wars: The Secret History of the CIA, Afghanistan, and bin Laden, from the Soviet Invasion to September 10, 2001*. London: Penguin, 2004.

Crile, George. *Charlie Wilson's War: The Extraordinary Story of the Largest Covert Operation in History*. New York: Atlantic Monthly, 2003.

Dreyfuss, Robert. *Devil's Game: How the United States Helped Unleash Fundamentalist Islam*. New York: Henry Holt, 2005.

Esposito, John L., and Dalia Mogahed. *Who Speaks for Islam? What a Billion Muslims Really Think*. Washington, D.C.: Gallup, 2008.

Fairweather, Jack. *The Good War: Why We Couldn't Win the Peace in Afghanistan*. New York: Basic, 2014.

Fury, Dalton [Thomas Greer]. *Kill Bin Laden: A Delta Force Commander's Account of the Hunt for the World's Most Wanted Man*. New York: St. Martin's, 2009.

Gentile, Gian. *Wrong Turn: America's Deadly Embrace of Counterinsurgency*. New York: New, 2013.

Gerges, Fawaz A. *The Far Enemy: Why Jihad Went Global*. 2nd ed. Cambridge: Cambridge University Press, 2009.

Glantz, Aaron, and Anthony Swofford, eds. *Winter Soldier: Iraq and Afghanistan*. Chicago: Haymarket, 2008.

Gopal, Anand. *No Good Men Among the Living: America, the Taliban, and the War through Afghan Eyes*. New York: Metropolitan, 2014.

Gordon, Joy. *Invisible War: The United States and the Iraq Sanctions*. Cambridge, MA: Harvard University Press, 2010.

Gould, Elizabeth, and Paul Fitzgerald. *Crossing Zero: The AfPak War at the Turning Point of American Empire*. San Francisco: City Lights, 2011.

———. *Invisible History: Afghanistan's Untold Story*. San Francisco: City Lights, 2009.

Gall, Carlotta. *The Wrong Enemy: America in Afghanistan 2001–2014*. New York: Houghton Mifflin Harcourt, 2014.

Grenier, Robert L. *88 Days to Kandahar: A CIA Diary*. New York: Simon & Schuster, 2016.

Hastings, Michael. *The Operators: The Wild and Terrifying Inside Story of America's War in Afghanistan*. New York: Blue Rider, 2012.

Horton, Scott (no relation to the author). *Lords of Secrecy: The National Security Elite and America's Stealth Warfare*. New York: Nation, 2015.

Johnson, Chalmers. *Blowback: The Costs and Consequences of American Empire*. New York: Holt, 2004.

———. *Nemesis: The Last Days of the American Republic*. New York: Metropolitan, 2008.

———. *The Sorrows of Empire: Militarism, Secrecy, and the End of the Republic*. New York: Metropolitan, 2004.

———. *Dismantling the Empire: America's Last Best Hope*. New York: Metropolitan, 2010.

Jones, Ann. *Kabul in Winter: Life Without Peace in Afghanistan*, New York: Metropolitan, 2007.

———. *They Were Soldiers: How the Wounded Return from America's Wars: The Untold Story*. Chicago: Haymarket, 2014.

Junger, Sebastian. *War*. New York: Twelve, 2010.

Kinzer, Stephen. *Overthrow: America's Century of Regime Change from Hawaii to Iraq*. New York: Times Books, 2006.

Kolhatkar, Sonali and James Ingalls. *Bleeding Afghanistan: Washington, Warlords and the Propaganda of Silence*. New York: Seven Stories, 2006.

Lance, Peter. *1,000 Years for Revenge: International Terrorism and the FBI—the Untold Story*. New York: William Morrow, 2004.

Lando, Barry M. *Web of Deceit: The History of Western Complicity in Iraq, from Churchill to Kennedy to George W. Bush*. New York: Other, 2007.

Lean, Nathan. *The Islamophobia Industry: How the Right Manufactures Fear of Muslims*. London: Pluto, 2012.

Ledwidge, Frank. *Investment in Blood: The True Cost of Britain's Afghan War*. New Haven, CT: Yale University Press, 2013.

Margolis, Eric S. *American Raj: Liberation or Domination? Resolving the Conflict Between the West and the Muslim World*. Toronto: Key Porter, 2008.

———. *War at the Top of the World: The Struggle for Afghanistan, Kashmir and Tibet*. Oxford: Routledge, 2010.

McDermott, Terry. *Perfect Soldiers: The 9/11 Hijackers: Who They Were, Why They Did It*. New York: Harper Collins, 2009.

Mueller, John. *Overblown: How Politicians and the Terrorism Industry Inflate National Security Threats, and Why We Believe Them*. New York: Free, 2009.

Novinkov, Oleg. *Afghan Boomerang: Notes of a Former Soviet Officer*. Houston: Novinkov, 2011.

O'Connell, Aaron B., ed. *Our Latest Longest War: Losing Hearts and Minds in Afghanistan*. Chicago: University of Chicago Press, 2017.

Pape, Robert A. *Dying to Win: The Strategic Logic of Suicide Terrorism*. New York:

Random House, 2005.

Rashid, Ahmed. *Taliban: Militant Islam, Oil and Fundamentalism in Central Asia.* New Haven, CT: Yale University Press, 2010.

———. *Pakistan on the Brink: The Future of America, Pakistan and Afghanistan.* New York: Penguin, 2012.

Scahill, Jeremy et al. *The Assassination Complex: Inside the Government's Secret Drone Warfare Program.* New York: Simon & Schuster, 2016.

Scheuer, Michael. *Imperial Hubris: Why the West is Losing the War on Terror.* Washington, D.C.: Potomac, 2007.

Shahzad, Syed Saleem. *Inside al Qaeda and the Taliban: Beyond bin Laden and 911.* Chicago: Pluto, 2011.

Soufan, Ali. *The Black Banners: The Inside Story of 9/11 and the War Against al-Qaeda.* New York: W. W. Norton, 2011.

Suhrke, Astri. *When More is Less: The International Project in Afghanistan.* Oxford: Oxford University Press, 2011.

Turse, Nick, ed. *The Case for Withdrawal from Afghanistan.* New York: Verso, 2010.

van Linschoten, Alex Strick, and Felix Kuehn. *An Enemy We Created: The Myth of the Taliban-Al Qaeda Merger in Afghanistan.* Oxford: Oxford University Press, 2012.

Wissing, Douglas A. *Hopeless but Optimistic: Journeying through America's Endless War in Afghanistan.* Bloomington: Indiana University Press, 2016.

———. *Funding the Enemy: How U.S. Taxpayers Bankroll the Taliban.* New York: Prometheus, 2012.

Woods, Chris. *Sudden Justice: America's Secret Drone Wars.* Oxford: Oxford University Press, 2015.

Woodward, Bob. *Bush at War.* New York: Simon & Schuster, 2002.

———. *Obama's Wars.* New York: Simon & Schuster, 2010.

Wright, Lawrence. *The Looming Tower: Al-Qaeda and the Road to 9/11.* New York: Vintage, 2007.

Zunes, Stephen, and Richard Falk. *Tinderbox: U.S. Foreign Policy and the Roots of Terrorism.* Monroe, MN: Common Courage, 2002.

Index

130-131, 140, 146, 147, 151,
   156, 164, 165, 175-176, 181,
   185-186, 195, 199, 200-201,
   215, 221, 234, 237, 240, 241,
   247, 248, 256, 259
Chandrasekaran, Rajiv, 168, 199
Chechnya, 42, 55
Cheney, Dick, 2, 30-31, 63, 70-
   71, 85
China, 22, 25, 42, 65, 78, 100,
   104, 110, 129, 132, 165, 177,
   218-219, 239, 257, 259-260,
   264
Christianity, 11, 15-16, 19, 21
Clapper, James, 151
Clark, Wesley, 57, 158
Clinton, Bill, 23, 33-34, 41-45,
   54, 100, 158, 264
Clinton, Hillary, 143, 146, 153,
   157-159, 164, 202, 263-264
Coats, Dan, 249, 254
Cockburn, Andrew, 32-33, 191
Cockburn, Patrick, 119, 124,
   131-132, 165, 230
COINdinistas, 158-160, 164-
   165, 181
Cold War, 24, 30, 33, 44, 56,
   103, 126, 264
collateral damage, 3, 137, 141,
   195
Council on Foreign Relations,
   159, 218, 249-250
counter-revolutionary war, 163
counter-terrorism, 3, 66, 69,
   103, 111, 113, 131, 144, 149,
   153, 183, 186, 200, 207, 218-
   219, 221, 255, 262
Counter-terrorism Plus
   Training, 186, 255
Counterinsurgency Field
   Manual, 3-24, 159, 181
Counterterrorism Pursuit
   Teams, 113, 182

Crocker, Ryan, 220-221
Crossing Zero, 220
Cruise missile strikes, 1998, 42,
   49
Crumpton, Henry, 63
Cruz, Ted, 4
Cullison, Alan, 52, 54
Curtis, Adam, 17-18
Curtis, Lisa, 260

D

Dam, Bette, 107, 168, 211
Dasht-i-Leili massacre, 89
David Kilcullen, 159, 167, 172,
   180
Davis, Daniel, 196-199
Dawood National Military
   Hospital, 122
Declaration of War Against
   Jews and Crusaders, 5, 15
Deep State, 104
Defense Inspector General, 122
Defense Intelligence Agency
   (DIA), 53-54, 146
DeLong, Mike, 64, 65
Demos, 14
Department of Defense (DoD),
   9, 11, 13, 38, 79, 81-82, 84,
   120, 122-123, 138, 201, 212,
   248-249, 254
Doctors Without Borders, 213
Dostum, Abdul Rashid, 60, 80,
   89
Dr. Strangelove, 83
drone wars, 130, 144
Drug Enforcement Agency
   (DEA), 173, 175
drug wars, 118, 173
dual containment, 33
Duffy, Kevin, 40
Dunford, Joseph, 217, 248
Durand Line, 91, 145, 165
DynCorp, 256-257

Marjah, 170-173, 178, 181, 220
Marshall Plan, 120, 226
Massive Ordnance Air Blast
    (MOAB), 249
Massoud, Ahmad Shah, 88-89,
    93, 169
Mateen, Omar, 232-234
Mattis, James, 62, 66, 159, 249,
    251, 256, 260-261, 262
Mazar-e-Sharif, 60, 214, 225
McCain, John, 46, 85, 146, 152,
    154, 155, 246
McChrystal, Stanley, 148-149,
    153-154, 156, 161, 165-166,
    168, 170-172, 175, 178, 180-
    181, 183-184, 185, 195, 218,
    220, 250, 265
McConnell, Mike, 130
McDermott, Terry, 7
McKiernan, David, 148
McMaster, H. R., 248, 252, 254,
    256-257, 260-263
MI-5, 13
MI-6, 37
Military Aged Male (MAM),
    135, 186
Military Industrial Complex,
    104
Miller, John, 4
Miller, Laurel, 253, 261
Miller, Paul D., 217-218
minerals, 101, 257
Mohammad, Binyam, 74
Mora, Alberto, 83
Mubarak, Hosni, 33, 75, 242
mujahideen, 27-29, 32, 38, 42-
    44, 48, 62, 89, 98, 111, 132,
    174, 200, 258-259
Mullen, Mike, 153-154
Murad, Abdul Hakim, 41
Mutassim, Agha Jan, 107
Muttawakil, Wakil Ahmed, 49,
    52, 107

N

Nagl, John, 159-160, 183, 227
Nangarhar Province, 65, 140,
    211, 222, 249
National Bird, 191
National Security Agency
    (NSA), 105, 237
National Security Council
    (NSC), 24, 59-60, 72, 100,
    151, 156-157, 173, 217, 248,
    260, 262
National Unity Government
    (NUG), 94, 121, 209, 216,
    225
NATO forces, 57, 101, 118,
    151, 156, 175, 258
NATO governments, 118
NATO occupation, 105
neoconservatives, 275
Nerkh District, 194
network science, 183
New Great Game, 98
New York, New Jersey sidewalk
    attacks, 235
Nicholson, John, 168, 222, 246
Nixon, Richard, 264
No Good Men Among the Living,
    106
No-fly zones, 6, 14, 32
Non-Governmental
    Organization (NGO), 92,
    110, 115, 117-118, 120, 123,
    164
Nordland, Rod, 36, 115, 172,
    190, 250
North Atlantic Treaty
    Organization (NATO), 25,
    57, 65, 92, 95-96, 101-103,
    105, 114-115, 118, 120, 126-
    127, 131, 140-141, 144-146,
    150-151, 156, 166, 168-169,
    175, 182, 185, 187, 189, 192,
    204, 222, 226, 234-235, 252,